FOCAL IMPULSE THEORY

MUSICAL MEANING AND INTERPRETATION
Robert S. Hatten, editor

FOCAL IMPULSE THEORY

Musical Expression, Meter, and the Body

John Paul Ito

INDIANA UNIVERSITY PRESS

This book is a publication of

Indiana University Press
Office of Scholarly Publishing
Herman B Wells Library 350
1320 East 10th Street
Bloomington, Indiana 47405 USA

iupress.org

© 2020 by John Paul Ito

Manufactured in the United States of America

Library of Congress Cataloging-in-Publication Data

Names: Ito, John Paul, author.
Title: Focal impulse theory : musical expression, meter, and the body /
  John Paul Ito.
Description: Bloomington : Indiana University Press, 2020. | Includes
  bibliographical references and index.
Identifiers: LCCN 2019050618 (print) | LCCN 2019050619 (ebook) | ISBN
  9780253049957 (paperback) | ISBN 9780253049933 (hardback) | ISBN
  9780253049940 (ebook)
Subjects: LCSH: Musical meter and rhythm. | Music—Interpretation
  (Phrasing, dynamics, etc.) | Music—Performance—Physiological aspects.
Classification: LCC ML3813 .I86 2020 (print) | LCC ML3813 (ebook) | DDC
  781.2/22—dc23
LC record available at https://lccn.loc.gov/2019050618
LC ebook record available at https://lccn.loc.gov/2019050619

1 2 3 4 5   25 24 23 22 21 20

To the servants of art

CONTENTS

ACCESSING AUDIOVISUAL MATERIALS

Focal Impulse Theory includes two types of supplementary materials, available online: sound examples and video examples. The official way to access these materials is through the Indiana University Press website listed below.

As a convenience to readers, access to these materials will also be provided via other websites, including my personal website and KiltHub, Carnegie Mellon University's online data repository. Internet searches on my name and *focal impulse theory*, possibly with added terms such as *KiltHub*, should bring these sites up easily.

Note that media examples are available both for streaming and as downloads from KiltHub, but as of this writing only for streaming from the Indiana University Press website; those concerned with obtaining the highest possible sound quality should use downloaded files.

Three additional items that are not officially part of the book are also found on KiltHub: they are annotated scores to a portion of the final movement of Schumann's piano concerto, op. 54, discussed in chapter 15, and to the first movements of Brahms's clarinet sonatas, op. 120, discussed in chapter 16.

Finally, the book includes references to a large number of commercial recordings. To the extent possible, given changes in platforms and business models, I plan to maintain mechanisms that will allow readers quick and easy access to these recordings. At the time of this writing, I am using Spotify playlists; my personal website will house whatever means of access are currently in use.

The audiovisual materials can be viewed online at https://media.dlib.indiana.edu/collections/jw827j548.

Sound 5.1. Haydn, String Quartet op. 74/2, i, mm. 9–20, Allegro spirituoso, one focal impulse per measure. Stéphane Tran Ngoc, violin, Wen-Lei Gu, violin, Matthew Michelic, viola, and Janet Anthony, cello. https://purl.dlib.indiana.edu/iudl/media/b19f16f46n.

Sound 5.2. Haydn, String Quartet op. 74/2, i, mm. 9–20, Allegro spirituoso, two focal impulses per measure. Stéphane Tran Ngoc, violin, Wen-Lei Gu, violin, Matthew Michelic, viola, and Janet Anthony, cello. https://purl.dlib.indiana.edu/iudl/media/c08h442tow.

Sound 5.3. Millöcker, *Der Bettelstudent*, Act I, No. 1, mm. 1–24 of the Moderato section. Kurt Pratsch-Kaufmann, baritone, the Chor der Deutschen Oper Berlin, and the Berliner Symphoniker, conducted by Robert Stolz. https://purl .dlib.indiana.edu/iudl/media/m214657c8p.

Sound 7.1. Haydn, String Quartet op. 33/2, iii, mm. 21–26, Largo sostenuto, focal impulses on quarter-note beats. Stéphane Tran Ngoc, violin, Wen-Lei Gu, violin, Matthew Michelic, viola, and Janet Anthony, cello. https://purl .dlib.indiana.edu/iudl/media/q37v63hxot.

Sound 7.2. Haydn, String Quartet op. 33/2, iii, mm. 21–26, Largo sostenuto, focal impulses on eighth-note beats. Stéphane Tran Ngoc, violin, Wen-Lei Gu, violin, Matthew Michelic, viola, and Janet Anthony, cello. https://purl .dlib.indiana.edu/iudl/media/n79h14cq7r.

Sound 7.3. Mozart, Viola Quintet K. 406, i, mm. 22–39, Allegro, focal impulses on half-note beats. Stéphane Tran Ngoc, violin, Wen-Lei Gu, violin, Matthew Michelic, viola, John Paul Ito, viola, and Janet Anthony, cello. https://purl.dlib .indiana.edu/iudl/media/q27z60g06q.

Sound 7.4. Mozart, Viola Quintet K. 406, i, mm. 22–39, Allegro, focal impulses on quarter-note beats. Stéphane Tran Ngoc, violin, Wen-Lei Gu, violin, Matthew Michelic, viola, John Paul Ito, viola, and Janet Anthony, cello. https://purl.dlib.indiana.edu/iudl/media/q085549r33.

Sound 9.1. Bach, Sonata for Viola da Gamba and Harpsichord BWV 1027, i, mm. 1–3, focal impulses on dotted-quarter-note beats. John Paul Ito, viola, and J. Andrew Olson, harpsichord. https://purl.dlib.indiana.edu/iudl/media /227m70pq4g.

Sound 9.2. Bach, Sonata for Viola da Gamba and Harpsichord BWV 1027, i, mm. 1–3, focal impulses on eighth-note beats. John Paul Ito, viola, and J. Andrew Olson, harpsichord. https://purl.dlib.indiana.edu/iudl/media /8418614p51.

Sound 9.3. Bach, Sonata for Viola da Gamba and Harpsichord BWV 1027, i, mm. 1–3, with secondary focal impulses. John Paul Ito, viola, and J. Andrew Olson, harpsichord. https://purl.dlib.indiana.edu/iudl/media /089227pp2h.

Sound 10.1. Schubert, "Auf dem Wasser zu singen," D. 774, mm. 9–16, Mässig geschwind, unitary impulse cycles. Patrice Michaels, soprano, and Michael Kim, piano. https://purl.dlib.indiana.edu/iudl/media/h440797538.

Sound 10.2. Schubert, "Auf dem Wasser zu singen," D. 774, mm. 9–16, Mässig geschwind, binary impulse cycles. Patrice Michaels, soprano, and Michael Kim, piano. https://purl.dlib.indiana.edu/iudl/media/r76fo6j415.

Sound 12.1. Robert Schumann, *Faschingsschwank aus Wien*, i, mm. 87–94, Sehr lebhaft, focal impulses shifted to reflect alternative heard meter. Anthony Padilla, piano. https://purl.dlib.indiana.edu/iudl/media/t44p58rk41.

Sound 12.2. Robert Schumann, *Faschingsschwank aus Wien*, i, mm. 87–94, Sehr lebhaft, focal impulses shifted and sustained to follow anticipations in the notated meter. Anthony Padilla, piano. https://purl.dlib.indiana.edu/iudl /media/x51h53zx32.

Sound 12.3. Robert Schumann, *Phantasiestücke*, "Grillen," mm. 59–72, Mit Humor, focal impulses following alternative heard meter shown in example 12.3. David Keep, piano. https://purl.dlib.indiana.edu/iudl/media/j13900qs82.

Sound 12.4. Robert Schumann, *Phantasiestücke*, "Grillen," mm. 59–72, Mit Humor, focal impulses as in example 12.5. David Keep, piano. https://purl.dlib .indiana.edu/iudl/media/r46q979s9v.

Sound 15.1. Brahms, Capriccio op. 116/1, mm. 1–9, focal impulses as in example 15.1. David Keep, piano. https://purl.dlib.indiana.edu/iudl/media/t44p58rk5b.

Sound 15.2. Brahms, Variations and Fugue on a Theme by Handel, op. 24, mm. 25–32, performance reflecting the notated meter, more overt version. David Keep, piano. https://purl.dlib.indiana.edu/iudl/media/445c38887x.

Sound 15.3. Brahms, Variations and Fugue on a Theme by Handel, op. 24, mm. 25–32, performance reflecting the notated meter, more subtle version. David Keep, piano. https://purl.dlib.indiana.edu/iudl/media/c87p68nf36.

Sound 15.4. Brahms, Capriccio op. 116/7, mm. 74–92, Allegro agitato, focal impulses as in example 15.3. David Keep, piano. https://purl.dlib.indiana.edu /iudl/media/c97k71qf5p.

Sound 15.5. Robert Schumann, Piano Concerto op. 54, iii, mm. 80–262, Allegro vivace, focal impulses as in examples 15.4, 15.5, and 15.6 and the supplementary online score. David Keep, piano, and William Davidson, piano. https://purl.dlib.indiana.edu/iudl/media/880v73dv16.

Sound 15.6. Brahms, Capriccio op. 116/7, mm. 21–46, Allegro agitato, focal impulses following the notated meter, with shifted focal impulses following the anticipations in the melody. David Keep, piano. https://purl.dlib.indiana.edu/iudl/media/z01069bc7k.

Sound 15.7. Brahms, Capriccio op. 76/5, mm. 86–94, Agitato, ma non troppo presto, focal impulses following the notated meter. David Keep, piano. https://purl.dlib.indiana.edu/iudl/media/593t84bf83.

Sound 15.8. Brahms, Capriccio op. 76/5, mm. 86–94, Agitato, ma non troppo presto, focal impulses as in example 15.11b. David Keep, piano. https://purl.dlib.indiana.edu/iudl/media/f16c08kj5c.

Sound 15.9. Brahms, Clarinet Quintet, op. 115, i, mm. 25–41, Allegro, focal impulses following the alternative metrical notation shown in example 15.13. Bixby Kennedy, clarinet, and the Verona Quartet, Jonathan Ong, violin, Dorothy Ro, violin, Abigail Rojansky, viola, and Warren Hagerty, cello. https://purl.dlib.indiana.edu/iudl/media/h63s85cc7p.

Sound 15.10. Brahms, Clarinet Quintet, op. 115, i, mm. 32–37, Allegro, second alternative version, omitting mm. 34–35, shown in example 15.15. Bixby Kennedy, clarinet, and the Verona Quartet, Jonathan Ong, violin, Dorothy Ro, violin, Abigail Rojansky, viola, and Warren Hagerty, cello. https://purl.dlib.indiana.edu/iudl/media/435g356f95.

Sound 15.11. Brahms, Clarinet Quintet, op. 115, i, mm. 32–37, Allegro, third alternative version, clarifying notated meter, shown in Example 15.16. Bixby Kennedy, clarinet, and the Verona Quartet, Jonathan Ong, violin, Dorothy Ro, violin, Abigail Rojansky, viola, and Warren Hagerty, cello. https://purl.dlib.indiana.edu/iudl/media/n30099156r.

Sound 15.12. Brahms, Clarinet Quintet, op. 115, i, mm. 25–41, Allegro, focal impulses following 1.5-length bars in mm. 25–33 and then following the notated meter. Bixby Kennedy, clarinet, and the Verona Quartet, Jonathan Ong, violin, Dorothy Ro, violin, Abigail Rojansky, viola, and Warren Hagerty, cello. https://purl.dlib.indiana.edu/iudl/media/z40k81mm23.

Sound 16.1. Brahms, Clarinet Sonata No. 1, op. 120/1, i, Allegro appassionato. John Paul Ito, viola, and David Keep, piano. https://purl.dlib.indiana.edu/iudl /media/207t64jh8f.

Sound 16.2. Brahms Clarinet Sonata No. 2, op. 120/2, i, Allegro amabile. John Paul Ito, viola, and David Keep, piano. https://purl.dlib.indiana.edu/iudl /media/d27880xq8j.

Video 8.1. Demonstration of singing hemiolas by Schumann with focal impulses following the hemiola vs. following the notated meter. https://purl.dlib .indiana.edu/iudl/media/781w42qc4x.

Video 9.1. Demonstration of two-arm exercise for feeling focal impulses that are shifted to follow anticipations and sustained into the strong beat. https:// purl.dlib.indiana.edu/iudl/media/425k324h61.

Video 9.2. Demonstration of partner exercise for feeling focal impulses that are shifted to follow anticipations and sustained into the strong beat, with Matthew Hettinga. https://purl.dlib.indiana.edu/iudl/media/d66v937621.

Video 9.3. Demonstration of single-arm exercise for feeling focal impulses that are shifted to follow anticipations and sustained into the strong beat. https://purl.dlib.indiana.edu/iudl/media/fo6go5hf7d.

Video 10.1. Demonstration of qualities of upward focal impulse. https://purl .dlib.indiana.edu/iudl/media/5547722g3s.

Video 10.2. Demonstration of the contrast between unitary and binary impulse cycles, using Fauré's "Les Berceaux." Daniel Teadt, baritone, and David Keep, piano. https://purl.dlib.indiana.edu/iudl/media/k81j52zb07.

Video 11.1. Demonstration of singing upward-oriented vs. downward-oriented unitary impulse cycles, using the *Pizzicato Polka* by Johann Strauss Jr. and Josef Strauss. https://purl.dlib.indiana.edu/iudl/media/613m90gtom.

Video 11.2. Demonstration of upward-oriented vs. downward-oriented unitary impulse cycles, using the Loure from Bach's Partita No. 3 for Solo Violin, BWV 1006. Paul Miller, violin. https://purl.dlib.indiana.edu/iudl/media/to5346gc9w.

Video 11.3. Demonstration of singing upward-oriented vs. downward-oriented binary impulse cycles, using the *Radetzky March* by Johann Strauss Sr. https://purl.dlib.indiana.edu/iudl/media/821g550j59.

Video 11.4. Demonstration of upward-oriented vs. downward-oriented binary impulse cycles, using the Loure from Bach's Partita No. 3 for Solo Violin, BWV 1006. Paul Miller, violin. https://purl.dlib.indiana.edu/iudl/media/999n109328

Video 11.5. Demonstration of upward-oriented vs. downward-oriented binary impulse cycles, using "Ach ich fühl's" from Mozart's *The Magic Flute*. Jennifer Miller, soprano, and David Keep, piano. https://purl.dlib.indiana.edu/iudl/media/to5346gdoc.

Video 11.6. Demonstration of mixed impulse cycles with upward-inflected vs. downward-inflected downbeats, using the Chaconne from Bach's Partita No. 2 for Solo Violin, BWV 1004. Paul Miller, violin. https://purl.dlib.indiana.edu/iudl/media/227m70q21j.

Video 12.1. Demonstration of the interactions among binary impulse cycles, metrical shifts, and hypermeter in the first theme and transition from the slow movement of Mozart's Piano Sonata K. 311. David Keep, piano. https://purl.dlib.indiana.edu/iudl/media/c67w62hbox.

PREFACE

*F*OCAL IMPULSE THEORY OFFERS AN ACCOUNT OF THE role of meter in musical performance. Focal impulses are bodily pulsations that musicians use to organize the motion involved in performance. Focal impulses often coincide with some prominent level of beat, so that musicians essentially perform from beat to beat at that level. This does not mean that meter dictates motion, however; focal impulses can diverge from the regularity of the beats, and sometimes multiple interpretations of the meter are possible. Performers have choices—about which beat level to invest in, and about when to open gaps between meter and motion. In this book, I show that these choices have consequences for the expressive shaping of the sound produced. The choice to feel a piece "in two" versus "in four," for example, will be a choice not only about what it feels like to play or sing the music but also about what the performance sounds like. In deciding how to place focal impulses, performers have a discrete set of options, each of which has holistic effects on the expressive character of the music. The details of the theory are worked out with reference to Western classical music of the eighteenth and nineteenth centuries, but the basic principles explored could well apply more broadly. (The potential of the theory to inform musics of other times and places is explored briefly in the concluding chapter.)

I understand this book as one component of a larger project addressing meter and hypermeter in eighteenth- and nineteenth-century Western classical music. The central component in this project is formed by *Focal Impulse Theory* and by a previous study on hypermeter (Ito, 2013a); together they address the most common patterns and compositional practices involving meter and hypermeter, with this book focusing primarily on the ways in which performers respond to metrical practices. The second component looks at the extraordinary development of the standard patterns in the music of Brahms. Its center of mass is a completed corpus study looking at metrical dissonance in all of Brahms's works with opus numbers. That study originated as the concluding part of this volume but grew to a scale requiring independent presentation. Portions of the work on Brahms that deal centrally with performance appear in this book as part 5; I intend to present the rest as a second book (Ito, in preparation c). Finally, the third component addresses the origins of the standard patterns in the first half of the eighteenth century. It is concerned especially with the emergence of the full notated measure as a meaningful compositional unit (as opposed to the use of half bars in early eighteenth-century compound meter) and with the rise of four-bar phrase construction from a genre-specific feature to a near-universal principle. The first results look especially at Bach (Ito, in preparation a).

The origins of this book lie in work at Columbia University with Fred Lerdahl, who knew when to push me hard and when to give me free rein. Among Fred's many contributions was the suggestion of the adjective *focal*. Others who helped make this book better in those early stages include Joe Dubiel, David Cohen, Joel Lester, and Robert Remez. For helpful conversations and pointers to literature over the many years of the book's gestation, I thank Daniel Barolsky, Ben Binder, Ken Bozeman, Mark Butler, Deanna Clement, Rolf Inge Godøy, Mark Gotham, Gérald Guillot, Dave Keep, Mark Latash, Daniel Leech-Wilkinson, Justin London, Scott Murphy, Stephen Neely, Richard Parncutt, Steve Rings, John Rink, John Roeder, David Rosenbaum, Heather Rusiewicz, Rebecca Simpson-Litke, and Chris Stover. I am also grateful for the assistance of a number of librarians, especially music librarians Kristin Heath and Antoinette Powell and ILL librarians Cheryl Kraft, Andrew Marshall, and Angela Vanden Elzen. During my time in New York, I was a member of the Neue Bach Band; working regularly with such wonderful musicians helped me with this book in many ways, most directly through a comment of Missy Fogarty's during a dress rehearsal at Queens College that inspired the scenario that opens chapter 1. Many teachers and collaborators helped shape the perspectives shared here; among them, David Epstein and George Neikrug were particularly formative influences. The book has also been shaped by the many students who have used its drafts in classes over the years; they have contributed much to the final form, and a good number will recognize that examples they submitted for homework have made their way into the book.

I have had the great good fortune to have the collaboration of a number of outstanding performers in making the sound and video examples that accompany the book; they are Janet Anthony, William Davidson, Wen-Lei Gu, Matthew Hettinga, David Keep, Bixby Kennedy, Michael Kim, Patrice Michaels, Jennifer Miller, Paul Miller, Matthew Michelic, J. Andrew Olson, Anthony Padilla, Daniel Teadt, Stephane Tran Ngoc, and Verona Quartet members Jonathan Ong, Dorothy Ro, Abigail Rojansky, and Warren Hagerty. I am deeply grateful for these examples; they are not just clear demonstrations but also beautiful artistic statements. Much credit for this is also due to the outstanding work of recording engineers Larry Darling at Lawrence University, Riccardo Schultz, Michael Bridges, Matthew Hettinga, and Wei Lim at Carnegie Mellon University, and Wei-Xiong Wang at Skillman Music, and of piano technicians Peter Stumpf and Bruce Ziesemer.

Stephen McCardell's fastidious work editing and formatting the musical examples gave them their elegance, and Justin Macey kindly ran a motion-capture session, the results of which are used in the cover illustration.

The preparation of materials for this book has received generous funding through a Distinctiveness Grant from the Office of the Provost at Lawrence University, a grant from the Berkman Faculty Development Fund at Carnegie Mellon University, and a publication subvention from the Society for Music Theory. A semester leave granted by Dan J. Martin, dean of the College of Fine Arts at Carnegie Mellon, was a great help in completing the final manuscript.

Robert Hatten has been the ideal editor to work with. I am grateful both for his support and enthusiasm for this project and for the many suggestions that have helped the book find its final form. David Lidov has been a great source of guidance and encouragement at several stages in this book's development; in particular, his decision to sign an early review has helped the book to see the light of day. Harald Krebs has also given helpful feedback on multiple occasions, both officially and informally. Finally, two anonymous reviewers also have my gratitude for the ways in which they helped me to refine this book. At Indiana University Press, Raina Polivka was extremely helpful at the stage of the proposal and initial contract, Nazareth Pantaloni III has offered valuable advice regarding copyright issues, and Janice Frisch has been unflagging in offering guidance and wisdom on innumerable issues both large and small.

This book's dedication may seem rather old-fashioned—fittingly, given that the book may be understood as a late flowering of writings on meter in performance from a hundred years ago and more (discussed in chap. 14). More fundamentally, the dedication reflects a sense that this book is a payment on a debt that I owe to the art of musical performance for all that it has given to my life. This is not meant to suggest that serving art is the highest, or the safest, of all possible callings. There are certainly masters who more consistently reward their faithful servants. (I think especially of the stunningly disparate fates of two amazing musicians whose paths intersected mine in unforgettable ways in Chicago when I was younger, Günter Wand and Elaine Scott Banks.) And it is certainly not meant to suggest that the true servants of art are those who will appreciate this book! Rather, the dedication pays tribute to all those whose labor in music, however imperfect, is directed to ends greater than themselves. It honors those whose efforts have been inspired by performances in which contingent, finite humanity somehow approaches something of transcendent meaning and value. If experiences of these sorts and their various human and textual sources have at times been distorted through deification, there are good reasons for this.

Finally, I give special thanks to my family, Sarah, Yuki, Mari, Sachi, and Elias. Sarah has had a central role in this project. She believed both in it and in my continued work as a scholar when the viability of each was called seriously into question. And considering her limited knowledge of the content of my tasks, her guidance has been astonishingly reliable as I have decided what to say no to and how to order the things I say yes to. All of you fill my life with love and joy, and you help me keep my work in perspective (including through quotes assembled in the personal section of my website). You deserve the dedication of this book and more, but I did not feel that this dedication was mine to give, and the next book in the works is spoken for as well. You are next after that, I promise! And given how unlikely it once seemed that this nerdy MIT graduate would one day find himself surrounded by beautiful women, a third book seems quite modest as an object of hope and expectation.

Pittsburgh, Feast of St. Thomas, 2018

COPYRIGHT ACKNOWLEDGMENTS

PART 1
INTRODUCTION

1

INTRODUCING THE FOCAL IMPULSE
AND ITS THEORY

1.1. The Focal Impulse

The musicians stop in the midst of their rehearsal. Somehow the music isn't feeling right. It seems stuck, grounded, unable to take flight. Should it be faster? No, the tempo seems about right. The problem is more elusive. "I think that we've been feeling the music too much in four, and the quarter-note beats are feeling like lead weights," says one of the musicians. "Let's try feeling it more in two." They try it, and they agree this solves their problem.

Like most musicians, these performers had goals about the sound of the music; they found some expressive qualities desirable, others undesirable. Their ears alerted them to the problem, and their ears evaluated the solution. But although the problem itself was one of sound, the solution they adopted made no reference to sonic parameters. In fact, their one discussion of the sound in concrete, nonmetaphorical terms occurred when they rejected tempo as a possible source of the problem. Instead, they spoke in terms of an abstraction—meter—and decided to shift some kind of primary investment from one level of beat to another. But what kind of investment is this? If I had been one of those musicians, I would have had a very physical understanding of what it might mean to *feel* the music more in two. I would understand an investment of much of my body in the half-note level; going well beyond pressing my toe against the floor to keep time, feeling the music in two would mean filling my body with a visceral pulse that would organize the motions I made in playing the music.

"A visceral pulse"—what exactly does that mean? Just what is it that changed between the two performances? What are musicians really talking about when they speak of feeling music in two or in four? In this book I argue that the difference is a matter of the placement of what I call *focal impulses*.

Example 1.1. Beethoven, Trio op. 70/1, i, "Ghost," mm. 1–5.

A focal impulse is a special kind of motion that not only produces direct, immediate results—often the playing of a note or a chord—but also sets the body moving in ways that facilitate subsequent motions. Focal impulses are used by performers in the organization of physical motion, and they commonly align with some level of the meter, especially in the eighteenth- and nineteenth-century Western classical music that is the primary focus of this book. What changed between the two performances in the story was the placement of focal impulses: the musicians went from placing them on the quarter-note beats to placing them only on the half-note beats. In general the placement of focal impulses influences the resulting sound in holistic ways; for example, it is not simply a matter of the notes produced by the focal impulses having sharper attacks. Changing the placement of focal impulses makes global changes in the expressive character of the music, and this is how the change to the half-note level solved the musicians' problem.

But this explanation is still rather abstract. To further pursue the concept of the focal impulse, let us consider the following three thought experiments. First, imagine playing, on any instrument, a single eighth note of any pitch, in a comfortable register, *forte* and with a strong accent. Imagine the physicality of this action, what it would feel like to play such a note.

Second, imagine playing the opening of Beethoven's "Ghost" Trio (ex. 1.1), playing any of the parts on any instrument. Again, focus on what it would feel like to play this music.

For the final thought experiment, again imagine playing the beginning of the "Ghost" Trio, but this time use only motions of the kind you imagined in the first thought experiment. That is, imagine constructing a performance out of a sequence of isolated, separate motions in which the only differences among the motions were the minimal changes needed to produce the different pitches. For string players, this would likely mean that all notes were played down-bow, attacked from the air. For a pianist, only one finger of each hand would be used, and each keystroke would probably start more than an inch above the keyboard. Singers and wind players would probably find this mode of performance particularly awkward: each note would require first a strong contraction of the abdominal muscles and then a relaxation in preparation for the next note, and the relaxation would probably need help from the diaphragm.

I feel safe in assuming that the results of the second and third thought experiments were quite different. Outside of contrived experiments, musicians rarely use isolated physical impulses for each note. In most cases, the physical motions involved in musical performance are integrated into sequences of motion, with focal impulses used only for some of the notes. In the first thought experiment, it seems most likely that the isolated note would be produced using a focal impulse. In the second thought experiment, with so many notes following each other in close succession, focal impulses would presumably be used to produce only some notes, with the other notes falling between the focal impulses. The third experiment asks for a very strange performance in which a focal impulse is used to produce each note in the passage. This strangeness underscores the fact that sequences of motion are organized in units of more than one individual motion; they cannot simply be assembled by producing isolated motions one after another.

The contrast between the second and third thought experiments does not arise from an equally strong contrast at the level of individual notes. For notes that are produced directly by focal impulses when the passage is played normally, the difference between the experiments would be less salient; at least for the start of the note, the performance in isolation would not be so different from the performance in context. For notes not produced directly by focal impulses, however, the difference between context and isolation would be stark. The way any one of these notes is played relates strongly to the ways in which the surrounding notes are played; remove one of these notes from its context and that note is no longer the same.

Approaching from a different angle, suppose that we leave out all of the notes not directly produced by focal impulses. For one possible way of performing the start of the "Ghost" Trio, this would yield example 1.2. If we play examples 1.1 and 1.2, there should be a basic similarity between the two

Example 1.2. Reduction of op. 70.

experiences—if we are indeed placing focal impulses on the notes shown in example 1.2. Example 1.1 should feel like an elaborated version of example 1.2. Music theorists commonly use reductions that show only the most important events from a perspective of harmony and voice leading. Example 1.2 shows a reduction that preserves important events from the perspective of the organization of physical motion, again based on one possible way of playing the passage.

Focal impulses often reveal their presence particularly clearly when they are placed on rests, as the performer will often move during the rest in a way that helps to set up the music that follows. Example 1.3 shows a passage in which this is likely, the opening melody from Bach's Harpsichord Concerto in A Major, BWV 1055. It will be easier to make the music sparkle out of the downbeats if the performer moves on the downbeats, making motions that do not seem necessary from the standpoint of sound production. The difference that meter makes to performance is highlighted in the simple recomposition shown in example 1.4, in which the music has been shifted to begin on the downbeat. This recomposition will likely sound different from the original and feel different to play. Take a moment to imagine how playing these two passages would differ, paying attention to the notes' accentuation, attack, and timing—and even more to the physicality of playing them. At a macroscopic level, the sequences of motions might be very similar, but the details of motion and the organization of that motion would be quite different.

Sometimes a melody seems to make a point of omitting strong beats, and such melodies have special rhythmic characters. Consider the principal theme from the final movement of Mozart's Concerto for Two Pianos in E-flat Major, K. 365 (ex. 1.5). The rests and ties found on so many of the hypermetrically

Example 1.3. Bach, Harpsichord Concerto BWV 1055, i, mm. 1–3.

Example 1.4. Recomposition of BWV 1055.

strong downbeats have tremendous energy because of their (silent) focal impulses. If the melody is recomposed to give those downbeats attack points, the result is flat and lifeless by comparison (ex. 1.6).

The effect of focal impulses on strong-beat rests is probably particularly salient to me as a violist because certain kinds of nineteenth-century orchestral textures frequently omit strong beats in the inner voices. Characteristic instances are given in examples 1.7 and 1.8, from Verdi's *La Traviata* and the overture to Johann Strauss Jr.'s *Die Fledermaus*. The violists' notes should sound like consequences of the strong beats, and that requires that the notes *be* consequences at a motional level; the notes must be produced by motions that flow out of focal impulses on the strong beats. In these cases, the silent focal impulses would probably be produced in the abdomen and bow arm, initiating states of motion conducive to playing the off-beat notes but not directly initiating any notes.

In these examples of focal impulses on strong-beat rests, the physical motion on the rest reveals the presence of the focal impulse. If we viewed performance as the stringing together of isolated motions, there would be no need to move on these rests—after all, when rests do not fall on strong beats, they do not usually inspire motion of this sort. The helpfulness of this motion can reside only in its influence on the motions that follow. We become aware of

Example 1.5. Mozart, Concerto for Two Pianos, K. 365, iii, mm. 1–16.

Example 1.6. Recomposition of K. 365.

this organizing role of motion because the motion occurs on a rest, but there is no reason to suppose that only motions on rests can play this role. If it is helpful to move this way on a rest, then the motions we make to play notes on strong beats may actually serve two functions, both producing the notes on the strong beats and helping to organize subsequent motion. Strong-beat rests are among the best clues to focal impulses—in fact, the long path that led to the focal impulse concept began with my attempts as a pit musician to give convincing shape to the off-beat "pah-pahs" in the waltzes of *Fledermaus*.[1]

The nature of the focal impulse is also illuminated by the contrast between strong attacks that are produced by focal impulses and strong attacks

Example 1.7. Verdi, *La Traviata*, Act I, mm. 116–119, Allegro brillantissimo e molto vivace.

Example 1.8. Johann Strauss Jr., *Die Fledermaus*, Overture, mm. 166–173, Tempo di Valse (nicht zu schnell).

Example 1.9. From Stravinsky, *Rite of Spring*, "Glorification de l'Élue," mm. 1–3. Adapted by permission from Ito (2013c), © Springer-Verlag Berlin Heidelberg 2013.

that are not. A helpfully extreme example is found in the "Glorification de l'Élue" from Stravinsky's *Rite of Spring* (ex. 1.9). The two parts shown are similar as sequences of rests and notes, approaching exact rhythmic canon; but if we assume that all but the last of the bass notes coincide with the strong beats in the mixed meter—and thus with the focal impulses—they will be very different in their physical execution. The bass players will feel a solid grounding that comes from playing on the beat, and their parts will be substantially easier. The wind players will need to produce not only vigorous focal impulses on the strong beats but also strong accents on the notes that follow, with their bodies constantly jarred as one or the other of these strong muscular contractions flies by. Where the bass players will feel stable and grounded, the winds will feel quite unsettled. As before, it will be helpful to imagine playing these parts, again on any instrument.[2]

This example shows that a performer's strong attacks are not all the same; strong attacks that align with focal impulses are performed quite differently from those that fall between focal impulses. It also shows us two things about the sound of focal impulses. First, strong accents either aligned with focal impulses or not are different not just in the way the motion is organized but also in their sound. Considering the nature of the motion involved, I would expect the accents in the wind parts to sound substantially more dynamic and unstable than the accents in the bass part. The possible uses of this distinction will be explored in chapters 7 and 12, which consider cases of metrical dissonance and metrically malleable music.

Second, the sonic traces of the physical demands of playing the wind parts will affect the expressive character of the passage, leading especially to greater intensity and instability in the sound. Music often creates this kind of sonic excitement through similar means: strong syncopated accents at fast tempo put the body through a rapid push and pull, and shifting asymmetrical meters prevent the establishment of a regular groove. Music that has these features will be exciting for many reasons, some of which are primarily cognitive; for example, we understand the conflicts between the syncopated notes and the metrical hierarchy, and we are unable to predict either the next accent or the next strong beat. But such music will also have a visceral excitement that is communicated from one spinal column to another via details of sound, as we intuit the bodily states that were involved in making the music.[3] This level of body-to-body communication allows us to understand emotion in sound across barriers of language, culture, and even species, and it is one source of the expressive effect of focal impulse placement. Focal impulse placement is a tool not only for the organization and coordination of motion but also for the expressive shaping of sound.

A detailed examination of the sound of focal impulses must wait until chapter 5, but it may be helpful to present an initial example of how music can sound different when played in two instead of in four. Example 1.10 shows the opening theme from *President Garfield's Inauguration March*, op. 131, by John Philip Sousa. As performed by "The President's Own" United States Marine Band (2014), the squareness of the articulations, the sharply pointed dotted rhythms, and the strong emphases given to notes falling on quarter-note beats all contribute to a strong sense of the march being performed in four. (As of this writing, this recording and all other commercial recordings referenced in this book are freely available on the internet on sites offering streaming audio or video. Full references for each example are given in the discography; as detailed in the section "Accessing Audiovisual Materials" at the front of the book, I also plan to maintain playlists to make examples more easily accessible. Listening to the examples is an integral part of reading the book, and using the best available playback equipment is strongly recommended.) I am told that connoisseurs of military bands consider European bands to have a lighter performing style than American bands, and this is borne out at least in the examples considered here. In the performance by the Central Band of the Royal Air Force, directed by Keith Brion (2012), the lack of emphasis on the second and fourth quarter-note beats and the much more relaxed treatment of the dotted rhythms are particularly clear signs of a performance in two. (I could easily believe, however, that the snare-drum player was feeling the music in four.) To be sure, this case is particularly clear—few contrasts presented in the following pages will be quite as salient as this one. But these recordings serve well as initial examples of how a performance can project a clear sense of being organized around a main beat level, with that organization reflected both in specifiable details of sound and in more holistic qualities of motion.

Example 1.10. Sousa, *President Garfield's Inauguration March*, op. 131, mm. 8–15, Tempo di marcia.

1.2. Focal Impulse Theory and Experience

This initial discussion has provided some sense of what I mean when I refer to a focal impulse. But what is a focal impulse, exactly? At this point, the best answer I can give is, come and see (and feel, and hear), as a fuller answer emerges over the course of parts 2 and 3. This long exposition is required because focal impulse theory is most centrally a theory about experience. What that means for the theory—for what the theory is and does, and for how one reads and uses it—is the topic of this section. Focal impulse theory also has a scientific side, and that is addressed in the next section. Because it is a theory about art, section 1.4 turns toward aesthetics, considering whether and to what extent the theory may value some performance options above others. (Readers whose primary interests are practical may want to skip ahead to this section.) Finally, the chapter closes by providing orientation for readers with various backgrounds and interests.

Returning to the question of how focal impulse theory relates to experience, there is a short answer and a longer answer. The short answer is that focal impulse theory is first and foremost a theory that explores experience on its own terms, and there are no shortcuts to experiential learning. Musicianship instruction offers some partial parallels; for example, beginning theory students can be taught about I, IV, and V chords in a single class session, but teaching them to identify the chords by ear takes much longer. This book will need to present a large number of examples, drawing on a wide variety of contexts, because they are needed if readers are to acquire the new experiential category of the focal impulse. There is furthermore an additional challenge relative to the ear training example, and that is the lack of an objective definition of the focal impulse. Focal impulses are most fundamentally things that the body produces by moving in certain ways, and they are known mainly through observation—observing how you move your own body as you perform music, observing how these ways of moving affect the sound, and observing what other musicians look like and sound like while performing music. A truly objective definition of the focal impulse would require a fairly comprehensive understanding of these ways of moving in terms of human movement science; as we will see, understanding even much simpler kinds of motion is quite difficult. I cannot concisely state what focal impulses are because, at the most fundamental level, I don't know.

In discussing the challenges of introducing the new experiential category of the focal impulse, it is important to be clear that while the category may be new, the experience itself is not. Based on my own experience and based on many conversations with musicians (including many while teaching the theory over the course of more than ten years), I believe that I am not introducing new ways of approaching performance but rather providing names for things that musicians do all the time. The fact that the experience existed before the category was acquired does not, however, mean that gaining the category leaves experience unchanged. Here again the analogy with ear training is helpful, as we know that it can sharpen and enrich our existing experiences. Similarly, the primary goal of this book is to have transformative effects on familiar aspects of listening to and performing music.

The beginning of a longer answer is found in Michael Polanyi's (1962, chap. 4) analogy between ideas and tools in his book *Personal Knowledge*. He discusses two kinds of awareness that we can have when using a tool. To illustrate, let us consider a pair of downhill skis as a tool for traversing a ski slope. In Polanyi's terms, the skier will often have "focal awareness" of the edges of the skis digging into the snow. The uphill edges will be the ones that cut grooves, and releasing those edges will result in a turn, so that the opposite edges become the uphill edges and begin to grab the snow. This awareness of the edge is central to skiing, and the skier will focus attention on the sensation of grabbing with the edge, using this sensation as an integral part of the activity. If we distance ourselves from the perspective of the skier, however, we immediately recognize that this focal awareness of the action of the edge of the ski is not what we have been representing it to be. The skier has no neural connections to the ski; the awareness is not really of the edge of the ski but rather of the forces exerted by the boot on the foot and lower leg, interacting with awareness of whole-body posture, balance, and motion. These forms of awareness, which are always present but usually in the background, Polanyi called "subsidiary awareness."[4] Polanyi was interested in tool use because he believed that we use ideas in the same ways that we use tools. Ideas can give us a (possibly erroneous) picture of the exterior world, and they allow us to interact with that world in certain ways. We can dwell in tools so that they effectively become extensions of our bodies, and we can likewise dwell in mental tools. Just like a pair of skis (or a blind person's cane, one of Polanyi's examples), the present theory is a tool that allows its users to dwell in it as a means of perceiving, thinking about, and interacting with some aspect of the world.[5]

One learns to ski though demonstration, through verbal description and instruction, and through trying it oneself. One learns to use a theory in the same way. And because focal impulse theory grew originally out of experience and seeks to return to experience, the learning process must live in the realm of experience. Polanyi (1962, 62–63) argues that the user of a tool is generally not able to specify either exactly how the tool is used or how it came to be adopted as a tool; the tool-user's learning process "relied on an act of groping which originally passed the understanding of its agent and of which he has ever since remained only subsidiarily aware, as part of a complex achievement" (63). For Polanyi, learning to use a tool involves a heuristic leap that irreversibly changes the perception of its user; this process mirrors the process of discovery of the tool, and it cannot be discretized into individual logical steps.[6] If this is so, then the only way that I can communicate the content of my theory is by leading the reader through a process of discovery that recapitulates my own.

It is not only the exposition of the theory that must rely on a process of discovery through examples but also its justification. For the most convincing evidence for the theory is precisely the experience of the user who discovers the power of using the theory as a tool.

My goal is to help the reader make an irreversible heuristic leap, to facilitate the reader's acquiring the theory as an intellectual tool. This process is not entirely specifiable, and how it happens—indeed whether it happens—will vary from person to person. As a result, I do not present my theory in the form of a step-by-step logical argument; instead, I attempt to stir up imagination and reflection on musical experience in ways that point toward the desired leaps. I certainly attempt to marshal persuasive evidence and to argue rationally from accepted principles; but the governing intent throughout is to aid readers in their own personal processes of discovery of the theory as a tool that can fruitfully inform perception, thought, and action.

Polanyi's concepts helpfully illuminate many important aspects of focal impulse theory, but he tends to assume objects of study that are simply given and "out there," such as physics and chemistry (two of Polanyi's main areas of interest). In contrast to the phenomena studied by the physical sciences, focal impulses and their patterns of use exist as a shared social practice among musicians. A helpful resource for conceptualizing the socially situated nature of the experience of focal impulses is Charles Taylor's (2004) concept of the social imaginary. Although the content of focal impulse theory is quite different, and although the defense of the theory proceeds along entirely different lines, a decent description of focal impulse theory is that it aims to make explicit one component of a musical social imaginary. Taylor understands a social imaginary to encompass "the ways people imagine their social existence, how they fit together with others, how things go on between them and their fellows, the expectations that are normally met, and the deeper normative notions and images that underlie these expectations" (23). This imagining is not primarily theoretical; rather, it is "that largely unstructured and inarticulate understanding of our whole situation, within which particular features of our world show up for us in the sense they have" (25). Crucially, "it is the practice that largely carries the understanding" (25), and as an instance of a "repertory" (25) of available social behaviors, Taylor considers initiating conversation with strangers in social settings, saying that "the discriminations we have to make to carry these off, knowing whom to speak to and when and how, carry an implicit map of social space, of what kinds of people we can associate with in what ways and in what circumstances" (25–26). From the standpoint of focal impulse theory, the most helpful part of Taylor's social imaginary is this conception of mostly tacit codes of conduct, transmitted largely through some sort of statistical learning process based on observation of others and on the responses to one's own behavior. It matches quite closely the ways in which I believe the norms of musical performance described by focal impulse theory are established and perpetuated.

1.3. Focal Impulse Theory and Empirical Science

Although focal impulse theory lives primarily in the domain of experience, it also has empirical implications. Considering the scientific side of the theory is a rather different enterprise from using the theory as an experiential tool; nonetheless, a helpful path into the scientific side also leads through experience.

Describing experience is not straightforward. Assuming that I have devised a scenario that leads you to have an experience that is sufficiently similar to mine, how do I call attention to the specific facets of experience that I want to discuss? How do I pinpoint the relevant facets, especially, when they involve subtle aspects of the way the body is moving? It seems inevitable that any attempt to speak of such experiences would have to involve some combination of straightforward description with a richer, more figurative use of language.

When I try to think about and describe the things that happen in my body as I play music, I tend, for reasons having to do with my own training and temperament, to use the language of physics and physiology. What is happening when I use this kind of language? I am trying to capture my best understanding, my best impression, my best guess of what is going on. I do not really know the extent to which the language I am using accurately describes what is happening. It is some blend of a hypothesis, a guess, an impression, and a metaphor, and the proportion of each is unknown.

The theory would not be incomplete if that were the end of the story. However, the same training and temperament that lead me to frame my observations in scientific terms also lead me to wonder how empirically accurate the theory would be if it were taken as a hypothesis about the motor organization of performance. More than wonder, I have begun to conduct experiments, attempting to move toward an answer to that question. Consequently, the theory has a kind of double existence. The primary existence is the one already discussed: the theory exists in relation to experience, intended to describe existing experience and, through focused attention, to transform experience. Secondarily, the theory suggests empirical hypotheses about motor organization. This double existence puts the theory in a somewhat strange situation. In its primary nature, its evaluation is essentially subjective, based on the perceived accuracy of its account of experience and on the richness of its contributions to experience. (A large number of evaluators can mitigate this subjectivity, giving some sense of the degree to which the theory resonates with a community and a tradition.) But in its secondary nature, the theory is to be evaluated based on its empirical accuracy. What happens if the judgments are not the same? What happens if it seems experientially helpful but proves to have limited empirical accuracy?

The story of an early experiment in music and motor control helps answer these questions. We will read in chapter 13 about a paper published in

1929 in which N. A. Bernstein and Tatiana Popowa disproved the theory that it is possible to play the piano relying only on the weight of the arms (i.e., not using muscular forces originating in the arms). Although they demonstrated more than eighty years ago that this is impossible for all but very slow tempi, many distinguished teachers continue to appeal to this theory; presumably the theory functions as a helpful guide to perception and action, even though the theory's own account of the way in which it is helpful is not accurate. For the present purposes, the key question is, how should a scientist respond to this result? One possibility would be simply to write off the theory and end the inquiry. The theory made predictions, the predictions were proven false, end of story. While I fully accept the validity of the experimental result, this response strikes me as unimaginative and uncurious. If piano teachers find it helpful to use this image, and if students find that it improves their playing, these experiences must have some source. If it is not a matter of using no active contractions of arm muscles, fine. But it does seem likely that the arms are somehow being used in different ways when playing "with the arms" or "without the arms." Can we find out what the difference is? And does the difference shed light on why the image is helpful? Fundamentally, the two responses to the experiment I have outlined differ in their understanding of how language is used. Is "play with the weight of the arms alone" only a description of the physical world that can be falsified empirically or is it also an image that points toward a certain experience without capturing the experience itself?

This example is helpful because focal impulse theory raises the same issues. When the time between focal impulses is relatively short, it seems perfectly credible (though by no means proven) that focal impulses could be organizing motion in more or less the ways proposed by the theory. However, for reasons detailed in chapter 13, this seems much less likely when the time span between focal impulses is somewhat longer (an approximate threshold that aligns with a number of empirical findings is around two to three seconds). With slower rates of motion, focal impulse theory seems likely to be metaphorical—but this is not at all to say that it is purely intellectual or just an interesting way of thinking about things. To the contrary, I would assert that at slow rates of motion, focal impulse theory describes an implicit, usually preconscious metaphor that is widely used by musicians to give coherence and direction to motions that unfold on challengingly long timescales. Musicians often practice fast passages slowly, attempting to transfer the precision that is more easily achievable at slow tempi to the actual performance tempo of the passage. As indicated by the results of Bernstein and Popowa, and as discussed further in chapter 13, musicians are mistaken if they believe that they are practicing the same motions, only slower. A large change in the rate of motion will often result in a change in the organization of motion; musicians can't do exactly the same thing, just twice as slowly, any more than runners can. Nonetheless, the fact that this practice technique is so widely seen as effective suggests that it does aid in transferring qualities of precision, even if the exact motion is not the same. I am making a parallel suggestion—that when performing slow passages, musicians implicitly attempt to transfer qualities of coherent relatedness among notes and among motions, qualities that are much more easily (and differently) achievable at faster tempi. In these situations, focal impulse theory is not making new suggestions about how to deal with slow music but rather providing new ways of thinking about things that musicians already do. What I am suggesting is similar to cross-domain mapping (Lakoff and Johnson 1980), but with the mapping being from one way of moving to another and with explicit, conceptual thought not necessarily playing a role. An example from outside of music would be swimmers using the mental image of swimming downhill. Clearly this example involves conceptual thought, but a certain way of moving in relation to the water and an awareness of what that way of moving felt like could easily have supported a feeling of "as if" that preceded the verbal formulation.

This discussion brings us back to the theory's double existence. Primarily, the theory is a tool in Polanyi's (1962) sense, to be used to open up new possibilities of action and perception in relation to music. When I use a phrase like "inject energy into the system," it represents my best guess and impression about what is happening; it will guide my own empirical investigations of the theory, and I want it to be taken seriously as an idea about the physical world. But such phrases are fundamentally pointers, opportunities for moments of recognition that can open doors to shared experiences and shared ways of perceiving. I could have replaced most instances of "is" with "seems to me to be" or "can be grasped by imagining it to be," but this language would have made the exposition leaden. Secondarily, for those who want to investigate the hidden reality behind the picture presented by the tool—for those who are curious about Polanyi's subsidiary awarenesses and the ways in which they constitute focal awareness—the theory can be taken as presenting informally phrased hypotheses about the motor organization of music performance. I am currently pursuing empirical examinations of the theory's claims, but they raise a very different set of issues. I have therefore chosen to pursue those investigations as a separate project, and I hope to report the results through standard scientific channels. The results so far are both interesting and promising, but in relation to the scope of the claims being made, the degree of empirical support gathered to date is quite modest. Chapter 13 situates the theory with respect to music psychology and human movement science and gives brief descriptions of some of my experiments; those interested in the details will want to consult the scientific publications. The final section of chapter 13 returns briefly to the epistemological status of the theory, which I explore further elsewhere (Ito, in preparation b).

1.4. How Music Is Performed, Could Be Performed— Should Be Performed?

A question about the nature of focal impulse theory concerns its relation to values. Does it merely describe the way things are, listing options among which performers freely choose? Or does it take a stand on aesthetic issues, advocating for some options above others?

It will be helpful to frame this question in terms of norms. When we say that something functions as a norm, we may mean one of two quite different things. We may simply be making an assertion of statistical prevalence, or we may be claiming that the norm is perceived as having greater value, even that it serves as a standard against which other instances may be judged. The position taken in this book blends the two approaches: because of their prevalence, the typical patterns will often (though not always) be more highly valued.[7] It will be left to the reader to judge the effectiveness of any given departure from the norms.

Throughout this book I will assume that focal impulses are always being used; there are no stretches of music in which organization in terms of focal impulses is not occurring. In empirical terms, this assumption is probably an oversimplification. As we will see in chapter 13, human motor control is prohibitively complex, and many ways of moving can result in the same basic action (e.g., grasping an object). It would seem extraordinary, then, for there to be only one way in which musicians organize sequences of motion. As already noted in the previous section and as discussed in chapter 13, I believe that the term *focal impulse* actually names at least two different ways of organizing motion, one used at faster rates of focal impulses and one used at slower rates. Beyond this, at least one other mode of organization exists: my earlier counterexample of simply stringing individual notes together, which, based on the testimony of countless inexpressive renditions of "Twinkle, Twinkle," is a common approach for beginners.[8] And an opposite approach to motor organization may sometimes be used, in which many motions fuse into unified wholes. (We may see indications of this when a musician has trouble beginning in the middle of a passage but instead must start at its beginning.) Furthermore, there is no reason to think that only two alternatives exist to organization in terms of focal impulses; the empirical questions relating to motor organization in performance are very much open. Nonetheless, the claim here is that their use is quite prevalent.

Typical focal impulse placements are norms in the sense of being prevalent; are they also norms the sense of being more valued? This is a complex question, and I will offer two main answers.

The first and most important answer to the question is that focal impulse theory is not primarily intended as a theory of aesthetic value. Rather, it is intended as a tool to guide perception and action. Its role is to make the user aware of a range of possibilities: what the options are, what each will sound like, and how the consequences of one decision may be relevant to others. The options a performer chooses are entirely outside the purview of the theory. If a performer is more satisfied about her choices regarding perception and action as a result of using the theory, the theory has served its purpose.

Although that answer is primary, it is incomplete in certain respects. Part of the theory's practical value is assumed to lie precisely in the correlation between statistics and aesthetics: if something is often done by good musicians, it will probably also be aesthetically pleasing—at least with respect to the communities, practices, and traditions in which those musicians are embedded. If so, then a statement such as "focal impulses are always placed on downbeats" should be translated simultaneously as "focal impulses are very frequently placed on downbeats" and as "many situations in which focal impulses are not placed on downbeats would be improved by adding focal impulses on the downbeats." But just which of those many situations would be improved? A musician may well say, "I don't think I'm placing focal impulses as described by the theory here. Does the theory say I'm doing something wrong?"

This more pointed version of the question elicits the second main answer, which considers three scenarios, each offering a different response.

First, I sometimes encounter musicians who tell me that they do not think their own focal impulse placements are as regular as I claim is normal. When I watch and listen to them play, I am often able to tell them that they have been misled by the salience of my initial examples and that focal impulses are often more subtle than they are expecting. They are indeed placing focal impulses as I predict, and I can point out specific aspects of sound and motion that help them identify the less salient focal impulses. In this case, the discrepancy is apparent and not real; the process of coming to understand and perceive the focal impulse is simply incomplete.

Second, there are cases in which I agree that musicians are not placing focal impulses as the theory indicates and in which I can point to specific aspects of their performance that could be facilitated by using more standard focal impulse placements. Often the musicians agree with me, finding the performance that fits the usual patterns more effective.

But there is a third possibility: that the performance uses something unusual to effective expressive ends.[9] A passage from a recording of Bach by Mischa Maisky, discussed in chapter 5, is an example of this phenomenon. Unusual performances may result from the performer having honed in on subtle aspects of the score that strain against the norms of compositional practice, and especially against the norms of meter. In other cases, a performer may take a particularly creative and active role in interpretation, placing performance emphases in sophisticated counterpoint with the score's salient structures. Either way, these choices can be aesthetically valuable.

There is no objective way to determine which of these three scenarios best describes an individual instance. Consequently, the application of focal impulse theory will be a matter of skilled practice, always possessing a subjective component. As with such matters generally, a community of skilled practitioners will be a helpful resource for those who would hone and exercise their skill.

Finally, beyond these two main responses to questions of value, I must also acknowledge that I am advancing aesthetic values in this book that are not part of the theory itself. At a certain level this happens almost constantly. I present examples that illustrate common ways of performing, and I offer interpretations that illustrate new possibilities that the theory reveals; naturally, I have chosen examples that I personally find appealing, interesting, and convincing.[10] And because I am a music theorist, it should not be surprising if my explorations of possibilities often involve analysis of the score, defining *analysis* simply as the art of making meaningfully interconnected observations about music. I hope it will be understood that I am using analysis as a way of enriching my engagement with the music and not as a source of exclusive, final judgements about the nature of a specific passage or the ways in which it might be performed.[11]

1.5. How Different Readers May Connect with This Book

Two main audiences may find this book of interest: music theorists and other humanistic scholars of music, and performing musicians. The details of the theory will be most relevant for readers who spend significant time with eighteenth- and nineteenth-century Western classical music, but I hope the broader strokes of the theory will resonate much more widely. (Some other musics are discussed briefly in the concluding chapter). Within those groups, readers who have a scientific outlook will form a significant subgroup; concerns specific to this subgroup have already been addressed.

The first audience is the primary one: my fellow scholars in music theory and related disciplines. Focal impulse theory overlaps with mainstream music theory in four main areas. The broadest two are (first) meter and rhythm, or time in music more generally (Lerdahl and Jackendoff 1983; Hasty 1997; Krebs 1999; London 2012), and (second) analysis and performance (Stein 1962; Cone 1968; Berry 1989; Dunsby 1995; Epstein 1995; Rink 1995b, 2002; Cook 1999; McClelland 2003; Barolsky and Klorman 2016; Klorman 2016). The third area is embodiment and gesture (Lussy 1874, [1885?]; Riemann 1884, 1903; Jaques-Dalcroze 1920, [1930] 1985; Whiteside [1955] 1997, 1969/1997; Zuckerkandl 1956; Lidov 1987, 2005; Cumming 2000; Hatten 2004; Le Guin 2006; Pierce 2007; Godøy and Leman 2010; Kozak 2015; Cox 2016; De Souza 2017; Kim and Gilman, forthcoming), which is discussed in chapter 14. Finally, the empirical side of the theory intersects significantly with music cognition, which is discussed in chapter 13. It is natural to examine phenomenology and its applications to music for connections with focal impulse theory, given their emphasis on experience and first-person perspective, but this area is something of a near miss. Phenomenological accounts of music, such as those by Clifton (1983), Lewin (1986), Fisher and Lockhead (2002), Benson (2003), Montague (2011), Kozak (2015), and De Souza (2017), often seem harmonious with focal impulse theory at a very basic methodological level, and several focus explicitly on the role of the body. Nonetheless, closer and more detailed connections cannot be made with either their content or their specific working methods.

Despite the intersections with active areas of research, this book is an outlier with respect to music theory—unusual both in its subject matter and its approach. But if some aspects of the book seem foreign to mainstream music theory, I hope that at least one aspect will seem very much at home, and that is its participation in what Mark DeBellis (1999) calls the "paradox of musical analysis." The paradox is this: we believe analysis when it seems true to our experience of the music, but we value analysis when it speaks into and transforms that experience. It seems that the two should be mutually exclusive, and yet that is exactly what good analysis does. In seeking to both describe and transform experience, the goals of analysis and the goals of focal impulse theory are the same.

The second audience to which the book is addressed consists of musicians and university-level music students. I hope to write a second book at some point that directly addresses this more general audience of musicians, omitting purely scholarly issues and providing additional examples and pedagogical exercises. That is not the book you hold in your hands, and if you are primarily a performing musician, I am grateful for your interest. More than that, I have taken several steps to enhance this book's appeal. First, I have attempted to minimize jargon and to make the discussion as readable as possible. Second, I have included chapter 2, which summarizes the few concepts from metrical theory and cognitive science that are essential for following the book's explorations of focal impulses. Third, I have tried to group together the more highly theoretical discussions so that a few whole chapters may simply be skipped, leaving the rest as practical and relevant to the performer as possible. The performer may wish to skip chapter 6, which discusses some theoretical issues raised in the basic exposition of the theory, and chapters 13 and 14 (pt. 4), which situate the theory with respect to various academic disciplines. In the remaining chapters, basic theoretical issues arise frequently but briefly, for the most part; they should not present significant obstacles to readers whose primary concern is practical application.

Whatever their perspectives and concerns, all readers should be prepared for a theory that fluidly blends description of the old and familiar with suggestion of the new and even surprising. They should also be willing to suspend judgment about certain aspects of the theory until they are confident that they have arrived not just at a conceptual understanding but also at a perceptual understanding of the focal impulse. In return, the book offers two opportunities: to get to know the focal impulse as an organizing agent in performance, shaping both motion and sound; and through doing so to expand the ways in which it is possible to experience and to act—both as a listener and as a performer of music.

Notes

1. Examination of personal experience is not the only kind of evidence for silent (or, as we will see, not-so-silent) focal impulses on strong beats that carry rests or ties. In a video of a master class available online, Yo-Yo Ma (2015, 1:30–2:00) says of a strong-beat rest that "the rest is actually a slap in the face." (The context is a cello quartet playing a Prokofiev march.) And in his recording of the first movement of Brahms's Cello Sonata No. 2 in F major with pianist Juhani Lagerspetz, cellist Truls Mørk (1988) sniffs quite audibly on the strong-beat rests and ties that he wants to spring out of. (Because of the metrical complexity of this theme, these strong beats are not all downbeats; see Ng 2006.)

2. The contrast between the parts described here raises a familiar question for twentieth- and twenty-first-century music (Copland 1943–44; Clarke et al. 2005, 40, 45, 47): What difference does the placement of the bar lines make? Clarke and his collaborators also mention the impact of a downbeat rest on the performer (45).

3. David Epstein (1990, 204) has a made a similar argument about the bodily state of the performer being reflected in the sound produced, as has Arnie Cox (2016).

4. As it happens, I call the muscular contractions that are organized by focal impulses "subsidiary impulses." Although I read Polanyi (1962) before starting work on this project, the resemblance between my terminology and his is coincidental.

5. Very similar accounts of tool use by Heidegger and Merleau-Ponty are discussed by De Souza (2017, 20–21).

6. This is one of the major thrusts of Polyani's (1962) argument, but see esp. 123, 143, 151, and 310.

7. This blending is related to the prototype category, one of the central tools of this book. Prototype perspectives understand that norms are statistically prevalent and that they serve as reference points, with other category members understood and interpreted in relation to them. Much humanistic scholarship, and much music theory, can be viewed as the assertion of central members of prototype categories, with this assertion resting on a scholar's deep and intimate knowledge of the category. I have argued elsewhere that it is profitable to frame such discussions explicitly in terms of prototype categories and that it is desirable to use empirical methods to support and refine those more informal judgments (Ito 2013a, 2014). This project is an example both of leaning heavily on introspective judgments about prevalence and centrality and of taking initial steps toward supporting those judgments empirically.

8. In a widely seen TED talk, conductor Benjamin Zander (2008) describes the development from beginning musician to accomplished artist in terms of a progression from using impulses on every note to using one impulse per phrase. Although I suspect that his use of the word "impulse" does not correspond exactly to the focal impulse as discussed in this book, there is clearly a close relationship.

9. Along these lines, Bruno Repp (1997, 1998) has created artificial performances by averaging the timing profiles of many recorded performances of the same works. These artificial performances are highly rated aesthetically, and performances by advanced students are often fairly close to the average. But performances by interpreters who are particularly known for their individuality are among the farthest from the average.

10. In sections 5.4 and 7.2, I also advocate on behalf of an older performance tradition whose rhythmic freedom has become unfamiliar as a result of the increasingly central place that precision has come to occupy since the late nineteenth century (Day 2000; Philip 2004).

11. This disclaimer is needed especially because such claims have been made in the past; they have been thoroughly critiqued in the past three decades or so (Rink 1990; Lester 1992, 1995; Cook 2013). Nicholas Cook has been particularly vehement in arguing against what he calls (borrowing from theater studies) a "page-to-stage" orientation in many music-theoretical writings that touch on performance, but I think there is some slippage in Cook's argument. Ostensibly, the problem is not with page-to-stage analyses in and of themselves but rather with an ideological orientation that, because of a particular understanding of the nature of music, privileges the theorist and denigrates the active, creative contributions of performers. Nonetheless, in practice, Cook seems to regard any use of that analytical approach as inherently problematic (39–40). For my part, I see no inconsistency between affirming the value of page-to-stage analyses and agreeing that other approaches are also needed (see Schmalfeldt 2016).

2

FOUNDATIONS IN MUSIC THEORY AND COGNITIVE SCIENCE

THIS CHAPTER DISCUSSES TERMS AND CONCEPTS THAT GO beyond the typical contents of an undergraduate core theory curriculum and that are needed as background for the rest of the book. The topics are the metrical hierarchy, the prototype category, terminology for syncopation and metrical dissonance, and hypermeter. Readers who are not already familiar with the metrical grid and the prototype category will want to read the first two sections of this chapter before proceeding. They will then have the choice either to continue through the remainder of the chapter in sequence or else to skip ahead to part 2 (the main exposition of focal impulse theory), returning to sections 2.3 and 2.4 when the topics of metrical dissonance and hypermeter arise.

2.1. The Metrical Hierarchy

The most generally accepted psychological theory of meter in music is that of Lerdahl and Jackendoff (1983, chaps. 2, 4). Their larger project is to describe how listeners understand music apart from notation; accordingly, they treat meter not in terms of meter signatures but in terms of a hierarchy of beat levels.

The most important background for Lerdahl and Jackendoff's theory of meter is their separation of meter and grouping. For them, meter has to do with the relative strength of beats within a hierarchy. Grouping has to do with how things group together, with what belongs together with what. Looking ahead to example 2.1b, for example, we can observe that the passage shown is a bounded unit, a four-bar phrase, and that it consists of two two-bar subphrases. We can further observe that the phrase begins with two measure-long motives, and we could have a conversation about whether the final eighth notes in measures 1–3 belong with the material that comes before or with the material that follows. All of these observations and discussions are about grouping. Grouping exists at all hierarchical levels in a piece of music. Individual notes group together, and at the highest level, a piece will divide into two or three main sections. Music theory usually names groups based on their function, and there are names for groups of many sizes: *motive, subphrase, phrase, period, theme group, exposition,* and so forth. In Lerdahl and Jackendoff's terminology, these terms can all be replaced with the bland but helpfully generic term *grouping unit*. Their distinction between meter and grouping is useful because it allows us to see that some apparently metrical concepts are really concerned with both meter and grouping. For example, the distinction between upbeat and afterbeat turns on whether notes on weak beats group more strongly with what has come before or with what follows.

Turning now to Lerdahl and Jackendoff's (1983) understanding of meter proper, we begin with meter as notated, but we will soon leave notation behind. Suppose we have some passage in $\frac{4}{4}$; it should be possible to tap along with a great many different beats—whole notes, half notes, quarter notes, eighth notes—depending on the tempo and on how slowly or quickly we are able to tap. These beat levels form a hierarchy: at the top level are the whole notes, the whole notes are subdivided to create the half notes, and so on. Each of these beats can be idealized as a point in time that has no duration. This leads to a close analogy with dimensionless points in space, and this in turn invites a spatial representation of this hierarchy of beats as a grid of dots, with each dot representing one beat, and a horizontal stream of dots representing a stream of beats of a certain duration.[1] Figure 2.1 illustrates this for a meter of $\frac{3}{4}$. Note a potential area of confusion regarding the different ways in which beat levels might be described as higher or lower. It is traditional, when speaking about hierarchies, to call the more important, larger, global levels the *higher* levels and to call the less important, smaller, local levels the *lower* levels, and this way of speaking about hierarchies of beat levels will be used in this book. But, as illustrated in figure 2.1, it is standard to arrange metrical grids with the fastest, hierarchically lowest beat levels at the top of the grid. This is done because the grids are usually placed below the staff, and putting the lowest levels on top, closest to the music, makes it easier to understand which dots align with which notes. But this means that levels that are lower hierarchically are higher visually.

This grid of dots provides a clear way of defining metrical strength: at any one beat level, the strong beats are those that are also beats at the next higher hierarchical level. As an example, consider the second quarter-note beat in each measure of figure 2.1. At the quarter-note level, this beat is weak because,

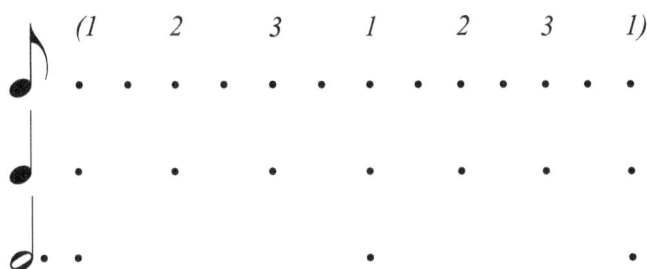

Fig. 2.1. A metrical grid for 3/4 (after ex. 2.8a from Lerdahl and Jackendoff 1983, 20).

unlike beat 1, it is not also a beat at the next higher level (the dotted-half-note level). But at the eighth-note level, this same beat is strong because it is also a beat at the quarter-note level.

This explanation is a somewhat complicated way of saying that the second quarter-note beats in $\frac{3}{4}$ are weaker than the downbeats but stronger than the weak-beat eighths. The metrical grid can be more cumbersome to talk about in words, but it has several advantages over conventional metrical notation, especially for cognitively oriented music theory. First, it is visually apparent from the grid how the beats relate to one another in terms of metrical strength. Second, it is easily credible that someone who listened to music but had never had any training in performance or music notation might have an implicit understanding of stronger and weaker beats quite similar to this hierarchy of beats. Concepts of meter that are based in notation quickly run into trouble for this kind of listener—why should they imagine that there are such things as measures? And even if they did, how would they decide what the main beat was, or how many beats there were in a measure? How would they know if the music was in $\frac{2}{4}$ or $\frac{4}{4}$?[2] These questions disappear when we use the metrical hierarchy. We understand the note values along the left to be convenient labels that help the reader relate the beat levels to the score; the only thing understood to be present in the mind of the listener is the hierarchy of beats. This hierarchy is called variously the *metrical hierarchy* or the *metrical grid*, and the representation of the hierarchy using dots is called a *dot diagram*. An example of dot notation applied to actual music is shown in example 2.1a; here the grid is extended rather obsessively down to the level of the sixteenth note, in response to the presence of two sixteenth notes in the passage. It is customary to omit the lower levels of the hierarchy, as in example 2.1b. Example 2.1b also illustrates dot notation's ability show us things that conventional metrical notation cannot, in this case that the downbeats are not all equally strong, every other downbeat being stronger.

a)

b)

Example 2.1. Metrical grids applied to the opening measures of Mozart's K. 331 (after exx. 4.4 and 2.21a from Lerdahl and Jackendoff 1983, 71, 33).

Two other aspects of the metrical grid are relevant to our concerns. First, Lerdahl and Jackendoff (1983), drawing on gestalt perceptual psychology, consider it axiomatic that groupings of various sorts always go by twos and threes. Their hierarchical treatments of meter and grouping both assume that when going from level to level in a hierarchy, single entities are always dividing into either two or three smaller entities. Therefore, beat levels in the hierarchy always relate to one another by multiples of two or three in the spacing between the beats. In their treatment of meter, this approach reflects the commonplace elements of basic theory: in $\frac{4}{4}$, the whole is two halves, a half is two quarters, a quarter is two eighths; in $\frac{3}{4}$, the dotted half divides into three quarters and a quarter divides into two eighths; in $\frac{6}{8}$, the dotted half divides instead into two dotted quarters, each of which divides into three eighths. We would be aware of something missing if we were to say that in $\frac{4}{4}$, the whole note divides into four quarters, with no half-note level and each of the three weak quarters being equally weak metrically; or worse, that $\frac{6}{8}$ divides directly into six eighths, with five equally weak eighth-note beats. With so many weak beats relating directly to just one strong beat, there would be a sense of vagueness, of underdefined relationships and an incompletely realized hierarchy.

The final aspect of the metrical grid to highlight is the anchoring of the hierarchy. In conventional metrical theory, the many beat levels are anchored by two structures: a main beat level (e.g., the quarter in $\frac{4}{4}$, the dotted quarter in $\frac{6}{8}$) and a measure that unites two, three, or four of the main beats. Lerdahl and Jackendoff's (1983) theory avoids any reference to notation, and so these anchors are not available—the listener often does not know what beat level she is tapping along with or whether there are two or four main beats in the measure. As an alternative, Lerdahl and Jackendoff use a term from renaissance metrical theory and speak of the *tactus* as the listener's main beat, the beat that the listener taps along with. Especially when the tactus is expressed physically in this way, it is easy to draw parallels between the tactus as something experienced by the listener in relation to meter and the focal impulse as something employed by the performer in relation to meter—and the parallel is even easier to draw if listeners use their own focal impulses. But there is no necessary correlation between the listener's taps and the performer's (or the listener's) focal impulses. The relationship between the two should become clearer as the focal impulse comes into focus (and the discussion of cognitive approaches to meter and timekeeping in chap. 13 should help). The question of a listener's focal impulses is touched on at the end of the concluding chapter, as an area of the theory in need of further development.

2.2. The Prototype Category

As a concept, the prototype category grew out of psychological research on prototype effects in mental categories, conducted mainly in the 1970s and associated especially with Eleanor Rosch (Rosch 1978; Mervis and Rosch 1981; Lakoff 1987, chap. 2). The cognitive linguist Dirk Geeraerts (1989) has identified four central tenets of categorization in cognitive linguistics, and this work in psychology is the source of the first three:

1. Prototype categories have graded typicality; not every member is equally representative of the category.
2. Prototype categories have fuzzy boundaries.
3. Prototype categories cannot be defined in terms of a single set of necessary and sufficient attributes.
4. Possible ways of structuring prototype categories include family resemblance and radial sets of clustered and overlapping models.

The first point is the heart of the prototype approach to categorization: some members of a category are "better" examples of the category than other members—that is, they are prototypical.[3] Prototype effects are seen in relatively external kinds of overt behavior; participants in experiments rate prototypical examples as such, and when asked to list members of categories, participants name prototypical examples sooner and with greater frequency.

But prototype effects are also revealed in less overt ways, including priming effects and the speed of learning artificial categories (i.e., categories invented for the purpose of the experiment). To use standard examples from the literature, a robin is a more prototypical bird than a hawk, and each is more prototypical than an ostrich. This concept can also be expressed in spatial terms by saying that categories have centers (or cores) and peripheries, often with fine gradations between the two. In discussing the placement of focal impulses with respect to meter in eighteenth- and nineteenth-century Western classical music, I will distinguish three main concentric regions: a core, an inner periphery, and an outer periphery.

The second point states that mental categories often lack clearly defined boundaries, so that it is impossible to specify the exact point at which examples cease to be members of the category. The categories *red* and *tall building* are basically clear in their content, but one could neither specify frequencies of electromagnetic vibration at which red becomes orange nor stipulate a precise height under which a building is not considered tall. It follows that when instances occur near category boundaries, judgments of category membership will often vary from person to person.

The third point is that prototype categories cannot be defined in terms of some set of necessary and sufficient conditions for membership; as this was the defining feature of classical categories as set down by Aristotle, prototype categories are not classical categories. An example of a classical category is the *positive odd number*. This category can be defined using two conditions. First, for N to be a positive odd number, there must exist some integer M such that $N = 2M + 1$. Second, for N to be a positive odd number, N must be greater than zero. These conditions are necessary because if we take one away, the set we have defined will not be the set of positive odd numbers. And the conditions are sufficient in that nothing that is not a positive odd number satisfies both conditions. In an equivalent formulation, these criteria specify all and only positive odd numbers. Note that classical categories also contrast with prototype categories on the first two of the four main characteristics discussed above; in classical categories no member is more prototypical than any other, and classical categories do not have fuzzy boundaries. Most prototype categories cannot be defined using necessary and sufficient conditions. A classic case is the chair; if you are familiar with a range of chairs and stools, especially those designed by artists and architects, you will see that no set of necessary and sufficient conditions includes all chairs but no stools.[4]

The fourth point gets at the structuring of categories. If they are not defined by necessary and sufficient conditions, how are they structured? Rosch

(1978) is quite explicit that "prototypes do not constitute a theory of representation of categories" (40). Rather, the first three points constrain the forms that theories of categories may take—whatever their particulars, theories about prototype categories should not make predictions that contradict the first three points. A number of answers to the question of how prototype categories are organized have been proposed over the past thirty years (Smith 2005); this question is the most disputed aspect of the prototype category.

Family resemblance, the way of organizing prototype categories used here, bases the understanding of a peripheral practice or object on an understanding of a more central one.[5] For example, in a phrase like "the mother of all water fights," *mother* is first understood metaphorically to refer to a source (connecting with central meanings of *mother*) and then inserted into a hierarchy, with the source having a higher place in the hierarchy than the things that flow from the source. Although family resemblance applies most obviously to the use of words and the categorization of objects, it can apply to any kind of voluntary behavior in which norms of practice undergo continual definition and redefinition in an evolutionary process.[6]

The composition of music is a voluntary behavior of that sort, and countless examples show composers knowingly playing off of established norms.[7] One example is provided by gavottes of Bach. Gavottes normally feature two upbeat quarter notes leading into a strong downbeat (Little and Jenne 2001), as in the gavotte from English Suite No. 5, shown in example 2.2a. In a pun on the usual practice that could have caused chaos had the gavottes actually been danced, in the gavottes from the Orchestral Suites Nos. 3 and 4, Bach introduces suspensions that delay the crucial downbeat, either in the bass or in the melody (exx. 2.2b and 2.2c). These movements extend the scope of the category *gavotte*.

If extensions of practice of this sort become standardized, they can themselves serve as points of departure for further extensions of practice, thus building a new space at the periphery of a category. An example is the common-tone diminished seventh chord. It started out as a by-product of neighboring motion embellishing a root-position triad, but it eventually became a familiar enough sound that it could depart from its origins—no longer sandwiched between two identical chords but rather standing more on its own, embellishing the motion into a chord from some other chord. This is how prototype categories are built up.

For our purposes, prototype categories are helpful because they provide a way of talking about practice in terms of graded centrality; some ways of doing things (e.g., placing focal impulses) are more typical than others. The

Example 2.2. Bach, Gavottes. (*a*) English Suite No. 6, BWV 811, Gavotte I, mm. 1–4. (*b*) Orchestral Suite No. 3, BWV 1068, Gavotte I, mm. 1–4, reduced score. (*c*) Orchestral Suite No. 4, BWV 1069, Gavotte, mm. 1–4, reduced score.

more typical instances occur with greater frequency, and they often function as norms, providing the terms we use to understand the less typical instances. They also function as models, with novel uses of focal impulses taking inspiration from standard ones. If we see the world through the lens of classical categories, we will only be able to see two things: either rigidly consistent patterning or else chaos. Prototype categories are a natural fit for what we expect with any kind of artistic practice: coherent patterning and clear general trends, but an absence of solid lines marking the boundaries between what is done and what is not done.

2.3. Terminology for Syncopation and Metrical Dissonance

Syncopation occurs when weaker beats are more strongly emphasized than stronger beats. Metrical dissonance occurs when syncopations form regular patterns that conflict with the meter and that could potentially be construed as implying some other meter or some other placement of bar lines. The term *metrical dissonance* is used both for cases in which the listener hears syncopation in the notated meter and for cases in which the listener shifts to a different heard meter.

The most commonly used terms for types of metrical dissonance come from the work of Harald Krebs (1999).[8] When the competing pattern fits the meter signature but suggests a different placement of bar lines, the term *displacement dissonance* is used, indicating that the patterning of the music has been shifted, or displaced, with respect to the notated meter. Displacement dissonance will often be discussed in terms of phase, a concept drawn from mathematics. In any pattern that has cyclical repetition, *phase* refers to a specific position within the cycle, often using a scale from 0 to 1 for the entire cycle. Thus we could speak of the third quarter-note beat in common time occupying the 0.5 phase position within the measure. Phase can also refer to the relative alignment of two cyclically repeating events; the events are in phase when they occur at the same time and out of phase when they occur at different times. For example, two metronomes set at 60 beats per minute (bpm) can be either in phase or out of phase, and metronomes set at 60 and 66 bpm will gradually drift between being exactly in phase and exactly out of phase. I will thus sometimes speak of a pattern of syncopations as being out of phase with the meter.

If the metrical dissonance suggests a different meter or, more precisely, a meter with a different metrical grid, the term *grouping dissonance* is used. This term indicates a different spacing of strong beats at some level and thus a different grouping of beats into larger units by the strong beats.[9] A hemiola in which, for example, two measures of $\frac{3}{4}$ are heard with strong beats corresponding to a single measure in $\frac{3}{2}$ is an instance of grouping dissonance, with the quarter-note beats grouped either in threes (in the notated meter) or in twos (in the hemiola).

2.4. Hypermeter

In example 2.1b, the metrical grid includes a beat level higher than that of the downbeats. At this level, the beat lasts two measures, and so the downbeats alternate between downbeats that are beats at this higher level and downbeats that are not; this means that there is an alternation between strong and weak downbeats. The term *hypermeter*—literally, *large meter*—describes any metrical organization on a scale larger than the notated measure.[10] For Lerdahl and Jackendoff (1983) and for most cognitively oriented music theorists, this definition captures all there is to hypermeter; it is simply that part of the metrical grid that involves longer timescales than the interval from downbeat to downbeat. But there is a much older way of looking at hypermeter that sees it mainly as the metrical organization of the downbeats and that gives special prominence to four-bar units. I refer to these two approaches, respectively, as the cognitive and analytical traditions.[11] In the following survey of hypermetrical analysis, I draw mainly on the analytical tradition and especially on my own extensions of the analytical tradition (Ito 2013a). Readers seeking either more depth or divergent viewpoints will find plenty of references in the notes. This discussion has two parts: the first looks at the basics of hypermeter, and the second looks at hypermeter in more complex contexts.

Basic Hypermetrical Analysis

For a description like "four-bar phrase" to be meaningful, we must have a concept of the measure, which the metrical grid lacks. We could appeal to notation and use the notated measures; this is often perfectly valid, especially when talking about the performer's point of view, as the performer will be looking at (or at least strongly influenced by) the score. But it is not difficult to develop conceptions of the measure and of the hypermeasure without recourse to notation; these concepts will help us when there is an alternative heard meter.[12] We can start by saying that the listener will perceive some main beat level—Lerdahl and Jackendoff's (1983) tactus. We can then say that the listener will hear *heard measures* consisting of between one and four tactus beats. This sense of orientation to a main beat and to heard measures is called *metrical orientation*. So far this account mostly shadows the structure of conventional metrical theory but without any role for notation; for any given listener, the tactus may or may not correspond to the meter's main beat, and the heard measures may or may not correspond to the notated measures. The downbeats of the heard measures are the *heard downbeats*, and when *hypermetrical orientation* is present, the heard downbeats function as the main beats (hyperbeats) in the hypermeasures, taking on roles that parallel the roles of the quarter-note beats in $\frac{2}{4}$, $\frac{3}{4}$, and $\frac{4}{4}$ measures. (Unlike measures felt in one, hypermeasures in one do not make sense; if the heard hypermeasures are the same size as the measures, hypermeter is absent.) Many hypermetrical analyses in this book will assume that the listener's heard measures are the same as the notated measures. Some analyses in chapter 12 depart from this pattern, however, allowing heard measures to stretch and contract as the heard downbeat moves back and forth between the notated downbeat and the

Example 2.3. Mozart, Piano Sonata K. 331, i, mm. 1–4.

middle of the measure. Even more complex variations in heard meter will be encountered in chapters 15 and 16.

We have already seen an analysis of the hypermeter of the first few measures of Mozart's K. 331 from the perspective of the cognitive tradition (ex. 2.1b); an analysis of the same passage drawing on the analytical tradition is shown in example 2.3. In the fractional notation, the numerator is the hyperbeat number and the denominator is the number of measures in the hypermeasure.[13] The notation "3/4" is pronounced not as "three quarters" but as "three of four" or as "third of four." Because the heard downbeat and notated downbeat do not always correspond, the hypermeter fractions will always be placed directly above the heard downbeat.

Because phrase construction in four-bar units is a very strong norm, many cases exist in which phrases of other lengths are understood in terms of a four-bar model. Examples of this arise later in this section, in the discussion of hypermetrical complexity, and further examples appear later in the book. But there are also cases in which we hear in terms of hypermeasures of other sizes, especially two- and three-bar hypermeasures. An example that can be heard in two-bar hypermeter is the opening of Mozart's Piano Sonata in C Major, K. 279, (ex. 2.4). It is also a good example of phrase and subphrase overlap because the events on the downbeats of measures 3 and 5 are simultaneously conclusions of prior material and new beginnings. Although it would be possible to hear the first four measures as a complete $\frac{4}{4}$ hypermeasure, the analysis shown in the example, in which those measures are two complete $\frac{2}{4}$ hypermeasures, better captures my hearing of the passage. The reason for this has everything to do with the "orientation" part of the phrase *hypermetrical orientation.* As an example of orientation in time, the work week gives shape to the week, with a sense of where I am now (Monday as I write this, setting out on my journey) and where I am headed (a weekend of rest, worship, family adventures, and odd jobs around the house).[14] Heard hypermeasures also mark a sense of orientation in time, an orientation that includes an amount of time I'm paying attention to now as well as a sense of when I expect this

Example 2.4. Mozart, Piano Sonata K. 279, i, mm. 1–8.

unit to end and the next to begin. Listening to music always involves multiple, simultaneous timescales; what I'm paying attention to now will often be, all at once, a beat, a hypermeasure, and a section of a movement. But if we're talking about the level of hypermeter, the level of a handful of heard measures, the opening music of K. 279 seems to me to lead toward the downbeat of measure 3 and from measure 3 on to measure 5. My awareness of a single arc from the beginning to the downbeat of measure 5 is much less vivid. Because my horizon of expectation uses a two-bar periodicity at this point, I hear two-bar hypermeasures. This horizon widens right away as measure 5 begins; I can tell that a longer-breathed hypermeasure is beginning. Turning now to triple hypermeter, the most famous example is the one labeled explicitly as such by Beethoven in the scherzo of the Ninth Symphony, using the words "ritmo di tre battute" (rhythm of three measures).[15] A more melodic passage in triple hypermeter, from the final movement of Brahms's Piano Trio in B Major, op. 8, in the original version of 1854, is shown in example 2.5.

Because the great majority of examples of hypermeter discussed in the book use four-bar hypermeter, I close this treatment of basic hypermetrical analysis by looking at typical patterns for the alignment of four-bar hypermeasures with four-bar grouping units.[16] There are four possible alignments; a grouping unit could start with any one of the four hyperbeats.[17] But two alignments are so typical that they can serve as templates to understand more complex cases, which is to say that they serve as schemas. Elsewhere I have summed up the schema as "a general pattern to which individual instances can be related, even when those individual instances relate to the schema only partially" (Ito 2013a, 50). As might be expected, schemas are closely related

Example 2.5. Brahms, Piano Trio op. 8, iv, 1854 version, mm. 104–116, Allegro molto agitato.

to prototype categories; the structure of prototype categories is often understood in terms of clusters of related schemas.

When four-bar hypermeter is found, the most common way for the music to align with the hyperbeats is for the first measure of the phrase to be the hypermetrical downbeat, as in example 2.3. This alignment between the grouping unit and the hyperbeats is described by the *1–2–3–4 schema*; shown in table 2.1, which originally appeared in Ito (2013a), it is also called the *beginning-weighted* schema or simply the *primary* schema. The hyperbeat numbers always refer to the usual numbering of beats, as in a conducting pattern, with the downbeat being beat 1. The four main columns of the table represent the four measures of the grouping unit in order of appearance. In this schema, the grouping unit begins with hyperbeat 1, making it beginning accented. The next row of the table indicates the relative metrical weight of each hyperbeat, and the final row shows each measure's role in the grouping unit, with the first measure initiating, the second continuing, and so forth. This schema will be helpful when we examine more complex cases of hypermeter, helpful especially because it allows us to identify hyperbeats based on a relatively course-grained hearing of metrical weight. Suppose

Table 2.1. Hypermetrical weight and grouping function for hyperbeats in the 1-2-3-4 schema

Type of Attribute	Hyperbeat			
	1	2	3	4
Degree of metrical weight	Primary weight	Unweighted	Secondary weight	Unweighted
Role in grouping unit	Initiation	Continuation	Continuation or beginning of conclusion	Conclusion or end of conclusion

that we are hearing in terms of the schema, and we encounter a measure that seems somewhat weighted, but it is not clear whether the measure has the primary weight of hyperbeat 1 or the secondary weight of hyperbeat 3. If we can tell whether its role is initiating or continuing (or beginning to conclude), we can tell if we are hearing that measure as a first measure or as a third measure in the schema. The schema helps us to hone in on what we are already hearing so that our analysis can both represent and sharpen our existing hearing.

The beginning-weighted schema can be used at any time, but it is found especially at the beginnings of movements or major sections of movements. This is because music that begins a section is likely to feel like a beginning; it will likely have its most characteristic and important material at the start of the phrase, with the cadence being somewhat more generic. Using the primary schema emphasizes this salient beginning with hypermetrical weight.

It is also possible, however, for music to emphasize ending and cadence. Such music is found especially at the ends of major sections—in closing theme groups from sonata forms or in codas or codettas, for example. It can also occur in the phrase extensions called postcadential extensions.[18] (As one example of a postcadential extension, the cadence that ends the transition in a sonata-form movement and that serves to mark the end of the first half of the exposition is often extended in this way.) The material found in such places sometimes has generic and conventional thematic content, in contrast to the beginning-oriented music described earlier; this is especially common in postcadential extensions. Closing themes often have a more distinctive thematic profile, but when they do, their beginnings often sound like middles. They will often contrast with first themes, particularly because the purpose of their existence is to lead us on to cadence. Where first and second themes sound comfortable commanding the stage, closing themes

Table 2.2. Hypermetrical weight and grouping function for hyperbeats in the 2-3-4-1 schema

Type of Attribute	Hyperbeat			
	2	3	4	1
Degree of metrical weight	Unweighted	Secondary weight	Unweighted	Primary weight
Role in grouping unit	Initiation	Continuation or subsidiary conclusion	Continuation or subsidiary initiation	Conclusion

are more in a hurry to get somewhere. In this vein, a friend of mine used to say that you could almost hear Beethoven waving goodbye in his closing themes.

End-oriented material of this kind is not served particularly well by the primary schema, given that the end of the unit, either a cadence or the conclusion of a subphrase, will be unweighted—and thus unemphasized—hypermetrically. For this reason, end-oriented material often lends itself to end-weighted hypermeter, with hyperbeat 1/4 closing, not beginning, the grouping unit.[19] This is described by the *2-3-4-1* schema, shown in table 2.2, also called the *end-weighted* schema. An example of end-weighted hypermeter, the closing theme from the last movement of Beethoven's Piano Sonata in F Minor, op. 2, no. 1, is shown in example 2.6. As shown in the table, the schema includes two options for the organization of the grouping unit: in one, the grouping unit is a continuous whole (the two middle measures both continuing); in the other, it divides into two parts (with the second measure a subsidiary conclusion and the third a subsidiary initiation). This is because those two ways of organizing grouping units are both commonly found in postcadential extensions. These options are illustrated by example 2.7, which shows the end of Chopin's Prelude in E-flat Major, op. 28, no. 19.[20] This prelude is in a simple ternary form, with the outer sections consisting of parallel periods, and when the period returns after the contrasting middle section, the second phrase is extended by one measure so that the cadence lands on a hypermetrical downbeat. This is the point of departure for the final postcadential extension, in which the two possibilities for the end-weighted schema alternate, with the music segmented in measures 50–53 and 58–61 and continuous in measures 54–57 and 62–65. It is also quite common for end-oriented music to consist of chains of overlapping five-bar phrases in which the first and the fifth measures are both weighted (because of the overlaps, the fifth measure of one phrase is the first measure of the next). In such cases, we speak of a *hybrid* schema. Examples of the hybrid

Example 2.6. Beethoven, Piano Sonata op. 2/1, iv, mm. 32–42, Prestissimo.

schema, like those of the end-weighted schema, are particularly common in closing groups, codas, and end-oriented music more generally. The second theme from the final movement of Schubert's Symphony No. 4 in C minor, shown in example 2.8, is more beginning-oriented than end-oriented, but the fourth measure of each little phrase (or subphrase?) both answers the third and leads strongly into the next beginning, creating an unusually continuous flow; this makes the passage a striking example of the hybrid schema, despite the less usual formal location.[21]

Example 2.7. Chopin, Prelude op. 28/19, mm. 41–71, Vivace, simplified and reduced score.

Example 2.8. Schubert, Symphony No. 4, iv, mm. 83–93, Allegro, reduced score.

Analysis of Hypermetrical Complexity

Meter within the measure is often a consistent backdrop for a movement. I will discuss plenty of exceptions over the course of the book, but in much music from the eighteenth and nineteenth centuries, whatever metrical pattern the music starts with continues until the end.[22] In contrast, hypermeter is quite variable and discontinuous. It is not uncommon to go from hearing in terms of four-bar hypermeter to three-bar hypermeter and back again, or to encounter a four-bar hypermeasure that is expanded to five or six measures or else left incomplete. A number of techniques lead to adjustments of hypermeter, some more consistently patterned and some more variable. I begin with the typical patterns and then move on to the freer cases.

Theorists have identified a number of consistently patterned adjustments to hypermeter; for our purposes, the most important are *hypermetrical reinterpretation, extended upbeats, successive downbeats,* and *split downbeats.*[23] These adjustments to hypermeter are based on widespread compositional techniques whose ranges of variation define prototype categories. To appreciate how a given instance fits into larger patterns of compositional practice, it is necessary to be familiar with those patterns.

The first pattern is the hypermetrical reinterpretation. Hypermetrical reinterpretation occurs at some phrase overlaps, when the cadence of the phrase, expected to be weak, is suddenly discovered to be strong, as new material begins at the moment of cadence.[24] The most frequently cited example comes from the first movement of Haydn's Symphony No. 104, at the overlap between the first theme and the transition (ex. 2.9). Note the contrast with the second theme from the final movement of Schubert's Symphony No. 4; there the overlaps occurred in the fifth bars of the phrases, which were expected to be strong. There were no surprises, and so there were no hypermetrical reinterpretations. In the Haydn example, the listener expects hyperbeat 4/4, but it is immediately evident that this moment is a new beginning and that it is metrically weighted. The arrow from 4/4 to 1/4 represents the listener's sudden readjustment. (The performer must make the surprise happen and thus must prepare for it. For the performer, there is simply a new hyperbeat 1/4, interrupting the previous hypermeasure.)

In their most standard form, hypermetrical reinterpretations result in hyperdownbeats spaced three measures apart that are heard within a framework of quadruple hypermeter. Hyperdownbeats every three measures arise most straightforwardly in triple hypermeter, and so triple hypermeter will often be a competing interpretation when there is a phrase overlap on the fourth

Example 2.9. Haydn, Symphony No. 104, i, mm. 17–35, Allegro, reduced score.

measure of a phrase. The competition is heightened when a regular three-bar periodicity is established; this can easily occur when four-bar phrases are chained together with overlaps. This possibility makes interesting parallels with five-bar phrases with overlaps that use the hybrid schema, which were illustrated earlier by the passage from the final movement of Schubert's Symphony No. 4. Example 2.10 shows the opening measures of Mozart's Piano Sonata in D Major, K. 311. If we listen from the start to the downbeat of measure 4, and from the downbeat of measure 4 to the downbeat of measure 7, we hear that the first two phrases work perfectly well as quadruple hypermeasures. But in each case there is a phrase overlap: the cadential tonic of one phrase also serves as the beginning of the next. Just as five-bar phrases chained with overlaps lead to hyperdownbeats four measures apart, we find hyperdownbeats every three measures in K. 311. If we compare this passage with example 2.5, from Brahms's op. 8, we see that the phrase overlaps are the crucial difference between Brahms's theme as an unambiguous example of triple hypermeter and K. 311 as a case in which hearing hypermetrical reinterpretations is a possibility. The Mozart passage is interesting in this regard because the case for the reinterpretations is somewhat equivocal. It is equivocal mainly because at the start of measure 4, we would seem to be hearing simply a weak-hyperbeat imperfect authentic cadence (IAC) concluding the first phrase; but in the second half of the measure, we hear a clear parallel with the first measure of the phrase, suggesting that the downbeat of measure 4 had

Example 2.10. Mozart, Piano Sonata K. 311, i, mm. 1–8.

been another hyperdownbeat. This possibility is greatly strengthened because the second phrase unfolds as a literal repeat of the first, adjusted only at its ends. But because measure 4 does not announce itself from the start as a new beginning, the interpretation in terms of a hypermetrical reinterpretation is undermined (of course, the performer has the option of bringing out—or concealing—the role of m. 4 as a beginning).[25] If I wanted to show how clear the case can be for chained reinterpretations spaced three bars apart, I would have chosen a different example, as I have done elsewhere (Ito 2013a, 72–73). The value of this more borderline case lies in showing just how far from the clarity of Haydn's Symphony No. 104 we can move and still retain the hypermetrical reinterpretation as a real potential hearing.

The second of the hypermetrical adjustments is the extended upbeat. In this case the term provides the definition, referring to extra measures that serve as extended upbeats to the main phrases that follow.[26] Example 2.11 shows the most frequently cited instance: the opening of the exposition from the first movement of Haydn's Symphony No. 101. A key feature here is that the upbeat measures could be removed, leaving the body of the phrase as a complete four-bar hypermeasure. Extended upbeats are always understood to represent extra hyperbeats in this way. If there is regular, uninterrupted cycling through the four hyperbeats, but with grouping units starting with 4/4 hyperbeats (as in the first waltz from Johann Strauss Jr.'s *Blue Danube Waltz* [Rothstein 1989, 6, 8–9]), these upbeat measures do not count as extended upbeats.

Example 2.11. Haydn, Symphony No. 101, i, mm. 24–33, Presto, reduced score.

Example 2.12. Mozart, Piano Sonata K. 333, ii, mm. 8–15, Andante cantabile.

Successive downbeats, the third of the regularly patterned hypermetrical adjustments, occur when one section ends with a hypermetrical downbeat and the next section begins with another hypermetrical downbeat in the following measure.[27] Example 2.12 shows an instance of successive downbeats, the seam between the transition and the second theme in the slow movement from Mozart's Piano Sonata in B-flat Major, K. 333. In the context of a large-scale point of articulation in the form, discontinuity of hypermeter is natural and unobtrusive.

Finally, the split downbeat occurs when a new section arrives with a hypermetrical downbeat, but the accompaniment texture precedes the melody by one measure, so that both the start of the section and the start of the melody are heard as hypermetrical downbeats. Example 2.13, from Gilbert and Sullivan's *H.M.S. Pinafore*, is typical. It also illustrates the source of the term *split downbeat*—it is as if a single measure, in which the melody and the accompaniment begin together, has been split into two, with the accompaniment coming in first. The same effect occurs even more frequently with a spacing of two measures; this is shown in example 2.14, from the slow movement of Schubert's Symphony No. 8 in B Minor. In cases like this, hypermeter is suspended until the entrance of the melody; there is no real continuation until forward motion resumes with the second part of the split downbeat.[28] In the example, the suspension of hypermeter is indicated using the abbreviation *H.M.T.*, which stands for *hypermetrical tunnel*. This term comes from a comparison of the absence of hypermeter to an experience of driving through a tunnel, in which we are unable to get a larger sense of orientation from the surrounding landscape and instead have an entirely local sense of where we are (Ito 2013a). The most typical case of the split downbeat involves the sense that a single event happens twice, and this requires that the two instances have the same harmony. But like most of our analytical categories, the split downbeat is a prototype category; as a result, it can also be heard in less typical contexts. In the first movement of Beethoven's String Quartet in A Minor, op. 132, the second theme proper enters in measure 49, following a cadence on a hypermetrical downbeat at the start of the previous measure and a bar of vamping accompaniment. In this context, a split downbeat makes sense, even though the accompaniment begins on tonic harmony and the melody begins on the dominant.

The simpler kinds of hypermetrical discontinuities that we have just surveyed all occur at boundaries between phrases. The more complex cases of irregular hypermeter are found inside phrases, when phrase lengths are not even multiples of four. We have already seen that some of these cases can be understood in terms of hypermeasures of a length other than four bars. But in many instances, we can still hear in terms of a four-bar schema; it is just that some hypermeasures are incomplete or have had beats added or subtracted.

The simplest of these cases occur when there is a deceptive cadence or an evaded cadence—when there was an "unsuccessful" attempt at an authentic cadence.[29] In such cases it is common to return to material that has just been heard (or to material that is similar or equivalent in function) and to redo the

Example 2.13. Sullivan, *H.M.S. Pinafore*, "The hours creep on apace," mm. 27–36, piano-vocal score.

Example 2.14. Schubert, Symphony No. 8, ii, mm. 60–69, Andante con moto, reduced score.

cadence, usually making the authentic cadence successfully the second time around. When this happens, it is natural to hear the second pass in terms of the first and to hear the parallel measures with parallel hyperbeats. A simple passage that can be heard in this way is shown in example 2.15, from the rondeau "La Badine" from the fifth *ordre* of François Couperin's *Pièces de clavecin*.

Hearing hypermeter in irregular phrases is more complex when there is no direct model for the added material—or when the irregularity is not necessarily the result of added material at all. In such cases, the schemas display their full utility. Example 2.16 shows the beginning of Chopin's Etude in

Example 2.15. François Couperin, *Pièces de clavecin*, 5th *ordre*, Rondeau, "La Badine," mm. 1–10.

Example 2.16. Chopin, Etude op. 10/3, mm. 1–5.

E Major, op. 10, no. 3. The opening phrase consists of five measures, but it can readily be heard in terms of a four-bar framework. The beginning and conclusion are clear, with the first measure a hyperbeat 1/4 and the final bar a 4/4; the bigger question concerns the middle measures. They all play continuing roles, and so hyperbeats 2/4 and 3/4 seem the obvious candidates. We can further observe of that of the three middle measures, all but measure 4 have syncopations across the bar line—and not just melodic syncopations but syncopations of harmonic rhythm, as the downbeats of these measures each repeat the final chords of the preceding measures. Because the downbeat of measure 4 is so much more strongly articulated than the downbeats of measures 2 and 3, it makes sense to hear measure 4 as hyperbeat 3/4 and measures 2 and 3 both as hyperbeats 2/4, a hearing further reinforced by the motivic similarity of those measures. This hearing is shown in example 2.16.[30]

Although considerations of hypermeter are absent from much of the book, we will return to hypermeter, and to complex cases that continue to show the utility of the schemas, at the end of part 3 and in part 5.

Notes

1. In the metrical grid, the kind of duration employed is not the actual performed duration, which is often quite variable. Duration is couched instead in terms of the listener's understanding of functionally equivalent durations (e.g., the duration from one main beat to another). These durational categories will often effectively reproduce the notated durations of the score.

2. I have proposed an approach to answering these questions that, although meant mainly for listeners who are musicians, is at least conceivable for listeners who are not (Ito 2013a); this approach is summarized in sec. 2.4.

3. Instances that are prototypes may or may not exist (Rosch 1978, 40).

4. If you ask people to name an odd number, they will almost always pick a number between one and nine (as opposed to some larger, or much larger, number). Even this seemingly classical category shows prototype effects as a mental category. Furthermore, it shows that the prototype category is itself a prototype category; the four characteristics listed are not necessary and sufficient conditions (Geeraerts 1989).

5. This is the interpretation used in cognitive linguistics; other meanings of this phrase have been proposed.

6. Two entertaining essays by John R. Taylor (2004, 2006), both dealing with the evolution of slang expressions, provide an excellent introduction to the development of prototype categories from the perspective of cognitive linguistics.

7. Although not making an explicit appeal to the prototype category, Hepokoski and Darcy's (2006) influential sonata theory is grounded in exactly this conception of compositional practice.

8. The concepts originate in Krebs (1987) and the terms in Kaminsky (1989).

9. This use of the term *grouping* is unrelated to its use by Lerdahl and Jackendoff (1983).

10. The term was coined by Edward T. Cone (1968), but the concept can be traced to the eighteenth century (see Bent 1987, 12–16).

11. William Rothstein's *Phrase Rhythm in Tonal Music* (1989) is the most developed expression of the analytic tradition, and its pt. 1 is the best introduction to that tradition.

12. This account of heard meter and hypermeter was originally developed in Ito (2013a).

13. Previous work in the analytical tradition assumed a four-bar framework while acknowledging the possibility of hypermeasures of other lengths; the fractional notation makes the size of the hypermeasure explicit. This is important because hypermeasures are often left incomplete or otherwise adjusted. Until I introduced this notation (Ito 2013a), a reader looking at an example in the analytical tradition would not know without consulting the text whether "1 2 3 1" referred to a complete three-bar hypermeasure or an incomplete four-bar hypermeasure.

14. The concepts of metrical and hypermetrical orientation draw on studies of temporal orientation, especially within the week, described in Friedman (1990, chap. 5).

15. Rothstein's (1989, 38) ex. 2.16 shows this passage with the hyperbeats labeled.

16. This account leans heavily on Ito (2013a), which also examines the antecedents of this approach within both the cognitive and the analytical traditions.

17. McKee (2004) examines each of the four possibilities.

18. A postcadential extension is material that is added after the cadence, which is to say after the real end of the phrase. This material serves to extend and confirm the cadence, to give it extra weight, and sometimes to allow more of the accumulated forward momentum to dissipate.

19. The correlation between formal endings and end-weighted hypermeter has been explored by David Temperley (1996, 2003), Samuel Ng (2012), and me (Ito 2013a). The terms *beginning-oriented phrase* and *end-oriented phrase* come from Epstein (1979).

20. Ex. 2.7 originally appeared in Ito (2013a, 74).

21. The distinction between the end-weighted schema in the Chopin example and the hybrid schema in the Schubert turns on the question of whether the cadences are heard as overlaps. In the Schubert, reasons not to hear the fourth measure of each unit belonging either only backward or only forward have already been discussed; I would only add the two-measure harmonic rhythm, which helps bind the third and fourth measures together. In the Chopin, the key factor is the leap after the downbeat in m. 49 followed by a very conjunct line. A good way to probe your own intuitions about overlapped versus nonoverlapped grouping boundaries is by singing with elongated pauses for breath. To project a cadence without overlap, breathe after the cadence. And to project an overlap, breathe just before the cadence—because the momentum into the cadence creates its own continuity, the break is less obtrusive before the first note of the new grouping unit than after. (Skipping forward to ex. 2.9 and singing the passage from the Haydn symphony in both ways makes clear that breathing before an overlap is more natural, and this principle will be involved in the discussion in n. 25 of contrasting grouping interpretations in recordings of ex. 2.10.)

22. Baroque composers often seem to have intended half measures as the real measures (Grave 1985); this adds a layer of complexity to my claim about consistency of meter, but it does not represent an exception because the meter of half measures was usually quite consistent. It has recently been argued that classical-era composers, building on this practice, would make unnotated changes in the size of the measure in the middle of a movement or even in the middle of a phrase (Mirka 2009). This is discussed further in sec. 6.2.

23. The following discussion draws heavily from Rothstein (1989), who catalogs these four adjustments to hypermeter and more, sometimes using slightly different terms.

24. Rothstein (1989, 52–56) uses the term *metrical reinterpretation*, and he cites treatises that discuss it (using various names) going back to 1754. It also receives sustained attention from Ng (2009), who argues that it can occur apart from the phrase overlap. Hypermetrical reinterpretation most often involves a weak final hyperbeat turning into a hyperdownbeat, but it is not uncommon to turn a hyperbeat 3 into a hyperbeat 1 (e.g., Rothstein 1989, 178). An example of something similar to hypermetrical reinterpretation taking place within the measure is discussed in chap. 12.

25. Good examples of contrasting recordings are those by Christoph Eschenbach (1968), who makes m. 4 continuous with the preceding phrase, and Daniel-Ben Pienaar (2009), who emphasizes the new beginning and thus the hypermetrical reinterpretation. For me, it is what happens later in the passage and later in the piece that makes the reinterpretation fully convincing. First, the second phrase has a much more obvious overlap with the start of the transition, and, given the parallel between the phrases, this enhances the status of the overlap in m. 4. Second, quadruple hypermeter is extremely prevalent throughout this movement, interrupted only a handful of times. And third, overlaps emerge as a feature of the piece in both sections of the closing group (mm. 24–36), where they are chained more standardly using the hybrid schema. The relationship between the closing theme and the first theme is highlighted

by the order of events in the recapitulation, which honors older norms from the city of its composition. The retransition doubles as the transition in the recapitulation (mm. 75–78), so that the recapitulation begins most obviously with the second theme in the tonic (mm. 79–86, altered to end with a half cadence, so that it acts more like a first theme group). The first-theme material is then inserted between the closing group (mm. 87–99) and the expanded codetta (mm. 105–112) so that the chain of overlaps in the closing group leads seamlessly into the chain of overlaps in the first theme.

26. Extended upbeats are discussed by Rothstein (1989, 30–40, 56–57, using the term "elongated upbeat") and by McClelland (2006).

27. Rothstein (1989, 58, 60–61) uses the term "successive downbeat" as an umbrella category that also includes, among others, the split downbeat to which we turn next. As a variant on the more usual practice, I have discussed a case in which successive downbeats are instead successive hyperbeats 2/4 across a section boundary (Ito 2013a, 74–75).

28. Like almost everything relating to hypermeter, these measures could be heard in other ways. For example, a listener might continue the four-bar template until it is interrupted by the new beginning of the melody, or the performer, knowing how long the vamp will last, could hear a two-bar hypermeasure. I prefer absence of hypermeter for such passages in part because this general way of hearing accommodates gaps of varying length between accompaniment and melody, including the three-bar separation when the waltz music first starts in "Un bal" from Berlioz's *Symphonie fantastique* and the many ad libitum vamps of operetta and musical theater.

29. Janet Schmalfeldt (1992) has paid close attention to this practice, focusing on the evaded cadence.

30. Rothstein (1989, 221–24) analyzes this passage in terms of an underlying four-bar phrase that has been transformed; however, because downbeats in the underlying version are not all downbeats in the transformed version, the analysis does not provide a way to hear hypermeter in the actual music. In general, Rothstein believes that some passages possess an underlying hypermeter (revealed through analysis) that is not actually heard, but no surface hypermeter—that is, no hypermeter that presents itself to the listener (1989, 97). For Rothstein, this phrase is among those passages. David Temperley's (2008, 316–17) hearing of the passage is also quite different from mine; attending to the strong syncopations, he hears the middles of the measures as stronger metrically than the downbeats. The reading offered here seems more compatible with that of John Rink (2015); although Rink does not discuss phrase rhythm, he makes syncopation (at smaller and much larger levels) central to his understanding of the piece. And related to the larger topic of this book, Rink also mentions the salient difference between feeling the piece in two versus in four.

More generally, it is common to encounter five-bar units like this in which we hear either an extra hyperbeat 2/4 or an extra hyperbeat 3/4. When an extra hyperbeat 3/4 is heard, it will result in two relatively strong hyperbeats 3/4 in a row; in such cases, the first is often heard as somewhat stronger than the second. Brahms's *Variations on a Theme by Joseph Haydn* offers a case study in the different ways in which five-bar units can be organized, and the theme offers a nice example in which it is easy to hear five bars as four with an internal expansion.

PART 2

BASIC FOCAL IMPULSE THEORY

3

THE BASIC CONCEPT OF
THE FOCAL IMPULSE

WHAT EXPERIENCE IS NAMED BY THE TERM *FOCAL IMPULSE*? And how does the focal impulse relate to other aspects of performing and hearing music? As discussed in chapter 1, there is no easily encapsulated answer to these questions. An abstract, general definition will soon be offered, but that definition will be too vague to be of much use by itself. To be truly meaningful, the concept must take on flesh, and it does this as we see its relation to other experiences and concepts, and as a variety of different contexts allow more of its aspects to emerge. This is what it means to acquire a new experiential category, and especially to acquire that category as a tool used in both perceptual and intellectual tasks. Presenting a picture of the focal impulse that is complete at a basic level is the central task of part 2, and especially of chapters 3 through 5. That picture will then take on greater depth in the remainder of the book.

We begin by reviewing the discussion from chapter 1. Focal impulses account for the difference between hearing music in two and in four; the difference lies in the beat level at which focal impulses are employed. If a note is played in isolation, it will probably be played using a focal impulse. Within continuous sequences of notes, focal impulses are used for just some of the notes. The notes played using focal impulses feel similar to the ways they would feel if removed from the sequence and played in isolation. The notes not played using focal impulses feel quite different within the continuous sequence from how they would feel in isolation. Passages with rests on strong beats often reveal the presence of focal impulses with particular clarity; this is because focal impulses are often used on empty strong beats. These silent focal impulses help the following notes respond to the strong beats in the desired ways, often springing out of the energy of the strong beats.

Example 3.1. Bach, Brandenburg Concerto No. 6, BWV 1051, i, mm. 1–3, soloists and continuo only.

Chapter 1 emphasized this last point with a renotated version of the opening melody from a Bach harpsichord concerto; in fact, Bach himself provided another example of this same point. In the first movement of his Brandenburg Concerto No. 6, the two solo viola parts are often in canon at the eighth note; as is apparent in example 3.1, the first viola part often sustains notes into quarter beats, resuming motion on the second sixteenth of the beat. In contrast, the second viola always articulates the quarter-note beat; the difference between the two parts is most salient in the dotted rhythms, figures that are syncopated for the first viola but not for the second. Using any instrument (or imagined instrument) to play these two parts—parts that differ only in their metrical placement, not in their sequence of pitches and durations—should help guide attention to events that occur (in most performances) on the quarter-note beats. These events, helping to organize the whole and also affecting the way it feels and sounds, here receive the name *focal impulse*.

3.1. Defining the Focal Impulse

The first step toward defining the focal impulse is defining the impulse. An *impulse* is a muscular contraction with a clearly observable moment of initiation. Tapping a finger usually involves impulses; relaxed breathing usually does not, because each breath's beginning is gradual, hard to pin down in time. In general, notes that are played or sung are initiated by impulses; notes within glissandos are the main exceptions.

What sets focal impulses apart from other impulses is their role in organizing motion over longer spans of time: in addition to (usually) initiating some notes directly, they create a context for other impulses and notes that follow. This organizational role is most apparent when the focal impulses *do not* initiate any notes—when they are placed on rests or ties. These cases reveal that the motional contexts created by focal impulses—setting the body in motion in certain ways—are crucial in helping the notes that follow to be shaped in the desired ways.

To more clearly distinguish between impulses that are and are not focal impulses, the latter will be called *subsidiary impulses*. Focal impulses may often be strong, even vigorous, at least in relation to the subsidiary impulses that follow, but the two cannot be distinguished purely on the basis of strength. The explosive syncopations seen in example 1.9 from the *Rite of Spring* show that subsidiary impulses can be powerful. This example reemphasizes the basic definition: although focal impulses may often be stronger than the subsidiary impulses that follow them, the primary difference is not one of strength but of a role in organizing motion. This organizing role comes down to context. Focal impulses are not dependent on the motional contexts bequeathed by preceding sequences of motion (at least they are much less dependent on context than subsidiary impulses). And they are able to create new motional contexts—that is, new initial states of the body and its various segments, involving especially momentum and energy. In terms of ongoing patterns of bodily motion, focal impulses effectively wipe the slate clean and begin anew. It is because of this lack of dependence on context that notes produced by focal impulses retain their character when played in isolation, removed from the passages in which they occur. In contrast, a subsidiary impulse relies heavily on context—specifically, on the context provided by the preceding focal impulse. As we have seen, if we remove the note on which a focal impulse falls, that focal impulse will still be needed to create context for the subsidiary impulses that follow. Without just the right context, subsidiary impulses cannot achieve their motional goals, those goals being the production of specific notes with specific patterns of timing, loudness, accentuation, articulation, and expressive shaping in general.

I call the span of time during which the focal impulse governs motional context the *consequent span*. The end of the consequent span occurs just before the next focal impulse. Focal impulses are generally placed on strong beats, so consequent spans correspond to units of the meter (e.g., measures and half measures; exceptions are discussed in pts. 3 and 5). When the theory is translated into scientific terms in part 4, we will see that the correspondence between meter and focal impulse placement generates a claim that the segments used in motor planning and motor organization are metrical units.

The basics of focal impulse theory are summarized as follows:

- Motion in performance is organized around and segmented by the focal impulses, with the performer playing or singing from focal impulse to focal impulse.

- Focal impulses tend to be aligned with the meter, so the segmentation often consists of metrical units.
- Each focal impulse helps to organize the motion that will occur during its consequent span. It creates initial conditions that will facilitate the production of the subsidiary impulses in such a way that the notes produced have the desired details of timing, articulation, and so forth.
- The momentum and energy with which various parts of the body are set in motion are central aspects of those initial conditions.

3.2. Notating the Focal Impulse

Focal impulses will be notated as vertical lines above the staff with the beginnings of slurs extending forward from their tops. This symbol is applied in a possible interpretation of the opening of the "Ghost" Trio in example 3.2 (the hemiola that motivates the focal impulse placement of mm. 2–3 is one of the special cases that will be discussed in pt. 3). The vertical line is intended to represent the salient, rapid beginning of the focal impulse, and the beginning of the slur represents the governing function of the focal impulse with respect to its consequent span. Because each consequent span ends at the next focal impulse, the consequent spans will not be notated explicitly. The dashed lines between staves in example 3.2 make it easier to see where the focal impulses fall throughout the texture. In most cases, the alignment of focal impulses with the meter will make it easy to see where focal impulses fall in lower staves, even though the analytical notations are placed above the system. The dashed lines will be used for special cases in which conflict with meter or ambiguity of meter makes the focal impulse placement less clear.

Some focal impulses are not placed on attack points, and in such cases the notation may not mark the beat on which the focal impulse is placed. When the focal impulse notation lacks a home in this way, a sequence of dots will be placed above the staff and below the focal impulse notations; the dots indicate the beat level on which focal impulses are placed, providing a clear visual indication of the placement of the focal impulses. The dots are intended to evoke the metrical notation of Lerdahl and Jackendoff (1983). In any measure in which they are used, one dot will be used for each beat at some metrical level. The level used will not be specifically notated because it will be evident from the number of dots in the measure (to see this notation in use, see ex. 4.2a).

Although not related to the notation of focal impulses, two issues are raised by the "Ghost" Trio example that may be helpful to highlight, previewing more thorough discussions later. First, the segmentation shown in

Example 3.2. Beethoven, Trio op. 70/1, i, mm. 1–5, with possible focal impulse placement.

example 3.2 is essentially metrical, which puts it in conflict with the grouping. This is because the focal impulses that initiate the consequent spans follow first the notated meter and then the hemiola; in terms of the organization of motion, the strong beats are beginnings. In contrast, in the grouping, all of the strong beats after the first are endings. Shouldn't the grouping be reflected in the performance? Don't most performances of measures 2 and 3 make the notes that follow the upward leaps sound like small-scale beginnings? And don't most performers want to make the descending eighths rush headlong down into the notes on the strong beats of the hemiola? Yes, of course, but when speaking of physical motion, causation must occur in the present and in the past, not in the future. When the eighths that follow the downbeat of measure 2 articulate a local sense of new beginning and then drive insistently toward the next strong beat, they do so by virtue of the context of motion created by the focal impulse on the downbeat. This issue is the main focus of section 6.1.

Second, different focal impulse placements can lead to different understandings of musical processes and to different expressive characters. It would be possible to perform the passage with an additional focal impulse on beat 2 of measure 1; this would create greater consistency, in that each pattern of four descending eighths would begin one eighth after a focal impulse. But that consistency would drastically change the drama of the passage. The focal impulse placement shown in example 3.2 emphasizes the first two beats of measure 2 as an unexpected contraction of the material presented in measure 1. It is unexpected in part because the quality of the descending eighths that end measure 1 will be different from the quality of the eighths that follow. The first instance, later in a longer consequent span, is likely to be lighter and more graceful, whereas the second may be more insistent, perhaps even driven. If the first measure offers no clue of the transformation to come, it will be possible to begin the phrase with a gracious elegance that makes a quick turn toward feverish obsession as the opening idea is contracted and its character intensified. The continuing intensification then comes to a similarly abrupt halt as the piece seems to reach an early crisis of uncertainty. With a focal impulse on beat 2 of measure 1, there is no transformation and thus no surprise, and the implied narrative of the opening measures will be rather different. Although examples of this sort of contrast between options will be found throughout the book, those found in chapters 7, 12, 15, and 16 will be particularly dramatic.

3.3. Making the Focal Impulse More Concrete: An Experiment and Two Analogies

This chapter concludes with three discussions intended to make the concept of the focal impulse more concrete. I first present a simple procedure for finding focal impulses, and then I offer analogies with half-pipe sports and with the choice of gear when cycling or driving.

Finding Focal Impulses

We have already seen that cases in which focal impulses fall on rests or ties are particularly helpful for illustrating the organizational role of focal impulses and for forcing them out into the open, so to speak, through motion that does not directly lead to sound. This effect scales with the rhythmic intensity of the music; the need for silent motion found in the canon in the Sixth Brandenburg is even more pronounced in the rhythmic canon found near the end of the scherzo of Brahms's Piano Quintet (ex. 3.3). The rhythm played by the first violinist and the violist is considerably more challenging than that played by the second violinist and the cellist, and the challenge is not only cognitive but also physical, given the tension and energy required to produce the focal impulses on the empty beats. (The pianist's focal impulses are discussed in chap. 9.)

Because active rests provide clues to the presence of focal impulses, they can serve as the basis of a simple procedure—an experiment of sorts—to find

Example 3.3. Brahms, Piano Quintet, op. 34, iii, mm. 176–180, Allegro.

Example 3.4. Beethoven, Overture to *The Creatures of Prometheus*, op. 43, mm. 17–20, first violin part.

out where we are placing focal impulses when performing a given passage. All we do is remove one note at a time; if motion is required on the new rest, we have found the location of a focal impulse.

Consider the second theme from Beethoven's overture to the *Creatures of Prometheus* (ex. 3.4). Suppose that focal impulses are employed once per measure. If this is the case, then we should be able to remove notes from any beat except the downbeat without disturbing the focal impulse placement of the passage. Examples 3.5a–3.5c show some possibilities. In none of these cases will the performer need to make extra motions during the rests that have been introduced. Suppose, however, that we remove the downbeat, as in example 3.5d. If focal impulse placement is to be preserved, then the performer will still have to produce a focal impulse on the downbeat, making some kind of motion during that rest to structure the motion during the consequent span.

Example 3.5. Some recompositions of op. 43.

To expand on a point made in chapter 1, analysis of focal impulse placement can be considered a form of reductional analysis. A simple two-voice, note-against-note progression can be revealed by a voice-leading analysis to structure a complex musical surface. In the same way, focal impulses can be considered the backbone of the physical motions involved in performing a passage of music. If all of the notes except those produced by the focal impulses are stripped away, playing the result reveals a simple sequence of motion; the motion needed to play the actual passage is an elaboration of this simple sequence.[1] In contrast, if we remove the notes produced by the focal impulses, then we will have to move silently on those now-empty beats, keeping the focal impulses in the absence of the notes they originally produced—assuming that we wish to preserve the character of the other notes.

Focal Impulse Theory and Half-Pipe Sports

An analogy with half-pipe sports can clarify the relationship between focal and subsidiary impulses. A half-pipe is a surface with an approximately U-shaped cross section, resembling a pipe that has been sawed in half lengthwise. First used by skateboarders, half-pipes take advantage of conservation principles to facilitate aerial maneuvers. Starting on one edge of the half-pipe, the skateboarder moves back and forth over the surface of the pipe, pushing off of the surface so that she flies into the air when she reaches each edge. While in the air, the skateboarder performs various tricks such as flips and rotations; these are the point of the sport. Snowboarders have adopted the half-pipe, and their surface, covered with snow, is angled downward lengthwise so that the snowboarder follows a zigzag path down the half-pipe. Half-pipe snowboarding was introduced into the Winter Olympics at the 1998 games in Nagano, Japan.

The dynamics of these sports offer some helpful insights into focal impulse theory. At the moment in which the athlete leaves contact with the surface and flies into the air, she loses the ability to influence the momentum or angular momentum of her center of mass. From this moment until the moment she lands, those parameters will be determined by their initial conditions and by gravity. Although her center of mass undergoes simple projectile motion, this is not the end of the story. If it were, half-pipe sports would not be spectator sports. While the athlete is in the air, she is physically active, and her motions can be impressive. But the muscular contractions that create the acrobatics are not capable of influencing the trajectory of her center of mass. She is only able to influence the trajectory of her center of mass during her push against the surface, and this ability ends when she leaves contact with the surface.

A more detailed look at the athlete's motion in the air only increases our appreciation for the centrality of the push against the surface. Many moves that a skilled half-pipe athlete can execute in the air are highly complex and require much more than a certain flight time or initial angular momentum about the center of mass. Many of these acrobatic tricks are so complex that their successful completion depends on the position, momentum, and angular momentum of each of the athlete's body parts having precise values at the moment she leaves contact with the surface. The values of these parameters at this moment will separate the moves the athlete knows how to do into two categories: those that can be done under these circumstances and those that cannot. Again, it is the push against the surface—including all of the details of a whole-body motion—that sets these parameters.

This picture of half-pipe sports, which could have been developed just as well from any type of aerial gymnastics, offers an excellent analogy with the dynamics of music performance. A focal impulse, like the push against the surface, both makes possible and establishes constraints for a further sequence of motion. It does this both at the coarse level of total energy and at the granular level of details of the initial conditions of the trunk and of limb segments. During the consequent span, equivalent to the flight time of the athlete, active motions are initiated by the subsidiary impulses, which may be quite forceful—strongly accented syncopations would be an example. But, like the motions of the half-pipe athlete in the air, they take place within a predetermined set of global motional constraints.

Focal Impulse Theory and Cycling

One way focal impulses organize motion is by injecting energy into the system. Among the musical examples seen so far, this is particularly evident in the Bach harpsichord concerto and the Verdi accompaniment pattern, both from chapter 1. The desired lightness of the notes in each case seems to require a lightness in the manner of playing and therefore also in the subsidiary impulses that produce the notes. For light, gentle motions to produce the notes, the body must already have been set in motion by some more vigorous impulse—a focal impulse. In each example, organizing the motion in this way is part of the challenge of playing the passage and part of what lends the passage a special kind of focus. When a focal impulse directly initiates a note, it is relatively easy to keep the motion going in subsequent notes, like a racquetball ricocheting back and forth across a court. When the focal impulse falls on a rest or a tie, the first few notes that follow are easy, but keeping the body in motion for subsequent notes gets harder. Two things are needed to keep the energy from running out: just the right motions in the silent focal impulse and the skillful stewarding of energy while playing the notes. With subtle balances in play, it is more like skipping a stone than setting a rubber ball bouncing. Natural sources of resistance within the body must be minimized, and motions must follow one another with particular fluidity. The focal impulse injects energy into the system and establishes a context of motion. Special skill is needed to maintain that context and to draw on the energy gradually enough, as both energy and context need to last until the end of the consequent span.

The idea that focal impulses introduce energy into the system amplifies the analogy with half-pipe sports, as energy is a crucial aspect of motional context in both cases. It also leads to a basic correlation, all other things being equal: the more there is to be done in a given time span (or in a given span of the meter), the more frequently we should expect focal impulses to occur. If a piece of music becomes more technically challenging, we would expect that shifting to more frequent focal impulses would make the new passage easier to play. (Indeed, student performances can become conspicuously more "beaty" when passagework is involved.) Similarly, we would expect that music at a slower tempo would have focal impulses placed more frequently relative to the measure in order to preserve the amount of time between focal impulses. (For example, if focal impulses are placed every half note at a tempo of quarter equals 104 bpm, they will occur with the same frequency as focal impulses placed every quarter note at a tempo of 52 bpm.)

A relationship exists between the tempo and the frequency of focal impulses relative to the measure, but it is not as simple as the number of focal impulses per measure necessarily decreasing as tempo increases. A fairly wide range of rates is comfortable for the production of focal impulses. Therefore, at moderate tempi, several focal impulse placements are likely to be reasonably easy to produce. In many cases, it is appropriate to adjust the number of focal impulses within the measure as tempo changes in order to keep the temporal rate of the focal impulses within a comfortable range; but there are also many cases in which this approach would not produce the desired musical effect. A very fast rate of focal impulses can make a fast tempo more driven and exciting, and a very slow rate of focal impulses can lend a special kind of focus and intensity to slow music. Both require special skills on the part of the performer.

I like to think of the relationship between the rate of focal impulses and the tempo in terms of an analogy with the relationship in cycling between the speed and the gear used. Tempo corresponds to speed in an obvious way, and there is a close fit between the number of focal impulses per measure and the gear. If we think of the measure as corresponding to one full rotation of the pedals, the number of focal impulses per measure is analogous to the number of teeth in the gear being used (fig. 3.1). My bike, like many, has

Pedals, high gear — 1 rotation

Rear wheel, low gear — 1 1/3 rotations

Rear wheel, high gear — 4 rotations

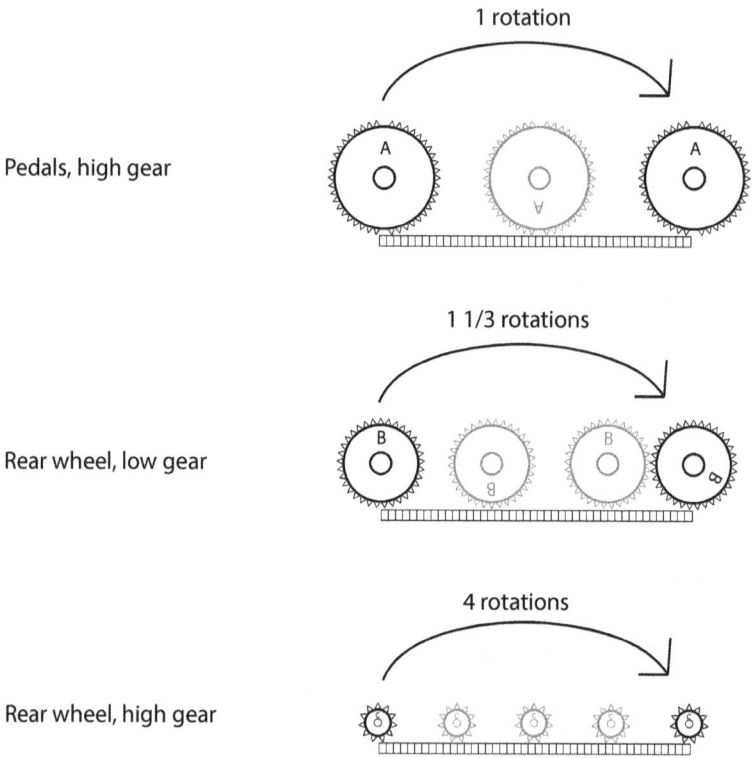

Fig. 3.1. Bicycle gear relationships.

two sets of gears; let us assume that the gears by the pedals are fixed on the highest gear, so that we can focus on the gears by the rear wheel. Let us suppose that my highest gear by the pedals has forty-four teeth. This means that turning the pedals one full rotation will move the chain through forty-four links. Turning to the gears by the rear wheel, let us further suppose that the highest gear has eleven teeth and the lowest thirty-three. This means that to turn the wheel one full rotation, I need to move the chain by eleven links in highest gear and by thirty-three links in lowest gear. Combining these sets of numbers, one full rotation of the pedals produces four full rotations of the wheels in highest gear but only one and one third in the lowest; I go three times farther per rotation of the pedals in the highest gear compared with the lowest.

The most efficient way to match speed with gear is by shifting to a higher gear (fewer teeth) when speed increases, just as the most comfortable way to match tempo with metrical frequency of focal impulses is by shifting to fewer focal impulses per measure as tempo increases. But efficiency is not always the only consideration; when sprinting, it is often easier to go faster by moving the legs faster than by pushing harder, so cyclists may stay longer in lower gears as they increase speed. The same dynamic is at work when driving a stick-shift car, as it can be exciting to accelerate to sixty miles per hour using only the lower gears. (Something of the sort is happening when you hear an engine roaring at very high pitch.) This puts a greater physical strain on the car and, if taken to excess, could push the rotations per minute so high that the engine would be damaged. It is also possible to drive in a gear that is higher than usual for the speed; this will stall the engine if the torque demanded is too high. The performer has a parallel range of options with regard to focal impulse placement.

In cycling and driving, additional variables can change the usual relationship between velocity and gear. If the vehicle is heavily laden or going up or down a hill, the relationship between torque and velocity will change; this, in turn, will shift the range of speeds at which each gear is most efficient. In general, the relationship will be that if the cyclist or the car needs to work harder, it will be advantageous to stay in lower gears at higher speeds.

Focal impulse placements work similarly. Returning to the basic definition, the focal impulse puts various parts of the body in physical states conducive to producing the subsidiary impulses in the desired manner. Given that the body is not an idealized physical system (e.g., one without friction or compressibility), the durations of such physical states are limited. Consequently, a focal impulse can organize only a limited span of time; after that, the system (the body) requires a new injection of energy. And if the system needs to work harder, the time span that can be organized by a single focal impulse will become shorter. Working harder in this case means organizing either more motion or more strenuous motion. A $\frac{4}{4}$ measure with quarter-note motion may work well with just one focal impulse in the measure, but if the measure has a complex rhythm including sixteenths, thirty-seconds, and some ties and syncopations, more focal impulses will likely be needed. Similarly, very heavy accents, especially if placed in subsidiary rhythmic positions, will be produced more easily with a higher frequency of focal impulses within the measure. In general, the length of time that can be organized by a focal impulse will be determined by what must happen during that time.

Just as the choice of gear will determine the kinds of strains put on the car and thus influence the character of the driving experience, so choices about focal impulse placement will strongly influence the degree and kind of physical strenuousness involved in performance. In turn, the details of physical exertion will often leave sonic traces; musical instruments are transducers, converting energy from physical motion into sound, and the details of the ways in which the motion occurs tend to leave traces in the details of the sound (Baily 1985, 242). These details are often recoverable by the listener; as a result, focal impulse placements contribute to a visceral sense of the quality and character of the physical motion that lies behind the music or that can be suggested by the music.[2]

A few examples of how placement of focal impulses might resemble gear choice are found in Tchaikovsky's Symphony No. 5. The first theme of the first movement, which is in $\frac{6}{8}$ marked "allegro con anima," could be felt either in one or in two (ex. 3.6). Feeling the music in two is, in some respects, the most obvious choice. This would put the main beat squarely within the range where music psychologists believe the most natural, or preferred, tempos reside; the dotted-half pulse would be possible but less preferred (London 2012; see chap. 13). But in this passage, a sense of world-weary detachment may be desired, as if the music enters already beaten down and in need of some time to summon more energy. In this case, feeling the music in one could be appropriate. The contours would be smoother, with less energy to invest in weaker beats; furthermore, the syncopations at the end of the idea would be more mumbling than insistent.[3] Conversely, if the desired qualities include rhythmic alertness and crispness, with a precise snap to the syncopations near the end, feeling the music in two would be the better choice. When this same material is heard in the coda, the expressive character is quite different,

Example 3.6. Tchaikovsky, Symphony No. 5, op. 64, i, mm. 40–45, Allegro con anima, reduced score.

Example 3.7. Tchaikovsky, Symphony No. 5, op. 64, i, mm. 505–10, Allegro con anima, reduced score.

and a different frequency of focal impulses could help bring this out (ex. 3.7). This passage is often heard along the lines of an unresolved struggle with fate that motivates the trajectory of the rest of the symphony. It is possible to perform this music with one focal impulse per measure, but this would tend toward a gracefulness and elegance that many interpreters would find out of place here. It suits the implacability of fate and the intensity of the struggle to use two focal impulses per measure, leading to a more insistent rhythmic character. With two focal impulses per measure, notes on weak beats can be given greater emphasis through dynamics and articulation, and the syncopations can have a driving intensity that would have seemed less clearly motivated in the earlier passage. Both focal impulse placements are possible

Example 3.8. Tchaikovsky, Symphony No. 5, op. 64, iv, mm. 1–4, reduced score.

for both passages; what is striking about the two options is that the higher and lower energy levels that they would suggest relate directly to contrasts of expressive character between the passages, doing so through the details of the sound produced.

A similar contrast between bookending statements, this time of the fate motto itself, is found in the final movement of the symphony. At the start of the movement, marked "andante maestoso," again two frequencies of focal impulse seem reasonably likely, four per measure or two per measure (ex. 3.8). The quarter-note pulse is more likely, given the slow pace of the half notes, but focal impulses on half notes are quite possible. Half notes would aid in the projection of that pulse as what Joel Lester (1986) has called the "primary metrical level"; they would help project a sense of calm confidence, the telltale sonic difference between the two options being the amount of rhythmic and articulatory energy given to the sixteenth notes. When this theme returns in the coda with the indication "moderato assai e molto maestoso," the character is markedly different (ex. 3.9). The accompaniment, which in the earlier passage articulated only half-note beats, now features martial eighths placed on quarter-note beats. Furthermore, a countermelody emphasizes the quarter note through dotted-eighth-sixteenth rhythms. Although half notes are, as before, more prominent in the melody, performing the melody with focal impulses on the quarter-note beats will give the sixteenths declamatory power that would be difficult to impart if feeling half-note beats.[4] This passage is almost always performed with strong focal impulses on the quarter-note beats; it gives the sense of something massive moving and points toward the power needed to create this heroic triumph, a reminder of the intensity of the struggle. To return to our gear analogies, the music here is like a powerful car screaming up a steep hill in second gear.

Example 3.9. Tchaikovsky, Symphony No. 5, op. 64, iv, mm. 472–77, reduced score.

Finally, we can see an opposite effect of focal impulse placement in the fourth movement's main contrasting theme (ex. 3.10). Given the many halves and quarters, especially in the latter part of the theme, focal impulses coinciding with the half-note beats of the alla breve meter would seem an obvious choice. But the long note that starts the melody can serve as a clue to a different possibility: using focal impulses only on the downbeats.[5] This quite slow

Example 3.10. Tchaikovsky, Symphony No. 5, op. 64, iv, mm. 128–35, Allegro vivace, reduced score.

rate of focal impulses, slow especially in comparison with the rhythms of the accompaniment, can help give this melody a sense of effortlessness. Played this way, it can feel like soaring down a hill on a bike with only easy pedaling, one of the closest things to flying without leaving the ground.

After reading chapters 4 and 5, or perhaps after finishing part 2, I recommend returning to this analogy between focal impulse placement and cycling and driving, and to the light it sheds on the interrelationships among tempo, focal impulse placement, degree and kind of activity, and qualitative sense of motion. Explore the range of possibilities with a few passages of music. Perform, sing (expressively, but without concern for technique), imagine performing, or conduct an imaginary ensemble that perfectly reflects your gestures.[6] Hold the rate of focal impulses per measure constant while changing the tempo and then do the same with a few other focal impulse placements.

Try as many different focal impulse placements as possible while holding tempo constant, and do this at a few different tempi. Then go back and experience this same space of options with different articulations, senses of weight, and degrees of accent. See how different focal impulse placements feel with light articulations versus heavy ones. See how they feel if you imagine that you are performing on a planet with much more gravity, where everything has much more weight, or if you imagine performing on the moon, with much less weight. Imagine that you are somehow performing while submerged in water, with the resistance of the water slowing down and smoothing out your motions. Imagine the same thing submerged in molasses, with the effect now greatly amplified. The point of imagining performing with different amounts of gravity or viscous resistance is to explore a range of expressive characters for the music and to see how these expressive characters, together with more straightforward parameters of accentuation and tempo, relate to a range of options regarding focal impulse placements. Getting to know the focal impulse experientially in this way is essential to understanding it.

Notes

1. Abby Whiteside ([1955] 1997, [1969] 1997) describes exercises that she calls "pulsing" and "outlining," in which a musician gradually adds notes to a skeleton resembling ex. 1.2, which showed only the notes produced directly by focal impulses in the opening of the "Ghost" Trio. The relationship between her approach and focal impulse theory is discussed in chap. 14.

2. The sonic traces discussed as resulting from the degree and kind of physical strenuousness involved in performance are not the same as the sonic traces left by the focal impulses themselves. The sonic traces of focal impulses lend themselves to more detailed discussion because they are patterned in more consistent ways; they are examined in chap. 5.

3. This discussion will touch on a number of aspects of the sound of focal impulses and of different kinds of syncopations that are dealt with in chaps. 5 and 7. Readers may want to return to this section after reading those chapters, as a number of the assertions about the results of focal impulse choices will have acquired more grounding at that point.

4. The clear reference to the topic of the march might seem like an additional reason to place focal impulses on quarter-note beats; however, as seen in the two contrasting performances of a Sousa march in chap. 1, such reasoning would have to consider specific traditions relating to the march, likely involving composition, performance, and specific styles of marching.

5. Less frequent focal impulses are practical for the sustained lines of the melody and supporting voices, but the rhythmically active accompaniment—and especially the parts with the off-beat quarter-note triplets—will probably need focal impulses on the half-note beats. Placing focal impulses differently in different parts of an ensemble is a special case covered in chap. 8.

6. For instrumentalists, expressive singing is a helpful way to connect with intuitive musicianship without potential interference from the technical concerns of performance. Singers can reap the same benefits if they sing like nonsingers; this involves some mental work that instrumentalists do not have to do.

4

FOCAL IMPULSES AND METER

The Simplest Cases

An important part of getting to know focal impulses is forming expectations about how their placement relates to meter. A tendency for them to be placed on strong beats has already been prominent, starting with the first examples from chapter 1, but this tendency is not absolute. The placement of focal impulses will be understood in terms of a prototype category, which is a basic form of patterning for much human cognition and voluntary behavior. The specific prototype category developed here is intended to describe eighteenth- and nineteenth-century Western classical music; different prototype categories would be needed to describe the use of focal impulses in other repertoires.

Because the prototype category has been invoked frequently in music theory in recent years, a basic level of familiarity will be assumed; readers wanting more information will find a summary in chapter 2. Here I simply state again that, as emphasized in chapter 2 through the example of the gavottes, prototype categories are by no means restricted to the organization of verbal categories or even to language more generally; they will be found anywhere that human imagination is at work making creative and flexible associations. Consequently, prototype effects should be expected in the ways in which focal impulses are used and in the ways in which features of the music influence their placement.

Prototype categories can be described in spatial terms by saying that they have centers (or cores) and peripheries, often with fine gradations between the two. In discussing the placement of focal impulses with respect to meter (in the target repertoire), we distinguish three main concentric regions: a core, an inner periphery, and an outer periphery[1]. In the core, there is a close (but not absolute) correspondence with meter—this represents the normal practice (i.e., the placements that are most frequently found) as well as the normative practice (i.e., the central cases with respect to which the peripheral cases are understood). The core is described in this section. The inner periphery is discussed in part 3; it contains cases in which the meter itself is more complex, the heard meter conflicts with notated meter, or a principled departure from meter occurs. In the outer periphery, other factors override the tendency for metrical alignment in ways that are more flexible and less predictably patterned than those discussed in part 3; we will see an example of this in chapter 5, and others will appear occasionally. Given this understanding of focal impulse placement as a prototype category, what follows should be understood not as a set of hard and fast rules but rather as an account of the most normal and normative cases, cases which anchor a much broader range of possibilities.

The first three chapters of part 2 are the most important for helping readers connect the focal impulse with their own musical experiences. To keep momentum through these chapters, a number of important theoretical discussions regarding the relationship between meter and focal impulses will be postponed until chapter 6. The discussion here gives priority to concise exposition over reasoned defense. And for the sake of that exposition, I will adopt the convenient fiction of a musician sitting back and going through a deliberate process of placing focal impulses. Such a process may occasionally occur when musicians have discussions such as whether to feel the music in two or in four, but in the majority of cases, focal impulses are placed without conscious reflection.

The basic unit of analysis for the placement of focal impulses is the notated measure.[2] Within a section with a consistent character of motion, placement of focal impulses will be consistent from measure to measure. The task of the musician is to decide on a placement of focal impulses for a general measure that will serve as a template for all measures within the section.

Within that template measure, the main task is deciding how deeply to populate the metrical hierarchy. Among the core cases, the downbeat always receives a focal impulse; as a result, when placed with minimum frequency, focal impulses occur once per measure, on the downbeats. If more than one focal impulse is desired, the additional ones will be placed on all beats either one or two levels below the metrical level of the downbeats, with the great majority of cases having no more than four focal impulses per measure.[3] Thus in simple duple and quadruple meters, there will usually be one, two, or four focal impulses, in $\frac{4}{4}$ falling on the whole-note, the half-note, or the quarter-note beats. In a triple meter, it is less likely that focal impulses will be placed two levels down from the measure level; in $\frac{3}{4}$ they usually fall on either

a)   b)

Example 4.1. (a) Johann Strauss Jr., *Emperor Waltz*, op. 437, Waltz No. 1, mm. 1–4, Tempo di Valse, reduced score. (b) Mozart, Menuetto K. 409, mm. 1–2, reduced score.

the dotted-half- or quarter-note beats. This amounts to saying that focal impulses tend to get placed at the beat levels that receive primary attention from performers and listeners, whether because of motives, figuration, harmonic rhythm, or other factors.[4]

In chapter 3, passages from Tchaikovsky's Symphony No. 5 illustrated some of these options for focal impulse placement: common time in two versus in four in examples 3.8 and 3.9 and alla breve in one versus in two in example 3.10. In triple meter, it is common to feel a waltz, such as Strauss's *Emperor Waltz* (ex. 4.1a), in one, whereas the more stately minuet will typically be felt in three, with focal impulses placed accordingly, as in Mozart's Menuetto K. 409 (ex. 4.1b).

The one real disjunction between focal impulse placement and meter within the core of most central cases becomes possible when there is a triple level one or two levels below the measure level (e.g., the quarter notes in $\frac{3}{4}$ or the eighth notes in $\frac{6}{8}$). In such cases, focal impulses can be placed unevenly within the triple level, effectively turning it into an unequal duple level. This corresponds to the simple observation that triple motion sometimes seems to limp along in unequal pairs, either "**one** (two) **three one** (two) **three**" or "**one two** (three) **one two** (three)." If the triple layer is two levels below the measure level, as in $\frac{6}{8}$, the unevenness should be consistent, for example, "**one** (and) **a two** (and) **a**," not "**one** (and) **a two and** (a)."

It is possible to make a number of connections with this way of feeling triple meter. It could reflect the intrinsic bias of the body toward two-fold division. It could relate to the understanding of triple meter as unequal duple, which was the norm in the sixteenth century and persisted among theorists through the middle of the eighteenth century (Houle 1987, chaps. 1 and 2). And it could be related to the qualitative distinctions among focal impulses

Example 4.2. Bach, Partita No. 2 for Solo Violin, BWV 1004, Chaconne. (a) mm. 1–2. (b) mm. 133–35.

that will be introduced in part 3. But the main reason for including this possibility is simply that these focal impulse placements occur with significant frequency; a consistent physical investment in just one of the two weak beats in triple meter is a familiar reality for musicians.

In the opening of Bach's chaconne from the Partita No. 2 for Solo Violin (ex. 4.2a), the sarabande character would make focal impulses on beats 1 and 2 appropriate, and this is how it is often played. But focal impulses on each quarter-note beat are also possible. The triple and quadruple stops lend themselves to a marked rhythmic character, and if particularly pointed eighths are desired—sharply articulated and decisively placed in time—this focal impulse placement would be a good option.[5] In contrast, the much gentler character of the start of the section in the major (ex. 4.2b) makes the even placement much less likely. The loure from the Partita No. 3 (ex. 4.3) offers the potential for the opposite unequal placement; Jascha Heifetz (1952) uses the unequal placement in his recording, whereas Sergiu Luca (1977) uses focal impulses only on the larger beats. An example that is often more heavily marked than the loure is Pamina's aria "Ach ich fühl's," from *The Magic Flute* (ex. 4.4). As we will see again in chapter 10 with additional resonance, the extra duration given to the stronger beat tends to make the music sound heavier and more grounded, and this can enhance affective qualities of sadness and enervation. Chapter 5, which discusses the sound of focal impulses, will include more examples of the uneven duple placement of focal impulses in triple meter.

In compound duple meters it is common to place focal impulses either on downbeats only (especially for fast, light music; e.g., tarantellas) or one level down (on the dotted-quarter beats in $\frac{6}{8}$). Among the examples from Tchaikovsky's Symphony No. 5 in chapter 3, instances of $\frac{6}{8}$ in one versus in two were seen in examples 3.6 and 3.7. Placement two levels down populates the triple level, the eighth notes in $\frac{6}{8}$; if this level is populated at all, it is most common to place the focal impulses unevenly, with two per larger beat and four per

Example 4.3. Bach, Partita No. 3 for Solo Violin, BWV 1006, Loure, mm. 1–2.

Example 4.4. Mozart, *The Magic Flute*, "Ach ich fühl's," mm. 1–5, reduced score.

measure. In $^6_8$, this means that consequent spans alternate in length between quarters and eighths, with either a long-short or a short-long pattern. Even placement on each triple subdivision of the main beat is possible but occurs less frequently (e.g., in a slow $^6_4$ by Brahms).

What is the maximum number of levels down from the measure level that will receive focal impulses in the core? This question receives a vague answer because the answer will vary with meter signature, resulting not just from general principles but also from specifics of cultural practice—as we would expect with a prototype category (Geeraerts 1997). Our guideline of a maximum of two levels down and a usual limit of four focal impulses total does fairly well, accounting for variations such as why the level two down from the measure level is used in $^4_4$ but not in $^3_4$, why the eighth-note level is rarely filled in $^6_8$, and why focal impulse placements involving subdivisions of the compound beat unit are rare in compound triple and quadruple meters. But the limits that culture places on the applicability of general principles are displayed in the different treatment of $\frac{2}{4}$ and $\frac{4}{4}$, which are indistinguishable from the standpoint of the metrical grid.[6] In $\frac{4}{4}$, two levels down from the measure level is the quarter note, one of the beat levels most likely to attract primary attention. But in $\frac{2}{4}$, two levels down from the downbeat is the eighth note. In some slow movements in $\frac{2}{4}$, the eighth-note level is extremely salient, and focal impulses on eighth notes would be likely; but the eighth note in $\frac{2}{4}$ remains far less likely to receive focal impulses than the quarter note in $\frac{4}{4}$. This comparison shows that the core is itself a prototype category, with graded centrality, fuzzy boundaries, and a lack of strict necessary and sufficient conditions for membership.

The discussion of basic template measures within the core of cases is now complete: focal impulses are placed at least every downbeat; they may also fill the metrical hierarchy either one or two beat levels below the level of the measure, with rarely more than a total of four focal impulses per measure; and if there is a triple level one or two levels below the measure, that triple level may be filled unevenly, as if it were a duple level with unequally spaced beats. Example 4.5 shows the possible core placements in $\frac{4}{4}$, $\frac{3}{4}$, and $\frac{6}{8}$. Two discussions remain. The first looks at how consistently this template measure is to be applied. Under what circumstances do musicians change from one focal impulse placement to another? And under what circumstances do different musicians within an ensemble employ different focal impulse placements? The second discussion looks at circumstances in which focal impulses are added or removed relative to the picture generated by the template measure.

The template applies within whatever portion of the music the performer feels should have a consistent character of motion. This character of motion will include characteristics such the degree of exertion, the amount of resistance encountered, and whether the motion is smooth or jerky, tense or relaxed. In a baroque figural prelude or dance suite movement, the whole movement could have a consistent character of motion. In an emotionally turbulent *scena* from a nineteenth-century opera, a consistent character of motion might last only for a few measures. Focal impulse placements are also assumed to be homophonic, consistent among members of an ensemble. Feeling focal impulses together is an important aspect of what it means to play together; sonic and visual cues make this possible, with a conductor (when present) often facilitating. Coordinating focal impulses helps musicians not only with synchronization but also with gestural aspects of how the music flows through time. Cases also occur in which different musicians within an ensemble place focal impulses differently, and we have already seen a potential

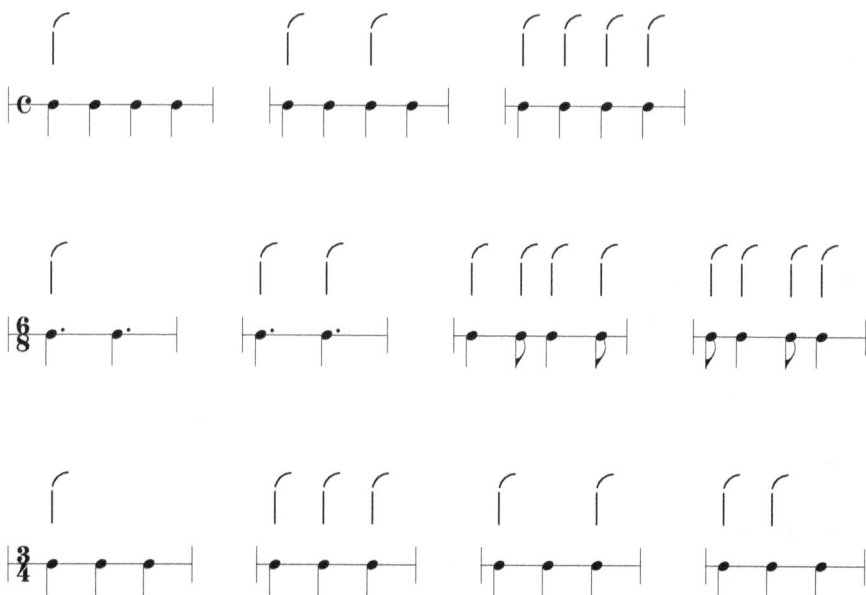

Example 4.5. Typical focal impulse placements for 4/4, 6/8, and 3/4 meters.

example (ex. 3.10). These cases of polyphonic focal impulse placement are not, however, included in the core of most central cases; rather, they are found in the inner periphery, discussed in part 3.

These two expectations about focal impulse placement—that they be placed consistently in a section of consistent motional character and consistently through an ensemble—are more frequently violated than the other norms discussed in this chapter. Some performers adjust their focal impulse placements fairly frequently, including within sections with a consistent character of motion. And when this happens with individual musicians within an ensemble, polyphonic focal impulse placements result. Many performances place focal impulses quite consistently, both within sections and throughout ensembles, but greater diversity of focal impulse placement is also common. These norms are nonetheless valuable, for two reasons. First, though they have more exceptions than the other norms, they do still describe general trends; a performance in which focal impulse placements changed haphazardly would be rather unusual. Second, they provide a helpful perspective, differently for different users of the theory. For analysts, they provide a simple baseline in relation to which more complex cases can be understood. And for performers, the norms provide spurs to look for placements that can serve an entire passage well. The freedom to change placements within a section or an ensemble is still there, but upon reflection they may come to value the gestural consistency that comes with observing the norms, the desired aspects of variety being achievable through other means. Like the average timing profiles mentioned in chapter 1, consistent focal impulse placement may be regarded as a safe option that usually works reasonably well. Departures from consistency are less predictable. Some may be brilliant interpretive choices, others basically equivalent alternatives; still others work against a convincing trajectory of musical motion.

Turning to deviations from the basic template measure, the core includes a case in which focal impulses are added beyond what would be implied by the template. This happens because the first focal impulse, which prepares for the first attack point, occurs before the music begins. In general, the physical motions involved in performance need to be prepared. For music to have the right sense of motion, and, in many cases, for it to be possible to execute the motions that produce the first notes, the body must already be in motion before the first sound is made. Performers do not generally start a performance directly from a state of rest.

There is nothing mysterious about these silent focal impulses that precede the music. They are the bow movements of a string quartet preparing to play, the synchronized breaths of a woodwind quintet, the motions that orchestral players make in joining the conductor's initial upbeat. They are simply the familiar physical impulses that musicians use to initiate performance. When musical examples include the beginnings of movements, rests will be added to show the placement of the preparatory focal impulses.[7]

Focal impulses generated by the template measure are also sometimes omitted; this happens when a focal impulse has no impulses to govern, appearing in the middle of a long rest or note. In such cases, focal impulses resume before (not simultaneously with) the next attack point; this gives the resuming motion the same preparation as the beginning. Occasionally it may be helpful to flag the fact that focal impulses are being omitted—for example, by placing dashed-line versions of the usual notation in the places in which focal impulses would otherwise have occurred (see the glossary, fig. G.1d). In practice, however, this notation is rarely needed because omitted focal impulses tend to be clear from context. Given this clarity, omitted focal impulses will almost never be indicated in the lower staves of multipart textures. When there are long rests in the top staff of a multipart texture, focal impulse notations will sometimes be shifted down to the highest active staff, usually shifting back up for the preparatory focal impulse before the reentry of the top-staff part. But there will also be rests in the top staff that are long enough to result in the omission of focal impulses but short enough that moving focal impulse notation to a lower staff would be visually obtrusive. In such cases, as with the omission of focal impulses in lower staves, the omission will simply be understood.

As already emphasized, the discussion in this chapter covers only the most normative performance situations—those found in the core of the category of focal impulse placements. Core placements are summarized as follows.

- Within a section with a consistent character of motion, focal impulses are placed consistently from measure to measure and consistently across parts within an ensemble.
- Focal impulses are placed at least on each downbeat.
- If multiple focal impulses are used, they fill beat levels evenly. They may be placed one level below the level of the downbeats, and in some cases they may be placed two levels below, depending on the meter. In most cases, there are not more than four focal impulses per measure.
- If focal impulses are placed on a triple level, it is possible to place them on only one of the two weak beats, so that the triple level is felt as if it were an unevenly spaced duple level. If this is done in a meter such as $\frac{6}{8}$, which has two triple units per measure, the focal impulses should fall consistently on either the second or third beat within each triple unit.
- A focal impulse always precedes the first attack point; notating this often requires adding rests before the beginning of a movement.
- If a focal impulse organizes no notes up to and including the next focal impulse (if it falls in the middle of a long note or a long rest), it may be omitted. Omitted focal impulses may be notated with a dashed-line version of the usual notation. Focal impulses must resume before the next attack point.

Notes

1. There is also a small middle periphery; see chaps. 11 and 12.
2. The reasons for the centrality of the measure will be discussed in chap. 6.
3. There is an interesting connection between the usual limit on the number of focal impulses in a measure and research into the spontaneous perception of quantity apart from counting, called *subitization* (Dehaene 2011, 30–59, 254–60). This ability is found in infants, and it extends to the number 3, with some evidence that adults may be able to subitize the number 4 in some cases. Although most studies have used visual stimuli, this same ability applies to the perception of numbers of sounds, including in three- and four-day-old infants (Bijeljac-Babic, Bertoncini, and Mehler 1993).
4. This is clearly related to Joel Lester's (1986) concept of the primary metric level. It is also related to the tactus, but the relationship of focal impulse placement to the tactus

is complicated. Focal impulses have freedoms that the tactus lacks because focal impulse placement can fail to correspond to any pulse level within the metrical hierarchy. The listener's tactus is also less likely than the focal impulses to track a slow pulse level, as we will see in chap. 13.

5. This discussion assumes sonic results of focal impulses discussed in chap. 5; if the claims about sound seem unclear or undersupported, it might be helpful to return to this chapter after reading the next one.

6. Problems with treating meter as a fully symmetrical hierarchy of beat levels have been discussed by Mirka (2009) and elsewhere by me (Ito 2013a).

7. Although these preparatory impulses are nearly ubiquitous, they may not always be strictly necessary. They *are* necessary when there is an upbeat figure, to organize the subsidiary impulses of the upbeat. But when the music begins with a focal impulse, it may be possible for the player to bring the muscles to the needed state of preparation in an arrhythmic way and then to begin with a focal impulse that releases this tension in initiating the first note; however, this approach would be highly unusual.

5

THE SOUND OF FOCAL IMPULSES

THE MAJOR CLAIM OF THIS CHAPTER IS THAT focal impulses leave characteristic sonic traces, so that choices about how many focal impulses to use
and where to place them will have important effects on the sound of a performance and on its expressive character. To some extent, these effects can be
decomposed into separate parameters of sound, and we can talk about ways
in which specific notes are marked differently by those parameters under different focal impulse placements. However, the most important effects are not
atomistic—this note a little louder, that note a little longer—but rather holistic.
With a different focal impulse placement, we change from one overall pattern
to another, a more subtle version of the kinds of perceptual changes that occur
when we switch understandings of classic ambiguous visual figures such as
the rabbit/duck. I think of this holistic pattern change as the primary reason
for performing musicians to care about focal impulses. It is a straightforward
way to transform the expressive shape of a performance. And because there
will often be only a handful of likely options for focal impulse placement, it
is like a dial that can be set to different options, with each option markedly
different from the others. This finite set of options can provide a helpful point
of grounding in an interpretive process that often provides a dizzying array of
choices—so many notes, and so many ways to shape those notes.

This central topic of the sound of focal impulses is discussed in the second section of this chapter. The first section provides a conceptual frame, the
third section discusses the visually observable effects of focal impulses, and
the final section argues that focal impulses facilitated the greater rhythmic
freedom of older performance traditions.

5.1. Preliminary Issues

Without taking away from the aural significance of focal impulses, it is also
important to stress that the sonic cues are not so unambiguous that focal

impulse placement can be known with certainty from the sound of a performance. Although there are characteristic sonic traces, these traces will not always be desired effects, and it is possible to minimize them. Furthermore, the same traces can come from other sources—for example, when loudness accents occur on strongly marked syncopations.[1] Consequently, while some cases seem quite clear, others leave us uncertain. A certain amount of guesswork is always involved. At times in this book, I may seem to make an absolute claim, but this is always an abbreviated expression of a more tentative position. (There is more certainty in the recordings produced for this book with the specific intention of demonstrating contrasting focal impulse placements.)

Findings from music psychology can help frame the issues. Most importantly, although performers can influence how listeners hear meter, they cannot determine it. John Sloboda recorded pianists playing simple melodies that had been carefully constructed to make sense when placed in varying meters (Sloboda 1983, 1985), and measurements of performance inflections suggest that the pianists placed focal impulses in accord with the meter, differently in the different versions. (They were not informed that some of the melodies they played differed only in the placement of the bar lines.) Listeners were shown the melodies with both notations and asked to match notations with performances. The listeners performed above chance levels at this task, indicating that there were sonic cues to the performer's understanding of the meter, but they were rather variable in their judgments. The fundamental issue is that listening is too actively constructive and inferential a process for the performer to be able to determine (as opposed to influence) the listener's experience. In work that resonates strongly with focal impulse theory, Mari Riess Jones and various collaborators have proposed a theory of *dynamic attending* (Jones and Boltz 1989), in which listeners can choose to pay attention to larger or smaller timescales. Like viewing a painting up close or from a distance, listeners get a different perspective on the same sonic input by following a slower or faster beat. (To illustrate this, chap. 13 presents an informal experiment demonstrating that subtle variations in timing, loudness, and articulation that are clearly audible when following a faster beat level recede noticeably when following a slower beat level.)

This tells us that we cannot assume that our initial hearing of a performance is actually the best fit to the sound, just because we have not encountered anything that directly contradicts it. For our chosen mode of hearing may be concealing the features that could incline us toward another hearing: if we follow faster beat levels, we may miss larger patterns of coherence; if we follow slower beat levels, some important but subtle details may recede in salience, even to the point of disappearing. Furthermore, although conducting along can be quite helpful, as moving with the beat improves the accuracy of temporal judgments (Manning and Schutz 2013, 2015), it also influences pattern perception (Phillips-Silver and Trainor 2005, 2007, 2008; Repp and Knoblich 2009; see further discussion in chap. 13). Accuracy is improved, but additional biases may be introduced.

If we are aware that our listening strategies may be skewing our perception, we can at least avoid being taken captive by a single hearing. We do this by purposefully trying out a variety of hearings, checking preferred hearings against ones at both lower and higher metrical levels to make sure that the very act of listening at one level has not prevented the perception of cues that point strongly toward another. And it is indeed helpful to conduct our hearings: specifically, beats should be conducted wherever focal impulses are being considered, using uneven duple patterns when focal impulses are omitted from a triple metrical layer (e.g., conducting ⁶⁄₈ in four). We just need to make sure to do both our listening and our conducting with multiple patterns. Sometimes we may decide that the cues are too ambiguous to permit even a tentative decision. But in many other cases, careful comparison of multiple hearings can lead to a firm conviction that one hearing is better supported than the others, despite observing clearly how each way of hearing skews perception in its own favor.[2]

If cautions about the uncertainties surrounding focal impulse placement seem to stand in some tension with the strong claims made earlier regarding the impact of focal impulses on the character of a performance, we should bear in mind just how important small adjustments can be in high-level music training. Even when the effects of focal impulse placement are subtle (and they are not always subtle), they can be highly significant for the engaged listener.

5.2. The Sound of Focal Impulses

A focal impulse usually produces a dynamic stress (an accent of loudness) and/or a more sudden attack, at least for instruments that can produce such variations. A clear example is the first half of the gigue from Bach's First Cello Suite (ex. 5.1), as played by Yo-Yo Ma (1983), in which prominent dynamic stresses on the dotted-quarter beats suggest focal impulses placed two per measure. (Internet searches should bring up playlists of each chapter's examples of commercial recordings.)

Example 5.1. Bach, Suite No. 1 for Solo Cello, BWV 1007, Gigue, mm. 1–8. Adapted by permission from Ito (2013c), © Springer-Verlag Berlin Heidelberg 2013.

In a more legato context, the accents will be less vigorous, sounding like weighty pulsations. Recordings of the opening of Beethoven's Quartet op. 130 (ex. 5.2) by the Alban Berg Quartet (1983) and by the Busch Quartet (1941) illustrate this, with the Alban Berg taking the music in three and the Busch Quartet in one. The articulation of the cello starting in measure 7 is particularly telling.

The effects of focal impulses can also be heard in the timing of notes. Two main patterns are frequently encountered. The first is caused by giving a sense of weight to the focal impulse; this results in the elongation of the note on which the focal impulse is placed, a gentle agogic accent. Put more precisely, the time span from the attack point of that note until the attack point of the next (referred to as the *interonset interval* [IOI] in the music psychological literature) is lengthened. This may result in lengthening the consequent span that contains the lengthened IOI, or other notes may be shortened to preserve the length of the consequent span. Yo-Yo Ma chose the first of those options in measures 1 and 5 of the gigue from the cello suite, both of which feature noticeable lengthening of the downbeat. The second main temporal effect involves rushing through the notes within the consequent span. With the first effect, a lengthened first note can lengthen the consequent span. But because musicians rarely contract time spans longer than a few notes, the rapid unfolding of the notes in the second effect does not shorten the consequent span but instead lengthens its final IOI. Physically, these faster notes result from a sense of release of muscular tension following a strong focal impulse. This makes sense given that control of the rate of a motion often involves muscles that oppose the motion. A strong sense of release following the focal impulse

Example 5.2. Beethoven, String Quartet op. 130, i, mm. 1–10, Adagio ma non troppo.

Example 5.3. Bach, French Suite No. 6, BWV 817, Allemande, mm. 1–4. Adapted by permission from Ito (2013c), © Springer-Verlag Berlin Heidelberg 2013.

may extend to these opposing muscles, so that motion proceeds more rapidly than it would otherwise. Faster initial notes can be heard in both consequent spans in measure 3 of the gigue.

Gustav Leonhardt's recording (1975) of the allemande from Bach's French Suite No. 6 (ex. 5.3) provides a striking example of the effects of focal impulses on timing. In this recording, Leonhardt sometimes combines the two effects: the first note of the consequent span is elongated, and the subsequent notes move forward even more than would be needed to get to the next strong beat on time, leaving a bit of extra time before the strong beat. This occurs very audibly in the left hand in the initial measures.[3] In attributing these timing details to certain ways of moving the body, I am not denying that they are conscious and deliberate. The lengthening of metrically strong notes is described in baroque performance treatises, and the rapid forward motion occurs at least in part to clear the sound: by reducing the amount of residual sound present when the new attack comes, Leonhardt creates the impression of a stronger attack on the next (metrically strong) note. But the fact that this way of playing is the result of a conscious choice does not mean that it is any less the product of patterned ways of moving the body.

Dynamic stresses and temporal effects combine as clues to focal impulse placement in Artur Schnabel's recording (1939) of the opening of the second

Example 5.4. Schubert, Piano Sonata D. 960, ii, mm. 1–4.

movement of Schubert's Piano Sonata in B-flat, D. 960 (ex. 5.4). The emphasis on the downbeats seems clear enough. And the loudness accents on the third beats, combined with the elongation of the third beats, lead me to conclude that Schnabel was using focal impulses on those beats as well. This example is the first in which triple meter is treated as an uneven duple, leading to alternation of long and short consequent spans. In contrast, Alfred Brendel (1971) sounds like he was using focal impulses only on the downbeats. The lengthening of the third beats in Schnabel's recording suggests the presence of focal impulses in particular because of the sense of rhythmic discontinuity with what came before; within each measure, the length of the third beat does not make sense as a consequence of the temporal flow of the earlier beats. Notes flow out from focal impulses like ripples spreading after a stone is thrown into the water; if we see a new pattern of ripples, this suggests that another stone has been thrown.

In Jessye Norman's and Geoffrey Parsons's (1985) performance of Richard Strauss's song "Wie sollten wir geheim sie halten," op. 19, no. 4, we can hear that for a singer, the dynamic stresses accompanying focal impulses can encompass both the consonant and the vowel; this is clearly evident in the opening measures (ex. 5.5). Later in this short song, temporal effects of focal impulses are also quite pronounced. Combining propulsive forward motion with a moderate rate of focal impulses, this performance is an excellent example of the sense of powerful soaring that can come with using fewer focal impulses, discussed at the end of chapter 3.

Loudness and duration provide us with the most overt clues to focal impulse placement. A note produced by a focal impulse may be louder, it may have a longer duration, and the duration that precedes it may be lengthened.

Example 5.5. Richard Strauss, "Wie sollten wir geheim sie halten," op. 19, no. 4, mm. 1–5.

Because focal impulse placement is strongly correlated with meter, we can predict that strong beats will be marked in these ways, and this prediction has been strongly confirmed by experimental psychologists. As discussed in chapter 13, in eighteen papers dating as far back as 1936, each describing multiple experiments, researchers reported finding at least one of these cues to meter; only one paper reported looking at both loudness and timing and failing to find metrical patterning in either one. This evidence for the theory of focal impulses is indirect, but it indicates significant consonance between predictions of the theory and the empirical literature.

These patterns are also widely attested in the literature on historical performance practice (Houle 1987; Brown 1999). From the seventeenth through nineteenth centuries, there was general agreement that notes on strong beats would receive some degree of dynamic stress. In the Baroque period, articulation and the lengthening of durations were also widely seen as marking metrical accents, and metrical theory further reinforced the importance of perceptual emphasis on metrically strong beats. This topic is examined in greater detail in chapter 14.

Although differences of loudness and duration are the clearest and most overt indications of focal impulse placement, they are not the only signs. Another clue is the sense that a note has been placed deliberately in time, as opposed to being allowed to fall more freely in time. Although this may sometimes be a matter of the precision of timing, such a perception can arise without noticeable timing variation. Therefore, I suspect that this sense of definite temporal placement is rooted primarily in articulation, with timing effects a secondary factor. Example 5.6 shows measures 9–20 of the first movement of Haydn's String Quartet op. 74, no. 2. Stéphane Tran Ngoc, Wen-Lei Gu, Matthew Michelic, and Janet Anthony perform the excerpt with focal impulses only on the downbeats in sound example 5.1 and with focal impulses on the half-note beats in sound example 5.2. In a few places, audible accents in the middle of the measure are a cue to focal impulse placement, as in measures 13 and 14 in sound example 5.2. Mostly, though, the differences are more subtle. Although both performances feature expressive timing, the notes on the third beats of each measure in the first violin part sound as if they have been placed more definitely in time in sound example 5.2 than in sound example 5.1; this may have something to do with the timing itself, but it also has to do with the sharpness of the articulation. There is also a subtle difference in the coordination of the instruments. In sound example 5.2, the instruments are all quite closely synchronized on both of the half-note beats; in sound example 5.1, the various parts are less precisely synchronized in the middles of measures, as each line is shaped temporally according to its own internal dynamics, with the parts coming together for the commonly felt downbeats. (This difference in synchronization is easier to hear when conducting in half notes along with the recordings.)

Although I believe that the features of sound that I describe are clearly audible, the performances of the Haydn quartet are more ambiguous than the performances of Bach discussed above; therefore, they allow us to return to the earlier discussion of the perceptual biases inherent in hearing in a meter, now with concrete examples. Returning to Leonhardt's performance of the allemande from the French Suite, it would seem odd to me if a listener, coming to the performance without preconceived expectations, were to hear this performance in four. But what if the listener does come with preconceived expectations? If we listen again to Leonhardt's recording, this time attempting to hear it in four, we find this task quite doable for the most part. Leonhardt's coupling of eighth-note pairs, typical of the historically informed baroque performance of his time, helps us in this task; and when the music becomes more sequential heading into the first cadence,

Example 5.6. Haydn, String Quartet op. 74/2, i, mm. 9–20, Allegro spirituoso.

Bach helps us as well. Leonhardt's rubato immediately following that first cadence will present one of the larger hurdles, as will the performance of the syncopations in measures 9 and 10. Similar listening experiments with Haydn's op. 74, no. 2, hearing each performance first in one and then in two (or vice versa), will encounter fewer obstacles. The rhythmic markedness of sound example 5.2 seems somewhat unusual when heard in one, especially in the first violin part in measure 11, and the temporal spread of beat 3 in measure 12 is salient when sound example 5.1 is heard in two, but in general,

Example 5.7. Bach, Suite No. 1 for Solo Cello, BWV 1007, Courante, mm. 1–4.

it is possible to hear each performance each way. Such cases reinforce the importance of listening both ways, staying alert to cues of successful and unsuccessful fit.

All of the sonic cues to focal impulse placement function only in context; none will necessarily, by themselves, give the listener the impression that a focal impulse was used in a certain location. This is particularly true for the articulation cues. In the Haydn example, short, light articulation was heard as a clue to the absence of a focal impulse. But in another context, especially if combined with a sharp attack, short articulation could point in the opposite direction, to the possible presence of a focal impulse. Eric Clarke (1985) noted this same ambiguity regarding the use of articulation as a cue to structural features of the score. Because cues of loudness and duration are somewhat more consistently patterned, they lend themselves more readily to empirical investigation. In contrast, the cues of articulation seem to require such subtle contextual interpretation that their use will remain a matter of judgment.

Having explored the typical patterns of correlation between sound and focal impulses, we can consider the counterexample to metrical placement promised in the previous chapter. The opening measures of Mischa Maisky's recording (1999) of the courante from Bach's First Cello Suite (ex. 5.7) offer an unusually clear example of focal impulses placed at odds with meter. To my ear, it sounds like focal impulses are placed on beats 1 and 2 in measures 1 and 2 but only on beat 2 in measures 3 and 4; however, it is possible that gentle focal impulses are also placed on the downbeats of those measures. This judgment of focal impulse placement is based on all of the parameters discussed: the notes posited to be produced by focal impulses are louder, more bitingly attacked, and separated in time from the notes that surround them by small (and not so small) IOI lengthening. I believe that the downbeats in measures 3 and 4 lack focal impulses because the notes on the downbeats are not sufficiently differentiated from the notes that surround them by any of those parameters. I hear no significant markings of the downbeat in measure 3 and only minor ones in measure 4—a small dynamic stress, and IOI lengthening before and after the downbeat, which, as part of the significant ritard into beat 2, does not reflect downbeat emphasis. Maisky's performance seems to me extremely unusual, not because of the degree of accentuation he places on the second beat but rather because I do not hear a significant bodily investment in the downbeat. Syncopations happen all the time; few performances subvert meter in the ways this one does. The striking character of this performance serves as evidence that focal impulses tend to be aligned with meter.

5.3. Visual Cues to Focal Impulses

One might expect that if focal impulses are used to organize longer spans of physical motion in performance, their effects should be not only sonic but also visual. I do often feel that seeing a performance in addition to hearing it is helpful in forming more confident guesses about the placement of focal impulses, but generalizing about visual cues is difficult. Torso motions can be helpful indications, but they often lack the consistency that I hear in the sound. In going through video recordings of performance, I can often find visual indications of most focal impulses, but the cues are highly contextual, changing in some cases from one measure to the next. My experience accords well with the limited and equivocal picture of correlation between meter and physical motion in performance available from the empirical literature, discussed in chapter 13.

A sampling of video recordings of performance is likely to yield many clear examples in which motions of larger parts of the body are synchronized with the meter, even if the specifics of the synchronized motions are variable. For reasons of performance culture, this is often more evident with soloists and chamber ensembles than in orchestras. (Within orchestras, wind players often move the most overtly; among string sections, that of the Vienna Philharmonic is particularly demonstrative.) Period-instrument ensembles are also relatively unrestrained in their physical movements; a recording of the Brandenburg Concertos by the Freiburger Barockorchester (2000), referred to in chapter 8, is a source of many clear examples. Although some phase drift can occur, there is often a correlation between body sway and meter. It is particularly interesting to observe the head motions of the harpsichordist in the cadenza from the first movement of Brandenburg Concerto No. 5 because, unlike most of the other motions observed, it would not be possible to claim that these motions existed primarily for the purpose of ensemble synchronization.

5.4. Focal Impulses and Older Performance Traditions

This chapter has equipped us to see that if a precise, literal rendering of the score is a main goal of performance, using more focal impulses will be advantageous. We have already observed that notes produced by focal impulses can give the impression of being placed more definitely in time; they are also placed more definitely in a literal way—notes produced by focal impulses receive both more attention and more intention. If literally precise rhythms are important, using more frequent focal impulses will help—both directly, because more of the notes are produced by focal impulses, and indirectly, because with shorter consequent spans that contain fewer notes, it is easier to control the timing of the notes produced by subsidiary impulses. We have also seen that ensemble synchronization is often more precise for the notes produced by the focal impulses, and so more frequent focal impulses will help in this area as well. Beyond timing, intonation and articulation are also more precise with more focal impulses. This observation converges with the work discussed earlier by Jones and Boltz (1989), who argue that listening while following faster beat levels is like zooming in on an image—a finer-grained level of detail comes into focus. Listeners (including those in the midst of performing) are more likely to notice mistuned notes or imprecise rhythms when giving attention to faster beat levels.[4] With both attention and action, shorter timescales enhance precision.

Gains in precision are not the only results of placing focal impulses on faster beat levels, however; there are also losses. Just as looking at a large painting at close range makes it difficult or impossible to appreciate the work as a whole, aspects of the music that unfold over longer timescales will receive less attention when following faster beat levels. And in terms of the details of performance discussed in this chapter, the trade-offs are particularly clear, because expressive shape is related to focal impulse use. It follows that precision and expressive shape are not independent variables. We cannot take a performance with free rhythms and inexact ensemble synchronization and make it more precise while retaining its distinct expressive character. If we use more focal impulses to achieve greater precision, we will have created a new performance, displacing the old one.

For musicians today, the value placed on precision is often high, in some cases even supreme. This situation has resulted from a marked increase in the importance of precision over the course of the twentieth century, itself the result of factors including the increasing prevalence and precision of recorded sound, modernist aesthetics, and modernist approaches to textual interpretation. Listening to recorded performances that span more than a century, enormous gains in precision have unquestionably been made; however, we can also observe that the music sounds qualitatively different, which means that something has been lost. Older performance traditions, in which music was often shaped in ways that were inconsistent with literal precision, have fallen out of use. Some aspects of these older traditions, such as the use of expressive intonation, are unconnected to the use of focal impulses. But others, having to do particularly with rhythm and temporal shape, are strongly related to the placement of focal impulses. As ways of performing that use fewer focal impulses have fallen out of use, so have the kinds of freedom that come with fewer focal impulses. In this section I will examine in detail a few passages from older recordings. The greater rhythmic freedom of styles of performance from before 1950 has often been noted; this observation is based on performance treatises, descriptions of famous musicians' performances, and, more recently, recordings (Philip 1992; Rosenblum 1992; Hudson 1994).[5] I offer a new perspective on some forms of temporal flexibility, showing that a strong relationship can exist between the timing profile and the use of focal impulses. In the present context, I am motivated to demonstrate these effects because many musicians today are unfamiliar with these older traditions and because I personally find their combination of rhythmic vitality with rhythmic freedom to be a highpoint of the art of performance.

We will start with chamber music, with two passages from the recording of Schubert's String Quartet in G Major, D. 887, made in 1938 by the Busch Quartet. Although this is a midcentury recording, the members of the quartet were all born in the nineteenth century, so their performance reflects training at the end of the nineteenth century and the very beginning of the twentieth. Adolf Busch, the first violinist in the quartet, was born in 1891, and his two principal teachers both studied with Joseph Joachim. As the most prominent non-Jewish German violinist of his time, Busch could have received a warm embrace from the Nazis; instead, he seriously damaged his career and his health as a consequence of his moral decision to emigrate to the United States (Potter 2010).

The final movement of the quartet is a tarantella in $\frac{6}{8}$ marked "allegro assai," and the lightness and ebullience of the Busch Quartet's performance (1938) is closely related to the many clear signs of the music being felt predominantly in one. An example of this is the effervescent theme that closes the A section in the sprawling sonata rondo form; the rhythm is particularly free when this theme returns in the development in measure 389 (ex. 5.8; 1938, 5:13). Focusing on the first violin part, this is a clear example of letting the notes following the focal impulse flow more quickly and then waiting

Example 5.8. Schubert, String Quartet D. 887, iv, mm. 389–93, Allegro assai.

Example 5.9. Schubert, String Quartet D. 887, iv, mm. 121–28, Allegro assai.

until the next strong beat; here, one of the intentions is probably to leave space between the grace notes that begin several of the measures and the eighth notes of the same pitch that precede them. (In some other performances, the rhythm of those measures can sound somewhat unclear.)

A similar rhythmic effect is found in the arpeggios that end the first main theme of the B section (ex. 5.9; 1938, 1:46). Here the middle of the measure in the first violin part comes conspicuously early and audibly earlier than in the second violin and viola parts. An approximate measurement of the timing, produced using the program Sonic Visualiser (Cannam, Landone, and Sandler 2010), indicated that in measures 125–132, the second beat came on average approximately 43 percent through the total duration of the measure (an evenly timed second beat would have occupied 50% of the measure). The Busch Quartet's performance has great gestural vitality, and part of that vitality comes from vigorous but relatively infrequent focal impulses. Strongly physical responses to the focal impulses, including letting the subsequent notes flow more quickly, are not restrained by literal or precisionistic understandings of the rhythm. This is a clear example of an older style of performance, quite different from how the movement is performed today.

Our other examples come from vocal music, specifically from Viennese operetta. It would seem that the particularly strong traditions in this repertoire have helped aspects of an older style to survive somewhat longer and more pervasively than they have elsewhere. The first examples come from a video recording of *Die Fledermaus* with Hermann Prey (1977) in the role of Eisenstein. At his first entrance, in no. 2 (ex. 5.10; 1977, 10:47 relative to the start of the opera), the second beats of measures 7 and 8 are noticeably lengthened. In contrast to the preceding examples, in which lengthening late in the measure resulted from a vigorous focal impulse on the downbeat, here the point seems to be to allow more time for the more important syllables in the second half of the measure and to give them stronger accentuation. In measure 18 (not shown), the first two eighths are very noticeably shortened, here to set off the shout-like leap up a major sixth and to make a particularly strong *h* at the start of the new word. Even more obvious, and more typical as a response to a strong focal impulse, is the rushing through the words "dagewesen" and "auserlesen" at the start of the final section of the following duo (no. 3; ex. 5.11; 22:59).

A final example comes from another famous operetta. In the recording of Carl Millöcker's *Der Bettelstudent* conducted by Robert Stolz (Pratsch-Kaufmann [1966?]), the exchange between a chorus of prisoners' wives and the jailor Enterich in the opening number of act 1 (ex. 5.12, sound ex. 5.3) illustrates how a singer can give a passage in tempo an almost recitative-like character; it also shows that no one parameter can be decisive in determining focal impulse placement. The synthesis of articulation, accentuation, and timing suggests that Kurt Pratsch-Kaufmann (Enterich) is singing in one while the chorus and orchestra are performing in two. Especially in the measures with the dotted rhythms, the sopranos place a sharp accent in the middle of the measure,

Example 5.10. Johann Strauss Jr., *Die Fledermaus*, Act I, No. 2, Trio, mm. 6–12, Allegro moderato, piano-vocal score.

Example 5.11. Johann Strauss Jr., *Die Fledermaus*, Act I, No. 3, Duo, mm. 5–10 of the concluding Allegro non troppo, piano-vocal score.

Example 5.12. Millöcker, *Der Bettelstudent*, Act I, No. 1, mm. 1–4 and 9–12 of the Moderato section, piano-vocal score.

suggesting the use of a focal impulse there, whereas Pratsch-Kaufmann places the middle of the measure much more freely and without accent. Interestingly, measurement reveals that both the sopranos and Pratsch-Kaufmann place the middle of the measure slightly early in the measures with the dotted rhythms; the rhythmic gesture seems clearly enough established that the uneven timing is used whether there are one or two focal impulses per measure. Pratsch-Kaufmann is both earlier in his placement of the middle of the measure and more variable in its timing; however, it seems likely that it is not timing alone but rather a combination of factors—with articulation and accentuation high on the list—that is responsible for the different impressions of focal impulse placement in the two passages.

In my experience, this kind of performance has become rare. My most vivid memories of it are from hearing Prey sing Eisenstein in the 1990s and from a performance of Bruckner's Symphony No. 4 by the Vienna Philharmonic in 2003. In one passage from the Bruckner, solo wind players moved expressively as they shaped their own lines, each according to its own internal dynamics; although the middles of measures were noticeably apart in time, they always landed on the downbeats together. Neither of those performances had a musty, museum-like quality, and I am certainly not calling attention to these practices in order to suggest that performers try to turn back the clock. Beyond being aware of these kinds of rhythmic freedom, I would hope that musicians might relax the demands of precision and find fresh ways of being harmoniously responsive to one another in time.

This chapter concludes the central portion of part 2; the most crucial experiential aspects of the focal impulse have now been discussed. The remaining two chapters move in opposite directions: first to more theoretical matters, with further discussion of the role of meter in relation to focal impulses and consequent spans, and then to practical application, with a taxonomy of syncopations based on focal impulse placement.

Notes

1. Chap. 1 claimed that, in some cases, auditory cues allow us to distinguish accented syncopations produced by subsidiary impulses from strong attacks produced directly by focal impulses. Chap. 7 will provide examples defending this idea.

2. The quality of sound reproduction can strongly influence judgments of focal impulse placement; therefore, the reader is encouraged to listen to the examples using the best equipment available. Also, downloaded media files are superior to streamed files.

102 | Focal Impulse Theory

3. Dirk-Jan Povel (1977) found exactly these durational patterns when he used a computer to measure timings in Leonhardt's performance of the first prelude from bk. 1 of *The Well-Tempered Clavier.*

4. As we will see in sect. 13.1, Jones's dynamic attending theory posits that following a beat consists in focusing attention at the moment the beat is expected; if this is so, a beat *is* attention, and so to follow a faster beat is to deploy attention more frequently.

5. Scholars of historical performance generally identify two main types of rhythmic flexibility (Philip 1992; Rosenblum 1992; Hudson 1994). The one that will be addressed here involves the use of flexible durations within a basically steady tempo; this practice became prominent in the late seventeenth century and reached a particularly high level of development in Chopin's piano playing. The second kind of rhythmic flexibility involves significant adjustment to the prevailing tempo; its ascendance in the nineteenth century is associated especially with Liszt and Wagner.

6

MORE ON FOCAL IMPULSES AND METER

THIS CHAPTER ADDRESSES THREE ISSUES REGARDING FOCAL IMPULSES and meter: the importance of meter as opposed to grouping, both for focal impulse placement and for the extent of consequent spans; the importance given to the notated measure; and the contrast between the depth of meter and the flatness of the impulse hierarchy. These discussions examine foundational aspects of focal impulses, but they are more theoretical than much of the rest of part 2. Readers with more exclusively practical interests may wish to skip to chapter 7, which applies the focal impulse in situations involving metrical dissonance.

6.1. Grouping versus Meter, Groups versus Consequent Spans

Focal impulse theory focuses on meter to the point of ignoring grouping almost entirely. At least two counterproposals could be made. The first would allow grouping boundaries to exert a strong influence on the placement of focal impulses. The second would grant that focal impulses tend to be placed on strong beats but argue that consequent spans should reflect grouping units rather than metrical units. I will address each counterproposal in turn.

Throughout this book, a great many of the discussions serve implicitly as evidence for metrical placement. Furthermore, chapter 13 presents extensive evidence (albeit indirect) supporting metrical placement from the literature of experimental psychology. In this discussion, I simply state two additional reasons to reject placing focal impulses based on grouping. First, meter is less ambiguous than grouping, more consistent, and much more predictable. From a psychological perspective, it would be much less demanding (and thus more efficient) to base motor organization on meter. And second, as we saw in the last chapter, focal impulses that are misaligned with meter tend to sound quite unusual, indicating that they belong in the outer periphery.

Example 6.1. Handel, Water Music Suite, Overture, mm. 1–3, reduced score.

Let us now consider the viewpoint that accepts metrical placement but argues that consequent spans should reflect grouping. The opening of the overture from the first suite of Handel's *Water Music* (ex. 6.1) provides a helpful entry point. In accord with Lerdahl and Jackendoff's (1983, 45) "Grouping Preference Rule 2 (Proximity)," the pick-up sixteenths group together with the quarter notes they precede. Under the present theory, although the pick-up notes begin a group, they end a consequent span. Before exploring this conflict further, it may be helpful to note that it is not unusual. The units of meter and grouping are often displaced, and both exist in a nested hierarchy in which a beginning or end at one level may be a middle at another. To claim that some sort of boundary separates two events is not to say that our primary hearing of their relationship may not be one of belonging together—this is simply business as usual in music. Furthermore, the theory as put forward does not attach any experience to the boundaries of a consequent span other than the focal impulse itself. It matters for the theory's account of how focal impulses do what they do that consequent spans end with the next focal impulse, but this claim does not carry any experiential freight. It would do so only if some competing version of the theory made experiential claims about the ends of consequent spans when focal impulses lie in their middles rather than at their beginnings and ends (e.g. "this is what the end of a consequent span sounds like" or "this is what it feels like").

Returning now to the passage from the *Water Music*, the claim that consequent spans should reflect grouping would note the strong sense of the pick-up notes belonging *physically* to the next quarter note. Each quarter note might be compared to a planet that draws the preceding sixteenth notes into its gravitational field like asteroids.[1] I agree with this description of how the sixteenth notes behave: they should flow smoothly into the quarter note with a sense of purposefully directed motion. But we should be clear that the quarter note that is the goal of motion can influence the manner of performance of the sixteenth notes only by being an input to a planning process; there is not any direct, physical causation from the quarter note to the sixteenths, for any such causation would need to operate backward through time. If the pick-up notes seem to flow toward the quarter notes in a particularly smooth, even necessary, way, this is because the preceding focal impulse successfully initiated a trajectory of motion that could have that sense of purposeful direction. The dependence of the sixteenths on some prior motion is clarified if we imagine an alternate version of this opening. Let the first attack fall on beat 2 following a quarter-note rest, shifting the passage by a quarter note. Focal impulses retain their placement with respect to the bar lines, but not with respect to the notes. In this new version, the sixteenths will still flow into the following quarter notes, but it will be evident that they have been set in motion by events on the strong-beat sixteenth rests. The analogy with half-pipe sports discussed in chapter 3 reinforces this understanding of physical causality. A half-pipe snowboarder who has just spun 360 degrees in the air may seem to approach the surface of the half-pipe with smooth, purposefully directed motion, but this impression results from her prior actions. (To see the importance of prior action for the goal-oriented quality of the descent, consider a contrasting scenario in which the athlete has been pushed unexpectedly off of a platform and is falling toward a snowbank.)

As we will see in chapter 13, the control of motion is extremely complex, and focal impulse theory is almost certainly an oversimplification from a scientific standpoint. This is true especially with respect to processes of motor planning, which likely unfold on multiple levels simultaneously. But for the phenomenological side of the theory, which aims to fruitfully inform listeners and performers, organizing the theory in terms of consequent spans that follow focal impulses is simple, theoretically coherent, and consistent both with experience and with basic physics.

6.2. The Salience of the Notated Measure

As indicated in chapter 4, bar lines are tremendously salient to performers. Regardless of the attention or lack of attention given to other levels of metrical structure, performers generally make a physical investment in the downbeat.

Why should this be? At the simplest level, the bar line is the mechanism of chunking that is built into the notation of common-practice music. Whether or not printed music is used in performance, this chunking will have had significant input to the musician's understanding of the music, making it plausible that this notated segmentation would influence mental representation. (To see the cognitive power of segmentation, try repeating your phone number rapidly with an unfamiliar chunking; for the United States and Canada a challenging one is 2 + 2 + 3 + 3.)

At a more fundamental level, bar lines are used by composers to mark a structurally important level of the meter. To arouse intuitions that confirm this claim, let us assume the negative—and in broadly sweeping form. Let us assume that the particulars of notation are entirely arbitrary: So long as the temporal proportions are preserved and the metrical hierarchy is respected, it does not matter what note values the composer uses, and it does not matter where the bar lines are placed. If this were the case, then the following two transformations, applied to any piece in duple or quadruple meter that has a regular duple or quadruple hypermeter, would have no effect on the music. First, apply either a doubling or a halving both to the bottom number in the time signature and to the note values. The measures will now contain the same segments of music that they did in the original, but the note values will be either doubled or halved. For the second transformation, again double or halve the time signature, but this time leave note values unchanged so that bar lines are either added or deleted. The measures now contain either twice or half the music that they contained in the original. I would argue that although both transformations change the music in significant ways, the effects of the second run deeper.

As a test case, consider the opening melody from Mozart's Piano Concerto in G Major, K. 453 (ex. 6.2). Under the first transformations, in which note values are changed, the implied differences include tempo, articulation, character, and sense of weight. Relative to the original (ex. 6.2a), the doubled note values of example 6.2b suggest a slower tempo and either a very heavy sound or else a floating sound, with the white notes in the latter case evoking the world of Renaissance polyphony. In example 6.2c, the halved values suggest a faster tempo and a lighter, even dainty character.

The second kind of transformation also changes the likely manner of performance. To take just one example, the third beat of measure 1 in the original could easily have a lightness that would be very strange on the downbeat of the second measure of the march-like example 6.2e. Similarly, the heaviest reasonable performance of that note in the original version would probably be too heavy as a performance of the third quarter-note beat of example 6.2d.

Both kinds of transformation change performance inflections, but the second kind implies structural changes that the first does not. Changing the amount of music contained by the measure changes the perspective from

Example 6.2. Mozart, Piano Concerto K. 453, i, Allegro, opening melody and some renotations.

which we view the music, and structural relationships look different from these new perspectives. In example 6.2d, for example, the melodic decoration of D in the first measure tends to fade into the background, the underlying pitch coming to the fore. But in example 6.2e, we have not so much a single D as a varied motive that insistently drives in repeated Ds. Examples 6.2b and 6.2c change the music's character, but examples 6.2d and 6.2e change the music's identity in some more fundamental way.

This demonstration suggests that composers use bar lines to mark a level of the meter that has a particular kind of structural importance. This idea makes almost no contact with the music cognition literature. Lerdahl and Jackendoff (1983) treat meter as a symmetrical hierarchy with only the tactus being singled out as having special significance. Justin London's (2012) more recent theory is similar; although it goes beyond Lerdahl and Jackendoff in positing a role for specific durations, the theory includes nothing that could correspond to a downbeat. Experimenters often look for differentiation between the downbeat and other beats as a test for the reality of metrical structures (as discussed in chap. 13), but they are probably simply assuming that the downbeat will be relatively strong; like Lerdahl, Jackdendoff, and London, they do not propose any specific cognitive role for the notated downbeat. Outside of music cognition, however, the traditional approach is to take the notated measure as a foundational unit, both for meter and hypermeter (see sec. 2.4, especially on Rothstein 1989). For example, when Robert Hatten (2004, 114–17; 2012, 21) proposes that strong beats generate gravitational attractions within the virtual environment of music (building on Larson [2012, 148–49] and paralleling the brief discussion in the previous section), the notated measure and the notated downbeat are the primary points of reference for agential interactions with these virtual musical forces.[2]

As a step toward providing a listener-oriented, cognitive grounding for this older approach to meter and hypermeter, I have proposed the existence of the heard measure (Ito 2013a; see also sec. 2.4), a mental construct used by listeners who are musicians and perhaps by others. The heard measure corresponds in many respects to the notated measure but without recourse to notation; instead, it is understood to unite between one and four tactus beats. The heard measure provides a sense of what I call metrical orientation. At a level of structure smaller than the phrase, it gives a salient answer to the question, "What am I hearing now?"—a question that will always have multiple, hierarchically nested answers.

For the performer, whose understanding of the music is influenced by the written score, it seems likely that the heard measures will often correspond to the notated measures. If this correspondence is likely for the performer, it is even more likely for the composer—and so this cognitive marking could help explain the greater consistency of metrical structures in relation to hypermetrical structures. Indeed, throughout much of the common-practice era, changes of meter signature within the body of a movement were rather unusual, whereas changes in the number of measures separating strong hyperbeats were quite common. This suggests that composers understood the measure as a basic unit. The basic units themselves came as fixed, unchanging entities, but the process of joining basic units together (to form hypermeasures) was open to variation.

This basic picture of the stability of the notated measure in common-practice music is complicated by the fact that baroque composers often used the half-measure as the fixed, basic unit. Theorists of the seventeenth and eighteenth centuries often talked about compound meters in the original sense, in which, for example, $\frac{4}{4}$ and sometimes $\frac{6}{8}$ were understood to consist of two measures of $\frac{2}{4}$ and $\frac{3}{8}$, respectively, with each measure carrying equal accentual weight. And with the exception of certain genres, including rondeaus, chaconnes, passacaglias, and some dance types, this use of compound meter is quite common in baroque-period works. (Grave [1985] offers a good introduction.) The questions of whether and to what extent this baroque conception of meter continued to influence compositional practice in the classical era, and related questions of how these conceptions may be applied analytically, have received increasing attention in recent years (Grave 1984; Maurer Zenck 2001; Rothstein 2008; Mirka 2009; Ito 2014), with Danuta Mirka going farthest in proposing that understood meter may change rapidly. Whatever the eventual verdict on these questions, the stability of the notated meter is not in question; this means that the amount of music enclosed by the bar lines remains available as a salient horizon of temporal expectation.[3] Given the strong visual role played by the notated measure, it would seem likely that the notated measure would have some cognitive salience even if, under these older ways of hearing and understanding music, the actual measure was understood to be some other size. Indeed, this salience probably played a role in the evolution of metrical practice, with compound meter in the seventeenth- and eighteenth-century sense gradually falling out of use.[4]

As a final note on this topic, cases exist in which focal impulses are not placed on notated downbeats. In dealing with the inner periphery, part 3 will include cases in which the heard meter is out of phase with the notated meter; in these cases, the heard downbeat will typically receive a focal impulse. There are also cases in which performers might want to mark only hypermetrically strong downbeats with focal impulses. We have seen a potential example in the long-breathed melody of the main contrasting theme from the finale of Tchaikovsky's Symphony No. 5 (ex. 3.10).[5] Such cases move beyond the inner periphery of focal impulse placements to the outer periphery; they are among the cases that depart most notably from general norms.

6.3. Flat Impulse Hierarchy, Deep Meter

A salient feature of the impulse hierarchy I have described is its flatness. A passage in $\frac{4}{4}$ meter featuring both motion in sixteenth notes and four-bar hypermeter would have a seven-level metrical hierarchy using Lerdahl and Jackendoff's (1983) theory. But under the present theory, it would be performed with a simple two-level impulse hierarchy, with impulses being either focal or subsidiary. Two comments are in order with respect to this contrast.

First, it is not an implication of focal impulse theory that the flatness of the impulse hierarchy leads to a corresponding flatness in the effects of meter on performance, as if the only metrical layer that could be brought out in performance were the one marked by the focal impulses. To the contrary, metrical levels not differentiated by impulse hierarchy are often marked by performers, both physically and audibly. Any two focal impulses will have at least one thing in common: each will play an organizing role for the motion that follows, doing so until the next focal impulse. But they may be different in many other ways, just as members of most categories can be. For example, I belong to many categories of person: people born in the 1960s, people with one brown eye and one hazel eye, members of the Society for Music Theory, people who commute by bicycle. Each category includes many people, and it would be easy, within any of them, to find two people who were very different from one another. When we say that two impulses are focal impulses, we are saying that both play a governing role in the organization of physical motion; the notes they produce may be quite different (e.g., in loudness, articulation, color). There is plenty of room to mark multiple levels of the metrical hierarchy in performance, by means of various kinds of differences among both subsidiary and focal impulses.

Second, the flatness of the impulse hierarchy can be taken as a virtue, because it focuses on one region within an otherwise largely undifferentiated hierarchy. The metrical hierarchy as developed by Lerdahl and Jackendoff (1983) is characterized by symmetry and abstraction. There is much that this theory of meter fails to account for, but the solution is not to discard the theory but rather to augment it, understanding it as basic cognitive scaffolding around which more particular practices are anchored. London (2012) argued for the importance of specific durations in constraining the roles that various beat levels may play, so that two pieces with identical metrical grids may correspond to different experiences of meter if the grids intersect differently with the ranges of preferred beat durations. He also proposed that specific patterns of expressive timing (e.g., the early second beat in the Viennese waltz) may, if performed consistently enough, become part of the meter itself. Furthermore, influenced by studies of meter in non-Western musics, he developed a general theory for meters in which there is no nominally isochronous smallest beat (a unit to which all other beats relate as even multiples). My own contributions to this broader perspective on meter include heard measures consisting of some small number of tactus beats, and hypermeter theorized in terms of the organization of heard downbeats, with schemas for four-bar hypermeasures specifying hyperbeat roles in ways that allow hyperbeats to be heard out of their usual sequence (Ito 2013a). With this book, I suggest that the texture of metrical hearing and acting should be understood as more granular still, with a special kind of physical investment (the focal impulse) marking some special level of the beat, not necessarily the tactus, and with a variety of ways in which space can be opened between the placement of focal impulses and meter.

The flatness of the impulse hierarchy, then, does not reflect a flatness of metrical understanding but rather the opposite. In the view advanced here, the metrical hierarchy is a basic framework in relation to which other more varied and more specific metrical processes play out. Focal impulses can interact with those other processes, both being influenced by them and influencing the ways in which they are more or less likely to be heard. The result is therefore not a flattening, as if the impulse hierarchy were the only hierarchy or as if all focal impulses were the same in intensity and character. It is, instead, an enhancement: of a view of meter as both deep and richly textured, and of an understanding of differing practices that are particular to specific sets of levels within the hierarchy.

Notes

1. Similar arguments are made by Larson (2012, 148–49) and Hatten (2004, 114–17; 2012, 21).

2. Together with Arnie Cox's (2016) work on embodied, mimetic responses to music, the present theory helps explain why a listener's responses to the gestures that arise from these interactions can be so visceral.

3. In terms of focal impulse placement, performers attuned to implied half-measure meters would be no less likely to mark the notated downbeats with focal impulses; rather, they would have an additional (midbar) downbeat to mark.

4. This question of the evolution of meter in the eighteenth century will be the focus of a future study (Ito, in preparation a).

5. This focal impulse placement would not work for the accompaniment, and the resulting polyphonic impulse placement (chap. 8) is another factor distancing this way of performing the passage from the core. Examples of what focal impulses every other downbeat can sound like are found in several recordings of Ollendorf's first aria, "Und da soll man noch galant sein" (No. 2), from Millöcker's operetta *Der Bettelstudent*, at the text "Ach ich hab' sie ja nur auf die Schulter geküsst," mm. 87–102, somewhat surprisingly given the unambiguous metrical implications of the waltz. The recordings are those by Fritz Ollendorff (1966, 1:42) conducted by Robert Stolz; Wolfgang Hellmich (1968, 1:26), conducted by Günther Herbig; and Henryk Böhm (2013, 1:42), conducted by Uwe Theimer.

7

FOCAL IMPULSES AND CHARACTERS
OF SYNCOPATION

THIS CHAPTER SHOWS THAT WHEN SYNCOPATIONS ARE EXAMINED from the perspective of focal impulse theory, a simple three-category taxonomy emerges, based on the relationship between syncopated notes and focal impulses. Each type of syncopation has its own characteristic sound, and each sonic pattern is familiar. The first section develops the taxonomy, and the second uses it to suggest new ways of hearing and performing metrically dissonant passages from Mozart and Beethoven.

7.1. A Taxonomy of Syncopations

In terms of the character of sound produced and the manner of performance, patterns of consistent, regular syncopation come in three varieties. These syncopations (or "displacement dissonances"; Krebs 1999) will be presumed not to subvert the prevailing meter.[1] Cases in which the performer hears a different meter will be discussed in part 3 and particularly in chapter 12.

Of the three characters of syncopation, the first is the *vigorous* character; in this case, the syncopated attack points occur with the same frequency as the focal impulses, the two being offset in time (ex. 7.1a). These kinds of syncopations are typically characterized by rhythmic vitality, often with vigorous attacks and early release of the sound. Sometimes this early release takes place just after the strong beat in the middle of the syncopation, with the sound having been more sustained until then. (Ways of moving that could be sources of this pattern will be discussed in chap. 9.) The timing of these syncopations may at times be somewhat imprecise. Example 7.2 shows measures 21–26 of the third movement of Haydn's String Quartet op. 33, no. 2. In sound example 7.1, Stéphane Tran Ngoc, Wen-Lei Gu, Matthew Michelic, and Janet Anthony play this passage with focal impulses on the quarter-note

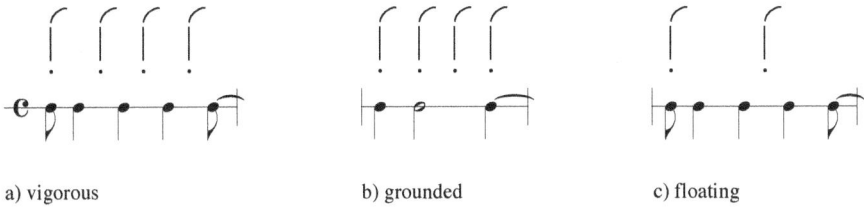

a) vigorous   b) grounded   c) floating

Example 7.1. Types of syncopation.

beats, resulting in vigorous syncopations that have rhythmically active attacks and early releases. As an extreme case, the passage from the *Rite of Spring* in chapter 1 also exhibits vigorous syncopations.

The second character of syncopation is the *grounded* character, in which enough focal impulses are used that the attack points of the syncopations coincide with normal placements for focal impulses (ex. 7.1b). The fact that the syncopated notes begin with focal impulses greatly reduces the sense of active rhythmic unrest that characterizes the vigorous syncopations. This alignment with focal impulses makes their often strong attacks sound grounded rather than conflicted. They feel much heavier than vigorous syncopations, and they usually lack the early release. In sound example 7.2, the passage from Haydn's op. 33, no. 2, is performed with focal impulses on eighth-note beats, resulting in grounded syncopations. The attacks of the syncopated notes are heavier, the sound is sustained longer, synchronization of parts is more precise, and there is a greater sense of the attack points being placed definitely at specific points in time.

In the third character, the *floating* character, the syncopated notes and the focal impulses are offset (as in the vigorous character), but there are at least two syncopated notes per focal impulse (ex. 7.1c). These kinds of syncopations typically have rhythmic energy, but they are less active than the vigorous syncopations. Their sound is characterized by a somewhat (but not too) insistent sustain, often followed by an early release; the release generally will not have the precise timing found in some vigorous syncopations. In contrast to the generally heavy grounded syncopations, floating syncopations are quite light, suggesting a suspended weight never fully released. Example 7.3 shows measures 26–39 of the first movement of Mozart's Quintet K. 406. In sound example 7.3, Stéphane Tran Ngoc, Wen-Lei Gu, Matthew Michelic, Janet Anthony, and I play this passage with focal impulses on the half-note beats, resulting in floating syncopations in measures 28–33 (the recording starts a few measures before ex. 7.3 begins). These

Example 7.2. Haydn, String Quartet op. 33/2, iii, mm. 21–26, Largo sostenuto.

measures have a quality of active rhythmic unrest, but in sound example 7.3 they lack the vigorous quality that is heard in sound example 7.4, which places focal impulses on the quarter-note beats. The most salient contrast is in the sharpness of attack; beyond this, tapping along with the eighth notes helps bring into focus the more precise ensemble synchronization in sound example 7.4—but the whole rhythmic feel of the passage is different generally.[2]

When the syncopations shift in measure 34 of the Mozart from quarter notes to half notes, we hear the expected shifts in type of syncopation

Example 7.3. Mozart, Viola Quintet K. 406, i, mm. 26–39, Allegro.

in the two recordings. Sound example 7.3, performed with focal impulses on half-note beats, has vigorous syncopations in measures 34 and 36; beyond a general sense of rhythmic activity and dynamism, we can hear this in the quality of the attack, the early release of the sound, and the slightly early onsets of the syncopated half notes. In sound example 7.4, with focal impulses on quarter-note beats, those syncopated half notes have a grounded quality.

Again, this is a matter of holistic character, but we hear specific traces of the focal impulses in the longer sustain, later onsets, and qualities of attack of those notes. In sound example 7.3, the syncopated half notes spring into motion; in sound example 7.4, they rest solidly on their heels.

Of the three characters, the vigorous syncopation is the most central; the other two flank it, standing on opposite sides both in terms of frequency of focal impulses and in terms of expressive quality. Vigorous syncopations come to mind first when thinking about syncopations, as they combine forcefulness with rhythmic unrest. This quality comes directly from their relationship to the focal impulses: they are powerful because each focal impulse needs to produce only one note, and the unrest arises because the notes and the focal impulses do not coincide. Relative to vigorous syncopations, grounded syncopations double the number of focal impulses. As with vigorous syncopations, each attack is the product of a focal impulse that has no other attacks to produce, and so the syncopations are similarly powerful; however, because the notes align with focal impulses, the sense of unrest is not present. Moving in the opposite direction from vigorous syncopations, floating syncopations double the number of notes; because notes and focal impulses do not align, the notes still sound unsettled, but because there are more notes per focal impulse, the attacks are less powerful.

In terms of focal impulse placements, these options for syncopations are discrete. But in terms of the sound produced, the possibilities lie along a spectrum, and distinctions are not always sharply etched; for example, if played gently enough, vigorous syncopations can be mistaken for floating syncopations. For each type of syncopation, I have discussed the sonic quality that is most likely to occur based on its pattern of motion; within each type, there is room for considerable variation in sound and expressive character.

One example of a gentler version of vigorous syncopations is found in a recording of the first solo episode from the last movement of Neruda's trumpet concerto (originally for horn, first two phrases of four shown as ex. 7.4) by Niklas Eklund and the Swedish Chamber Orchestra conducted by Roy Goodman (1999, 0:26). In most measures of this example, the soloist and orchestra seem to be placing focal impulses three per measure, on the quarter-note beats (A prominent exception is the first two measures in the solo part, where focal impulses seem to be placed on the first and third beats only.) Clear indications of this focal impulse placement are found in the degree of accentuation of the quarter-note beats, with specific instances including the cellos when they have unslurred quarter notes; the strings in their unison interjections between the trumpet's phrases; the definition of beat 3 in the solo part in the third phrase,

Example 7.4. Neruda, Trumpet Concerto (orig. for horn), iii, mm. 23–30, Vivace, reduced score.

when it begins descending sixteenth notes (0:38–0:42); the definition of beat 2 in the solo part, when it follows triplets on the downbeat in the second motivic idea of the fourth phrase (0:47–0:54); and the final two bars before the concluding cadence in the solo part. Given focal impulses on quarter-note beats, the many syncopated quarter notes in the solo part should sound like vigorous syncopations, and indeed they do, albeit rather gentle and lyrical ones: the attack of each note is just slightly more defined, and the sense of rhythmic placement more the product of specific intention, than would be expected with floating syncopations.

This distinction is best appreciated by comparing Eklund's performance with a performance that is felt in one, that of Tine Thing Helseth and the Norwegian Chamber Orchestra (2007, 0:28). Some of Helseth's quarter-note articulations are quite pronounced, especially in the first measure, which I could as readily believe was felt in three as in one. In the second measure of the episode, the quarter-note beats are again well articulated, but this is quite possible with subsidiary impulses, and there is a freedom to the rhythmic placement that results in small asynchronies with the orchestra; as a result, I find one focal impulse per measure more likely than three. When syncopations start in measure 27, they lack the sense of propulsive, insistent forward motion that Eklund's have. Most passages highlighted in Eklund's recording sound quite different in Helseth's performance, with quarter-note beats less pointedly defined and/or more freely placed. For the quality of Helseth's syncopations, I would point in particular to the passage with the triplets (0:51–0:58) as showing very legato floating syncopations and helping to clarify Eklund's as gentle vigorous syncopations. Finally, her approach to the final cadence is again quite marked, but the lack of synchronization with the orchestra leads me to believe that these measures also were felt in one.

The classification of syncopations begins to demonstrate what can be done with the theory of focal impulses. It also underscores the general point behind the discussions of sound examples. As indicated at the beginning of chapter 5, hearing focal impulses is not about detached, forensic sleuthing. The analyses call attention to minute details of sound not for the sake of the details themselves but because of their relationship to the overall character of the performance. That character would usually be described in macroscopic terms, perhaps using simile or metaphor. Such accounts can seem rather subjective, but by calling attention to details of sound, I am demonstrating that large-scale, holistic aspects of character can be grounded in those sonic details. More than this, when those details are observed from the perspective of focal impulse theory, patterns of coherent covariance emerge.

7.2. Applying the Taxonomy

The taxonomy of syncopations can be used to suggest interpretive possibilities, as one of the characters may fit expressive goals better than the others. In exploring this, we begin with some passages from Mozart; the opening of the "Little" G-Minor Symphony, K. 183 (IV/11/4, 87), is a particularly clear example.[3] Overall half-note patterning is evident until the second theme begins, as motives and harmonic rhythm consistently emphasize either the half note or the measure. Focal impulses on half-note beats would make the initial syncopations floating syncopations, and this fits well with the harmonic and melodic stasis of each measure. There is no apparent reason to emphasize each of the repeated notes, and deemphasizing them helps focus attention on the measure-long units at this point. Curiously, close listening to a sampling of recordings of this passage indicates that floating syncopations are not widely used; the insistence of the attack points and the degree of ensemble synchronization point toward vigorous syncopations in many recordings (although these vigorous syncopations are usually smoothed over). I suspect that ensemble synchronization is a main reason for this choice. In light of the discussion in chapter 5 of the development of performance style, I would guess that today's performers instinctively gravitate toward the greater precision of vigorous syncopations in this exposed passage.

If this guess is correct, I would suggest that the tail is wagging the dog. These performances often have a manic, caffeinated quality, and the pinging attack points draw attention down to small beat levels at which there is little substantive musical action. Given the initial measure-by-measure unfolding, I would think that a performance that placed focal impulses on half-note beats, using sustained and insistent floating syncopations, would be able to bring out more of the drama and pathos of this opening. The switch to half-note patterning in measure 5 would then represent a speeding up, anticipating further speeding up into the cadence as the quarter note finally receives substantial articulation. A performance with focal impulses on half notes throughout can accommodate this shape easily; a performance that starts in quarter notes is likely to shift to half notes in measure 5, in which case the rate of focal impulses will slow down just as the melodic material is speeding up. Performances along the lines I suggest seem to be quite unusual; the recording by Bruno Walter and the Columbia Symphony Orchestra (1954) is the only clear example I have found.

A similar case is found in the opening of Mozart's Piano Concerto in D Minor, K. 466 (V/15/6, 3). As in the "Little" G-Minor Symphony, harmonic rhythm and texture mark the measure or the half note, but here the melody moves at the (syncopated) quarter-note level. A scan through the major themes of the movement to evaluate the relative importance of half-note and quarter-note levels shows that motives and harmonic rhythm are consistent in marking the half-note level. And the cadences all fall on downbeats, making the use of eighteenth-century compound meter unlikely as a source of support for the quarter-note level. Nonetheless, as with K. 183, close listening to recordings tends to indicate (gentle) vigorous syncopations, with the same evidence of quality of attack and precision of synchronization. In this passage, the aesthetic case for half-note focal impulses and floating syncopations seems, if anything, even stronger than in the symphony, as the almost jazzy vigorous syncopations seem utterly out of place in the affective world of this theme. The sense of brooding unease that this music can project seems far better served by an enigmatic melody that twists and turns unevenly with a somewhat vague sense of relation to the meter, a natural outcome of using floating syncopations in this passage. Although not found in the majority of performances, these features can all be heard in the recording by John Gibbons and the Orchestra of the Eighteenth Century, conducted by Frans Brüggen (1986).[4]

A particularly rich set of syncopations is offered in the introduction from the overture to *Don Giovanni* (II/5/17, 5). This music is often played quite slowly, with focal impulses on the quarter-note beats and grounded syncopations. If the idea is to paint a picture of the statue of the Commendatore, this makes sense, as this option will allow the loudest sound and the most powerful attacks. If, however, this music is a picture of the Commendatore's statue *moving*—specifically, coming to drag Don Giovanni down to hell—then the greater drama, dynamism, and accentual conflict of vigorous syncopations will be a better fit. There are clues to this interpretation from motives, texture, and harmonic rhythm, and the indication of andante in cut time suggests a somewhat quicker tempo than is traditional; indeed, a quicker tempo is needed to give vigorous syncopations the requisite power and intensity. Focal impulses on the half-note beats will also make the *sforzando* outcries of measures 15 and 16 vigorous syncopations, contrasting with the more stolid character they usually have as grounded syncopations. And the syncopated quarter notes of measures 11–14 will then be floating syncopations, with a character appropriately similar to the opening melody of K. 466 (at least if performed as I suggest)—appropriate especially because they are not truly melodic but rather an expressive component of the texture. The start of the overture to *Don Giovanni* is performed in the way I describe somewhat more frequently than the other Mozart passages I have discussed (although it is still clearly a minority option). Good examples include recordings by Yannick Nézet-Séguin and the Mahler Chamber Orchestra (2011), Claudio Abbado and the Chamber Orchestra of Europe (1997), and Georg Solti and the London Philharmonic Orchestra (1996).[5]

We now turn to some well-known passages of metrically dissonant music from the first movement of Beethoven's Symphony No. 3, passages that have also been discussed by Harald Krebs (1999, 74–77) and Yonatan Malin (2005). These passages are more complex than the Mozart excerpts for two reasons: in Krebs's terms, they feature grouping dissonances in addition to displacement dissonances; and these grouping dissonances can lead us to understandings of the meter that conflict with the notated meter. Their greater complexity anticipates chapter 12, which looks at metrical dissonance beyond simple syncopations.

The most climactic of these passages is found in the development section. As shown in example 7.5, this passage has two forms of metrical dissonance. In measures 276–77, there is a simple displacement dissonance; and in measures 278–79, there is both grouping and displacement dissonance, coming from a periodicity of two quarter notes that begins on the (weak) second beat of measure 278 (focusing on the higher strings, which I take to carry the primary melodic line at this point).

What are we to make of this passage, and how might we perform it? If we simply stay with the notated meter, the qualities of the melodic accents will change as they shift in and out of phase with the notated meter, sometimes having the quality of strong accents performed using focal impulses and sometimes having the quality of strong accents performed using subsidiary impulses (recall the discussion of the passage from the *Rite of Spring* in chap. 1). Something that seems consistent will be performed inconsistently. Another strategy is to implicitly follow Lerdahl and Jackendoff's (1983)

Example 7.5. Beethoven, Symphony No. 3, op. 55, i, mm. 276–281, Allegro con brio, reduced score.

metrical preference rules and adopt a heard meter that makes strong attacks and long notes into strong beats. All strong melodic attacks align with strong beats under this hearing, but there are new problems, the foremost being the absence of any elegant way to transition in and out of the shifted heard meter.[6] Furthermore, this hearing would presumably turn Cooper and Meyer's (1960, 139) "loudest silence in musical literature" on the downbeat of measure 280 into a simple weak-beat rest (see also London 1993). In this case, I believe that the strategy of turning salient events into strong beats is exactly backward; given the clear syncopations within the notated meter of measures 276 and 277, it would make the most sense to treat measures 278 and 279 as a hemiola in phase with the notated meter but containing syncopated attacks. If focal impulses are aligned with the hemiola's strong beats (see chap. 8), all longer notes in the melody will then be vigorous syncopations, giving the passage both consistency and dynamism. This interpretation is applied to a fuller version of the passage in example 7.6.

This hearing preserves Cooper and Meyer's (1960) loudest silence, the chords themselves being loud either way. Furthermore, the chords will acquire a special intensity when heard as metrically dissonant.[7] This effect is intensified if the metrical interpretation is actually performed. To return again to themes sounded in the discussion of Stravinsky in chapter 1, in a performance that places focal impulses on the strong beats of the unshifted hemiola, the performer will need to produce both focal impulses coinciding with the rests and strong subsidiary impulses to play the chords; in this case, the production of silent focal impulses will provide a physical, embodied analogue to

Example 7.6. Beethoven, Symphony No. 3, op. 55, i, mm. 272–281, Allegro con brio, reduced score.

loud rests. This process is more physically intense than simply producing the chords with focal impulses, and the physical intensity will leave sonic traces.

An interpretation of this sort can rarely claim to be anything more than one possible reading of the passage. In this case, however, a passage from the exposition strongly suggests that Beethoven intended this hearing and that he built it up for us step by step.

The passage begins in measure 113 (ex. 7.7). In measures 113–16, sforzandi and agogic accents on the second beats create a consistent emphasis on beat 2. These syncopations are the first instances of metrical dissonance in this passage, and they do not threaten the notated meter. For the performers, the most likely option will be focal impulses only on the downbeats (with forceful subsidiary impulses on beat 2 to be sure); the use of focal impulses on one or both of the weak beats in the measure seems less likely, given how many of the features of the music combine to suggest that this movement is felt mainly in one.

After almost unalloyed metrical consonance in measures 117 and 118, Beethoven brings back the syncopation, now combined with a hemiola. The hemiola of measures 119–22 is clearly defined by a motivic pattern consisting of four eighth notes; as with any hemiola (as we will see in the next chapter), this presents a choice of whether to adjust the heard meter (and the focal impulses) to follow the hemiola.[8] Paradoxically, it is the sforzando on the downbeat of measure 120 that points most decisively toward the hemiola meter.

Example 7.7. Beethoven, Symphony No. 3, op. 55, i, mm. 113–133, Allegro con brio, reduced score.

When hemiolas are not syncopated, it is easy to hear and perform them as cross rhythms, retaining the notated meter. But, as measure 120 illustrates, retaining the notated meter for a syncopated hemiola requires mental contortionism. In a more standard context, the focal impulse and the accented attack point would work together to reinforce the notated downbeat. But here only the focal impulse reinforces the notated meter. The accented attack point is an afterbeat following a strong beat within a cross rhythm, and so we must hear the accented note as having very little to do with either the downbeat or the focal impulse, even though all three occur at the same moment in time. As in the passage from the development, hearing and performing the syncopated hemiola is simpler and more consistent in the hemiola $\frac{3}{2}$ than in the notated $\frac{3}{4}$. Under such a hearing, the accents are all weak-beat syncopations, following the pattern from measures 113–16 and extending it by the introduction of the hemiola. Especially with some help from the conductor, the orchestra would have no trouble placing focal impulses on the strong beats of the hemiola so that the sforzandi would all be produced by energetic subsidiary impulses.

Measure 123 marks a return to the notated meter; weak-beat accents continue, and a new element is added in the next measure: silence on the downbeats. Although the silent downbeats greatly intensify the displacement dissonance, I would argue that listeners will continue to hear the notated meter. The key is found in measure 123. Following the clear downbeat—unquestionably heard as a downbeat in its context—the second and third beats receive a new kind of accentuation from the triple stops in the violins. This accentuation involves more than the number of notes sounding; the mechanics of playing the triple stops will give those chords greater weight, in terms of both articulation and timing. Flowing directly from measure 123, the chords in measures 124–27 come therefore with a preformed understanding: those weighty triple stops are weak-beat accents. And when we get to the chords in measures 128–31, the context of the music since measure 113 provides them with a natural interpretation. Beethoven first introduced syncopations (mm. 113–16) and then syncopations within hemiola (mm. 119–21); then he returned to syncopations in the notated meter, intensified by silent downbeats (mm. 124–27). Following this progression, it makes perfect sense to hear measures 128–31 as weak-beat accents in a hemiola that has silent strong beats.[9] Compared with hearing and performing these measures in the notated meter, this is a more consistent interpretation—but one that makes the passage even more dynamically volatile.

The syncopation within the hemiola is relatively easy to hear in example 7.7 because of the way Beethoven prepares it. But this is not the first occurrence of this rhythm in the movement; as can be seen in example 7.8, this earlier appearance of syncopation within a hemiola may be the most challenging for the listener to sort out. In this first appearance, after only one statement of the basic pattern in measures 25 and 26, the syncopation pattern starts out of phase with the meter: the downbeat of measure 29, the downbeat that will initiate the second hemiola, is itself anticipated in measure 28. This anticipation has consequences for the performance of the entire passage as analyzed. But to see how this works, and to understand the focal impulse notation above

Example 7.8. Beethoven, Symphony No. 3, op. 55, i, mm. 23–37, Allegro con brio, reduced score.

the staff, we need some of the resources of part 3, which expands the basic treatment of the focal impulse found in part 2. We will return to this passage in chapter 12.

Notes

1. Krebs's terminology is explained in sec. 2.3.

2. Another example of flexible timing in floating syncopations is found in mm. 9 and 10 of Leonhardt's recording (1975) of the allemande from the French Suite No. 6, just a few measures after the end of ex. 5.3. The syncopated quarter notes are subtly delayed, and the first two lag slightly behind the sixteenths in the left hand.

3. For the remaining examples from Mozart in this chapter, readers are referred to the *Neue Mozart Ausgabe* (NMA), available online (http://dme.mozarteum.at/DME/nma/). Citations are given in the form used by the NMA.

4. This performance does seem to shift focal impulses to the quarter-note level in the final approach to the cadence, resulting in vigorous syncopations in the upper strings and winds. Some performances come close the character of performances in two but seem likely to have been in four, based on the insistent quality of the repeated notes in the syncopated melody at subphrase endings.

5. Features that differentiate these recordings from most others include the degree of synchronization and the character of the attack in the vigorous (or grounded) syncopations and

the smoothness of articulation in the floating (or vigorous) syncopations. Another good clue to performance in two versus in four is the character of the pervasive rhythm of dotted quarter followed by eighth that follows the initial chords. Performance in four is often evident from a heavy and defined quality given to the eighth notes, indicating the presence of focal impulses on the preceding weak quarter beats.

6. Both Frisch (1990, 152–53) and Downs (1970, 590, see also 595) offer examples with alternative barrings for related passages in the movement. Those of Downs show the awkwardness of the transitions with particular clarity, and Frisch seems to acknowledge this by using a question mark in square brackets in place of a meter signature for one measure. Frisch cites Hauptmann on the difficulty of hearing syncopations as syncopations when the strong beats are not articulated on the musical surface.

7. In Krebs's taxonomy, the chords are dissonant under either hearing because they do not align with the notated meter. But if the listener hears a $\frac{3}{2}$ in phase with the notated meter (in which the chords are syncopations), this will produce an indirect dissonance, clearly more salient than the subliminal dissonance that results from a shifted $\frac{3}{2}$ (in which the chords are on the beats).

8. Sforzandi are placed on weak beats with respect to an aligned hemiola; as in the development, this could open the possibility of hearing a shifted hemiola meter, but here this possibility seems more theoretical than real. No features of the music other than the sforzandi push toward hearing the middle of the pattern as a strong beat, and the sforzandi do not seem nearly sufficient to overcome the strong implications of having heard the pattern start with a clear downbeat (m. 119). The options on the table, then, are the notated meter and an unshifted hemiola.

9. Measures 128–31 are a culmination of metrical dissonance also at a hypermetrical level because the start of this new pattern establishes mm. 123–27 as a five-bar unit; together with the parallel passage in the recapitulation, this is the only place in the movement where a duple alternation of strong and weak measures is disrupted. Similar processes of intensification of metrical dissonance are described by Krebs (1999, 91–108).

PART 3
EXPANDING FOCAL IMPULSE THEORY

8

SPECIAL CASES OF FOCAL IMPULSE
PLACEMENT

CHAPTER 4 DISCUSSED THE MOST CENTRAL CASES OF focal impulse place-ment, those in which focal impulse placements follow the meter in sim-ple and straightforward ways. If focal impulse placement in eighteenth- and nineteenth-century Western classical music is understood in terms of a pro-totype category, those cases constitute the core. This chapter presents most of the inner periphery of the category. The topics discussed are impulse po-lyphony, asymmetrical meters, conflicts between notated and heard meter, and hemiola. They are presented in order of increasing complexity, beginning with the possibilities that stand more on their own and progressing to those that tend more strongly to involve other members of the inner periphery. The next chapter will discuss two additional features of the inner periphery: an-ticipations and secondary focal impulses.

8.1. Impulse Polyphony

Among the core cases of focal impulse placement, focal impulses are placed homophonically, with all members of an ensemble using focal impulses in the same places (except for simple exceptions; e.g., long rests in some parts).[1] Impulse polyphony, in which different members of an ensemble place focal impulses differently, occurs when there are contrasts between strands of a texture that make homophonic placement unsatisfactory.

One of the most common grounds for impulse polyphony is the juxtapo-sition of a long-breathed melody with a rhythmically active accompaniment. The opening of the last movement of Bruckner's Symphony No. 8 (ex. 8.1) provides a striking example. To produce a true *fortissimo* (and to be heard above the brass), the strings will need to use focal impulses on each of the grace notes preceding the quarter notes. In contrast, the brass instruments

Example 8.1. Bruckner, Symphony No. 8, iv, mm. 1–7, reduced score.

have no reason to use so many focal impulses; one per measure would seem more likely for them.

Similar factors are at work in a passage from the slow movement of Mozart's G-Minor Viola Quintet, K. 516 (ex. 8.2). The second violin and second viola will probably want to place focal impulses on the eighth-note beats for the sake of their off-beat thirty-second notes, both to help with synchronization and to give them crisp rhythmic energy. It would be possible for them to play with focal impulses every quarter, but their figures would sound much less incisive. (This is because of physical limitations on the ability of focal impulses to organize the metrically subsidiary portions of their consequent spans, discussed in chap. 3.) The cellist will probably also place focal impulses on eighth-note beats to help the inner voices coordinate their offbeat

Example 8.2. Mozart, Viola Quintet K. 516, iii, mm. 30–32, Adagio ma non troppo.

figures. If the melody lines were to use that many focal impulses, however, they could easily sound rather stodgy. The first violinist and first violist will probably find that their lyrical lines are better served by focal impulses on the quarter-note beats. In addition to avoiding excessive heaviness on the paired sixteenths, this choice allows the important weak-eighth-beat syncopations to be vigorous rather than grounded; as vigorous syncopations go, these will be rounded and singing rather than forceful and explosive, but the vigorous character will still lend the notes a more expressive quality than they would receive as grounded syncopations.

The main contrasting theme from the final movement of Tchaikovsky's Symphony No. 5 (ex. 3.10) is similar, especially in the off-beat accompaniment figures. Parallel choices would lead to focal impulses on half-note beats for the accompaniment and on downbeats for the long line of the melody. (The more unusual, outer-periphery placement of every other downbeat is also possible.)

Impulse polyphony has a strong relationship to questions of agency (Cone 1974; Monahan 2013; Klorman 2016; Hatten 2018). When different parts place focal impulses at different levels within one metrical grid, I usually have the impression of a single persona behind the music, but one with superhuman capabilities. In the examples discussed above, the slow rates of notes and of focal impulses in the melodies receive my primary attention; by themselves, these slow rates could simply imply slow metaphoric motion. But the much faster notes in the accompaniment modulate this impression; we must be hearing rapid motion, but rapid motion in which traversing long distances requires only occasional moments of primary effort. In the Mozart and especially in the Tchaikovsky, the impression is somewhat like a large bird soaring in the sky. But the more frequent focal impulses produced by the accompaniment voices do not merely index a rate of metaphorical motion; instead, I hear them as products of the overarching persona, now a superhuman persona that can direct energy and intention farther down into small metrical levels than a human performer ever could, at least with the focal impulse placement of the melody.[2] This quite visceral sense of superhuman agency is, I believe, part of the special expressive focus and intensity that these passages share, despite a number of significant expressive differences. In the Bruckner, with a much more declamatory melody and with extremely pointed and forceful attacks in the strings, the image of a soaring bird seems less apt and the sense of superhuman agency even more extreme; this passage seems more like a giant taking enormous strides through a forest, crushing trees with every step.[3]

Impulse polyphony has different implications for agency when the multiple placements reflect conflicting meters. In my view, the most compelling cases for focal impulses following simultaneous contrasting meters occur when different meter signatures are used; these cases are found mainly in music written after the nineteenth century. The scherzo of Ravel's String Quartet from 1902–3, in which some parts play in $\frac{3}{4}$ while others play in $\frac{6}{8}$, is the earliest example I know of in which different notated meters seem to demand different focal impulse placements, leaving aside obvious outliers like the multiple dance bands playing at Don Giovanni's party.[4] As it is not possible to hear two metrical frameworks at once (London 2012, 66–67), a listener will always experience a degree of estrangement from a performance that projects multiple meters at once. In this movement, whether we understand the music in terms of multiple agents or in terms of a single agent with abilities we lack, the result is a tantalizing dance that we can never entirely join in with.

The thornier cases are those in which the metrical conflict is not reflected in different meter signatures, arising instead from alternative heard meters. In these passages the potential conflict would result from some parts projecting an alternative meter while others project the notated meter. (Section 8.3 discusses simpler cases, in which the musicians all project an alternative heard meter; some listeners may still hear the notated meter, but any ambiguity is not reinforced by conflicting interpretations from the musicians.) An interesting argument for having different players within a chamber ensemble promote different meters has recently been advanced by Edward Klorman (2016), using a conception of multiple agency. I can certainly find this kind of performance fully convincing; two examples are discussed in section 8.4, and I will examine more in future work on Brahms (Ito, in preparation c).[5] Nonetheless, while I have tremendous respect for Klorman's work and find his analyses insightful and engaging, I rarely choose to play or hear music with a single meter signature as projecting multiple, conflicting meters; other ways of responding to the score's conflicting cues usually seem more persuasive.[6] The root issue for me is full apprehension of the music—can we understand it all at once, or are we aware that following one part requires cognitive estrangement from another? In common-practice music, meter and harmony usually provide a unifying perspective, even when the music projects various senses of multiple, even conflicting, agency. Full apprehension is a strong enough norm for this music that I will choose it unless another possibility seems clearly more convincing. Perhaps, as Klorman suggests, this perspective reflects excessive influence from nineteenth-century German music aesthetics. In any case, the choice of where to draw the lines between passages that are or are not enhanced by impulse polyphony reflecting different meters will need to be made by the reader.

8.2. Asymmetrical Meters

Cases of asymmetrical meters, such as $\frac{5}{4}$ or $\frac{7}{8}$, could be treated in the same way as the more straightforward meters of the core; this would mean that the downbeat must receive a focal impulse, focal impulses could also be placed up to two levels lower in the metrical hierarchy, and triple metrical layers could have a focal impulse on only one of the two weak beats. But actual practice seems to be much more constrained.

Asymmetrical meters are defined by a specific relationship between two adjacent layers in the metrical hierarchy. In the faster moving layer, referred to here as the *substrate level*, beats are equally spaced; this level generally has the note value identified by the lower number in the meter signature. In $\frac{7}{8}$, for example, the substrate level is the eighth-note level, in $\frac{5}{4}$ the quarter-note level. In the slower layer, the *mixed level*, beats have varying duration, with some consisting of two beats at the substrate level and some consisting of three.[7] In $\frac{7}{8}$ the mixed level consists of quarters and dotted quarters, in $\frac{5}{4}$ of halves and dotted halves.[8]

Focal impulses will generally be placed on the mixed level, and all beats at this level will receive focal impulses. If the mixed level is triple with respect to the next slower level (as in $\frac{7}{8}$), all three beats will receive focal impulses; in asymmetrical meters, the omission of one of the focal impulses in a triple level will not generally occur. Pieces in quintuple meters—for example, the second movement of Tchaikovsky's Symphony No. 6 (ex. 8.3) or Rachmaninoff's tone poem *The Isle of the Dead* (ex. 8.4)—will use two focal impulses per measure, the first falling on the downbeat and the second falling on the second beat at the mixed level (i.e., on the third or fourth beats at the substrate level).

The reasons for placing focal impulses on the mixed level intertwine cognitive and expressive issues, both relating to the clarity of the metrical hierarchy. In the usual symmetrical meters, inference can be relied on for a decent amount of information. If we hear a whole-note beat and an eighth-note beat, we can infer quarter- and half-note beats. If we hear a dotted-half-note beat and an eighth-note beat, we will need more information to determine whether the intermediate beat is the quarter note or the dotted quarter; once this beat is determined, however, it is likely to be fairly stable, counterexamples such as "America" from Bernstein's *Westside Story* lying outside the main stylistic confines of this study. In contrast, a $\frac{7}{8}$ measure has three different possible beat spacings for the level one down from the measure: 3 + 2 + 2, 2 + 3 + 2, and 2 + 2 + 3. And even if the meter signature is kept stable (as usually happens until

Example 8.3. Tchaikovsky, Symphony No. 6, op. 74, ii, mm. 1–4, reduced score.

Example 8.4. Rachmaninoff, *The Isle of the Dead*, op. 29, mm. 5–8, Lento, reduced score.

the early twentieth century), the beat spacings may change from measure to measure (e.g., mm. 43–47, 6–10 after [2], in *The Isle of the Dead*). The listener may well need some help from the performer to figure out the metrical organization, and focal impulses on the mixed level facilitate this. In terms of expressive effects, focal impulses on the mixed level will produce the most sharply etched contrasts between durations, and pieces with asymmetrical meters often highlight the conflict between the beats on the mixed level.

The impact of this combination of perceptual clarity and expressive excitement is underscored by considering the alternatives. If focal impulses are placed on the substrate level, the mixed level is likely to be somewhat vague. An example in which this effect works well is the second movement of Victor Ewald's Brass Quintet No. 1; the outer sections of the movement are in $\frac{5}{4}$, marked "adagio non troppo lento" (ex. 8.5), and because of the slow tempo, they are often played with focal impulses on the quarter-note beats. As would be expected, because the half-note and dotted-half pulses are not emphasized

Example 8.5. Ewald, Brass Quintet No. 1, op. 5, ii, mm. 1–4.

in performance, and because the durations involved are so long—well outside the range of preferred durations discussed in chapter 13—the meter can easily seem vague and underdefined. This mode of performance helps give the music a free, rhapsodic character; it also fits the score, because there is no strong marking of a beat level intermediate between the measure and the quarter note, whether through duration, harmony, or other factors. A performance with focal impulses on the mixed level would give the music a very different shape, clarifying a level of metrical organization that is usually left underdefined. The middle section is much clearer, consistently projecting 2 + 3 as it keeps the same meter signature, now with a tempo of allegro vivace; as would be expected, this section tends to be performed with focal impulses on the mixed level.

To find examples of focal impulses placed less frequently than every two or three beats at the substrate level, it is often necessary to consider cases in which the mixed level is spaced more widely than every two or three substrate-level beats, in violation of Lerdahl and Jackendoff's (1983) metrical well-formedness rules.[9] One such instance is the flute's first statement of the gently flowing main theme from the first movement of Henri Dutilleux's Sonatine for Flute and Piano (ex. 8.6), with a focal impulse placement that is heard in several recordings (e.g., Pahud and La Sage 1997, 0:25). In the first of the measures, the contour and the beaming both strongly support hearing the $\frac{7}{8}$ meter as 4 + 3—an uneven duple meter—and this can be reflected by using two focal impulses for the measure (this metrical interpretation is also indicated by dashed bar lines when this material is first heard in m. 1 of the piece).

Example 8.6. Dutilleux, Sonatine for Flute and Piano, i, mm. 10–11.

In the very next measure, however, rhythm and contour lead some musicians to interpret the $\frac{7}{8}$ as 3 + 2 + 2, an uneven triple meter.

This juxtaposition highlights two ways in which this passage (in the performance described) lacks the clarity that would come with focal impulses placed on a more normal mixed level.[10] First, the 3:2 ratio used in the second measure involves starkly contrasting durations; it is not mistakable for either 1:1 or 2:1, and a trained musician could hardly fail to be aware of hearing this ratio. In contrast, the 4:3 ratio of the first measure is much less sharply etched, and even with each eighth-beat articulated on the musical surface, it is not obvious how the durations of the main beats relate. Second, because the duration of four eighths is twice the duration of two eighths, the question of the true main beat level is muddied. Was the 4 + 3 really a duple measure or, instead, a 2 + 2 + 3 triple measure in which only the first and third beats were emphasized? Conversely, in the second measure, was the 3 + 2 + 2 really a triple measure, or was it a 3 + 4 with a strongly articulated subdivision of the second main beat? When main beats are clearly occurring every two or three substrate beats, these questions do not usually arise. In a passage like the conclusion of Bartók's *Dance Suite*, such absences of clarity would not serve the character that most performances want to project. But in a movement like Dutilleux's, they can contribute effectively to a gently elusive character, tinged with mystery.[11]

8.3. Conflicts between Notated and Heard Meter

Sometimes the score opens the possibility of hearing in a meter other than the notated meter, and sometimes the score makes hearing in another meter

Example 8.7. Mozart, Viola Quintet K. 516, iv, mm. 38–42.

virtually inevitable, at least for the listener. In such cases, the performers will generally place focal impulses in accord with the meter that they hear, whether or not this meter is notated.

In the most common cases of alternative heard meters, the heard downbeat simply shifts to the middle of the measure in a duple or quadruple meter; sometimes whole sections of movements are notated this way.[12] Examples include the main thematic material from the final rondo movement of Mozart's G-Minor Viola Quintet and the second trio from Schumann's Piano Quintet, shown in examples 8.7 and 8.8. (Here, follow the focal impulse placements shown as option *a*; option *b* will be explained in chap. 12.) In both cases, I find that harmonic rhythm, primacy effects of starting on the second beat, and grouping cues in the melody combine to give a clear sense of shifted meter. When the heard meter differs from the notated meter, bold-face dots are placed under the focal impulses on the heard downbeats.

I am claiming that performers are likely to play these passages in a manner that assigns the physical investment in the downbeat to the perceived, rather than the notated, downbeat. It might be objected that this way of playing the music essentially eliminates an anomalous feature of the score that was surely deliberate (Mirka 2009, 88–89). I strongly agree with the spirit of the objection, but dealing with this issue will require the qualitative distinctions among focal impulses introduced in chapter 10; this topic (and these specific examples) will return in chapter 12, when we return to performance options for standard kinds of metrical dissonance.

Example 8.8. Schumann, Piano Quintet op. 44, Trio II, mm. 1–4.

Example 8.9. Brahms, Violin Concerto op. 77, i, mm. 304–308, Allegro non troppo, reduced score.

While shifts of the heard downbeat to the middle of the measure are by far the most common cases of conflict between notated and heard meters, many other possibilities exist. A well-known example comes from the first movement of Brahms's Violin Concerto, starting in measure 304 (ex. 8.9). Although there is no notated change from the movement's $\frac{3}{4}$ meter, the grouping clearly projects units lasting five quarter-note spans. Taking grouping cues in the bass line as more significant than those in solo violin part, it is commonly performed as $\frac{5}{4}$ divided 3 + 2, one of the standard options for a (heard) asymmetrical meter.

8.4. Hemiola

Although the term has come to be used much more generally, *hemiola* refers most properly to cases in which six beats that would be heard as two groups of three in the notated meter are given a cross rhythm that suggests three groups of two (e.g., in $\frac{3}{4}$, accentuating every other quarter note for two measures to suggest a $\frac{3}{2}$ measure). Hemiola is interesting because it can be heard and performed in multiple ways. In some cases it is heard purely as a cross-rhythm within the notated meter, and performers wanting to project that option would presumably place focal impulses in accord with the notated meter. It is also possible to switch to a heard meter that aligns with the hemiola; if this is the hearing of the performers, it becomes a special case of conflicts between notated and heard meters, and the standard option would be to place focal impulses following the hemiola meter. A third possibility involving a more complex kind of metrical hearing will be discussed after looking at examples of the simpler cases.

The first musical example from Chapter 1, the opening of Beethoven's "Ghost" Trio, included a hemiola that most performers would choose to follow with their focal impulses, using the placement shown in example 3.2. Although it would not be physically awkward to perform the music following the notated meter, with focal impulses on each downbeat throughout, this would rob the passage of much of its sense of impetuous, headlong forward motion and, in turn, make the interruption of that motion less dramatically arresting.

Opposite cases, in which it would be unusual for performers to let the hemiola influence their focal impulse placement, include the third waltz of the *Blue Danube* by Johann Strauss Jr. and the presto giocoso section from the scherzo of the Brahms Sextet No. 2 in G Major, op. 36 (exx. 8.10 and 8.11). In each case, only the melody and some of the supporting voices have the hemiola; the bass line and nonmelodic inner voices remain clearly in the notated meter. The waltz feel—explicit and refined in the Strauss, implicit and rustic in the Brahms—makes staying with the notated meter especially likely.

Often there may be no compelling arguments either way on the question of whether or not to adjust focal impulse placement to the hemiola. In such cases, I would expect different performers to decide the question differently. In practice, however, many well-known passages have much stronger performance traditions than I would have predicted, so that focal impulse placements are almost uniform. More open choices between notated and hemiola focal impulse placements can be found, but the passages involved are usually less widely familiar.

Example 8.10. Johann Strauss Jr., *Auf der schönen blauen Donau*, Waltz no. 3, mm. 1–8, reduced score.

Example 8.11. Brahms, Sextet op. 36, ii, mm. 121–128, reduced score.

Among the well-known passages, a good example is the first reprise of the menuetto from Mozart's *Eine kleine Nachtmusik* (ex. 8.12). Consider the recording by Gidon Kremer and the Kremerata Baltica (1999); the placement of focal impulses with the hemiola in measures 6 and 7 seems very clear. I do not see any reason why the hemiola needs to be marked in that way, however, or why it needs to be marked in any way at all—I would have no problem with a performance that ignored the hemiola altogether. But after listening to a great many recordings, the closest I can find to a performance that stays in the notated meter is the recording by Concerto Köln (2005). The cellos and basses clearly feel the hemiola, but the violins' performance is more neutral; if primary attention is given to the melody line, it is at least possible to hear the performance as being in the notated meter.

I indicated earlier that possibilities exist for the listener other than simply retaining the notated meter or shifting to the hemiola meter, and the example from *Eine kleine Nachtmusik* provides a good entry point to this discussion. The prompt to find another option comes from the hypermeter. As indicated

Example 8.12. Mozart, Serenade "*Eine kleine Nachtmusik*," K. 525, iii, mm. 1–8.

in the account of hypermeter in chapter 2, and as we will see in more detail in chapter 12, if we are truly hearing in a meter other than the notated one, our hearing of hypermeter follows our hearing of meter, so that heard downbeats are heard hyperbeats. This creates a potential dilemma. It is common for hemiolas to be embedded within four-bar units in the notated meter, whether or not they are usually heard in the notated meter (e.g., exx. 8.10–8.12); presumably such units should all have quadruple hypermetrical organization, but when the hemiola meter is the heard meter, they contain only three heard downbeats.[13]

In these cases we would ideally be able to bring out the hemiola by means of focal impulses while retaining the framework of the notated meter for hearing hypermeter; this can be done in various ways. For example, we could continue to hear in the notated meter but place focal impulses in conflict with the meter, placing them instead on the main beats of the hemiola. A better alternative would be to orient to the hemiola meter as the main heard meter—and to place focal impulses accordingly—while retaining an awareness of the notated meter in the background, as a stable frame from which we have temporarily departed. The measures in this stable frame would then continue to carry the hypermeter. To experience this effect, return to the passage from *Eine kleine Nachtmusik*. First, sing the passage (ideally at a fairly brisk tempo) while conducting the heard meter, conducting in one for most of the passage but shifting into three for the hemiola. When this hearing is well established, sing the passage again; let the singing retain the same expressive shape, focal impulse placement, and heard meter that was used before, but shift the conducting to a pattern in four, conducting the hypermeter with beats corresponding to the notated downbeats. In this performance, the

Example 8.13. Robert Schumann, Symphony No. 3, op. 97, i, mm. 1–9, reduced score.

focal impulses used in singing and the beats conducted do not align during the hemiola. With practice, one can achieve a state of balance in which one is aware of the internal integrity of both metrical frameworks at the same time.[14] Bold-face dots for heard downbeats are not needed to resolve ambiguity when focal impulses follow the hemiola meter, and for listeners pursuing the kind of both/and hearing just described, they could overemphasize the hemiola meter. For these reasons, they will not generally be used when focal impulses follow the hemiola meter.

The opening of Schumann's Symphony No. 3 (ex. 8.13) is another passage in which an apparently free choice of whether or not to invest in the hemiola meter is rarely exercised. From the time I first got to know this piece by ear, before I had the concept of hemiola, I have been aware that different performances seem to project two different understandings of the meter, which I now understand as the notated meter of $\frac{3}{4}$ and the $\frac{3}{2}$ hemiola meter. I demonstrate the two possibilities in video example 8.1, which also shows the parallel options for a passage from the last movement of Schumann's Piano Concerto; that passage is discussed in chapter 15.

Given my early awareness of these options, it has come as a surprise to discover that it is difficult to find recordings in which it seems likely that the performers were consistently feeling the notated meter. Some performances seem to plant a flag clearly for the hemiola meter; the recording by Stanislaw Skrowaczewski and the Deutsche Radio Philharmonie (2007) is a clear example, and the performance by Neville Marriner and the Academy of St. Martin in the Fields (1998) is similar, in some ways more extreme. Others are more legato and can be heard either way; it is probably these that I used to think of as projecting the notated meter. A clear instance is the performance by Peter Lilye and the Moscow RTV Symphony Orchestra (2015). While I am prepared to believe that the opening measures were felt in the notated meter, and while I can hear recordings like this in the notated meter if I choose, I am no longer

Example 8.14. Brahms, Cello Sonata No. 2, op. 99, iii, mm. 112–16, Allegro passionato.

convinced that the whole passage was performed in the notated meter. For me, the main clues are the figures in measures 4 and 6 of dotted quarters on beat 2 followed by eighths, figures that fall on the third beats in the ³⁄₂ hemiola meter. These figures usually sound like they are initiated by focal impulses on the dotted quarters; this is because of the degree of accentuation and the sense of being bound together in leading into the next downbeat. The one recording I found that makes these gestures sound like responses to focal impulses preceding them is by Carl Schuricht and the Stuttgart Radio Symphony Orchestra (1960); the projection of the notated meter, coming in part from the way those figures are played, is also helped by what seems to be an errant tympani stroke on the downbeat of measure 6.[15]

One passage in which performers are more evenly divided in their treatment of a hemiola comes from the third movement of Brahms's Cello Sonata in F Major, op. 99 (ex. 8.14). Although this work is hardly off the beaten path, the passage in question is relatively inconspicuous, probably helping it to have a less clearly established performing tradition. In the recording by Alban Gerhardt and Markus Groh (1997, 1:55), the notated meter is strongly projected in particular by the sense of conflict that characterizes the passage. This is heard especially in the uneven durations of the quarter notes and the relatively loose synchronization between the instruments, factors that can be made particularly vivid by conducting along with the quarter notes. In contrast, the smooth articulation and even timing of the quarter notes in the recording by Torleif Thedéen and Roland Pöntinen (2006, 1:52) clearly project the hemiola meter, probably felt with one focal impulse per measure.[16]

This section closes with a consideration of two ways in which hemiolas can lend themselves to subtler treatment than simply shifting focal impulses to the hemiola meter or not. Even more complex situations involving

Example 8.15. Bach, Brandenburg Concerto No. 1, BWV 1046, iii, mm. 11–17, Allegro, violin 1 and continuo only.

hemiola, drawn from the music of Schumann and Brahms, will be examined in chapter 15.

The first of these discussions concerns cases of impulse polyphony in which some musicians in an ensemble shift to the hemiola meter while others stay in the notated meter. As discussed in section 8.1, impulse polyphony reflecting different metrical interpretations is quite different from impulse polyphony in which different levels are emphasized within the same grid, and I am not personally convinced that its use in warranted in many passages. A hemiola passage that does invite this treatment is the end of the opening ritornello of the third movement of Bach's Brandenburg Concerto No. 1 (ex. 8.15). Here the melody instruments have a clear hemiola meter of $\frac{3}{4}$ for two measures, while the bass line stays unambiguously in the notated $\frac{6}{8}$. Two factors make impulse polyphony seem more likely here than in the examples from Strauss and Brahms in which melody and accompaniment featured the same contrast. One is simply that hemiolas are particularly likely to be performed as such in baroque music. The other, weightier factor is that in the Strauss and the Brahms the melody slips out of the hemiola for the cadence; in this passage, the bass line joins the melody in the hemiola for the cadence. In a video recording by the Freiburger Barockorchester (2000, about 20 seconds into the third movement, which is about 8:25 after the start of the concerto), some musicians can be seen performing the passage (and a similar, later one) in

Example 8.16. Brahms, String Quartet No. 2, op. 51/2, iv, mm. 1–24.

this way. It is clear that the violists are staying in the notated meter until near the cadence, and although the camera pans to the violins late in the passage, they appear to be in the meter of the hemiola, and this energetically enough to suggest that they have been in the hemiola for some time (the sound also supports them having felt the hemiola throughout). Later in the video, around 1:26 after the start of the movement, the violins are clearly feeling the hemiola throughout a later, parallel passage.[17]

An even more remarkable example is found in the performance by the Amadeus Quartet (1959) of the opening of the last movement of Brahms's String Quartet in A Minor, op. 51, no. 2 (ex. 8.16). Even before performance considerations come into play, this example is already more complex because the hemiola in $\frac{3}{4}$ meter is embedded within a triple hypermetrical context, so two measures of hemiola alternate with one measure clearly in the notated meter.[18] In the first statement of the theme, first violinist Norbert Brainin seems to be in the hemiola meter in the relevant measures; conducting along with the hemiola meter helps clarify that there are no indications of metrical dissonance or physically complex motion in his straightforward performance. Because the rest of the quartet is clearly in the notated meter, this is a good example of impulse polyphony. In the second statement of the theme, however, violist Peter Schidlof's performance is much more ambiguous; although less clearly in the notated meter than some of the examples we have heard, the dotted half notes have a distinctively sustained quality that, to my ear, makes a performance in the notated meter more likely than one in the hemiola meter. Especially in light of the accompaniment, which no longer clearly projects the notated meter, even in places mildly reinforcing the hemiola, this is an interesting performance choice. In this recording, the first statement of the theme projects strong metrical conflict through impulse polyphony between melody and accompaniment, but then the second sublimates the conflict—lacking the accompaniment's stand for the notated meter, the conflict moves into the violist's body, as focal impulses on downbeats clash with the hemiola, creating embodied metrical dissonance. The result is a striking juxtaposition of interpretations of the hemiola between two consecutive thematic statements.

In the second of the more complex hemiola treatments, focal impulse placements are manipulated in and around the hemiola to create more vivid shapes. In the opening ritornello of the aria "I know that my Redeemer liveth" from Handel's *Messiah* (ex. 8.17), two potential hemiolas invite this treatment in different ways. The first of these, in measures 13 and 14, seems to be signaled in advance by the continuo group's reversal of the otherwise long-short rhythm. It is almost as if the continuo wants to warn the violins that their three-note motive is about to shift rhythmic emphasis as a result of the hemiola, something they might overlook given its unchanging position with respect to the bar lines. If the continuo group shifts to the focal impulse placement of the hemiola early—putting a focal impulse on the second beat of measure 12, as indicated in the example—this prodding effect will be given a visceral emphasis. The hemiola in measures 16 and 17 is rather different. Although the third beat of the hemiola figure (beat 2 of m. 17) is marked clearly enough, the second beat (beat 3 of m. 16) is not. There is no motion in the bass, no implied change of harmony, and only surface motion in the melody—the ascent to the E and back is a decoration of the structural tone B that gathers momentum for the descent that is about to occur. The cessation of motion at an underlying harmonic and contrapuntal level for three and a half

Example 8.17. Handel, *Messiah*, "I know that my Redeemer liveth," mm. 1–18.

beats suggests a stopping of time, and the floating sense that this could induce would be disturbed by a focal impulse on beat 3 of measure 16. This suggests the possibility of omitting the focal impulse from the second beat of the $\frac{3}{2}$ measure implied by the hemiola—an unusual instance of feeling triple meter as an uneven duple, using only two focal impulses on the triple level of the meter. (When focal impulses follow a hemiola, each beat of the hemiola usually receives a focal impulse.) As indicated in the example, the focal impulse on the downbeat of measure 16 can organize a consequent span that lasts for four quarter-note spans, with the second focal impulse of the hemiola hypermeasure falling on the large beat 3 (beat 2 of m. 17). I suspect that few hemiolas will invite this kind of treatment; in this case, however, it allows a sense of rhythmic direction to be suspended for a few beats, only to come back with

Example 8.18. Brahms, Piano Quartet No. 3, op. 60, i, mm. 236–43, Allegro non troppo.

renewed force in the second part of measure 17 as we realize that we are in a hemiola moving toward a cadence only when it is already two-thirds over.[19]

For a final example we return to Brahms. In the first movement of the Piano Quartet No. 3 in C minor, Op. 60, Marcus Thompson and Mihae Lee (1990, 7:14) of the Boston Chamber Music Society feel the second theme in the recap primarily in one in their tender rendition (ex. 8.18); this is indicated by gentle emphasis on the downbeats and by rubato in measures 238–39 that leads to subtle asynchrony between the instruments on the second and third quarter-note beats. In measures 240–41, Thompson and Lee make the unusual choice to feel only the first two beats of the hemiola, a choice that is not at first glance clearly motivated by the score. The effect, however, is striking; especially with the slight extra time they take, it is as if the theme has suddenly been captivated by some arresting vision. Why does this interpretation work so well? Part of the reason must be the surprising arrival of the second beat of the hemiola on a retrogressive IV chord, displacing the usual resolution of the dominant; temporal disruption is driven by harmonic disruption. This ensemble does not, however, mark any other statement of this material in this way; perhaps this particular IV chord possesses this magnetism because its root is the global tonic that is being so perversely resisted at this point in the form. Should we conclude then that Brahms has issued a subtle invitation to just this performance? I tend to think not. More likely, this inspired choice is one more sign of the richness of the partnership between performer and composer.

Notes

1. As discussed in chap. 4, this is an idealization; performers probably depart from impulse homophony fairly frequently, almost certainly more than from other core criteria.

2. To use a concept introduced in chap. 9, it is as if the persona's secondary focal impulses had the power of normal focal impulses.

3. That we might make a mimetic identification with this superhuman persona is pointed out by Cox (2016), and it could be part of the appeal—even part of the danger of the appeal—of this music. I am reminded of an anecdote he relays in which one of his brothers repeatedly exclaimed, "Feel the *power!*" while watching a hydraulic wood splitter in action (39).

4. Juxtapositions of time signatures that are compatible, at least at the tactus level and above, are more common in the eighteenth and nineteenth centuries than juxtapositions such as $\frac{6}{8}$ and $\frac{3}{4}$. Examples of $\frac{2}{4}$ and $\frac{6}{8}$ used as compatible time signatures include a passage from the final movement of Beethoven's Quintet op. 29 (Krebs 1999, 5) and Brahms's "Walpurgisnacht," op. 75, no. 4.

5. In the most extreme case, the opening section of the vocal quartet "Warum?," op. 92, no. 4, the notated meter of common time is used as a point of notational reference in the manner of Messiaen: the piano projects $\frac{5}{4}$, and the vocal parts alternate freely between common time and $\frac{3}{2}$, often failing to align with one another.

6. Readers wishing to make a direct comparison between Klorman's (2016) reading of a metrically dissonant passage and mine can look at our treatments of a theme from Brahms's Sonata in E-flat, op. 120, no. 2, discussed in his chap. 6 and here in sec. 16.2.

7. This understanding of the most common kind of asymmetrical meter found in Western classical music is widely shared; for example, Gotham's (2015, 2.3) term for what is here called the substrate level is the "common fast pulse," and he assumes it is grouped in two's and three's. London's (2012, chap. 8) discussion of nonisochronous meters includes a wider range of possibilities, but he affirms that this practice commonly occurs and offers reasons why.

8. The assumption that beats at the mixed level will contain either two or three beats at the substrate level is valid for Western classical music from the eighteenth through the early twentieth centuries; we will encounter an example below of more recent music in which this assumption does not hold.

9. London (2012, chap. 8), who considers a much wider set of musics than Lerdahl and Jackendoff (1983), allows for this possibility.

10. Both issues are considered in depth by London (2012, chap. 8).

11. The scherzo from Bartók's String Quartet No. 5, Sz. 102, marked "alla bulgarese," is another piece in which the composer seems to invite focal impulses placed more than two or three substrate-level beats apart, as the meter signature of ($\frac{4+2+3}{8}$) suggests three different

durations for the main beat. By London's (2012, 125, 129) criteria this cannot be the actual meter, as it violates the metrical well-formedness rule of maximal evenness.

12. Alternative heard meters do not necessarily have different implied meter signatures; given the importance of the bar line and of the downbeat, I also understand alternative heard meters to include cases in which the only metrical change is a shift in the location of the heard downbeat.

13. There are cases in which hypermeter seems to work best following a hemiola meter; such cases involve contracted heard measures (e.g., heard $\frac{2}{4}$ in notated $\frac{3}{4}$) more often than doubled heard measures ($\frac{3}{2}$). We will see one such case in chap. 16, and I will discuss more in my future work on Brahms (Ito, in preparation c). David Lidov (personal communication) has pointed out that as a well-entrenched metrical idiom, hemiola may enjoy an exemption from the usual rules of meter, paralleling ungrammatical idioms in language.

14. Some controversy surrounds the question of hearing in two meters at once. The influential position of London (2012) is that it is not possible, but many musicians, especially pianists and performers of musics of Africa and the African diaspora, claim that it is. Poudrier and Repp (2013), who both survey the empirical literature and present new findings, find some limited support for its being possible. I would not describe my own experience as truly hearing in two meters at once but rather as having a secondary awareness of a second meter. I will discuss this possibility in more depth in my work on metrical dissonance in Brahms (Ito, in preparation c), making an analogy with hearing *Stufen* as qualia—for example, hearing the final chord of the first reprise of a binary form simultaneously as the tonic chord in the key of the dominant and as the dominant chord in the home key.

15. An interesting indication of the strength of the tradition of feeling the hemiola meter can be seen in video recordings of this passage available online. Some conductors clearly project the hemiola meter (although not by conducting half notes in three). Others, including very distinguished conductors, use gestures rooted strongly in the notated meter while the orchestra feels the hemiola, judging by the sound and by bodily motions. It is a good reminder that there is plenty of room for divergence in focal impulse placement (and in many other areas) between conductor and orchestra.

16. Although cornerstones of the repertoire, Bach's cello suites are well known for being open to multiple interpretive possibilities, and numerous good examples of hemiolas that can be brought out or not are found in the Courante from Suite No. 5. Recordings that show clear contrasts in the treatment of the potential hemiolas in this movement are those by Pierre Fournier (1960) and Mischa Maisky (1999).

17. A more complex kind of impulse polyphony involving hemiola arises when two offset hemiolas are juxtaposed. As may be surmised from the discussion in chap. 7, I believe that syncopation within hemiola is far more common than impulse polyphony involving multiple hemiola meters. Nonetheless, examples exist in which this seems well justified. One of the clearest is found near the start of the trio from the third movement of Brahms's Piano Quartet in A Major, op. 26, mm. 223–25. Here the combination of a strong hemiola with a canon at the measure between the piano and the strings sets up offset dueling hemiolas in which impulse polyphony seems fully appropriate. I will discuss similar passages in my future work on Brahms (Ito, in preparation c).

18. Hemiolas of this sort, which occupy two thirds of a triple metrical unit, are discussed by Richard Cohn (2018), who refers to them as "Balkan hemiolas." The various implied meters of this movement are discussed by Scott Murphy (2009, 40–53). In the present passage, hemiola continues to be a factor in the third measure of each unit; in each case, although there are no credible threats to the notated meter, articulation and grouping both imply a reverse hemiola patterning, equivalent to a $\frac{6}{8}$ meter.

19. Edward T. Cone (1985, 151) looks at these two hemiolas from a different perspective and reaches the opposite conclusion about which is more overtly signaled.

9

ANTICIPATIONS AND SECONDARY
FOCAL IMPULSES

THE SPECIAL CASES OF FOCAL IMPULSE PLACEMENT DISCUSSED in chapter 8 move focal impulses but do not change the experience of producing them. This chapter covers two topics from the inner periphery in which the experience of the focal impulse is different. In the case of secondary focal impulses, their role in the organization of movement is also different, because they occupy an intermediate hierarchical position between regular focal impulses and subsidiary impulses.

9.1. Performing Anticipations with Shifted Focal Impulses

As explained in chapter 1, the first task in setting forth focal impulse theory is helping the reader to identify the relevant slice of experience. Here and in chapter 10, more than in the rest of the book, the slices of experience in question involve subtle distinctions, and I have found that this material presents greater challenges on an initial encounter than any of the other topics (although once the basic experiences have been grasped, using the concepts is straightforward). For this reason, in addition to extensive verbal descriptions, I offer exercises and video demonstrations intended to help make focal impulses placed on anticipations experientially real to the reader. I take a similar approach in chapter 10.

Anticipations occur when a note or chord that would be expected on a strong beat arrives early, on a weaker beat. If a focal impulse would normally fall on a beat that is anticipated, performers sometimes shift the focal impulse to the attack point of the anticipation.[1] While there may be many reasons for such a shift, it will be particularly likely if the anticipation is loud or has a pointed attack. When focal impulses are shifted in this way, the notation will be placed above the anticipation, with an arrow pointing to the beat on which the focal impulse would otherwise have occurred.

There are two possible options for marking the beat on which the focal impulse would normally have been found. In the first, the musician makes a small muscular contraction on the beat to keep track of the meter. This muscular contraction has primarily cognitive purposes; it does not seem likely to be important for motor coordination. It might, for example, consist of pressing the toes against the sole of the shoe. The second possibility is that the musician adapts the profile of the focal impulse to give it two salient time points—an onset at the start of the note and an offset on the anticipated beat. Recall the basic definition of an impulse: a muscular contraction with a saliently rapid beginning or onset. Nothing is stipulated about the release; it may follow hard on the heels of the onset, resulting in the impulse having a narrowly spiked profile, or the release may be extended in time, with the contraction often diminishing gradually. In the case under discussion, the onset of the focal impulse leads to a relatively static contraction, looking like a quick rise to a plateau. This plateau lasts until the anticipated beat, at which point there is a sudden release. This offset may be complete or it may be partial, an initial steep drop-off transitioning to a more gentle slope. Either way, the shape of the contraction looks approximately rectangular. This rhythmicized release of tension in the offset creates a second focal point in time, coinciding with the strong beat that has been anticipated. The sound produced is likely to mirror the shape of the muscular contraction: a forceful attack, then an intensely sustained sound, and finally a sudden release on the beat.

The scherzo from Beethoven's Cello Sonata in A Major, op. 69, thematizes its anticipations; it affords opportunities for shifted focal impulses of either kind. The cello's first entrance is shown in example 9.1 with shifted focal impulses. If the first option described above is used, so that the shifted focal impulses are felt without a substantial physical investment in the downbeat, this will likely result in each note being released fairly quickly, not necessarily sustaining the note into the downbeat at all. Performed in this way, each note will probably sound more like an isolated unit than like part of a longer line; in more expressive terms, each anticipation can sound like a surprise, giving the passage a breathless quality, unsettled and even somewhat off balance. Yo-Yo Ma and Emmanuel Ax (1983) sound like they were performing the passage in this way, and the sense of disorientation is made very effective musically.

If the cellist uses shifted focal impulses that do not invest in the downbeats, the cello part will likely sound as if it is constantly being pushed along by each new chord in the piano. In contrast, in the second kind of performance, in which the shifted focal impulses are sustained into the downbeats,

Example 9.1. Beethoven, Sonata for Cello and Piano op. 69, iii, mm. 8–16, Allegro molto.

the cello part will tend to sound as if it were forcefully driving forward, dragging the piano along with it. In this performance, the notes will likely have more intensity, sustaining until a rhythmic point of release on the downbeat. They will also cohere more clearly into a long line with purposeful forward motion. The recording by Pierre Fournier and Friedrich Gulda (1959) provides a clear illustration of this way of performing the passage.[2]

Both ways of placing shifted focal impulses aligned with anticipations feel different experientially from focal impulses aligned with the meter. If the peak of the contraction is sustained until the next strong beat, the contrast is obvious because normal focal impulses are not sustained in that way. (The exercises in the next section will help clarify what sustaining this focal impulse will feel like.) If there is no substantial physical investment in the strong beat, the difference is more subtle. The focal impulse itself seems quite similar to a focal impulse aligned with the meter, but it feels somehow less stable and grounded. We might make a comparison with the difference between two kinds of swings with a tennis racquet or a bat. In the first kind, comparable to the shifted focal impulses, your timing is off and you start the swing too late, putting in a strong muscular effort but swatting at the ball in a way that will not be able to produce a solid connection. In the second kind, more similar to focal impulses on strong beats, you are able to prepare well, anticipate the moment of contact, and connect in a way that transfers power and momentum to the ball. The curiously unsettled quality of shifted focal impulses that are not sustained is a key part of their expressive effect.

9.2. Exercises for Performing Sustained, Shifted Focal Impulses

This section presents two exercises that are intended to help the reader learn to feel shifted focal impulses that are sustained into the next strong beat. The first exercise targets the basic form and feeling of the motion, using a second arm to generate resistance. (Later that resistance will be generated within a single arm.)

- Start by raising your dominant hand with the palm open, facing outward, by your shoulder, as if you were about to slap palms with someone. Slapping palms is a helpful image, but the trajectory will be lower. The palm stays approximately level with the shoulder, putting the arm in a better position mechanically to push against resistance.
- Raise your other hand, palm open and facing yourself, reaching over so that it is across from the shoulder of your dominant arm; the non-dominant hand will be turned 90° relative to the dominant hand. Place it so that contact will take place when the elbow of the dominant arm is extended about halfway, to an angle a little smaller than 90°.
- Next start a quick and strong motion forward with the dominant arm.
- Make a solid impact with the nondominant hand, and let the two arms resist each other, pressing against each other with strong contact. Given the initial momentum of the dominant arm, its greater strength, and the mechanical advantage that comes from this posture, it will be natural to let the dominant arm prevail. Even as the arms resist one another, the dominant arm continues to extend, just much more slowly than before the impact. Conscious attention should be focused mainly on the dominant arm, especially on the exertion of the upper arm pushing outward. During this phase, in which there is a resisted push, the dominant arm should feel like it is pushing against a revolving door that has significant mass and friction.

- When the dominant arm is about halfway between the point of impact and full extension, with the elbow open to an angle somewhere in the vicinity of 135°, suddenly move the nondominant arm away, removing the resistance. Both arms should spring out of this moment of sudden lack of resistance. The nondominant arm continues to move away from the body until it bounces out of a point close to full extension; it then returns rapidly to the position at which it waits for impact from the dominant hand. Because the dominant arm was still pushing strongly when the resistance was removed, it continues its extension quite rapidly. It also bounces out of its maximum extension (probably just over 135°) and returns to its initial position by the shoulder, gradually slowing down.

Eventually these motions will be strung together, but first practice isolated sequences of contact, push, and release until a convincing feeling has been found. The goal is to feel these as shifted focal impulses that sustain until the point at which they would normally have occurred. The moment of contact is the focal impulse, the push against resistance is the sustain until the strong beat, and the moment of resistance suddenly going away is the release on the strong beat. This exercise is demonstrated in video example 9.1. Note that while the passage from Beethoven's op. 69 that is looped in this video (and subsequent ones) uses anticipations with only some downbeats, the demonstration shows continuous sequences of anticipations.

The key to these motions is the strong push, especially feeling that it exists in relation to just two simple moments in time: the moment of impact and the moment of resistance being released. It should feel like pushing hard against a heavy revolving door; it hardly moves at first, but then it suddenly gives way, turning much more freely and flying ahead of the pushing hand. It is crucial that the push begin just as suddenly as it ends and that the hand move toward the contact fully prepared to push firmly from the moment of impact.

If possible, this exercise is good to do with a partner. In this case, you stand facing each other with dominant arms aligned. Each person should start by finding the angle of the elbow that feels strongest—the ideal position for starting to push against the revolving door. With elbows bent to the preferred angles, stand so that the palms meet and then move a few inches apart. Now lean forward so that the palms meet again; leaning into each other just a bit will help make a solid contact between the palms. The person learning from the exercise does the motions described as being done by the dominant arm while the other person takes the role of the nondominant arm (but using their dominant arm).[3] This allows the person learning from the exercise to focus only on the motion that simulates the shifted focal impulse. I demonstrate the partner exercise with Matthew Hettinga in video example 9.2.

When I do this exercise in the classroom, I find a number of typical errors; correcting them usually leads fairly quickly to the correct form of motion.

- The push is too hard. The moment at which contact is established should not be too hard; it should not be like the moment of impact when hitting a baseball deep into the outfield. It is the whole push that will get the object moving, not just the moment of first contact; there should be nothing violent about the motion. The push should be firm and purposeful, expecting resistance from a heavy object with significant friction; but because of this resistance, the motion will be smooth and fairly slow once contact has been established.
- The push is too weak. Sometimes the motion is not convincing as a push against a heavy object, being closer to flicking a flyswatter. (This becomes especially important in the second exercise, when the person pushing must believably mime a push against heavy resistance.)
- The moment of impact and the push are separated into two different motions. In this case, there is something like a slap at the moment contact is initiated, with a small rebound in which the arm muscles relax, followed by a sustained push. Instead, there should be one motion: from the moment at which there is contact with the other hand or with the partner's hand, there must be continuous, firm pushing.
- When the resistance is removed, the arm does not fly forward by itself; rather, a new, fast motion must be initiated. This can be seen from a time lag between the sudden removal of resistance and the acceleration of the pushing arm. The need for new initiation reveals either that the push was not firm enough or else that the push let up in intensity at the last moment, anticipating the removal of resistance. With a strong, firm push that is smooth and continuous, the arm will fly forward by itself when the resistance is removed. The arm's sudden new motion will result from muscular activity that has been sustained for some time, not from a newly initiated muscular effort.

When you are confident that you are performing the exercise as described, either alone or with a partner, and when you can string these motions together in a continuous sequence, you are ready for the second exercise. The second exercise is crucial for performing anticipations with sustained, shifted focal impulses in actual musical performance.

In the second exercise, the form of the motion is the same, but the resistance comes from the muscles within the dominant arm of the person doing the exercise. It is not contact with another hand but a sudden contraction of the biceps that slows the motion and provides the resistance during the push, and the sudden cessation of this contraction removes the resistance, causing the arm to fly forward. For this variant to be effective, one side of the arm must not know what the other side is doing—the push forward has to be just as smooth, sustained, and consistent as it was when pushing against a partner or against the nondominant arm, so that the same dynamics of motion are produced. The only difference must be that the resistance comes from within the arm itself. The second exercise is demonstrated in video example 9.3.

When the second exercise can be performed both consistently and correctly, with multiple anticipations strung together in a continuous sequence, this kind of motion can be transferred to an instrument. For notes played on a keyboard or played down-bow on a string instrument, the transfer will be fairly direct.[4] For notes played up-bow, the roles of the muscles will be reversed, and for singers and wind and brass players, the form of the motion will have to be transferred to the diaphragm and abdominal muscles.

When preparing to play a passage using shifted focal impulses that sustain into the strong beat, start by singing the passage while doing the first exercise (resistance from a different arm), then sing the passage while doing the second exercise (resistance from within the same arm), and finally move to actual performance. Any time that the correct form of motion seems elusive, it will be helpful to back up one stage, returning to a simpler exercise. This backing up may need to happen several times until the anticipations can be performed consistently in a way that is both clear and convincing.

With the exercises having clarified what is involved in the various ways of performing shifted focal impulses, it may be helpful to consider another example focusing on the two kinds of shifted focal impulse and how they relate to syncopations. Example 9.2 shows an excerpt from the marche hongroise (Berlioz's version of the Rákóczy march) from *La damnation de Faust*.[5] While it could conceivably be taken in four, the meter is alla breve and the metronome marking is based on the half note; performances in two will be assumed here. Its dotted-quarter-eighth rhythms are effectively elaborated syncopated half notes; when felt in two, these will be vigorous syncopations. The passage has three possible performances: unshifted focal impulses or shifted focal impulses with or without sustain to the downbeat.

If the focal impulses are not shifted, the attack points will be produced with strong subsidiary impulses in the parts of the body that directly produce the notes; the focal impulses on the (silent) strong beats will probably be produced in some other part of the body. For string players, for example, the

Example 9.2. Berlioz, *La damnation de Faust*, "Marche hongroise," mm. 96–106, Allegro marcato, reduced score.

subsidiary impulses would be produced in the arm and shoulder; for wind and brass players, they would be produced in the abdominal muscles; and for both, focal impulses might well be located in the torso, especially in the back muscles. The visceral conflict between the strong subsidiary impulses and the focal impulses would be key contributors to the familiar sound of vigorous syncopations.

If focal impulses are shifted but not sustained, with only minimal physical investment in the strong beat, the performance will have the somewhat off-balance, disorienting sound described above in relation to the Beethoven scherzo. This performance is the simplest physically, in that for each pattern, only one moment in time is marked with significant bodily motion. But it may be the most complex cognitively, in that the body is not moving in synchrony with the metrical grid. This sense of being cast adrift from the more stable temporal markers seems likely to lie behind the particular expressive quality of this kind of performance. In the marche hongroise, it is likely to give the impression that the music is being buffeted by the strong forces at play, not driving and directing them. Focal impulses that are shifted but not sustained will offer an atypical version of grounded syncopations; focal impulses align with attack points in a straightforward way, but the misalignment between meter and focal impulses results in a much less stable feeling and sound.

As discussed in chapter 7, vigorous syncopations sometimes have an insistent sustain until the downbeat, at which point the sound decays rapidly. It should now be clear that the possibilities for vigorous syncopations include focal impulses that are shifted to follow anticipations and that are sustained into the strong beat. For performers who want to give the passage an aggressive, even ferocious quality, this may be a good option. The notes produced by sustained, shifted focal impulses will have both powerful attacks and energetic releases that propel the music into the next attack, and they will give the music an appropriate sense of headlong forward momentum.

9.3. Rearticulated Anticipations and Extended Cases

Anticipations are embellishing tones that precede the chords to which they belong; their pitches then continue to be heard once the chords arrive, with the notes either tied over or rearticulated. So far we have assumed that anticipations are tied over, which is the more straightforward motivation for shifted focal impulses. If the notes are rearticulated on the strong beats, the obvious procedure is to place the focal impulses on the strong beats.

Nevertheless, it is possible to perform rearticulated anticipations with shifted focal impulses, and a passage from Bach's Brandenburg Concerto No. 2, shown in example 9.3, presents a good opportunity. If the trumpet player shifts the focal impulses as indicated, her part will have a rhythmically lively character, with a syncopated emphasis reminiscent of big-band jazz. Given the relatively light character of this piece, the trumpet player would probably choose not to sustain the shifted focal impulse into the next strong beat. Another opportunity to use shifted focal impulses for rearticulated anticipations is found in the piano part from the excerpt from the Brahms Piano Quintet discussed previously as example 3.3. As shown in

Example 9.3. Bach, Brandenburg Concerto No. 2, BWV 1047, i, mm. 22–25.

that example, the pianist could move his focal impulses to the attack points of the chords in the right hand and to the beginning of the slurs in the left hand. Because the left hand changes pitch over the bar line, it does not seem to use anticipations at all, but it is clear that we are dealing with chordal arpeggiations in which the most important bass tones (F and C) have been shifted to just before their usual positions, with the chords themselves anticipated.[6] We can understand the actual piano part to be derived from a simpler texture in a three-step process, starting with block chords on the beat, progressing to broken chords corresponding to the actual part but starting on the beat, and finally shifting everything earlier by one sixteenth note to produce the actual part. This motivates the use of focal impulses that are shifted to follow what are now understood as anticipations in both hands.

The shifted focal impulses that are found in the inner periphery of focal impulse placements are used for anticipations in some fairly direct sense. The anticipations may be tied over, they may be rearticulated (as in the Brandenburg), or a chord may be anticipated, with specific pitches changing on the strong beat (as in the piano quintet). It is also possible to use shifted focal impulses in cases in which anticipation is understood in a more extended sense, as a metaphor for the gesture that unites the notes, but such uses belong among the more freely patterned cases of the outer periphery.[7]

9.4. Secondary Focal Impulses

This section describes a third level in the impulse hierarchy, one that is intermediate between focal and subsidiary impulses. These intermediate impulses are called *secondary focal impulses*, and the spans they govern are called *secondary consequent spans*. Where it is helpful for clarity, focal impulses may be referred to as *primary* focal impulses; no new level of hierarchy is implied. The notes within a secondary consequent span will have a sense of grouping together gesturally, similar to the way the notes within a primary consequent span hang together. These smaller groupings are heard to exist within the larger groupings of the primary consequent spans, however, and the secondary focal impulses will be audibly weaker than the primary focal impulses that organize them. Because secondary focal impulses exist within the consequent spans of primary focal impulses, they are not necessary for organizing motion. When performers use secondary focal impulses, it is to bind some cluster of notes together as a miniature gesture, making them sound like a unified whole within a larger unified whole. Secondary focal impulses are added for the sake of the character they generate, creating both emphasis on a beat and the sense of a metrical unit as a motional unit.

Within focal impulse theory, a hierarchical relationship between impulses always implies that the hierarchically higher impulse provides a necessary motional context for the hierarchically lower impulse. Primary focal impulses provide an organizing motional context both for secondary focal impulses and for subsidiary impulses, and when secondary focal impulses are used, they create a motional context for some subsidiary impulses. When this happens, those subsidiary impulses have a doubly organized motional context: the secondary focal impulse provides immediate context, but the secondary focal impulse exists within a context established by the primary focal impulse.

Secondary focal impulses will always be placed one or two metrical levels below the level at which the focal impulses are placed. Unlike primary focal

Example 9.4. Bach, *St. Matthew Passion*, "Ich will mit meinem Jesu wachen," mm. 1–2, oboe part only.

impulses, which must fill the metrical level on which they are placed unless that level is triple, secondary focal impulses never need to fill metrical levels. This is because secondary focal impulses are not needed for coordination in the way that primary focal impulses are. The primary focal impulse already organizes all of its consequent span, and so the secondary consequent span may simply end; the subsidiary impulses then go back to being organized directly by the primary focal impulse.

Secondary focal impulses will be notated as smaller versions of primary focal impulses. Because the end point of a secondary consequent span is not necessarily fixed by the position of the next focal impulse, the slurs coming from the symbols for the secondary focal impulses will be extended to cover their entire secondary consequent spans. Example 9.4 demonstrates this notation along with several features of secondary focal impulses. Primary focal impulses are placed on half notes here, and secondary focal impulses are placed two levels below, on the eighth-note beats. The eighth-note level is not filled evenly, however; this is particularly sensible in this case because a secondary focal impulse on the fourth eighth-note would have no other impulses to organize.

Another passage in which secondary focal impulses might be used is the opening of the first movement of Bach's Sonata for Viola da Gamba and Harpsichord in G Major, BWV 1027, shown in example 9.5. A performer wishing to emphasize the coupling implied by the slurs might play the passage as in example 9.5a, with secondary focal impulses on most of the weak eighth-note beats. (This focal impulse placement applies to the viola da gamba only.) It would be possible to play the music as in example 9.5b, without the secondary focal impulses, but this would make it harder to give the coupled sixteenths much of a lilt. In sound example 9.1, the focal impulse deployment of example 9.5b is demonstrated in my own performance on viola with harpsichordist J. Andrew Olson; the performance includes the second and third measures. It would also be possible to put primary focal impulses on all of the

Example 9.5. Bach, Sonata for Viola da Gamba and Harpsichord BWV 1027, i, m. 1.

eighth-note beats, as in example 9.5c, and such a performance can be heard in sound example 9.2. This focal impulse placement is challenging to perform well because there is a significant risk of sounding clumsy or excessively heavy. We attempted to avoid these dangers by giving the music the character of a stately dance; the result makes the music sound as if it were written in $\frac{3}{8}$ rather than $\frac{12}{8}$. The use of the intermediary level of impulse is a good way to produce a sound that is intermediary between the performances heard in sound examples 9.1 and 9.2. Sound example 9.3 presents this middle way, using secondary focal impulses as indicated in example 9.5a. Note that not all secondary focal impulses in example 9.5a have subsidiary impulses to organize; secondary impulses were assigned to the weak-beat eighth notes so that they and the other notes with secondary focal impulses would receive equal weight. If that were not desired, those secondary focal impulses could have been omitted.

Readers interested in a masterful display of the shapings possible with secondary focal impulses in this movement should consult the recording by Laurence Dreyfus and Ketil Haugsand (1985). They create an astonishingly rich variety of phrasings while projecting a clear sense of motional hierarchy: eighth-note beats are organized by dotted-quarter beats, and weaker metrical positions are organized by eighth-note beats.

Notes

1. This understanding of anticipations relates to David Temperley's (1999; 2001, 243–53) "syncopation shift rule," proposed for rock music, which infers unsyncopated deeper structures under the surface of a melody.

2. For an example of what shifted and sustained focal impulses can look like, see the video recording of the first movement of Brahms's Symphony No. 3 by the Vienna Philharmonic Orchestra conducted by Leonard Bernstein (1981). Details of the first oboist's motion in the passage in question (mm. 52–55, around 7:26 from the start of the video) are discussed in sec. 12.2, which also considers the possibility of hearing shifted meter. The exercises presented in sec. 9.2 will help clarify how shifted and sustained focal impulses relate to the motion seen.

3. The partner must remove resistance very crisply to create the sudden offset of the focal impulse. The partner must also move the arm rapidly out of the way to avoid the arm of the person doing the exercise as it flies forward. The partner must then move rapidly back into the starting position in order to be waiting there for the moment of contact. If the partner's hand is in motion at the moment of impact, the hands will likely bounce off of each other, when what is wanted is a continuous push from the beginning. At faster tempi, this will require very quick motions.

4. There may be some skepticism regarding this mode of performance on keyboard instruments, given that the sound cannot be altered once the key has been struck. While it is true that a keyboard instrument will not produce the characteristic insistent sustain followed by sudden decay that a string or wind instrument would produce, sonic traces—especially the attack and timing of each note—can still encode the characteristic aspects of the motion. This is true especially when the anticipated notes are found in context and can be compared with nonanticipated notes. If a pianist were playing the cello part in the Beethoven sonata, it might not be possible to distinguish types of shifted focal impulse or to tell the difference between that passage and one renotated with attack points on downbeats. But in the first eight measures of the movement, in which the pianist has both the melody with the anticipations and the accompaniment part, it is in fact possible to convey the distinction between shifted focal impulses that do or do not sustain through to a significant physical investment in the downbeat. Indeed, in their 1959 recording, Friedrich Gulda's anticipations have the kind of same insistent attack and sustain that Pierre Fournier's do.

5. Similar examples come from another march by Berlioz, the brassy, major sections (e.g., mm. 62–69) of the march to the scaffold from *Symphonie fantastique*.

6. This is particularly clear in m. 180; given the cello part, the C-minor chord is evidently in root position. And although the cello has a B natural on the downbeat of m. 178, it moves to an F for the rest of the duration of this chord, a plagal Neapolitan embellished as an augmented-sixth chord (at least if the movement is heard to end in C minor). As Peter H. Smith (1997, 190)

has also observed, it is possible to hear the scherzo ending either with a Picardy third in C minor or on a dominant chord in F minor; both options receive confirmation from music that follows, one from the trio and the other from the final movement.

7. An example is the first phrase of the menuetto from *Eine kleine Nachtmusik* (ex. 8.12) in the recording by the Hagen Quartet (1994). Responding to the beginnings of the slurs and to the trills, their focal impulses on the second two beats of the hemiola precede the strong beats in the manner of anticipations (not in this case sustaining the focal impulses), using the gesture of the anticipation without any of its customary harmonic groundings. That the accents are so clearly syncopations is also interesting; despite the focal impulse on the downbeat of m. 7, there is no confusing this performance with one that stays straightforwardly in the notated meter.

10

INFLECTING FOCAL IMPULSES
DOWNWARD AND UPWARD

U P UNTIL THIS POINT, NO PRINCIPLED DISTINCTIONS HAVE been made among focal impulses. Two focal impulses might have salient differences— for example, in intensity or in shape of beginning and release—but these differences have not been marked through the use of different terms. This chapter introduces a qualitative distinction among focal impulses, a way in which differences of character can be created by inflecting hierarchically equivalent focal impulses.

Qualitatively differentiated focal impulses will be categorized in terms of a descriptive image: it is as if they are moving in relation to gravity, either pulling upward and gathering tension or moving downward and releasing tension. It is important to stress at the outset that this distinction is qualitative. Focal impulses that gather tension and focal impulses that release tension are hierarchically equivalent: neither governs the other or provides a motional context for the other's consequent span. From a conceptual standpoint, instead of talking about different types of focal impulse, it would be preferable to talk about one type of focal impulse, with focal impulses acquiring different qualities when used in coordination with various characteristic patterns of muscular tension. Referring to different types of focal impulse treats them like different flavors of ice cream; it might be more accurate to treat the differences like different toppings added to vanilla ice cream. The reason for referring to different types of focal impulse is simply that the alternative is more cumbersome: it is easier to refer to one thing than to two, and more economical to use a single analytical notation for an inflected focal impulse rather than one notation for the focal impulse and a second for the inflection.

In line with the approach taken throughout the book, the first section leads the reader into the experience of inflected focal impulses and then presents a more formal account of their various kinds and interrelationships. The two middle sections continue the exposition of inflected focal impulses, addressing metrical placement and sonic qualities, and the chapter closes with an overview of the impulse hierarchy. The theory's complexity increases noticeably in this chapter, and the experiential distinctions in play become more subtle.

10.1. Focal Impulses and the Gathering and Release of Tension

We begin with the familiar textbook patterns for conducting in one and in two. These patterns provide two helpful experiential distinctions: one is between motions that predominantly gather or predominantly release tension, and the other is between ways of stringing these motions together in larger sequences.

Begin by conducting in one, at a moderate tempo, with a light, springy beat inserted into an otherwise flowing legato. After a few measures, switch to conducting in two, at the same beat rate and with a similar quality of motion. After a similar amount of time has gone by, begin to alternate between the two patterns, going back and forth every few measures or so.

Our two distinctions are already evident. First, there is a basic difference between motions oriented downward toward releasing tension and motions oriented upward toward gathering tension. The downbeats in the two patterns are much more similar to one another than either is to the upbeat in the pattern in two. Second, the unit of the measure is encoded in the motion, requiring that the beats occupy fixed positions within their patterns. A measure in one was never followed by an upbeat in two, nor was a downbeat in two followed by a downbeat in one. Take a moment and try both of those strange beat successions. They feel awkward, mainly because each involves a resetting of position; in general, the downbeat in one and the upbeat in two both leave you ready to start a new downbeat, either in one or in two, and the downbeat in two leaves you ready only for an upbeat in two. Any other beat succession will require an interruption of the usual trajectory and a quick relocation of the hand. Our initial discussion of the different qualities of focal impulse will be organized around these two observations, addressing one at a time.

The experience of gathering and releasing tension in the conducting patterns is closely related to the mechanics of the patterns themselves. Both patterns are oriented around vertical motions; as the arm moves to the top of the pattern, the place of readiness for the downbeat, it increases its gravitational potential energy. This usually involves increasing muscular tension as well, because the muscles need to work in order to resist the pull of gravity. As the arm moves down into the lower position, much of this gravitational potential energy turns into kinetic energy, and much of the muscular tension in the arm is released. The arm muscles will usually be active in the downbeat, but they are working with, not against, the pull of gravity. To experience just how much downward motion can be accomplished simply as a result of releasing the potential energy stored in the arm, conduct an upbeat and freeze at the top of the arm's trajectory. Take a moment to observe the effort this requires of muscles in the arm and shoulder. Then suddenly let the muscles in your arm and shoulder go limp. Observe the speed of the arm as it passes the normal point for the downbeat and the force with which it hits your leg.

Both patterns are organized around these two positions; the differences between the patterns lie in how they continue out of the downbeat and in how they construct the motion that brings the hand from the lower position back to the upper position. In the pattern in one, the hand travels up from the lower position, returning to the upper position. Although this is one motion, it has two different but partially overlapping phases. At first the upward motion is a continuation of the release of the downbeat, a springy bounce out of the lowest point in the descent. This initial stage of the upward motion is more a passive rebound than an active pulling. In the middle of the motion, though, this gradually changes. Without a salient beginning—and so without an impulse, in our terms—an upward pull is added to the passive rebound. The two coexist for a while as the rebound gradually fades out, and by the end of the upward motion the active pull predominates, resisting gravity and gathering tension. The reality of this transition can be verified by letting the arm go limp just after the downbeat; there is some upward motion following the downbeat (showing that the upward motion begins as a ballistic rebound out of the downbeat), but the arm never gets back to the starting position. Instead, it falls until it slaps against the body, showing that active pulling is needed to complete the usual upbeat. Speed and character of motion will make this transition occur earlier or later within the motion, but the basic picture will hold consistently. The upstroke starts as a bounce and ends as a pull, with no identifiable point at which the process changes from one to the other. As the arm reaches the apex of its motion, it comes to rest in a state of gathered tension, but without a distinct moment that initiated the gathering.

The conducting pattern for measures in two continues out of the downbeat quite differently. The hand makes a fairly small motion up and to the right, staying fairly close to the lowest position. This motion continues out of the downbeat's release of tension, and it never regathers much tension. From this position, and out of this state, the upbeat is initiated.

The upbeat has two tasks: it must produce a beat, and it must return the arm to the position of readiness, the upper position out of which the next downbeat will be initiated. The first step is to produce the beat, which is done by making a small initial downward motion for the ictus, located near the position of the downbeat ictus. The hand next travels upward, gathering muscular tension and returning to the upper position. There are two main ways in which this may occur.

The most salient difference between upbeat and downbeat is found when the upbeat has a more sustained quality, actively pulling throughout the upward motion. In contrast with the release of the downbeat, the muscles of the arm are constantly working to gather tension and pull the arm up, pulling it farther from its rest position. In this kind of motion, the muscles often do more work than is strictly necessary to raise the arm. The extra work comes from miming a sense of pulling against more resistance than just gravity, as if returning to the upper position involved stretching a bungee cord, with opposing muscle groups contracting together to create the extra resistance.

The other way of producing the upbeat is more similar to the downbeat, and especially to the downbeat in one. Here, the ictus sets the arm on an upward, ballistic trajectory. The snap of the beat essentially throws the arm upward, and, like the upward motion in the conducting pattern in one, there will be a seamless transition between the passive rebound out of the beat and a more active pulling at the top of the motion. The snap will often use an upward jerk, driven mainly by the biceps, similar to tossing a ball vertically into the air.[1]

A few simple exercises can help the reader to experience the similarity of these various ways of performing an upbeat and to feel the contrast with the downbeats. First, string upbeats together, without downbeats. This is essentially an alternative way of conducting in one, with the beat directed upward instead of downward; this way of conducting is often said to be common among opera conductors. Let the upbeat be the main beat, using any kind of upbeat already described, and instead of pausing momentarily in the upper position, allow the hand to fall down again. Using the biceps, gradually cushion the fall of the arm so that it decelerates into the lower position, from which it will initiate the next upbeat. As with the upward motion in the regular pattern in one, this downward motion has a seamless transition between ballistic motion at the beginning and controlled motion at the end.

When you are comfortable with this pattern, start to switch among the various possibilities for the upbeat, either pulling continuously or else snapping the beat and flying up. Try to feel what these motions have in common—the "up-ness" of each kind of upbeat.

As a next step, move freely among various beat patterns, including the regular pattern in one, the pattern in two, and the pattern in one with all upbeats, including each type of upbeat in both patterns that include upbeats. Pay attention to those things that unite downbeats and that unite upbeats, and to those things that make upbeats and downbeats as categories different from each other. Video example 10.1 demonstrates the different kinds of upbeat and samples the range of characters that each can have.

The motion of the downbeats is the more neutral motion; borrowing from semiotics, we might call it unmarked. Beyond the general sense of release, it has no special character to which our attention is directed. The upbeats contrast with the downbeats as the marked member of the pair; they are characterized by upward-directed motion that gathers tension. This gathering of tension may be smooth and continuous in the case of the pulling upbeat or concentrated into a much shorter span of time in the case of the tossing upbeat; in either case, there is a quality of up-ness that contrasts with the more neutral character of the downbeat.

When characterizing focal impulses in terms of upward and downward motion, these qualities of releasing and gathering tension are the important characteristics. The actual directions of motion involved may be quite different, but the qualities of releasing and gathering will translate as a consistent element, characterizing both motion and sound.

Having dealt with the contrasting qualities of upbeats and downbeats, we can now turn to our second basic observation about the conducting patterns—much more briefly, as we have already seen the ways in which the various beats do and do not follow one another. A gesture that is organized around the production of a downbeat can either bounce back to a place of readiness for another downbeat (as in the pattern in one) or remain in the lower position, requiring an upbeat to return to the upper position. Similarly, an upward motion can either return to the lower position, ready for another upbeat (as in the modified pattern in one, with all upbeats), or remain in the upper position, requiring a downbeat to return to the lower position. Downbeats are initiated from the upper position, upbeats are initiated from the lower position.

We have then four basic options for beats; they result from two prevailing directions of beats (downward and upward) and two ways of continuing

Table 10.1. Categories of qualitatively inflected focal impulse.

	No bounce from goal	Bounce from goal back to initial state of the focal impulse
Oriented toward release of tension	↓	↻
Oriented toward gathering of tension	↑	↺

out of the beat (either remaining in the target position or else bouncing back to the point of origin). The downward beat that stays down is the downbeat in two, and the downward beat that bounces back up is the downbeat in one. The upward beat that stays up is the upbeat in two, and the upward beat that bounces back down is the less standard of our options, the one that resembles conducting in one with all upbeats.

We can now lay out the basic theory of qualitatively differentiated focal impulses. Focal impulses that correspond in character to the beats of the pattern in two are called *downward* and *upward* focal impulses; they are notated using downward and upward arrows (↓ and ↑, respectively). Focal impulses that correspond to the usual conducting pattern in one (i.e., the pattern in one that uses downbeats) are called *cyclical* focal impulses, and they are notated with a U-shaped bent arrow (↻). Focal impulses that correspond to the upbeats in the alternative, upward-oriented pattern in one are called *upward cyclical* focal impulses, and they are notated by turning the notation for cyclical focal impulses upside down (↺). For clarity, the term *downward cyclical* focal impulse will sometimes be used to specify the regular (as opposed to upward) cyclical focal impulse. Table 10.1 presents the four kinds of focal impulse as entries in a 2 × 2 grid, reflecting the two binary choices.

Corresponding to the usual patterns in one and in two, qualitatively differentiated focal impulses come in complete *impulse cycles* that contain exactly one complete sequence of release and gathering of tension. Here we will assume that tension is first released and then regathered, ending in a place of gathered tension that is ready to release again. This choice reflects an assumption that the release of tension (corresponding to the downbeats in the conducting patterns) will generally correlate with greater metrical strength. As a result of this assumption, upward cyclical focal impulses will recede in prominence; although they are one of the four basic possibilities, they are understood in practice to be a less commonly used variant, reserved for the periphery (not the core) of uses of inflected focal impulses. (Chap. 11 discusses the use of upward cyclical focal impulses, the nature of impulse cycles that start with gathering tension and end with release, and the possibility of reversing the correlation between metrical strength and release of tension.)

If cyclical focal impulses are used, each focal impulse contains a complete impulse cycle; this kind of impulse cycle is called a *unitary* impulse cycle. If downward and upward focal impulses are used, a complete cycle consists of a downward focal impulse followed by an upward focal impulse; in this case, we speak of a *binary* impulse cycle. As a result of leaving aside the upward cyclical focal impulse, our symmetrical arrangement of four possibilities turns into an asymmetrical arrangement of three possibilities. From the place of gathered tension, two kinds of tension-releasing focal impulse can be initiated, the downward focal impulse or the cyclical focal impulse; but from the place of released tension, only the upward focal impulse can be initiated. The place of gathered tension is thus the place of readiness, from which either kind of impulse cycle can begin. Once the impulse cycle has begun, the only option is to complete the cycle, returning to the place of gathered tension.

The examples and exercises that follow in the remainder of this section broaden the scope beyond conducting to include other activities of music making and daily life. They are intended to further clarify qualitatively differentiated focal impulses by forging more links with lived experience.

The basic patterns of release and gathering of tension that we have charted so far can be found in many common activities. Consider hammering a nail downward. As one way of organizing the motion, it is easy to lead fluidly from one stroke to the next; in this case, the hammer rebounds after each stroke, and the hammerer continues the motion of the rebound so that it leads back to its starting position. There is only one impulse for each cycle of motion, the impulse given as the hammer hits the nail. But the motion could also be organized differently. Instead of capitalizing on the bounce to lift the hammer back to the ready position, you could allow it to bounce a couple of times and then come to rest. From this position it will have to be lifted—as a separate motion—back to its starting position. A similar pattern of motion now requires two separate main impulses, one for the downward, releasing motion and one for the upward, gathering motion.

The examples could be multiplied almost without limit, as many human physical activities can be analyzed in terms of the same patterns. Exhalation is capable of greater forcefulness and explosiveness than inhalation, and runners experience the two patterns in their breathing as they start to become winded, moving from active exhalation and passive inhalation to more labored breathing in which both phases are active. Particularly prevalent are motions that parallel the conducting pattern in one, in which only one phase of motion is used to produce results and the other is a recovery phase. These motions are almost always directed outward from the center of the body, and in most cases a joint extension is involved, whether of the elbow (e.g., throwing, swinging a bat or racquet) or the knee (e.g., running, cycling, kicking, rowing). These powerful motions correspond to cyclical focal impulses, and this fact reinforces both the character of downward-inflected focal impulses and the primary, default status of the downward-inflected character: when only one kind of focal impulse is used, it will usually be the (downward) cyclical focal impulse, corresponding to the downbeat in the conducting pattern in one.

Patterns of release and gathering of tension corresponding to unitary and binary impulse cycles can be found throughout the domain of human movement, in almost any case in which motion has a back-and-forth alternation between positions or states. Given their ubiquity, these patterns have the potential to function as primitives for the character of movement. This means that we can perceive their presence even when a literal, physical back and forth is absent—and in music performance through the progression from one focal impulse to the next.

Many cases of music performance present red herrings when we begin to look for these patterns. For singers, wind players, and brass players, for example, contractions of the abdominal muscles would be first places to look for these patterns of tension, based on their centrality to the production of sound and reinforced by the observations about breathing made above. But this approach quickly runs into a dead end: although respiration is a two-phase process, inhalation is not generally used to produce sound. Therefore, we must seek other expressions of the patterns, focusing not on opposing muscle groups but on qualities of motion distributed holistically over spans of time (i.e., over the consequent spans of the focal impulses). Downward focal impulses could involve muscular contractions that have a steep onset followed quickly by a partial offset, producing a spike followed by a somewhat lower plateau. And upward focal impulses might involve more gradual onsets that proceed directly (i.e., without a spike) to a sustained contraction (at least in the case in which there is a continuous, active pull). These patterns of muscle activation could occur in a variety of places, although the abdominal muscles would be a first place to look, again, because of the direct connection with sound production.

Because pianists also use only one direction of motion to produce sound, their use of inflected focal impulses will parallel that of singers and wind players. (Pianists have a particularly ready resource, as most of the arm can be traveling upward even as the tip of the finger moves downward to depress the key.) In contrast, string players present the opposite false pointer: back and forth motions in which both phases produce sound are extremely prevalent, but they often fail to make a one-to-one correlation with the focal impulses. Consider any passage in which a violinist plays running sixteenth notes, such as the opening of Bach's Brandenburg Concerto No. 5. If we assume that the violinist changes bow direction for every note, then the simplistic correlation of cycles of motion of the elbow joint with impulse cycles would lead to the impulse cycles occurring every eighth note. With unitary impulse cycles, this would mean focal impulses every eighth note, and with binary impulse cycles, this would mean focal impulses every sixteenth—both far too frequent. What might it mean, then, to use inflected focal impulses at a more reasonable rate? If we chose binary impulse cycles with focal impulses every half measure, for example, the overall tension pattern could be generated by varying the muscular tension in the bow arm, a variance that would likely lead to a more sustained sound during the half measures initiated by the upward focal impulses.

It is also possible for conductors to deploy focal impulses in a variety of ways in relation to the standard patterns. Just as notes can be produced by subsidiary impulses, so can a conductor's beats, so that a pattern in two can be produced using focal impulses (of whichever kind) on only the downbeats, or a pattern in four can be produced using focal impulses on only beats one and three. Consequently, common time could be conducted in four but felt in two using binary impulse cycles; what would be necessary would be a sense of pulling through from the third beat until the release of the first. Similarly, when a conductor wants to show focal impulses on only two beats of a triple meter, she will probably use the pattern in three but with one of the beats produced by a subsidiary impulse. Treating beats like notes, conductors have the same range of options for using focal impulses, and for using the various sorts of inflected focal impulses, as other performers.

These examples from everyday activities and from music making are intended to clarify the different qualitatively inflected kinds of focal impulse and to help the reader connect with them at an experiential level. The most helpful next step will be to experiment with the exercises that follow below, progressing gradually from settings that facilitate play with the various sorts of focal impulse to using them in actual performance. Exploring the range of variation possible within each quality will reveal just how different two focal impulses of the same type may be. The exercises involved are quite similar to those described at the end of chapter 3: the basic idea is to vary the quality of motion and the sense of resistance to motion in as many ways as possible.

Returning to conducting, begin by selecting a piece that can be felt with a range of characters, and then sing while conducting along in one or in two. (Singing allows access to a direct form of music making, unhampered by technical concerns. If you are a singer, you will want to sing as a nonsinger would, like marking in a rehearsal but with more expression and focus on musical shape.) Conduct the beats that receive focal impulses; this means that the measures of the beat patterns will not necessarily correspond to the notated measures. Vary both the conducting pattern used and the character of motion, and try to get a match between the character of your conducting and the character of your singing. In the singing, the parallel to the quality of motion of the gestures will probably be mainly a matter of subtleties of articulation. Try lighter and springier renditions and versions that are much more legato and sustained. For the legato versions, experiment with a variety of mental images: conducting in a swimming pool, conducting while submerged in molasses, conducting with elastic bands that slow down and smooth your motions. As you play with these variables, explore the range of character that is possible within each category, but also look for the commonalities shared by members of a category—the things that make two different upward focal impulses both nonetheless upward focal impulses.

As you do this exercise, try to get close correspondence between the character of your conducting and the character of your singing. Notice how adding resistance enhances the pulling quality of the upward focal impulse but also softens the release of the downward and cyclical focal impulses; if the softening of release is more pronounced than the intensification of gathering, it may draw the two qualities closer together—but a difference between the two should still be clear. These same exercises can gradually be brought closer to actual performance, first miming and singing, and then actually playing. For these later stages, however, the exercises may be most effective if the reader returns to them after completing the next two sections, which deal with how the qualitatively differentiated focal impulses are used in relation to meter and with the sound of the various types of focal impulse.

10.2. Inflected Focal Impulses and Meter

The introduction of a qualitative differentiation among focal impulses does not change the picture of metrical placement of focal impulses developed so far; for example, downward focal impulses will not be used in places where uninflected focal impulses would not have been. This is a logical consequence of the differentiation being qualitative and not hierarchical. What is needed is an account of how the inflected impulses will be distributed across the existing patterns, again following the prototype structure of the category of focal impulse placements.

The core placements using inflected focal impulses will be the same as the core placements discussed in chapter 4, with two main stipulations added. First, the impulse cycles used are the primary ones developed in the previous section, those which begin with the release of tension. Second, release of tension will generally correlate with metrical strength: when binary impulse cycles are used, the downward focal impulse will usually fall on the stronger beat (the downward and upward focal impulses may also fall on equally strong beats). The inner periphery of the category using inflected focal impulses is covered in chapter 11 and the small middle periphery in chapters 11 and 12.

With the introduction of qualitatively differentiated focal impulses, we see further entrenchment of the contrast between focal impulse placements on duple versus triple metrical levels, with greater flexibility accorded to triple levels. This makes sense because the basis for differentiation among types of focal impulse is their relation to the two-phase process of releasing and gathering tension. The body already has a bias toward duple patterns; many aspects of the body's organization emphasize duple divisions, and no bodily structure can serve as the basis for a natural three-fold differentiation. In addition to the mirror symmetry about the body's vertical axis emphasized by Parncutt (1989), joints have either two directions of motion or an infinite number—so no joint produces an intrinsically three-phase motion. Expanding beyond joints to other systems that move, such as the respiratory system and the eyelids, we continue to see binary motions. It seems therefore logical that motion in duple meter would be more regularly patterned and thus more highly constrained, as the body finds natural and obvious ways of moving in duple meters. In nonduple meters, the body encounters a situation to which it is less naturally suited and must find ways of adapting. As with mathematical modeling in the physical sciences and engineering, when ideal solutions are possible, they are few in number, and when approximations and compromises are needed, the possibilities are many.

The first and most basic principle governing the use of inflected focal impulses in the core is that the only impulse cycles used are those that start with release of tension (i.e., unitary and binary impulse cycles) and that cycles are generally complete. Because cycles are complete, cyclical focal impulses and upward focal impulses may be followed by either cyclical or downward focal impulses; downward focal impulses may only be followed by upward focal impulses. The only exceptions to complete cycles come when the flow of focal impulses is beginning or ending: at the beginning or end of a movement, or at the start or end of a long pause or long note. In such cases, the first focal impulse can be an upward focal impulse, and the last focal impulse can be a downward focal impulse.

The next principle is the general correlation between metrical strength and the release of tension. This correlation is not absolute because sometimes successive focal impulses are placed on beats that have equal metrical strength; examples include focal impulses placed on successive downbeats and focal impulses placed on beats two and three in triple meter. The precise form of the principle, then, is that focal impulse placements may not contradict the correlation of metrical strength with the release of tension: if a binary impulse cycle is used, the upward focal impulse may not fall on a stronger beat than the downward focal impulse does. It should be emphasized again that the correlation of downward focal impulses with greater metrical strength does not imply greater hierarchical importance. They have equal roles with respect to the organization of motion, and the downward focal impulse governs only its own consequent span, playing no role in the organization of the consequent span of the upward focal impulse.

The final constraint on the placement of qualitatively differentiated focal impulses within the core concerns when it is possible to use both unitary and binary impulse cycles and when it is necessary to choose just one kind. With one exception, only one kind of impulse cycle will be used; this reflects a sense that there would be something quite unusual about a measure felt in four with two unitary impulse cycles followed by a binary impulse cycle. The exception can occur when focal impulses are placed on a triple level of the meter, with focal impulses on each of the three beats. When this occurs, it is possible to use only cyclical focal impulses; however, if binary impulse cycles are used, they will alternate with unitary impulse cycles. This alternation is needed to respect the correlation of metrical strength with downward-inflected focal impulses; otherwise, in a triple meter with three focal impulses per measure, every other downbeat would have an upward focal impulse. The result would be a sort of motional hemiola performed against the notated meter—potentially effective but not found among the core placements.

When this mixed placement on a triple layer occurs, the most common option will be to place the cyclical focal impulse on the downbeat and the downward and upward focal impulses on beats 2 and 3. The reason for this is

Example 10.1. Sibelius, Symphony No. 2, op. 43, iv, mm. 39–44, Allegro moderato, reduced score.

that the sequence of an upward focal impulse into a downward-inflected impulse will create the most salient emphasis on the downward quality within the measure; it makes sense to place this emphasis on the downbeat. A passage that lends itself well to this pattern of focal impulses, from the fourth movement of Sibelius's Symphony No. 2, is shown in example 10.1. The harmonic rhythm, together with the accents and the pesante, *fortissimo* context, makes a focal impulse on each half note appear likely. The melodic sequence makes the second two half notes in measures 42 and 43 group together with the half notes on the following downbeats very strongly, and cyclical focal impulses on the downbeats will accentuate the phrasing break. Downward and upward focal impulses on the second two half notes foster a sense of direction and continuity within each group, and the propulsive harmonies on the third beats fit well with the pulling quality of the upward focal impulse.

The qualitative inflection of focal impulses greatly increases the possibilities for focal impulse placement. Example 10.2 is an expansion of example 4.5, which showed the most typical possibilities for the placement of focal impulses in quadruple, compound duple, and triple meters. For each focal impulse placement listed in example 4.5, example 10.2 displays the possible ways in which inflected focal impulses could be used. (Note that if focal impulses are placed one per measure and binary impulse cycles are used, the basic template will consist of two measures, not one, because downward and upward focal impulses will alternate from measure to measure.) Three focal impulse patterns are in parentheses, indicating that they are not expected to occur frequently. Binary impulse cycles with one focal impulse per measure will be rare in $\frac{4}{4}$ and $\frac{6}{8}$ because of limits on the abilities of focal impulses to organize their consequent spans. The patterns of tension and release of binary impulse cycles would introduce an additional motor demand, and few pieces of music are likely to be fast enough and have little enough going on in each measure

Example 10.2. Typical uses of qualitatively differentiated types of focal impulse for 4/4, 6/8, and 3/4 meters.

to make binary impulse cycles with one focal impulse per measure practical. And in triple meter, if mixed impulse cycles are used, the unitary impulse cycle will usually precede the binary impulse cycle for the reasons discussed.

Note that if unitary impulse cycles are used exclusively, the extra rules and guidelines presented add no restrictions and open no new possibilities; placement of focal impulses is as it was in chapter 4. Thus unitary impulse cycles may be considered to represent the basic form of the focal impulse, with binary impulse cycles an optional form of supplemental organization.[2]

10.3. The Sound of Qualitatively Differentiated Focal Impulses

The sonic differences that result from the use of different types of focal impulse are often more subtle than the sonic differences between notes initiated by focal and by subsidiary impulses. This is in part because the difference in character is distributed more thoroughly over the whole of the consequent span, rather than being mostly confined to the immediate vicinity of the note initiated by the impulse in question. This section will present relatively clear examples of each of the different types of impulse cycle; I do not claim that a random sampling would have yielded instances with so few ambiguities.[3]

Because hearing qualitative distinctions between impulses cycles is based on holistic properties of the sound, it is harder to identify discrete sonic cues when examining focal impulse type than when only the placement of focal impulses is in question.[4] Consequently, the discussions of the examples will be less detailed than those found in chapter 5. In general, my approach is to discuss pairs of performances, usually of the same music, that highlight the contrasting sounds of binary and unitary impulse cycles. My hope is that readers will be able to form impressions of the typical sounds of the types of impulse cycle by synthesizing their own musical experiences, the examples of motion described above, and the sound examples. As with the sound examples discussed in chapter 5, it may be helpful to try hearing each example in multiple ways, searching for the way of hearing that best fits the sound. It may also help to conduct along with the examples—in one, if trying to hear the example with unitary impulse cycles, or in two, if trying to hear it with binary impulse cycles. (Again, the measures conducted in this way will often not match the measures as notated.) A sense that the patterns in the sound either do or do not fit well with the physicality of the motions may aid in decisions about which impulse qualities are being heard—and thus in forming impressions about the sonic differences among types of impulse cycle. As in chapter 5, conclusions are provisional except for those regarding the original recordings produced for the book.

Throughout the discussion, the sound of unitary impulse cycles will be identified more by the absence of specific characteristics than by their presence; this is because unitary cycles are in some ways the default option, lacking a difference in character from one consequent span to the next. It is the alternation of the consequent spans between two different characters that identifies binary impulse cycles, with the consequent spans of the upward focal impulses often having a more sustained quality. As we have seen, the gathering of physical tension that occurs as a result of an upward focal impulse often leads to a sustained, pulling character, but its character can also be evocative of a light object being tossed into the air. Common to both possibilities is the fact that the state initiated by the upward focal impulse is not a stable rest state. Whether we imagine an object lifted or an object thrown, some kind of descent is expected. A downward focal impulse, by contrast, provides a sense of a descent leading to a stable resting state. The release of tension involved will often result both in a crisper attack and in more of a release in the sound. (Beware, however, of equating louder notes and stronger accents with downward focal impulses; the correlation is common but by no means universal.) In terms of character, we find a tendency opposite to that of the consequent span of an upward focal impulse: little other motion would, on its own, continue after the consequent span, and a new infusion of energy is needed if the music is not to come to rest.

Turning now to the examples, many instances of binary impulse cycles in duple meters will be cases of compound duple meters. Perhaps because of associations with lilting peasant dances, binary impulse cycles are often appropriate for compound duple meters, and they are often particularly audible when they are used.

The performance by Trevor Pinnock and the English Concert of the gigue from Bach's Orchestral Suite No. 3 (1978), shown in example 10.3, seems a clear case of unitary impulse cycles. Although the musicians use stronger accents on the downbeats than on the half measures, I hear no suggestion of the qualitative differences in consequent spans that would signal the use of binary impulse cycles. In the recording by Sigiswald Kuijken and La Petite Bande (1982), we again find stronger accents on the downbeats than on the half measures, but now there is an audible alternation of release and sustain. To my ear, this gives the music a significantly more dancelike character and makes this recording an unusually clear example of the use of binary impulse cycles.

I find the contrast particularly evident in two passages. The first is measures 5 and 6, and especially the character of the motion from the second beat of measure 5 into the downbeat of measure 6. In Kuijken's recording, the second beat of measure 5 has a real sense of lift, as if the short articulation were an upward toss of some object, and the downbeat of measure 6 gives the clear impression of a landing. Heard on its own, Pinnock's recording is a bit ambiguous there, and I could potentially hear an upward focal impulse leading to a downward focal impulse. But in comparison with Kuijken's recording, Pinnock's sounds quite neutrally shaped, pointing to the use of cyclical focal impulses. This seems particularly likely coming out of measures 3 and 4; the consistent feeling of downward release on each dotted-quarter-note beat in those measures leaves little doubt that they were performed using cyclical focal impulses, and so the use of a binary impulse cycle in measure 5 would be a change motivated by relatively subtle changes of gesture and texture. The second passage is measures 13–16, focusing especially on the bass line. Both recordings have a clear dynamic contrast between the downbeat and the middle of the measure, but in Pinnock's, the beats all have an even (and tension-releasing) character, with a bouncy quality similar to dribbling a basketball. Kuijken's recording has a remarkably clear sense of alternation between a lifting character on the upbeats, sounding like an upward toss, and a releasing character on the downbeats; it is as if the cellists, bassoonists, and bass players of La Petite Bande were going back and forth between juggling on the upbeats and dribbling on the downbeats.

Gigues from Bach's solo suites provide additional clear examples because the sonic traces of performers' motor behavior are easier to read when a single player is the source of all of the sound. When the performer is a string player, though, slurring half measures can lead to the suspicion that the sonic results are merely an artifact of bowing, as the binary schema is present quite directly in the dynamics of down-bow and up-bow. For example, in the gigue from Suite No. 4 (ex. 10.4), one might be inclined to attribute the sense of alternation in Yo-Yo Ma's recording (1983) solely to bowing. But the same bowing is frequently used in his performance of the gigue from Suite No. 1 (ex. 10.5), and the impression there is predominantly of unitary impulse cycles. (The video examples in chap. 11 include contrasting performances in which releasing and gathering focal impulses are exchanged while preserving bowings.)

Another clear example from the cello suites, this time from the beginning of the prelude to Suite No. 4 (ex. 10.6), is found in the recording by Heinrich Schiff (1984). The first two measures sound like Schiff may be using one cyclical focal impulse per measure, but starting in the third measure, it is

Example 10.3. Bach, Orchestral Suite No. 3, BWV 1068, Gigue, mm. 1–24, reduced score. (*Cont.*)

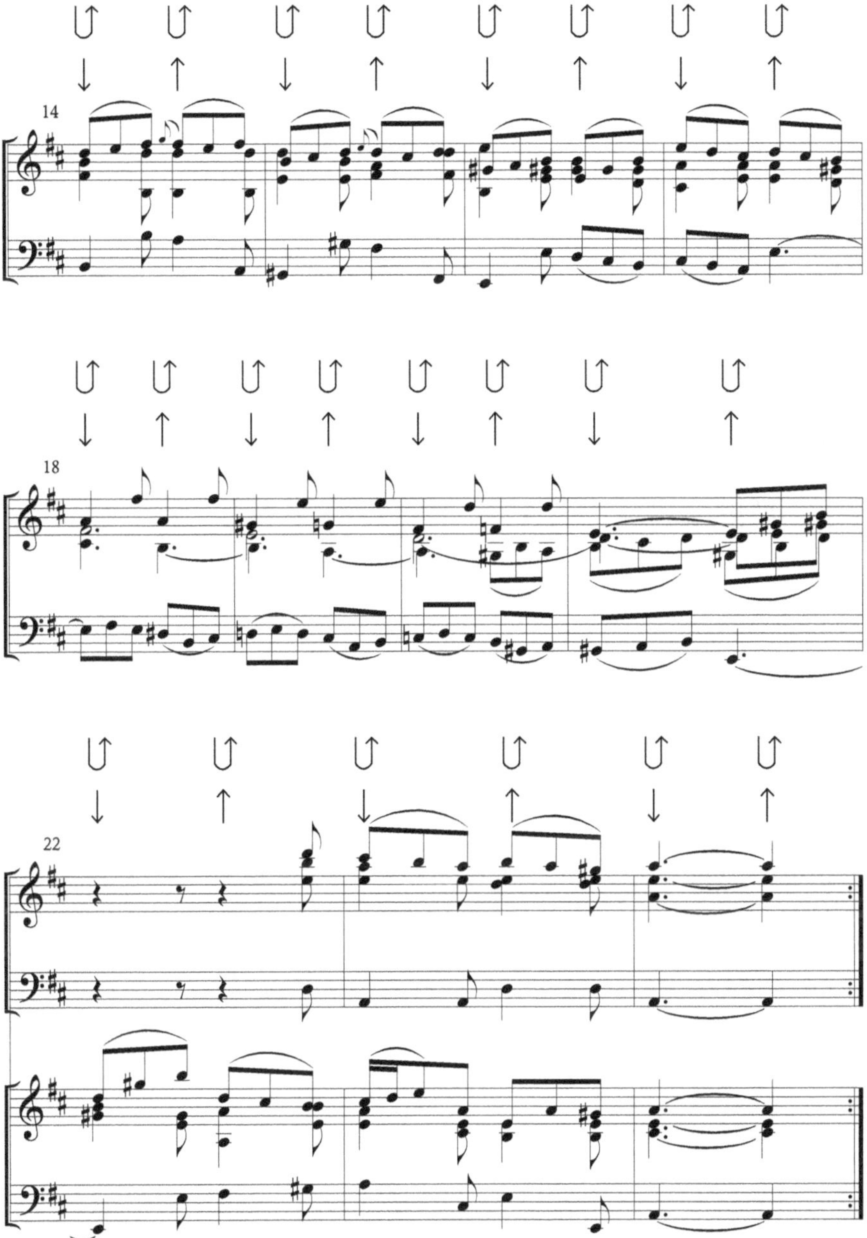
14
18
22

Example 10.4. Bach, Suite No. 4 for Solo Cello, BWV 1010, Gigue, mm. 1–4.

Example 10.5. Bach, Suite No. 1 for Solo Cello, BWV 1007, Gigue, mm. 1–8.

clear that Schiff is also using a focal impulse in the middle of the measure, indicated by loudness and especially by duration. The vivid contrast between the gruff release of the downbeats and the more gentle and sustained emphasis given to the midbar eighths strongly suggests the use of binary impulse cycles. In contrast, in the recording by Kivie Cahn-Lipman (2014), the focal impulse placement seems to be the same as in Schiff's performance, but while the downbeat and the midbar are clearly differentiated in loudness and articulation, I do not hear a similar contrast of focal impulse quality.[5]

Like Yo-Yo Ma in the gigues from the cello suites, Gustav Leonhardt (1975) creates contrasts between gigues by means of different types of impulse cycle in his recording of the French suites, also connecting with the time signatures in interesting ways. The gigue from Suite No. 2 (ex. 10.7) is in $\frac{3}{8}$, and the strong and relatively even accentuation-by-clearing given to each downbeat, together with the lack of alternation in character of motion between measures, are consistent with unitary impulse cycles. In the gigue

Example 10.6. Bach, Suite No. 4 for Solo Cello, BWV 1010, Prelude, mm. 1–4.

from the Sixth French Suite (ex. 10.8), the $\frac{6}{8}$ meter seems strongly reflected in the performance, although it is harder to explain just why this is. Certainly no level of the meter receives the kind of consistent emphasis that Leonhardt put on the measure in the gigue from French Suite No. 2. Reasonably frequent stresses on the measure and the half measure lead me to conclude that there are two focal impulses per measure, and, although I have trouble attributing my reaction to specific features of the sound, I have a sense of alternating character at the level of the half measure—somehow binary impulse cycles seem a better fit than unitary. This is a good example of a holistic property of an extended sound sequence being difficult to decompose into specific cues.

Qualitative differentiation of focal impulses is also possible in vocal performances. Example 10.9 shows the first phrase of Schubert's song "Auf dem Wasser zu singen." In sound example 10.1, soprano Patrice Michaels sings this passage as in option *a*, with unitary impulse cycles and two focal impulses per measure, giving most beats a relatively uniform quality. The recording displays some of the uncertainties of attributing focal impulse placement, as much of it would also be consistent with a performance with one focal impulse per measure. In sound example 10.2, the second halves of many measures have an intense sustained quality; this is the main cue to binary impulse cycles, shown as option *b*. The emphasis given to a number of the consonants on beat 2 also contributes to the vividness of this use of inflected focal impulses. (Pianist Michael Kim performed in each recording with a third pattern of focal impulses, using one focal impulse per measure; this is a case of impulse polyphony, as discussed in sec. 8.1.) In the second recording, the binary impulse cycles are used to bring out the dynamism of this sentential phrase. Each initial pair of measures ends with a longer duration, which, when performed with binary impulse cycles, receives a sustained, pulling quality. In the fifth and sixth measures of the phrase, Schubert discards the material

Example 10.7. Bach, French Suite No. 2, BWV 813, Gigue, mm. 1–7.

Example 10.8. Bach, French Suite No. 6, BWV 817, Gigue, mm. 1–8.

from the initial measures of the preceding pairs; long durations now occur twice as frequently—again (in a performance using binary impulse cycles) with a dynamically pulling quality. In contrast, the sixteenth notes that be-gin these measures do not lend themselves to strongly emphasized downward focal impulses. If the singer responds to this by downplaying the releasing quality of these downbeats, the first six measures will feature an increasing emphasis on the upward focal impulses, with their active quality bringing out both the gradual ascent of the melodic line and the doubling of the fre-quency of motivic succession. The seventh measure of the phrase can then represent a gestural arrival, as the melody completes its ascent and returns to the rhythm that was omitted in the fragmentation. With a longer duration

Example 10.9. Schubert, "Auf dem Wasser zu singen," D. 774, mm. 9–16, Mässig geschwind.

and a prominent pitch, the downbeat of the seventh measure is a good place for a salient downward focal impulse. This focal impulse can represent not only a literal release of tension from the upward focal impulse immediately preceding it, but also a larger release of the tension that has been accumulated by the confluence of binary impulse cycles, contour, and phrase design.[6]

An unusual opportunity to contrast choices of inflected focal impulses in commercial recordings by the same singer is presented by two of Jessye Norman's (1980, 1981/1982) recordings of Brahms's song "Geistliches Wiegenlied," op. 91, no. 2 (first vocal statement in ex. 10.10). In the recording with Ulrich von Wrochem and Geoffrey Parsons (1980), the quality of the beats is extremely consistent, vividly illustrating unitary impulse cycles, shown as option *a* above the staff. The recording with Wolfram Christ and Daniel Barenboim (1981/1982) is quite different, very frequently showing some contrast between the two main beats, sometimes in dynamic stress, sometimes in the quality of release of the downbeat, and sometimes in a pulling quality given to the midbar beat. As an example of binary impulse cycles, shown as option *b* above the staff, this is somewhat subtle on its own, but the contrast with the other recording is striking. It is a remarkable testimony to the collaborative nature of song performance that two recordings made so close in time by the same singer could have rhythmic conceptions that are so internally unified and so different from each other.

As a final example from duple and quadruple meters, in video example 10.2, baritone Daniel Teadt demonstrates the contrast between unitary and binary impulse cycles using Fauré's song "Les Berceaux"; I conduct the impulse cycles to make them visually apparent. Because of the consistent figuration in the piano part, David Keep used unitary impulse cycles in both performances. For both listener and performer, this song lends itself to particularly clear awareness of the differing qualities of unitary and binary impulse cycles; I return to it when discussing further exercises at the end of the section.

Moving on to triple meters, binary impulse cycles will be used most frequently when there are two focal impulses per measure, one on the downbeat and the other on either beat 2 or beat 3. As we will see, this use of binary impulse cycles creates special expressive possibilities. Because the discussion of that longer topic will close this section, we first deal briefly with mixed impulse cycles (in which each beat receives a focal impulse), the more unusual case of binary impulse cycles in triple meter.[7] Returning to the passage from Sibelius's Symphony No. 2 shown in example 10.1, the recording that I found that comes closest to the mixed cycles of the example is that of Leonard Bernstein and the New York Philharmonic (1966, 1:15). Measure 42 was probably

Example 10.10. Brahms, "Geistliches Wiegenlied," op. 91, no. 2, mm. 13–16, Andante con moto.

performed with just one focal impulse, but the following measure has timing patterns that strongly suggest three focal impulses, and the motion from beat 3 of that measure into the downbeat of the a tempo sounds like an upward focal impulse moving to a focal impulse that releases tension.

Proceeding to binary impulse cycles in triple meter with two focal impulses per measure, an example can be heard by revisiting an example of unequal consequent spans presented in chapter 5, the slow movement from Schubert's B-flat-Major Piano Sonata (ex. 5.4). In addition to using unequal consequent spans, Schnabel's performance (1939) also sounds like it uses binary impulse cycles. The lengthening of the third beat (which is more than 10% longer than the preceding beats on average) is a pulling back of the tempo, and the intensity that beat receives can easily be heard as a pulling in other senses as well. Hearing binary impulse cycles here is partly a matter of the touch on the first and third beats, but another important cue is the relative neutrality of beat 2, which adds to the sense that the tension of beat 3 was released on beat 1. At a straightforward level of analysis, if a piano key is being held down, it is impossible to influence the rate of decay of the note, to make one chord have a more insistent sustain and let another decay more rapidly. But performers can move their bodies in different ways in relation to the keyboard, and those different ways of moving leave traces in the patterns of timing and touch across a musical gesture—patterns that, in this case, lead to the impression of a flow of upward and downward focal impulses.

Performances of the first reprise of the sarabande from Bach's Suite No. 5 for Solo Cello (ex. 10.11) by Yo-Yo Ma (1983) and by Anner Bylsma (1979) give

Example 10.11. Bach, Suite No. 5 for Solo Cello, BWV 1011, Sarabande, mm. 1–8. Adapted by permission from Ito (2013c), © Springer-Verlag Berlin Heidelberg 2013.

us the opportunity to compare two different deployments of binary impulse cycles applied to the same work. Ma seems to take cues from a slurring common to several editions (including the one used as the basis for ex. 10.11), using binary impulse cycles and placing the upward focal impulse on the third beat. Here the cues to focal impulse placement are patterns of dynamic stress; those to focal impulse quality are an alternation between a pulling, lifting sound and a release of weight. Judging by the same aspects of sound, Bylsma, using one of the slurrings from the hard-to-read and seemingly inconsistent Anna Magdalena Bach manuscript, employs the upward focal impulse on the second beat, probably motivated by the tendency of sarabandes to place emphasis there.

Ma's and Bylsma's different placements of the upward focal impulse create striking differences in expressive quality; these differences are characteristic when unevenly spaced binary impulse cycles are used in triple meter. Although upward and downward focal impulses can each have a wide range of shapes, there is always a contrast in character between upward and downward focal impulses; when the consequent span that one governs is twice as long as the other, it makes one character or the other come to the fore.

In Bylsma's performance of the sarabande, the upward focal impulses have the longer consequent spans; if we imagine a protagonist as the source of the music, the active quality of the upward focal impulses will give the impression of a present and engaged protagonist, one whose overall orientation toward active striving (the upward focal impulses) is interspersed with moments of rest (the downward focal impulses). Although this movement tends strongly toward an elegiac character, Bylsma's rendition paints a more hopeful picture of grief. If we imagine a figure walking with a limping gait, corresponding to the focal impulses, we can see someone sinking down on the shorter step on the downbeat but then pushing actively up on the longer step that occupies beats 2 and 3 (actually walking this way is helpful). In contrast, Ma's performance, in which the downward focal impulses have the longer consequent spans, sounds weary and burdened. We can hear that moving forward musically is almost too much for an enervated protagonist and that progress can be made only haltingly. Here our limping figure sinks down on the downbeat for two quarter beats, possibly with a deep sigh, and effort is required to push himself up on the third beat. As should be expected, Artur Schnabel's performance of the Schubert is closer affectively to Ma's Bach than to Bylsma's, but clear contrasts also show how much room each possibility has for expressive variation. Schnabel's upward focal impulses have more force behind them than Ma's; we hear this from their intensity and from the way they are able to disrupt the temporal flow. The grief we hear seems therefore more intense and more present, with a greater sense of active emotional conflict. In comparison, we hear in Ma's performance a more distanced grief, a more muted affect.

A look back at examples of uneven placement given in chapter 4 can further expand a sense of the expressive possibilities of binary impulse cycles in triple meter. Pamina's aria "Ach, ich fühl's" (ex. 4.4) is similar to the examples just discussed if two binary impulse cycles are used in each measure, and a performance could potentially be made even more extreme, taking heaviness to the point of despair. The excerpts from the chaconne (ex. 4.2) are quite different, contrasting both with each other and with Bylsma's performance of the sarabande, which they would parallel in placing the upward focal impulses on beat 2. In the opening, the triple and quadruple stops, combined with the active quality of those upward focal impulses, would give the passage a restless, Promethean character. But at the start of the maggiore section, the much simpler texture, the slow, simple, singing melody, and the sweetness of the imperfect consonances would make gently imploring upward focal impulses more apt, giving the passage the quality of a tender embrace.

As discussed in chapter 1, the primary task in coming to grips with focal impulse theory is arriving at an experiential understanding of the various categories discussed, so that the right slices of experience attach to the right terms and concepts. This process involves irreversible heuristic leaps, and it will look different for different readers. The routes to understanding are particularly variable with inflected impulse cycles; in teaching this material, I have found that some students immediately connect with the concept, while others require more exposure. But most do eventually come to have a clear sense of the distinction between binary and unitary impulse cycles, both in listening and in performance. The key is simply having exposure to enough examples, just as it is in other cases of real distinctions that can be hard to quantify, such as the difference between the accents of Australians and New Zealanders.

To the reader who is slower to connect with this concept, I make the following recommendation. Go over the sound and video examples repeatedly, also looking forward to those of chapter 11, and, if possible, discuss them with someone who already grasps the distinction well. Try to find more examples that display the sound quality of binary impulse cycles clearly. Experiment with performance, returning to the exercises described at the end of section 10.1. Find a few passages in which a preferred focal impulse placement seems fairly clear, and then experiment with the two kinds of impulse cycle and with the two characters of upward focal impulse. In my teaching, I have found Fauré's song "Les Berceaux," used in video example 10.2, particularly helpful. As you work with your chosen passages, go back and forth between unitary and binary impulse cycles. Preceding the playing with conducting and singing will probably be helpful, conducting either in one or in two. (Again, conduct impulse cycles, not necessarily measures.) As the downbeats are fairly similar, give close attention to the contrasting, upward-inflected character of the upward focal impulses and of the second beats in the two-beat conducting pattern. With sufficient practice and exposure, musicians have, in my experience, come to a point at which they are able to use this distinction fluently—and at which they find that it helpfully illuminates their performing and listening.

10.4. Overview of the Impulse Hierarchy

This chapter and the preceding one have both introduced distinctions among focal impulses, hierarchical ones in chapter 9 and nonhierarchical ones here. It may be helpful to summarize the nature of the various relationships.

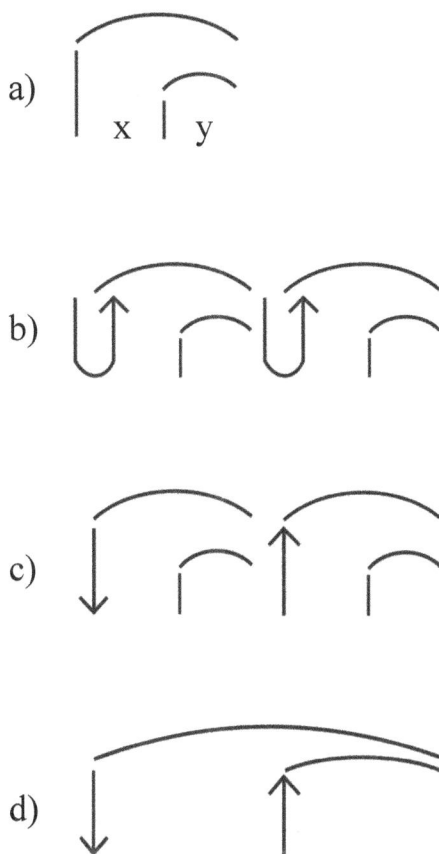

Fig. 10.1. Real and hypothetical focal impulse hierarchies.

Let us start with the hierarchical relationships. The hierarchy has three levels: focal impulses, secondary focal impulses, and subsidiary impulses. Figure 10.1a shows a case in which both primary and secondary focal impulses are used; throughout this example, slurs will cover the entire consequent spans of both primary and secondary focal impulses in order to make the hierarchical structure clearly visible. As is always the case, the primary focal impulse has an organizing role for all of the impulses within its consequent span. More specifically, it organizes the secondary focal impulse shown, and if a subsidiary impulse were placed at point *x* in the example, it would also organize that subsidiary impulse. If a subsidiary impulse were placed at point *y* in the example, it would be governed directly by the secondary focal impulse and indirectly by the primary focal impulse, because the secondary focal impulse and all of its secondary consequent span are included within the primary consequent span of the primary focal impulse.

In contrast, the relationships among the qualitatively inflected focal impulses are not hierarchical—none governs any of the others. Within the constraints discussed regarding placement of the various types (complete impulse cycles, etc.), any of them can replace any uninflected focal impulse in an assignment of focal impulses. The focal impulse deployments shown in figures 10.1b and 10.1c are hierarchically equivalent both to one another and to that in figure 10.1a, even though they feature, variously, uninflected focal impulses and different types of inflected focal impulse. (The secondary focal impulses in figs. 10.1b and 10.1c are included to display the hierarchical relationships; in most cases they will not be present.)

The hierarchic equivalence of focal impulse types may seem questionable in the case of binary impulse cycles. Because an impulse cycle is conceived as a unit, and because the downward focal impulse is correlated with greater metrical strength, it might seem reasonable to make upward focal impulses hierarchically intermediate between primary and secondary focal impulses. Figure 10.1d diagrams this possibility. With the three-quarter-height upward focal impulse representing an intermediate hierarchical position, the consequent span of the upward focal impulse is included within the consequent span of the downward focal impulse, implying the same hierarchical relationship of downward focal impulse to upward focal impulse that a primary focal impulse has to a secondary focal impulse. This inclusion of consequent spans is a necessary aspect of hierarchical inequality within the theory. In focal impulse theory, "is hierarchically superordinate to" always implies "governs and organizes the motional context of."

Why should downward and upward focal impulses not relate as in figure 10.1d, as this seems to point toward a cogent alternative version of the theory? The theory is formulated as it is because of my conviction, grounded in my own experience of performing binary impulse cycles, that the downward focal impulse does not play any organizing role in the consequent span of the upward focal impulse. Recall the role of energy in the definition of the focal impulse. The injection of fresh energy is often a key factor in overcoming the previously existing motional context and creating a motional new beginning. To claim that the downward focal impulse is superordinate to the upward focal impulse is to claim that the upward focal impulse's introduction of fresh energy is not sufficient to overcome the motional context established by the previous downward focal impulse. This is contrary to my experience, which indicates that upward focal impulses are as vigorous and energetic as downward focal impulses. Furthermore, many binary impulse cycles probe the limits of the ability of the downward focal impulse to organize its consequent span. As the end of the downward focal impulse's consequent span approaches, it becomes apparent that the energy in the system is running down and that a new focal impulse is needed if activity is to continue. This feeling that the energy provided by the previous focal impulse has been spent and that a fresh injection of energy is needed is a clear sign that the end of the consequent span has been reached. Because this feeling can be experienced just before an upward focal impulse is used, upward and downward focal impulses should be hierarchically equal (as shown in fig. 10.1c), each representing a type of primary focal impulse. Because of the interrelationships among hierarchy, organization, and energy, I can draw no other conclusion without radically reinterpreting this experience.

Notes

1. In a variant, the motion is more similar to projecting the arm upward by a quick downward push against a surface such as a table top, except that here the biceps provide the resistance instead of a surface.

2. Many connections exist among qualitatively differentiated focal impulses, the history and scholarship of meter, and the history of performance practice, starting with the Greek concepts of arsis and thesis, generally understood to indicate upbeat and downbeat but referring literally to the raising and lowering of dancers' feet. An association of upbeat and downbeat with the literal directions up and down was strengthened by the up-and-down conducting of the late Renaissance, and this basic shape has been preserved in the standard modern conducting patterns, as discussed above. More recently, Wallace Berry (1976) used arrows, clearly based on the motions of the standard conducting patterns, in his metrical analyses in *Structural Functions in Music*, but it is clear that these were not intended to have physical or gestural implications (328). In contrast, Steve Larson (2012, 148–49) explicitly connects conducting patterns with gravity in claiming that meter can be understood in terms of a metaphorical force analogous to gravity. In response to an article by Jonathan Still (2015), Robert Hatten (2015) tackles an important question of tension between theory and practice, the theory being Larson's metrical gravity and Hatten's (2004, 114–17; 2012, [21]) own use of the concept in terms of a virtual environment, and the practice being the actual motions of dancers, in particular when there is upward motion on the downbeat and downward motion on the upbeat. This issue is related to (but distinct from) the correlation between metrical strength and the releasing quality; as discussed in chaps. 11 and 12, the reversal of this usual correlation is a valuable expressive tool.

3. Although the specifics are quite different, in proposing that characteristic ways of moving can establish distinct categories within expressive profiles of pulses, focal impulse theory connects with the work of Manfred Clynes (1977, 1995).

4. It is often the case in auditory cognition that cues may be either discrete and localized or holistically distributed; identifications of specific instruments or speakers also depend on a wide variety of cues, some of which are more discrete than others (Handel 1989, chap. 8).

5. Another contrast between unitary and binary in the cello suites can be found within a single recording. In differentiating the two renditions of the first half of the allemande from Suite No. 3, Mischa Maisky (1999) uses (mostly) binary impulse cycles the first time and unitary cycles the second.

6. Chap. 11 discusses a case in which a similar shape is possible on a much larger scale.

7. When binary impulse cycles are used with one focal impulse per measure in a triple meter, this corresponds to the cases of compound duple meter already discussed.

11

MORE ADVANCED USES OF INFLECTED
IMPULSE CYCLES

THIS CHAPTER PRESENTS USES OF INFLECTED IMPULSE CYCLES that go beyond the basic patterns described in chapter 10. The first section discusses uses of inflected cycles in the inner periphery of the category of focal impulse placements, and the second section looks at a larger-scale use of the contrast between gathering and releasing tension.

11.1. Inflected Impulse Cycles in the Inner Periphery

The use of inflected impulse cycles in the inner periphery divides into two topics: the use of inflected impulse cycles with the placements discussed in chapters 8 and 9 and the use of impulse cycles in which the stronger beats are inflected upward. Of these topics, the first is more straightforward because most uses of inflected focal impulse cycles for placements from chapters 8 and 9 flow in obvious ways from the discussion of metrical placement in chapter 10. With impulse polyphony, for example, core uses of inflected cycles are found in all parts; and when heard meter conflicts with notated meter, core uses are employed in relation to the heard meter. Only two other comments are in order. First, when inflected impulse cycles are used with asymmetrical meters, the options for placement will be based on the number of beats per measure at the mixed level, paralleling common meters having that number of beats, with the further stipulation that all mixed-level beats receive focal impulses (i.e., not skipping one in a triple layer). Second, secondary focal impulses are not themselves inflected. Like primary focal impulses, secondary focal impulses come in widely varied shapes. But I have not observed consistent patterning in these variations comparable to the patterning of inflected focal impulses.

The use of tension-gathering impulses on stronger beats is a more involved topic. To summarize the basics of inflected impulse cycles, focal impulses can be inflected either downward or upward, focused mainly either on releasing or on gathering tension. The downward focal impulse and the cyclical focal impulse are focused on releasing tension, and the upward focal impulse and the upward cyclical focal impulse are focused on gathering tension. Downward and upward focal impulses stay in the released and gathered states respectively; cyclical and upward cyclical focal impulses return to the state from which they began. It is natural that downward-inflected focal impulses would tend to be used on stronger beats, given their greater maximum strength and the intrinsic stability of the state of released tension.

The usual correlation between metrical strength and downward inflection can easily be reversed, however. For binary impulse cycles, the upward and downward focal impulses simply trade places, with the upward focal impulses moving to the stronger beats. When this happens, we speak of *upward-oriented* binary impulse cycles. Unitary impulse cycles require the use of upward cyclical focal impulses in place of the usual (downward) cyclical focal impulses. (Upward cyclical focal impulses are notated by turning the notation for cyclical focal impulses upside down: ⋂.) The impulse cycles that use them are *upward-oriented* unitary impulse cycles.

Because the body is moving differently, the use of upward-inflected focal impulses on the stronger beats leads to differences in the sound of the music and in its expressive character, with gathering tension coming to the fore. With unitary impulse cycles, exclusive use of upward cyclical focal impulses replaces exclusive use of downward cyclical focal impulses, and with binary impulse cycles, the upward focal impulses become the more salient ones, partly because (as we will see in chap. 13) listeners focus more attention on stronger beats.

As a first step toward exploring the qualities of upward-oriented impulse cycles, we return to the discussion of conducting in one with all upbeats, which is to say that we start with the upward cyclical focal impulses. Recall from chapter 10 that upbeats can have either a tossing or a pulling character; this was demonstrated in video example 10.1. With the tossing character, the upward-inflected impulse can be quick, with sudden onset and rapid decay; this kind of upward cyclical focal impulse works well when the music should have a light and buoyant character. The initial theme from the *Pizzicato Polka* by Johann Strauss Jr. and Josef Strauss, shown in example 11.1, is a passage that could be well served by upward cyclical focal impulses that resemble light tosses. Video example 11.1 demonstrates singing the passage and conducting the impulse cycles, first this way and then with downward-oriented unitary cycles.

Example 11.1. Johann Strauss Jr. and Josef Strauss, *Pizzicato Polka*, mm. 5–8, reduced score.

Example 11.2. Bach, Partita No. 3 for Solo Violin, BWV 1006, Loure, mm. 1–2.

It is also possible for upward cyclical focal impulses to have the more sustained, pulling quality, as if pulling up on a bungee cord that is attached to the floor. The loure from Bach's Partita No. 3 for Solo Violin, discussed already as example 4.3, is a good candidate for gently pulling upward cyclical focal impulses. In video example 11.2, Paul Miller demonstrates upward and then downward cyclical focal impulses in the loure, and (as in the rest of the video examples featuring real performances) I conduct to help in visualizing the impulse cycles. Upward cyclical focal impulses are shown as option *a* in example 11.2.

In contrast to the muscular contractions involved in the tossing character, which are light and quick with rapid onsets and offsets, those used in the pulling character are more sustained, and they rise and abate more gradually, giving the pulling character a gently throbbing quality. But these characters should be understood as extreme points on a continuum, not as discrete categories; plenty of ways of moving may be found somewhere in the middle. Furthermore, even the more extreme cases have a wide range of qualities of motion. It is helpful to play with this range of possibilities as part of getting to know upward cyclical focal impulses; paralleling some of the exercises discussed in chapter 10, a good way of exploring is by imagining changes in the physical parameters of the imagined scenarios of motion. A ball can be lighter or heavier, a bungee cord can be looser or stiffer, and the activity can take place in fluids of varying viscosity.

The same possibilities for the upward cyclical focal impulse can be used for the upward focal impulse in the upward-oriented binary impulse cycle. In the case of the tossing quality, we can let the hand stay in the upward position after the toss and then move abruptly down to catch the ball again. Relative to the downward focal impulse placed on the stronger beat, this downward motion will be more like a passive letting go, less like a forceful downward motion. Relative to the upward cyclical focal impulse, the strong-beat upward focal impulse will have kept a bit more muscular tension after the offset following the toss, tension that is needed to keep the hand in the upper position; this tension is then abruptly released with the weak-beat downward focal impulse.[1] There may also be an active component to this downward motion, but in cases in which that active component is stronger, it will often be balanced by a more vigorous upward toss, as if tossing a heavier ball, in order to reflect the metrical hierarchy in the dynamics of motion. In all cases, the sense of priority between the two motions will be reversed. In the regular binary impulse cycle, the upward focal impulse exists to prepare for the salient downward focal impulse. But in the upward-oriented binary impulse cycle, it is the downward focal impulse that exists to prepare for the upward focal impulse that is the central event of the cycle.

A piece that could work well with upward-oriented binary impulse cycles that have a tossing quality is the *Radetzky March* by Johann Strauss Sr., a brief excerpt of which is shown in example 11.3. This music nicely demonstrates the contrasts between binary and unitary impulse cycles and between downward- and upward-oriented impulse cycles. Unitary impulse cycles will give the music a bouncier, jauntier feeling, and binary impulse cycles will have a more martial quality, lending themselves to a held-back beat in which the beat arrives at the last possible moment. Downward-oriented impulse cycles will sound heavier and upward-oriented cycles lighter. The two orientations of binary impulse cycle are demonstrated in video example 11.3.

When strong-beat upward focal impulses have the more pulling quality, the patterns of relationship with the weak-beat downward focal impulses will parallel those seen with the tossing character. After reaching a point of maximum velocity in stretching the bungee cord, the hand will slow down but

Example 11.3. Johann Strauss Sr., *Radetzky March*, op. 228, mm. 5–8, reduced score.

remain in the upper position, maintaining relatively static muscular contractions in order to continue resisting the bungee cord. (As ever, it is the characters of muscular contraction—the patterns of onset, sustain, and release—that transfer from the imagined scenarios of motion to actually making music.) These contractions will be released all at once as the hand moves rapidly to the lower position, preparing to pull again for the next strong-beat upward focal impulse. Because this downward motion is a focal impulse, some active muscular contractions will likely be involved, but they will generally be less intense than the contractions that create the upward focal impulses.

The loure was one of the first examples of uneven placement of focal impulses in triple meter in chapter 4; performed in that way, it can work nicely with either upward-oriented binary impulse cycles (shown as option *b* in ex. 11.2) or downward-oriented binary cycles. Both are demonstrated by Paul Miller in video example 11.4.

Pamina's aria "Ach Ich fühl's" from *The Magic Flute* (ex. 4.4) returns in video example 11.5, in which soprano Jennifer Miller and pianist David Keep demonstrate the same contrast between impulse cycles, now with the second focal impulse on the third beat of the triple metrical layer. Although the upward-oriented cycles are, for me, the most compelling option for this passage, the performance of downward-oriented cycles is noteworthy for projecting downward orientation clearly while avoiding the excessive heaviness that could easily come with it.

The norms for the metrical placement of upward-oriented impulse cycles are straightforward: where unitary impulse cycles would normally be used, upward cyclical focal impulses are used in place of the standard downward cyclical focal impulses, and where binary impulse cycles would be used, the positions of the upward and downward focal impulses are reversed. The one more complex case arises when unitary and binary impulse cycles are both used, which normally happens only when all three beats of a triple metrical layer receive focal impulses. As seen in example 10.2 and as demonstrated in

Example 11.4. Bach, Cantata "Wachet auf, ruft uns die Stimme," BWV 140, i, mm. 1–6, reduced score.

example 10.1, the most usual arrangement is for the cyclical focal impulse to come first, followed by the downward and then upward focal impulses. This arrangement is driven by the logic of putting the change in character from upward to downward inflection across the bar line. When upward-oriented impulse cycles are used, the same logic leads to the same sequence of unitary and then binary impulse cycles; this places the downward focal impulse on the third beat, so that the transition from downward to upward orientation marks the downbeat. This use of mixed upward-oriented impulse cycles is shown in example 11.4, from the opening movement of Bach's Cantata BWV 140, "Wachet auf."

This placement of focal impulses brings to the fore a feature of upward-oriented impulse cycles that has been implicit until now: upward-oriented impulse cycles are understood to begin and end at the point of released tension. Consequently, the requirement of complete impulse cycles stipulates that the units that follow one another are complete upward-oriented unitary and upward-oriented binary impulse cycles, each starting with upward-oriented impulses. In terms of individual focal impulses, this means that upward cyclical and downward focal impulses may each be followed either by an upward cyclical focal impulse or by an upward focal impulse, but an upward focal impulse may be followed only by a downward focal impulse.

Freer combinations of the various inflected focal impulse types can occur when we relax the requirement of complete impulse cycles, whether upward- or downward-oriented; this greater freedom puts these uses in the middle periphery. The most obvious motivation for freer combinations occurs in triple meter. In normal mixed impulse cycles, the first two focal impulses are inflected downward, and the third is inflected upward (or vice versa in the case of upward-inflected cycles). In the core, putting the contrast of inflection between beats 1 and 2 requires using only two focal impulses in the measure. If we want to have three focal impulses in the measure, and we also want to have the contrast of inflection occur between beats 1 and 2, we must use incomplete cycles. The opening of Bach's chaconne from the Partita No. 2 for Solo Violin, first seen in example 4.2a, offers opportunities for this. If the downbeat is given a downward character, beats 2 and 3 can contrast with it by using an upward character; as shown as option *a* in example 11.5, the sequence of focal impulses within the measure is then ↓ ∩ ↑. Here the sequence of (metrically strong) downward focal impulse followed by upward cyclical focal impulse violates the usual requirement for complete impulse cycles.[2] This same approach can also be used with the upward character falling on the downbeat, in which case the sequences used is ↑ ∪ ↓, as shown as option *b* in the example. Paul Miller demonstrates both ways of performing the passage in video example 11.6.

In the outer periphery, even greater freedom in the use of inflected focal impulses can lead to interesting expressive shapes. A mild example is the mixture of unitary and binary impulse cycles from measure to measure, violating the core's requirement of consistent placement. A passage that invites this is the famous first waltz from the *Blue Danube Waltz* by Johann Strauss Jr. The first measure of each four-bar unit is a 4/4 hypermetrical upbeat, and this can be brought out effectively with one focal impulse per measure in the pattern ↑ ∪ ∪ ↓. Given that this pattern repeats, the impulse cycles are eventually completed. This use of focal impulses fits the music better than consistent binary cycles would, given the harmonic and melodic stasis of the second through fourth bars of each unit. And while it may seem that the final bar breaks away from cyclical focal impulses for purely mechanical reasons, to prepare for the next upward impulse, the focal impulses

Example 11.5. Bach, Partita No. 2 for Solo Violin, BWV 1004, Chaconne, mm. 1–4.

used actually reflect distinctions among the measures, with the second and third continuing in motion and the fourth coming to a more settled resting place.

A larger departure from norms is suggested by Daniel Barolsky's (2007) discussion of Sergei Rachmaninoff's (1930) performance of the opening of the final movement of Chopin's Piano Sonata No. 2 in B-flat Minor. Barolsky (2007, [29], fig. 1) notes that Rachmaninoff's performance brings out a syncopation in the grouping, with a new measure-long unit beginning in the middle of measure 3.[3] Although the combination of poor sound quality and extremely fast tempo make focal impulse attributions uncertain at best, it is possible to hear Rachmaninoff's performance as suggesting a cross rhythm of three half-note beats starting in the middle of measure 3, felt against the background of the movement's alla breve meter, a more complex case than an alternative heard meter. Breaking out of the prevailing binary impulse cycles, this triple unit receives the usual treatment for triple meter using mixed impulse cycles, ↻ ↓ ↑. If this seems too uncertain to be called an analysis of Rachmaninoff's performance, it can be taken as a possibility inspired by his recording. Barolsky's work responds to Joel Lester's (1995) call to allow performance to inform analysis; we can follow the loop further around and allow recorded performance and published analysis to inform new performance. As might be imagined, these two examples only hint at the possibilities found in the outer periphery.

11.2. A Larger-Scale Contrast of Impulse Quality

Given an appropriate context, it is possible to use inflected impulse cycles to create more extended contrasts between gathering and releasing than are possible within a single inflected cycle. We saw a relatively modest example of this with Schubert's "Auf dem Wasser zu singen" (ex. 10.9); here the same thing unfolds on a much larger scale, suggesting a kind

Example 11.6. Tchaikovsky, Symphony No. 5, op. 64, i, mm. 170–74, reduced score.

of physical motion behind performance that would exceed the bounds of possibility.

Example 11.6 shows the beginning of the second theme from the exposition of the first movement of Tchaikovsky's Symphony No. 5. Binary impulse cycles are effective in giving this theme a tender, pleading quality, and if the pulling character of the upward focal impulse is allowed to affect the tempo, it can create a tenuto lengthening at the ends of measures 170, 171, and 173 that can be an expression of the indicated molto cantabile ed espressivo. The feature of the score that allows the character of the upbeat focal impulse to dominate this passage is the absence of melodic attack points on downbeats in the twenty-eight measures devoted to this theme in the exposition; all downbeats are either rests or ties from the previous measure. Inner voices also frequently lack downbeat attack points, especially in the earlier part of the passage.

In the first sixteen measures of the theme, the pulling of the upward focal impulses can be languorous, and the musicians can linger over this melody, pulling back in places to savor nonharmonic tones.[4] In measure 186, however, the upward focal impulses acquire a new function, as the music seems to be jolted out of reverie and begins to move insistently toward cadential closure (ex. 11.7). Now the upward focal impulses drive the increasingly headlong motion of the music, no longer pulling back but rather pulling forward, as the tempo and the dynamics both increase into the closing material in measure 198, with the wedge-shaped voice leading of the outer voices writing the crescendo large on the page. The tension created by this increasing weight of harmonic expectation—a sense of expectation that is heightened to the extreme

Example 11.7. Tchaikovsky, Symphony No. 5, op. 64, i, mm. 186–99, Molto più tranquillo, reduced score.

by effects of tempo, dynamics, register, and stretto—can be embodied in the sound itself by emphasizing the active, pulling character of the focal impulses. And, as noted previously, an emphasis on the upward focal impulses over against the downward focal impulses is facilitated by the fact that throughout this entire passage, the melody never places an attack point on a downbeat and never fails to place an attack point on an upbeat. If the music is played with binary impulse cycles aligned with the measures, the listener will hear the sound of downward focal impulses in each measure, sometimes in very forceful and characteristic ways, but always in accompanying voices, never in the most salient part of the texture.

In the final four measures of the second theme, coinciding with the arrival on the dominant pedal, the balance begins to tip toward the downward focal impulses. In measure 194, the horns and trombones introduce a fanfare motive based on the first theme. Although starting solidly on the downbeat, it is placed in the middle of the register, and the ear is still drawn primarily to the main melodic voice with its emphatic arrival on the high A. By measure 196, though, it is clear that the main melody has become a decorated pedal tone. Attention is easily captured by the powerful downward focal impulses used by the trumpets and oboes as they take up the fanfare motive in a higher register, marking the resolution of the cadential 6/4 and driving the harmonic expectation to a peak.

Although salient, the downward focal impulses of measure 196 are merely a foretaste of what will come in measure 198 with the arrival of tonic harmony. For the first time in this passage, the entire orchestra places attack points on the downbeat, and these attack points are marked triple *forte* and initiate fanfares and hunting calls. To emphasize the releasing character of this music, and because of the static repetition of the motives, cyclical focal impulses are used; tension-gathering upward focal impulses seem out of place on the second beats of these measures. In the passage that follows, the two kinds of impulse cycle will alternate. Massive though it is, this outburst does not seem sufficient to release the accumulated tension from twenty-eight measures of upward pulling, and so these figures are repeated over and over again throughout the twenty-eight measures of closing material and transition to development that follow, gradually subsiding in intensity of orchestration, dynamics, and register.

In some respects, the use of focal impulses in this passage has been extremely typical—focal impulses fell on dotted-quarter beats, and binary impulse cycles were aligned with the measures in ⅞. And yet, because of specifics of the construction of the music, the passage has the potential to suggest a huge twenty-eight-bar upbeat leading to a twenty-eight-bar downbeat. Beyond the interest this has for the performance of the specific passage, it can also partially rehabilitate an aspect of Cooper and Meyer's (1960) rhythmic theory that has often been criticized. Cooper and Meyer extended metrical processes to the highest levels of a composition, at which there might be, for example, a single downbeat followed by an afterbeat. Most contemporary metrical theorists agree that hypermeter is psychologically real only at relatively low levels, and they have tended to be critical of this aspect of Cooper and Meyer's theory—in many ways, rightly so. And yet this passage can produce effects similar to the ones Cooper and Meyer discussed. As in their theory, what we experience is not an upbeat time point that leads twenty-eight measures later to a downbeat time point but rather the character of upbeat and downbeat each distributed over lengthy spans of time. Although this does not blunt the main force of the usual critiques, it does show that some of the intuitions behind Cooper and Meyer's theory can be grounded in a theory of musical time and musical motion that operates on relatively short timescales.

This analysis has demonstrated that the strategic use of focal impulses can add a visceral dimension to a passage in which an increasingly intense and passionate yearning leads eventually to a cathartic release, with aftershocks that serve to further dissipate the accumulated tension. Belief in a connection between emotion and the physical motion of the body goes back to antiquity, and the more specific hypothesis that the physiological effects of emotions leave instinctively recovered traces in the sounds we make is now more than 150 years old (Spencer 1857). Given that emotional responses to music are extremely complex and come from many different sources, I would not want to claim that focal impulses account for more than a small part of the total picture. Nonetheless, focal impulse theory has the potential to illuminate certain aspects of a motional/emotional nexus of experience, a form of experience open not only to performers but also to listeners who perform along, their active engagement fueled by preconscious images of motion (Cox 2016).

Notes

1. The downward focal impulse that is mainly a release of tension within an upward-oriented binary impulse cycle raises the possibility of an adjustment to the basic definition of the focal impulse. Focal impulses were stipulated to be special kinds of impulses, with impulses defined as muscular contractions with noticeable onsets. But could a strong and salient offset of a muscular contraction also be considered an impulse, and could it serve the functions of a focal impulse? Although I do not think it happens frequently, it seems possible, especially if the release of tension results in the release of significant potential energy, as when the arm is released after being held in an upper position. If enough potential energy is converted to kinetic energy, it could easily fulfill the functions of a focal impulse, including injecting energy into the system and changing the momentum of the relevant body parts enough to largely erase any existing context of motion.

2. Note that it does not, however, violate the logic of succession that is based on the various impulses starting and ending at points of either gathered or released tension.

3. Although still quite limited in sound quality, versions of this recording are freely available online that are noticeably clearer than the mp3 clip included in the online article.

4. The rhythmic patterning of the melody, a syncopation within a hemiola (here usually felt in the notated meter), receives attention in chaps. 7, 12, and 15.

12

PERFORMING METRICAL DISSONANCE

CHAPTER 7 OFFERED AN INITIAL LOOK AT HOW focal impulses relate to the performance of metrical dissonance and discussed some simpler cases (syncopation and hemiola). With the resources of chapters 8–11, we now return to this topic. (Still more complex cases will be seen in chaps. 15 and 16.) Of the authors who have discussed metrical dissonance, Harald Krebs (1999) has given the most extensive consideration to performance issues.[1] (Readers unfamiliar with Krebs should consult the summary in sec. 2.3.) Krebs's expectations regarding performers and listeners are quite different. He believes that listeners will switch rapidly to whichever surface meter is dominant; he does not seem to think that there are any circumstances in which listeners could be expected to maintain a previously established meter when accents (broadly defined) tip a balance of evidence away from that meter (Krebs 1999, 45–47).[2] In contrast, Krebs seems to believe that performers should always hear in the notated meter. He is not explicit about the performer's hearing of meter as a perceptual orientation, but he emphasizes that in cases of metrical conflict, the performer should always "continue to *feel* the notated downbeats," and he makes clear that he means that the downbeats are to be felt physically (Krebs 1999, 181; emphasis in original). As should be clear at this point, I differ with Krebs regarding both performer and listener, but the disagreement results from building differently on a shared premise—namely, that conflicts between notated and surface meters are often purposefully used by composers to communicate with performers, and that such conflicts present opportunities to create more finely textured performances than would be likely had the music been notated more straightforwardly.

In the following discussion I consider three main cases: displacements in triple meter, displaced hemiolas, and half-bar displacements in duple meters. Before delving in, I explain my approach to these cases.

12.1. The Centrality of Hemiolas and Half-Bar Displacements

My basic claim regarding metrical dissonance is that hemiolas and half-bar displacements are the two most central cases: hemiolas are the most common grouping dissonances, and half-bar displacements are the most common displacement dissonances. (For displacement dissonances, the focus is restricted to cases in which a shifted meter is heard; simple series of syncopations within the notated meter were covered in chap. 7.)

Hemiolas are the most common grouping dissonances for the simple reason that they are least disruptive to the metrical hierarchy. Most metrical grids that have some triple layer have only one, and thus it is easy for this layer to trade places with an adjacent duple layer, leaving the rest of the grid intact. For example, the triple layer that is two levels below the downbeats in $\frac{6}{8}$ (the level of the eighths, at which every third eighth note is strong) may trade places with the duple layer above it to make $\frac{3}{4}$ (so that the triple organization shifts up one level from the eighths to the quarters). This change is not particularly disruptive because only two levels of the metrical hierarchy are involved; the downbeat level is the same, as are any higher, hypermetrical levels. (The reverse hemiola has this same property; reverse hemiolas are less common than hemiolas for contingent, style-historical reasons.) In contrast, if the duple layer of the quarter notes is made triple in $\frac{4}{4}$, this change will disrupt both the half-note level and the measure level, as well as any nontriple hypermetrical levels.

The reasons that half-bar displacements are the most common displacement dissonances are more complex. Generalizing from the viewpoint of Krebs (1999, 57), I assert that the disruptive effect of a metrical dissonance will have an approximately inverse relationship with the denominator of the fraction that describes the metrical shift as a phase shift. This makes a 1/2 phase shift in a duple meter the least disruptive (understanding *duple* loosely to include any meter that has a duple layer beneath the level of the downbeats). Next come 1/3 and 2/3 phase shifts in triple meters, and shifts involving finer-grained fractions (with larger denominators) follow. This basic picture is similar to Mark Gotham's (forthcoming) formal mathematical model of the strength of various metrical dissonances, and it is strongly supported by a statistical survey of metrical dissonance in Brahms's music (Ito, in preparation c).[3] Based on this picture, the main challenge to the centrality of half-bar displacements in duple meters would come from displacements by a third of a bar in triple meters; taken as fractions, the denominators are similar, and both involve shifting the heard downbeat to the metrical level one below the downbeats. I have two reasons for maintaining that half-bar displacements should stand in category by themselves; one is cognitive and the other historical.

The cognitive reason for a distinction between half-bar and third-of-a-bar displacement dissonances is that the greater number of weak beats per strong beat in triple meters reinforces the salience of the hierarchical distinction. In triple meters, the perception of the two weak beats as equally weak enhances the perception of difference between strong and weak beats; in duple meters, the fact that there is only one stronger and one weaker beat reduces the disparity between them. A social analogy may clarify this point. In $\frac{4}{4}$ and $\frac{3}{4}$ meters, let us take the level of the measure and the two metrical levels below this level and assign to each beat a military rank. In $\frac{4}{4}$, the first quarter-note beat is a sergeant, the third is a corporal, and beats 2 and 4 are privates. In $\frac{3}{4}$, the downbeat is a sergeant, the two weak quarter-note beats are corporals, and the weak eighth-note beats are privates. The $\frac{4}{4}$ measure has a sergeant, a corporal, and two privates; I would expect this to tend to flatten toward a two-level hierarchy, with the sergeant and the corporal grouped together above the two privates. Although they would retain their difference in status, the sergeant and the corporal, lacking company at their own rank, would tend to be lumped together as noncommissioned officers. In $\frac{3}{4}$, by contrast, there would be one sergeant, two corporals, and three privates. This arrangement would tend more to retain its structure as a three-level hierarchy. Because the two corporals each have another person to see as equal in terms of rank, the otherness of the sergeant will be enhanced.

The historical reason is that duple meters have a history of baroque-era metrical displacements that triple meters lack. As discussed briefly in section 6.2, much baroque music is rooted in the original use of the term *compound meter*—rather than indicating triple subdivision of the main beat, it expressed the understanding that some notated measures were compounds of two smaller "real" measures. For example, $\frac{4}{4}$ and $\frac{6}{8}$ could be understood as concatenations of two $\frac{2}{4}$ or $\frac{3}{8}$ measures, each of which had downbeats of equal metrical weight. Because phrase lengths (in units of half measures) were often quite irregular, the relative metrical strength of notated downbeats and mid-bar strong beats would shift back and forth, creating what would appear, from a modern perspective, to be displacement dissonances. In the first ritornello from the first movement of "Spring" from Vivaldi's *Four Seasons*, for example, the material first heard starting on the downbeat of measure 7 is immediately repeated in measure 10, but now it starts on beat 3. Arbitrary metrical shifts of this sort are extremely common, and an interpreter who is aware that the full common-time measure is hardly ever a meaningful frame of reference in a Vivaldi concerto will not understand this as a true displacement dissonance.[4] Over the course of the later eighteenth and earlier nineteenth centuries, this practice of composing in half bars gradually fell out of use, but shifts of metrical weight from the downbeat to the middle of the measure never entirely disappeared in the common-practice period. In triple meters, there is no parallel for this rival to the downbeat, either in theory or in practice. Theorists did not write of $\frac{3}{4}$ as a concatenation of three equally strong measures of $\frac{2}{8}$, and it was not common practice for baroque composers to write music that displaced the understood downbeat to a weaker beat in triple meter (hemiola being a different beast altogether—a grouping dissonance rather than a displacement dissonance).

Because simple cases of hemiola were considered in chapter 8, this chapter is fundamentally about various kinds of displacement dissonance. Based on the argument that 1/3 and 2/3 displacements of the heard downbeat in triple meter are relatively uncommon, it begins with cases of strong displacement dissonances in triple meter, finding ways to respond to the dissonance in performance while retaining the notated meter. It then considers examples of displaced hemiolas, similarly looking for alternatives to hearing and performing them as hemiolas within a displaced heard meter. The chapter closes by bringing the resources of chapter 11 to bear on the performance of half-bar shifts of heard meter. In chapters 15 and 16, we will encounter a variety of more complex cases, including additional displaced hemiolas and more subversive sorts of displacement and grouping dissonances.

12.2. Displacement Dissonances in Triple Meters

There are certainly cases in which the downbeat does shift in triple meter and in which it would probably be futile for the performer to try to keep the listener (or herself, for that matter) in the notated meter.[5] But especially given how unusual it is to encounter passages in which shifting is a foregone conclusion, it seems worthwhile to examine borderline cases closely to see if there are possibilities for feeling and projecting the notated meter. What might it mean to follow Krebs's (1999) direction to continue to feel the notated meter while vividly embodying metrical conflict? And is it true, as he asserts, that keeping the listener in the notated meter is a lost cause?

The most broadly applicable way for the performer to respond to displacement dissonances in triple meter while holding on to the notated meter

Example 12.1. Robert Schumann, *Faschingsschwank aus Wien*, i, mm. 87–94, Sehr lebhaft.

is by using shifted focal impulses, playing the displacement dissonances as anticipations. The first example of shifted focal impulses in chapter 9, from the Beethoven cello sonata, was an instance of this, and another good example is found in the first movement of Robert Schumann's *Faschingsschwank aus Wien*, a piece that receives extended attention from Krebs (1999, 213–19). In measures 87–94 (ex. 12.1), the downbeats are entirely suppressed, and it might seem natural to play these measures with focal impulses placed as if the meter were shifted to begin on the notated beat 3. Pianist Anthony Padilla plays the passage this way in sound example 12.1. But it is also possible for the performer to keep the notated meter and play the chords on the third beats as shifted focal impulses that sustain until a release on the downbeat, as in the analysis above the score. A performance with this kind of sustained leaning followed by a sudden release of weight is heard in sound example 12.2. I cannot explain just how a different physical approach to the passage led to differences of touch and timing, but the two performances clearly have significant expressive differences. To my ear, there are strong clues to the actual manner of performance in the quick releases after the attacks on beat 3 in the first recording and in the sustained quality of the third beats in the second recording. Again, conducting while listening helps bring the differences into focus; I suggest that readers conduct along in two ways with each of the recordings, conducting in one, either in phase or out of phase with the notated meter.

An alternative way of relating to this performance with sustained focal impulses is to use shifted and sustained focal impulses (as before) but to allow the heard downbeat to shift to beat 3. This hearing does not seem probable for the listener because it does not have any clear motivation in terms of the heard meter. But for the performer, this choice makes it possible to maintain a visceral link to the notated meter while hearing a shifted meter. Furthermore, because the physical behavior is the same for this option and the performance in the notated meter, it can be a good way to play both sides of the fence if the location of the heard downbeat is truly ambiguous. A good example of this is found in a video recording of the first movement of Brahms's Symphony No. 3 by the Vienna Philharmonic Orchestra conducted by Leonard Bernstein (1981). In measures 52–55, around 7:26 from the start of the video, we see what it can look like when focal impulses are shifted and sustained as the first oboist moves his head, torso, and arms while playing the offset dotted half notes.[6] The emphasis on quarter beats 3 and 6 that begins at the end of measure 50 will likely be heard initially as a gentle syncopation; however, as the passage proceeds, it becomes increasingly likely that the heard downbeat will shift backward to the final quarter beat of the bar, so that by the time the hemiola arrives at the end of measure 56, hearing shifted meter is virtually inevitable. The use of shifted, sustained focal impulses by the first oboist in the video can thus be understood as contributing to both sides of the ambiguity, just before the shift of metrical emphasis in the bassline that is likely to be a tipping point for many listeners. As will be discussed in my future work on Brahms (Ito, in preparation c), this way of performing has applications beyond triple meter; it can be used for any metrical shift by an amount other than half a bar.

This same solution, of using shifted, sustained focal impulses, can also be used when the emphasis is on beat 2, but in this case the metrical conflict is more intense, at least in part because the focal impulse must be sustained for so long with so little time for recovery. We will see an example of this, from the last movement of Robert Schumann's Piano Concerto, in chapter 15.

12.3. Shifted Hemiolas

In the previous section, the rarity of non-half-bar metrical shifts motivated the search for ways to perform triple-meter displacement dissonances in the notated meter. For the same reason, I now look for ways to preserve the notated meter (or at least an unshifted hemiola meter) when encountering shifted hemiolas—that is, hemiolas in which the strongest accent of the hemiola pattern does not coincide with the corresponding strong beat of the meter (e.g., a hemiola in $\frac{3}{4}$ that starts on notated beat 2, so that it is beat 2 of the implied $\frac{3}{2}$ hemiola meter, not beat 1, that is placed on a notated downbeat).

We have already seen one instance of a shifted hemiola understood in terms of an unshifted hemiola meter, in the discussion of Beethoven's Symphony No. 3 at end of chapter 7. Now we return to the strand left hanging at the end of that discussion. Recall the sforzando on the third beat of measure 28 in example 7.8, which we lacked the tools to deal with in chapter 7. We can now see that this sforzando would work well as a shifted focal impulse that responds to the anticipation. Given the way that it leads into a consistently syncopated passage, the sforzando invites the consistent use of shifted focal impulses shown in the example, with the other syncopations being understood as anticipations in a more extended sense.[7]

Another shifted hemiola is found in the movement "Grillen" from Robert Schumann's *Phantasiestücke*. As shown in example 12.2, which draws heavily on example 2.16 from Krebs (1999, 49), measures 61–66 feature a fairly consistent two-quarter-note periodicity, with periodic moments of alignment with the notated bar lines that arrive in the middles of subphrases, not at their beginnings. Example 12.3 shows one possible way of understanding the meter based largely on this two-quarter-note periodicity, with focal impulses based on the heard meter; in sound example 12.3, pianist David Keep performs the passage in this way. In measures 61–66, the heard meter is based directly on the two-quarter-note periodicity, with downbeats falling on the beginnings of the subphrases. In measures 69 and 70, the relationship between surface patterning and meter is more complex, with the two-quarter-note periodicity understood as a syncopation within a $\frac{3}{2}$ meter. There are two reasons for this. The first is the strong arrival of dominant harmony on the downbeat of measure 71, which clearly asserts itself as metrically strong (and which reasserts the notated meter). The second is the harmonic stasis of measures 69 and 70; because the strongly accented attack points do not bring chord changes, it is easy to hear them as syncopations.[8]

This way of understanding the passage is sensible, and many commercial recordings project a similar understanding of meter. Nevertheless, one aspect of the notation of the passage makes me suspect that this is not what Schumann intended, and that is the change of meter to $\frac{2}{4}$ for measure 68. If Schumann was willing to change the notated meter for a single measure, and if he intended this hearing of the passage, why didn't he make measure 60 the $\frac{2}{4}$ measure?[9] This would have "fixed" the seam between the first and second sections of the movement and turned the understanding expressed in example 12.3 into a simple aligned hemiola, making it much easier to perceive the implied meter.[10]

A clue to a different understanding of meter is provided by the simple observation that the beginning of the passage is based on an ascending circle-of-fifths sequence; as often occurs, the third iteration of the sequence, which would have contained the dissonant vii° chord in root position, is omitted, so that IV follows vi directly. Because each pattern in the sequence lasts for two measures and contains two chords, this suggests an underlying harmonic rhythm of one chord per measure. Example 12.4 shows a derivation

Example 12.2. Robert Schumann, *Phantasiestücke*, "Grillen," mm. 59–72, Mit Humor, annotations based on ex. 2.16 from Krebs (1999, 49). Adapted by permission from Ito (2013c), © Springer-Verlag Berlin Heidelberg 2013.

Example 12.3. Robert Schumann, *Phantasiestücke*, "Grillen," mm. 61–72, Mit Humor, rebarred, measure numbering based on the original. Adapted by permission from Ito (2013c), © Springer-Verlag Berlin Heidelberg 2013.

Example 12.4. Two-stage derivation of mm. 61–64 of "Grillen" from *Phantasiestücke* by Robert Schumann. Adapted by permission from Ito (2013c), © Springer-Verlag Berlin Heidelberg 2013.

of the passage from the bare ascending-fifths sequence. The starting point, shown in example 12.4a, is the sequence itself. In Example 12.4b, embellishments are added—harmonized neighboring motion in the first iteration, and a secondary chord and a more active bass line in the second. As a final step, the actual passage is generated by adding anticipations, bringing in the first chord of each iteration one quarter note early.[11]

Understood in this way, the notated meter is the heard meter, and focal impulses can be placed accordingly. In example 12.5 shifted focal impulses are used for the anticipations, and in sound example 12.4 David Keep performs the passage in this way. The differences between sound examples 12.3 and 12.4 are quite subtle; indeed, it is possible to hear either performance in terms of the shifted meter shown in example 12.3. But it is significantly easier to hear sound example 12.4 in the notated meter than sound example 12.3. This seems to be due mainly to the heaviness of the quarter notes in the middle of each iteration of the sequence in sound example 12.3, heaviness which results directly from the focal impulse placement.

This passage vividly illustrates the malleability of surface patterning. One of its shifted hemiolas is best understood as a syncopation within a hemiola, but others can be heard in multiple ways. As most commonly performed, the surface patterning dictates the heard and performed meter, so that the heard meter has both grouping and displacement dissonances with respect to the notated meter. But it is also possible to treat the surface patterning as a chimera that arises as the result of multiple adjustments to an underlying harmonic template that reflects the notated meter—and to perform and hear the passage on the basis of that understanding.

Together with the example from Schumann's *Faschingsschwank*, this passage also provides the first illustration of a basic principle: when surface patterning strongly conflicts with the notated meter, hearing the meter implied by the surface patterning is almost always possible, no matter how the passage is performed; in contrast, hearing the notated meter often requires

Example 12.5. Robert Schumann, *Phantasiestücke*, "Grillen," mm. 61–72, Mit Humor, focal impulse placements following the notated meter. Adapted by permission from Ito (2013c), © Springer-Verlag Berlin Heidelberg 2013.

that the performer be rooted in the notated meter, sometimes even that the performer try to project the notated meter. The asymmetry of these options contrasts markedly with the usual ambiguity in which, given two possible focal impulse placements, a performance can be heard either way. Here, it is not the case that the way the performer hears it simply may or may not be the way the listener hears it; rather, the performer gets to choose the degree to which the hearing of others will be constrained. If the performer chooses to let the heard meter follow the surface patterning, the listeners will likely be dragged along, no matter what their preferences are. Martha Argerich's (1979, 1:00) recording of the passage from "Grillen" is a clear instance of this; it would be difficult, if not impossible, to hear this performance in the notated meter. If the performer prefers the alternative meter, she can be confident that the listener will hear her performance in this way too. But if the performer prefers the notated meter, she has much less ability to impose this interpretation on the listener. David Keep's performance in sound example 12.4 can be heard perfectly well in the meter implied by the surface patterning; his performance opens the option of hearing in the notated meter, but it cannot insist that the listener choose this option. Moreover, I doubt that it would be possible for any performance to close the door to the meter implied by the durational pattern. In general, I prefer performances that take a strong interpretive stand: I am likely to have more appreciation for a performance that decisively advances a reading that I disagree with than for one that tries to leave everything up to the listener. I want to fully affirm the performer who makes a purposeful choice to embrace an alternative heard meter in this or any other passage. At the same time, it is helpful to recognize that the performer's choice of how to hear the passage is not just a choice about her own hearing: it is also a choice about how strongly to influence the experience of the listener, and of whether to open up options or to close them down.

12.4. Upward-Inflected Focal Impulses on Shifted Downbeats

My suggestion for the performance of half-bar shifts is to use the less standard form of inflected impulse cycles, with upward-inflected impulses on the stronger heard beats. This allows performers to place focal impulses in standard locations within the heard meter while also responding to the unusual notation. Using upward-inflected cycles for shifted meter can be particularly helpful when the location of the heard downbeat shifts back and forth repeatedly.

This practice gives the performer two seemingly incompatible advantages. On the one hand, from the listener's perspective, a shifted heard meter is not fundamentally different from an unshifted heard meter, and so it makes sense to employ an option that would also have been available had the music been notated as heard. But on the other hand, as mentioned earlier in this chapter, Krebs (1999) argues that such passages should not be performed exactly as they would be had they received more standard notation, and I agree—surely the composer had some purpose in selecting the alternative notation. By taking a less common option for inflected impulse cycles, we are making the performance different—different not in the sense of choosing something that we would never have chosen had the music been notated in the heard meter, but different in the sense of reversing the usual trends and choosing what is usually a less standard option.

Both examples from chapter 8 of half-bar shifts in the heard meter can be performed in this way. For the passage from the last movement of the Mozart quintet, upward-oriented binary impulse cycles are shown as option *b* above the staff in example 8.7. Relative to a more normal use of binary impulse cycles, this example reflects a double transformation. First, the heard down-beats are shifted to the middle of the measure; following the core practice, the focal impulses are also shifted. But then upward-oriented binary impulse cycles are used, and so the downward and upward focal impulses trade places. Like a double negative, these two transformations cancel themselves out, leaving downward focal impulses on downbeats and upward focal impulses on upbeats, just where they would most normally have been.[12] Again, bolded dots under the focal impulse notations indicate the heard downbeats. This kind of performance could be especially helpful for this passage. Given how squarely the repetitive rhythms fit into the simple hypermetrical frame, the downward quality could easily seem overemphasized if standard binary impulse cycles were used, conjuring up the hammering images from chapter 10 in a rather unwelcome context. (In imagining this, it is helpful to visualize the music re-barred to fit the heard meter.) In contrast, the alternative performance could be given the character of a light object repeatedly being tossed into the air, caught, and tossed again.

The fact that the double transformation results in upward-oriented focal impulses in the middle of the measure is one of the strongest of the arguments in favor of using upward-oriented impulse cycles for half-bar metrical shifts. We already have an association between the middle of the measure and upward-inflected motion, and this focal impulse placement essentially understands the metrical shift as transferring that quality to the heard downbeat. There is of course nothing necessary about the correlation of upward-oriented focal impulses with the middle of the measure. Downward-oriented focal impulses are often found there in the core, for reasons including the use of unitary impulse cycles and the use of two binary impulse cycles per measure. And in the periphery, they can result from the use of upward-oriented impulse cycles in an unshifted meter. Nonetheless, it is common to have a sense of lift in the middle of a measure, and our English-language terms *upbeat* and *downbeat* can be traced back to the arsis and thesis of Renaissance music, with *up* and *down* understood literally in terms of the arm motion of a choirmaster leading an ensemble (and even further back to similarly literal Greek meanings involving dancers' feet). There is then a strong intuitive resonance when we respond to half-bar metrical shifts by using upward-oriented impulse cycles.

The second example of half-bar shifts in chapter 8, the opening of the second trio from the scherzo of Robert Schumann's Piano Quintet, presents an opportunity to use upward cyclical focal impulses for a shifted meter; this is shown as option *b* above the staff in example 8.8. The basic figure here is less square than the one in the Mozart quintet, but it is repeated obsessively. Obsession could easily be emphasized in a performance using downward cyclical focal impulses, giving the music an aggressive, driving character.[13] In contrast, a performance using upward cyclical focal impulses would likely be lighter and more elegant. Both performances could work well, and the choice would probably depend on larger-scale interpretive decisions about the movement and the quintet as a whole.

In movements in which it is possible to hear shifted midbar downbeats, it is common for the heard downbeat to shift back and forth between the notated downbeat and the middle of the measure. This practice may well be a holdover from the arbitrary displacements of the downbeat in Baroque music discussed in sections 6.2 and 11.1, displacements that are better understood as hypermetrical than as metrical, resulting from the combination of half-bar measures with irregular phrase lengths. In later music, however, such arbitrary displacements are no longer the norm, and thus we have good reasons as interpreters to treat half-bar shifts of the heard downbeat as meaningful aspects of the music. In such cases, it is often effective to employ binary impulse cycles with two focal impulses per measure, switching to upward-oriented binary impulse cycles when the downbeat shifts to the middle of the measure. Doing this creates continuity, with the downward focal impulses always on the notated downbeats and the upward focal impulses always in the middles of the measures. The alternation of downward and upward qualities then becomes a stable background against which the heard downbeat can shift back and forth.

The last movement of K. 516 can work well this way. It is a sprawling sonata rondo, and the material shown above—the main thematic material from the A sections—is usually shifted, with other material in the A sections and the remainder of the movement heard in the notated meter. The third movement from the Schumann Piano Quintet is also a possible candidate for this treatment because the scherzo and the second trio are both heard shifted, the first trio and the end of the final coda residing in the notated meter. This movement is often heard in one, however; a performer who is drawn both to the regular alternation of downward and upward focal impulses and to a rate of one focal impulse per measure must choose between the two options.

When the metrical shifts take place at close enough quarters, interesting interactions can occur involving focal impulse placement, the length of the heard measure at the point at which the meter shifts, and hypermeter. In the opening measures of Sibelius's Symphony No. 2, shown in example 12.6, harmonic rhythm and (in some cases) melodic organization strongly point

Example 12.6. Sibelius, Symphony No. 2, op. 43, i, mm. 1–26. (*Cont.*)

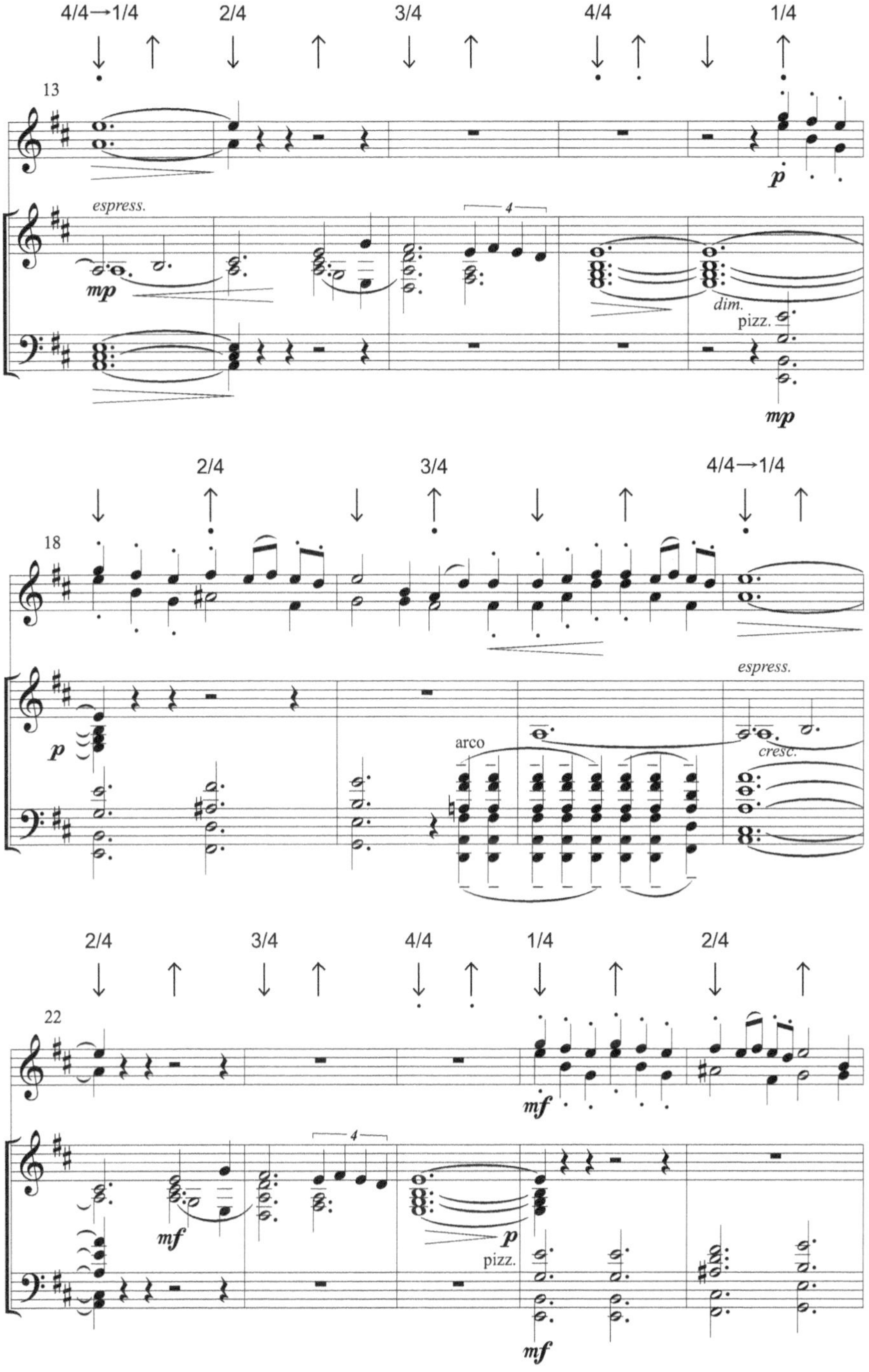

4/4→1/4
2/4
3/4
4/4
1/4
13
espress.
mp
dim.
pizz.
mp
p
2/4
3/4
4/4→1/4
18
p
arco
espress.
cresc.
2/4
3/4
4/4
1/4
2/4
22
mf
p
pizz.
mf

Example 12.7. Mozart, Piano Sonata K. 311, ii, mm. 1–11.

toward lengthened measures at the shift points.[14] As shown in the example, although the heard measures are consistently heard to expand, the hypermeasures alternately contract and expand, with a hypermetrical reinterpretation at the overlap on the half cadence.

The beginning of the slow movement of Mozart's Piano Sonata in D Major, K. 311, shown in example 12.7, offers a contrasting case, in which the metrical adjustments mainly contract the heard measure. In measure 8, the overlap between the cadence and the postcadential extension is placed unusually, and surprisingly, in the middle of the measure, so that we hear not a hypermetrical reinterpretation but a metrical reinterpretation, with the expected weak beat becoming strong.[15] Everything about the downbeat of measure 8, including the dominant harmony with cadential 6/4 and the preparation for a melodic descent from scale-degree 3, suggests that this is indeed a downbeat, specifically, the downbeat of the fourth hyperbeat in the hypermeasure, as indicated in the example. We expect a weak-beat cadence, paralleling the end of the first phrase. But the following beat becomes an early downbeat, so that the final measure of the phrase is contracted. And the end of the postcadential extension is similar, with the fourth heard downbeat again setting up a weak-beat cadence that is instead made strong (at least the first time, when the repeat is taken). This is demonstrated in video example 12.1, in which David Keep plays the piano and I conduct to make impulse cycles (right arm) and hyper-meter (left arm) visible. (In the video, we continue into the second theme, where notated meter is restored, now with an expanded heard measure.) The shifts to upward-oriented impulse cycles bring with them changes of color that I find particularly effective. In this example and in the Sibelius, use of binary impulse cycles serves to enhance both continuity and contrast when the heard meter shifts. It enhances continuity because of the regular alternation of downward and upward focal impulses, which serves to ground the music in something more stable than the heard meter. And it enhances contrast because the shifts in meter come with shifts in character, with differing metrical settings emphasized by differing orientations of binary impulse cycles.

Finally, an emphasis on the gathering of tension in the weak part of the notated measure can also help in dealing with cases in which the middle of the measure is emphasized without shifting meter. For example, when William Rothstein (1995) writes of a "shadow meter" in the final song of Beethoven's *An die ferne Geliebte*, he is explicit that he has in mind a consistent emphasis on the weak beat, not a new heard meter.[16] If performed with binary impulse cycles, these emphasized second beats will all have the pulling character of the upward focal impulse, nicely complementing the yearning that is both implicit and explicit in the text.

Notes

1. William Rothstein (1989) also gives substantive consideration to performance, but he does so by offering extremely sensitive ideas about the performance of particular passages—nothing that he says transfers easily to other contexts.

2. Krebs does believe a choice is necessary when there are multiple, conflicting meters available to be heard; Justin London (2012, 203n2) reports personal communication from Krebs clarifying that Krebs agrees with London's strongly argued case that listeners cannot simultaneously hear in two meters but must choose one.

3. An important contrast is that Gotham seems more oriented toward displacement dissonances with respect to a stable frame of reference than toward shifts of heard meter.

4. Put more precisely, it is not that the common-time notated measure is hardly ever relevant but that it hardly ever has an absolute priority that goes beyond local context; units of motivic construction lasting two half measures are quite common, and "Spring" starts off with several of them. This probably results from some combination of the notated measure as a salient frame of visual reference and the gestalt principle of grouping by twos and threes, with grouping by twos (in this case two half measures) the simplest option.

5. A number of such passages will be discussed in my future work on Brahms (Ito, in preparation c); an example in which a triple-meter shift is virtually inevitable is found in mm. 136–51 in the first movement of the Second Symphony.

6. Judging by ear, I would say that the first oboist is performing the C-sharp and the C in m. 53 an octave lower than notated. This same registral adjustment can be heard in all recordings of this movement made from the 1970s through the 1990s by the Vienna Philharmonic that I have consulted, and I have not found it in recordings by any other orchestras.

7. The accompaniment voices sustain the notes with the sforzandi into the following strong beats, so they actually are anticipations. And the melody is a compound melody, with the notes with the sforzandi understood to continue in the upper voice except at the end of m. 26.

8. In advocating for a hearing quite similar to this, Hatten (2002, 278–79) emphasizes the contrast between hearing mm. 69–70 as syncopation within a hemiola (retaining the notated meter) and Krebs's implication of a shifted hemiola meter in phase with the attack points.

9. Krebs comments in detail on how surface patterning makes m. 68 a strange place for a $\frac{2}{4}$ measure.

10. It would also greatly increase the likelihood of hearing and performing the passage in the notated $\frac{3}{4}$ (with that repositioning of the bar lines), and advocates for the understanding expressed in ex. 12.3 might well argue that this was the reason for the unusual notation.

11. This understanding also addresses two other issues with the hearing in a shifted $\frac{3}{2}$: the curious lack of parallelism among the beats and the ambiguity concerning the location of the downbeat. In the first and third iterations, any one of the three half-note beats could be heard as the stronger one; the factors at play are whether the first or the second chord in the underlying sequence is metrically stronger, and whether the second half-note beat extends the first chord or begins the second. The second iteration is almost as ambiguous, although there is probably a preference not to hear the secondary chord as metrically strong, especially because it is not included in the other iterations. It is mainly the continuation into the $\frac{6}{4}$ measure in ex. 12.3 that tips the balance in favor of the bar lines shown there, aided by a preference to hear beginnings as metrically strong. In the hearing that stays rooted in the notated meter, these issues are all addressed by the derivation shown in ex. 12.4.

12. Because of the double transformation relative to core placements, this use of upward-oriented impulse cycles belongs in the middle periphery of the category of focal impulse placements. Other similarly complex middle-periphery placements include anticipations used within a hemiola and the use of upward and downward focal impulses in ways that do not form complete impulse cycles, mentioned at the end of sec. 11.1.

13. The accents on the notated downbeats are tantalizingly elusive. Are they indications to the performer to stay in the notated meter, the listeners being most likely a lost cause? Or are they winking double negatives, weak-beat accents that end up on notated strong beats because of the metrical shift?

14. This is particularly clear at the end of the first statement in the horns, as the downbeat of m. 17 is not marked in any way. And although it is possible to hear a downbeat in the middle of m. 12, continuing the pattern established at the start of the movement, each heard downbeat since the entry of the winds has been marked by a harmonic change, and this one is not. Furthermore, the next beat, the first notated downbeat that is also heard as a downbeat, brings the first move away from the tonic pedal in the bass and the most strongly articulated harmonic change so far with the move to the root-position V chord for a half cadence. It is therefore easy to hear the middle of m. 12 also as the continuation of a $\frac{9}{4}$ measure. Interestingly, like the better known autograph to Mozart's duet, "Bei Männern," from *The Magic Flute*, discussed in n. 15, the autograph fair copy indicates that shifted heard meter was not part of Sibelius's initial conception, as bar lines fit the heard meter of the opening. Furthermore, the melody in the horns in m. 13 did not originally coincide with the final note of the oboe's phrase but rather followed it by half a bar, eliminating the shift of heard meter (Kilpeläinen 2000a, 218; 2000b, 207–8; Kallio 2001).

15. As mentioned in chap. 2, n. 24, Rothstein (1989) originally used the term *metrical reinterpretation* for the phenomenon that I call hypermetrical reinterpretation. Overlap with metrical reinterpretation within the measure happens a few other times in Mozart's music. In the second theme from the first movement of his Symphony No. 25 in G Minor, K. 183, we can add the (hyper)metrical reinterpretation at the overlap between the first and second thematic statements to the evidence offered by Grave (1985, 42–44) that Mozart was composing in half measures in this theme. There is a similar overlap of a weak-beat cadence (in the heard meter) in the coda of the duet "Bei Männern welche Liebe fühlen" from *The Magic Flute*. In this case, the heard and notated meters have been out of phase since the beginning, so the reinterpretation establishes the notated meter for the first time in the composition. This duet has received extensive attention because Mozart originally notated it with heard and notated meters corresponding until the reinterpretation; he later crossed out and rewrote all of the preceding bar lines (Laskowski 1990; Nowotny 1996; Perl 1998). Finally, Norman Wick (1994) has drawn attention to an example that makes a particularly close parallel with what happens at the end of the opening theme of the slow movement of K. 311. At the end of the first movement of the Piano Sonata in A major, K. 331, the coda is introduced by a metrical reinterpretation that moves the heard downbeat to the middle of the bar for the remainder of the movement.

16. Rothstein (1995), quoting the term "shadow meter" from a conference paper by Frank Samarotto, uses it to describe any regular conflicting pattern that may or may not rise to the level of an alternative heard meter. Samarotto (1999), in the published version of his earlier paper, is clear that he intends the term to describe only alternative meters that are actually heard as the main meter.

PART 4

CONNECTING FOCAL IMPULSE THEORY

13

CONNECTIONS WITH PSYCHOLOGY

AS DISCUSSED IN CHAPTER 1, THE THEORY OF focal impulses has an ambiguous status in relation to science, both attempting empirically accurate description and offering an extended metaphor. This chapter situates the theory with respect to existing work in psychology, starting to map out the areas of greater harmony and greater tension. The chapter begins with selected topics in music psychology: dynamic attending theory, studies of sonic and visual correlates of meter in performance, and the ways in which moving or watching motion may influence what we hear. It continues by looking at human movement science, examining three approaches and three particularly relevant experiments, and then moves on to speech science. Along the way, it briefly sketches the experiments that are being carried out to begin to test focal impulse theory. The final section explains more fully why the theory seems likely to be primarily metaphorical for longer timescales, and it explores how and why a mental image of the sort that focal impulse theory makes explicit could be helpful in projecting large shapes at slow tempi.

13.1. Dynamic Attending Theory and Studies of Metrical Hierarchy

Psychological approaches to musical meter generally affirm the reality of Lerdahl and Jackendoff's (1983) metrical grid, introduced chapter 2. Experimentally, it has received direct confirmation from Palmer and Krumhansl (1990), who found that listeners perceive the various beat positions within the measure using a similar hierarchy. And theoretically, it is central to the most thorough psychological account of meter, Justin London's *Hearing in Time* (2012).

The most prominent recent psychological investigations of the metrical grid involve the dynamic attending theory developed by Mari Riess Jones and various collaborators (Jones 1976; Jones and Boltz 1989; Large and Jones 1999; for accessible introductions, see Jones 1992, 2016). According to dynamic attending theory, meter is fundamentally about the deployment of attention in time. When a regular temporal context results in a listener following one or more hierarchically nested beat levels, attention is focused at the times at which beats are expected. In the model of Large and Jones (1999), tunable nonlinear oscillators produce periodic pulses of attentional energy; the more regular a temporal sequence and the longer it persists, the narrower these pulses become, representing the focusing of attention in narrower bands of time. This is depicted in figure 13.1, which is reproduced from Jones (2016); see especially the left-to-right progression of the lower layers. As indicated in the example, multiple oscillators with different periods may be simultaneously active; this hierarchical nesting is understood in dynamic attending theory to undergird the nested beat levels that we hear. More recently, in response to a growing consensus that auditory beat tracking involves the motor system, researchers both inside and outside the dynamic attending approach have proposed accounts of just how the two may relate (Patel and Iversen 2014; Large, Herrera and Velasco 2015; Todd and Lee 2015). They suggest that the phenomenon of beat tracking developed originally in relation to periodic bodily motion, and that virtual (perhaps abstractly imagined) motion is now able to substitute for actual physical motion. This helps explain why periodic motion is so common in response to music, and it also harmonizes well with focal impulse theory's perspective on the physicality of meter.

Dynamic attending theory is particularly relevant to focal impulse theory because it holds that attention can be selectively focused at higher or lower beat levels. Jones and Boltz (1989) coined the terms "future-oriented attending" for following slower beat levels and "analytic attending" for following faster beat levels; Jones (1992) makes the helpful analogy with looking at a work of art from different distances. Where focal impulse theory calls attention to the ability of the performer to put physical emphasis on various beat levels, dynamic attending theory calls attention to the ability of the listener to put attentional emphasis on those beat levels.

Taken as a whole, dynamic attending theory has strong resonance with focal impulse theory. Any support is tempered, however, by the fact that the focusing of attention on different beat levels is one of the least developed areas of work on dynamic attending, both theoretically and experimentally. As Jones (2016) acknowledges, the computational model of Large and Jones (1999) makes a deterministic mapping from sensory input to perceptual output, with no room for a listener's choice. This is not a retreat from claims about voluntary shifts of attention (Jones 2016, 133). There is no question that listeners are able to voluntarily change the way they hear metrically and that

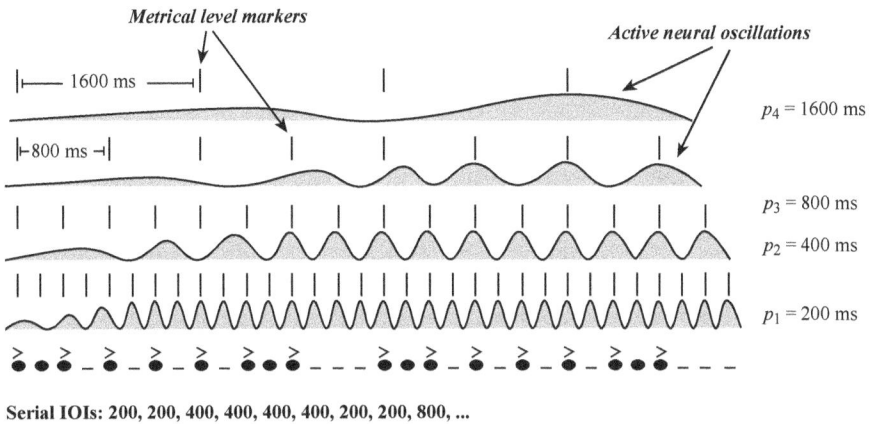

Fig. 13.1. Multiple levels of neural oscillation entraining to a rhythmic stimulus. Figure 9.3 from Mari Riess Jones, "Musical Time," in *The Oxford Handbook of Music Psychology*, 2nd ed., ed. Susan Hallam, Ian Cross, and Michael Thaut, p. 129, © Oxford University Press 2016. Reproduced with permission of the Licensor through PLSclear.

this changes their experience of the music.[1] Like all models, the model of Large and Jones (1999) is simply incomplete.

Experimentally, the central question about voluntary attentional shifts is perceptual: Do changes in attended beat levels lead to measurable differences in attentional acuity? This is an open question. Of the many experimental papers published by Jones and her associates over approximately forty years, I have identified only three in which the experimental conditions look at perceptual contrasts involving metrical hierarchy (as opposed to, e.g., the simple presence or absence of a regular beat or the contrasting subdivision of a single main beat); of these, only the most recent one approaches relevance to the question of attending to different beat levels (Jones, Boltz, and Kidd 1982; Jones 1984; Jones and Yee 1997). Nevertheless, the dynamic attending literature offers helpful models for possible experiments. Listeners could follow beat levels indicated at first by simple auditory cues, and because moving with a beat helps direct attention, they could move an arm smoothly in time with the beat. (Smooth motions help with feeling the span of time between beats, and slower beats are easier to feel with larger body segments.) Listeners would have to render some sort of judgment—for example, responding to out-of-tune or mistimed notes. I predict that following faster beat levels would be correlated with finer sensitivity to deviations, particularly those at weaker metrical positions.

When teaching about meter, I use a simple demonstration inspired by this kind of experiment. I play the start of the track "Move" from the path-breaking album *The Birth of the Cool* by the Miles Davis Nonet (1949), directing attention to the very fast quarter-note level (over 280 beats per minute) of the walking bass. I then direct attention to the typical swing ride-cymbal rhythm of a quarter note followed by two eighths; in the swing feel, it is typical to swing the eighths, alternating longer and shorter eighths. Restarting where the trumpet solo begins (0:35), I ask students to conduct in two (in half notes), and I ask whether drummer Max Roach is swinging the eighth notes. At the end of the following alto solo, I stop and let them listen again, this time conducting quarter-note beats (in four). Many students hear swung eighths when following the quarter-note beats but not when following the half-note beats, or hear them more obviously swung when following quarter-note beats. Readers can try the same thing to see if attunement to subtle differences is more sensitive when following faster versus slower beat levels. (As discussed in chap. 5, such gains involve trade-offs.) As it happens, the eighths are swung, but rather subtly. I have measured the average duration of the ride-cymbal eighths during the trumpet and alto solos, and on average they divide the beat 60/40. At such a fast tempo, the difference is challenging to hear, and shifting to a faster beat level can make a noticeable difference.

13.2. Traces of Focal Impulses in Sound and Visually Observed Motion

The second area in music psychology that relates to focal impulse theory is expressive performance. Meter is known to pattern sound and motion, and these patterns could be traces left by focal impulses. Because this research does not address the organization of motion, it is not direct evidence for focal impulse theory. But the patterns that emerge can lend support to the theory—or, in some cases, raise questions that challenge the theory. We will look at sonic patterns, at visual observations of motion, and at the ways in which these patterns can influence listeners.

Recall from chapter 5 the most straightforward sonic correlates of focal impulses: notes produced by focal impulses will often be louder, and durations that begin and/or end with focal impulses may be lengthened. Because focal impulses are so often placed on strong beats, this amounts to a parallel claim about notes on strong beats, and this claim is well supported. As markers of meter in performance, these patterns feature prominently in the surveys of psychological research on performance by Palmer (1997) and Gabrielsson (1999), and they have been used in algorithms for computer simulation of expressive performance (e.g., Livingstone et al. 2010). The patterns are widely accepted because they have been consistently observed: in the many experiments listed here, at least one of the patterns has been found, unless explicitly noted otherwise. The first group of studies involves laboratory performances of musical passages devised for the experiments (Gabrielsson 1974; Sloboda 1983, 1985; Clarke 1985, see also 1988; Edlund 1985; Talley 1989; Drake and Palmer 1993; Palmer, Jungers, and Jusczyk 2001).[2] The second group involves laboratory investigations using real music (Henderson 1936; Shaffer 1981, 1984; Palmer and Kelly 1992; Drake and Palmer 1993; Windsor and Clarke 1997; Penel and Drake 1998; Windsor et al. 2006).[3] Among investigations of laboratory performances of real music, only Todd (1992), looking only at loudness, did not find the predicted patterns at all. A final trio of studies looks at timing only in commercial recordings of keyboard music (Povel 1977; Repp 1990, 1998), with Repp (1998) looking at 115 recorded performances of the opening measures of a Chopin etude.[4] Only Gabrielsson (1987) looked for both timing and loudness patterns in commercial recordings, and he did not find them with significant frequency in five commercial recordings of a Mozart piano sonata.

In general, these results are consistent with a picture in which focal impulses, placed either on the downbeats or one metrical level below the downbeats, lead to loudness accents on the notes on which they occur and to lengthened durations on either side of those notes. The majority found the predicted patterns marking downbeats in $\frac{3}{4}$, marking downbeats and half measures in $\frac{6}{8}$, and marking either downbeats alone or downbeats and half measures in $\frac{4}{4}$.[5]

Rather than thinking of the experimental measurements as offering indirect evidence for the theory, it may be more interesting to think of the theory as offering an explanation for the patterns revealed by the measurements. In most cases, these patterns of variation have been understood in cognitive communicative terms, as aiding the listener in understanding the meter (Henderson 1936; Sloboda 1983; Clarke 1988). As we will see in more detail below, it is clear that they can indeed fulfill that role (Sloboda 1983). According to focal impulse theory, the patterns are also sonic traces of the ways in which physical motion was organized by the performer.[6]

Related to studies of sonic correlates of meter in performance but yielding more equivocal results are examinations of effects of meter on tapping. Among Bruno Repp's (1999a, 1999b, 1999c, 2002) many tapping experiments are some in which listeners tapped along with the fastest metrical level in very slow music. Because they were tapping below the level of a performer's main beat, it is possible that their taps were organized by focal impulses at a higher level. Repp's results are consistent with that scenario, with lengthenings just before and (less frequently) just after quarter-note beats.[7] This was not all the result of following along with a human performer; in many conditions, these effects arose while tapping along with metronomic, computer-generated performances, and in two cases while imagining the music and hearing only metronomic clicks (Repp 1999a, 2002). There is no way to know whether participants were actually placing focal impulses on quarter-note beats, but it is striking that the results conform to the corresponding timing patterns.

These results raise two questions: How does meter make a difference in tapping behavior, and are the sonic correlates of meter also found in tapping responses? Patel and his coauthors (2005) found that when participants tapped along with sequences that strongly induced both a regular beat and a consistent implied measure, downbeat taps were significantly better synchronized with the stimulus. In contrast, Repp (2005a) failed to find consistent markers of meter in either synchronization of taps or the variability of tapping when participants were instructed to vary locations of taps and of heard beats independently among various sixteenth-note subdivisions of the main beat; however, several factors suggest that some participants were consistently aligning the heard beats and the taps, against instructions. Regarding performance inflections, Repp and Saltzman looked in a 2002 unpublished study for both timing and intensity patterns when participants tapped rhythms that had strong implications of beat and meter, and they failed to find either. These tapping studies support the predictions of focal impulse theory much less consistently than the studies of actual performance. It remains to be seen if this points to flaws in the theory or whether the results stem from some specific aspect of the tapping task.

Turning now to visual observation of motion, recall from chapter 5 that while focal impulses seem to be overtly visible in many cases, there are also many cases in which they are not. And where they can be seen, they are often inferred from holistic patterns that do not yield a consistent set of cues; although they may sometimes line up with things like repetitive body sway, just as often the visible signs will take different forms over the course of a single phrase. Consequently, there is no short list of visible traces of focal impulses to complement the audible traces. It is therefore not surprising that the few studies of physical motion in performance that examine meter have had disparate results.

In the one study looking at meter that predates motion-capture technology, Clarke and Davidson (1998) found that although the period of a pianist's upper torso sway was not in synchrony with any level of the meter, gestures that were identified by viewers as carrying meaning tended to occur across bar lines. Among motion-capture studies, Wanderley (2002) found that the motions of clarinetists playing a passage from a Brahms sonata were heavily correlated with meter, but he regarded this as an artifact in relation to his main concern with expressive movement. As a result, Wanderley and his collaborators (2005) turned to an unmetered piece by Stravinsky; nonetheless, they report that in some passages, the beaming of notes had strongly metrical implications, and that this was reflected in the motions of one of the performers. Finally, in a paper by Windsor and his collaborators (2003) cited in Windsor (2011), two pianists had approximately circular motions of the head and shoulders at a period of one or two measures, and a third pianist nodded on each downbeat without moving the upper body.

One promising approach to visual correlates of meter in performance comes from a motion-capture study of dancing to music by Toiviainen, Luck, and Thompson (2010). Using mathematical techniques to extract prominent periodicities (Eigenmodes), they found significant periods equal to the quarter note, the half note, and the measure in $\frac{4}{4}$, with a tendency for larger and more proximal body segments to be involved in the slower-period motions. These results were confirmed and extended in a follow-up study (Burger et al. 2014). This approach could be used to look for longer periods of motion in music that moves predominantly in shorter note values, such as Baroque figural preludes, and I hope to apply this technique in analyzing the motion data from one of the experiments that I have conducted.

Some remarkable parallels with focal impulse theory are found in Rolf Inge Godøy's (2017a, 2017b, 2018) work on sound objects, goal points, and key postures. Godøy focuses on sound objects as sonic gestalts, which are understood to involve actual bodily motion in performers and (at least) images of bodily motion in listeners; these sound objects unfold on timescales similar to those of consequent spans (0.5 to 5 seconds). He focuses on the organization of physical motion in performance as central to sound objects, conceptualizing this organization hierarchically in terms of key postures that occur on goal points, with goal points occurring on downbeats and at other accented moments. Motion capture studies have been integral to the development of this perspective. Although only a few small examples have been published so far, this approach holds great promise for clarifying the nature of the events understood here as focal impulses.

Our final topic in this section is the effect of sonic and/or visual correlates of meter on listeners. Sloboda (1983, 1985) constructed melodies that could be understood in multiple meters and had pianists record each version. He found that listeners could match performances with intended metrical interpretations at better-than-chance rates, with performances by professionals more consistently matched than performances by students. Similarly, more experienced listeners made more successful identifications. Edlund (1985), in looking at notational variants of "Twinkle, Twinkle," also found many cases in which listeners could successfully identify the meter by ear. Palmer, Jungers, and Jusczyk (2001) found that musicians, nonmusicians, and infants could all distinguish performances of short, metrically malleable passages based on sonic cues to meter.[8] In a result that resonates with my recommendations for listening for indications of focal impulses, they found that musicians were particularly good at identifying performances of these passages when they were placed in mismatched metrical contexts, as the mismatch heightened the salience of the performance inflections. The greatest cautions about correlating performer intention with listener response come from the work of Martens (2012), who coached a student ensemble in performing passages with the same tempo but different main beats. Because Martens focused not on metrical interpretation but on choice of tactus, his work is particularly relevant. He found that an energy-based algorithmic frequency analysis of both video and audio recordings indicated that the quartet had been successful in shifting emphasis toward the chosen tactus. In a tapping experiment, however, only combined audio-video and video-only conditions led to significant differences in the tactus choices of participants (the audio-only condition also trended toward successful influence of performers' intended tactus, but the results were not statistically significant). Taken as a group, these experiments indicate that listeners are significantly influenced by the measurable differences in the sound and the appearance of a performance that result from performers' intentions about meter and tactus. When performing, more experienced musicians mark meter more consistently, and when listening, they have an advantage in detecting the audible signs of a performer's intention. Even in the most successful cases, however, significant numbers of listeners hear in ways that do not reflect the performer's intention, indicating that performers can influence—but not determine—listener responses. The listener retains considerable freedom in interpreting what she hears.

13.3. Influences on Hearing from Movement and Vision

This section looks at research indicating that our attempts to hear focal impulses may be influenced, and possibly even distorted, by some of the things that are meant to aid in the process—namely, moving with a beat that may carry the focal impulses and watching the motion of the performer where this is possible. This discussion amplifies the warning already raised in chapter 5. Again, I argue that we do not need to conclude that hearing focal impulses is nothing but a self-imposed feedback loop.

In a series of ingenious experiments, Phillips-Silver and Trainor (2005, 2007) demonstrated that bodily motion while hearing a metrically ambiguous rhythm significantly influences the metrical interpretation assigned to the rhythm. They presented both seven-month-old infants and adults with neutral performances of a rhythmic pattern that could be heard in either $\frac{3}{4}$ or $\frac{6}{8}$ and had participants make full-body motions while hearing the pattern; motions followed the beat in either $\frac{3}{4}$ or $\frac{6}{8}$. They later presented participants with two performances of the same rhythm in which the strong beats were marked with loudness accents; the two versions corresponded to the $\frac{3}{4}$ and $\frac{6}{8}$ interpretations. Participants had a strong tendency to indicate that they had previously heard the version corresponding to the meter that they had bounced to, showing that the motion had strongly influenced the interpretation of the ambiguous rhythm.[9] Similarly, Repp and Knoblich (2009) looked at the role of the keyboard in pianists' perception of the tritone paradox (Deutsch 1986), a psychoacoustic effect in which two computer-generated tones presented sequentially can be heard as either ascending or descending. They found that when pianists played the tones by pressing keys on an electronic piano keyboard and then were asked to judge whether the pitch motion was ascending or descending, a left-to-right sequence of keys pressed significantly biased them toward hearing ascending pitch motion. This effect persisted both when pressing keys on a computer keyboard that had a left-to-right progression and when watching the experimenters press the keys on the piano keyboard. As a result of the strong mapping that skilled pianists have between left-to-right motion and ascending pitch height, both making that motion and watching others do so can influence perception.

Looking at the influence of vision on auditory perception, Schutz and Lipscomb (2007) exploited a controversy among marimba players as to whether duration can be controlled separately from loudness by making a longer preparatory stroke. Based on their acoustic analysis, and in agreement with previous work, they found no difference in note length between notes prepared by long and short gestures. They then created videos in which video components of performances of notes intended as long and short were matched variously with the audio components of the same performances. Experimental participants consistently rated acoustic note duration based on the video component, despite having been warned that there could be mismatches between audio and video and having been instructed to base ratings on audio alone. Seeing a longer gesture created an auditory illusion of a longer note. Saldaña and Rosenblum (1993) performed a similar experiment, showing that seeing a cellist bowing or plucking a note can influence the perception of a sound as either bowed or plucked. Experimental results along these lines led Maes and his collaborators (2014) to theorize an interpenetration of processes of planning, executing, and perceiving movement.

This body of work should lead us to be cautious about interpreting what we hear. In particular, these studies reinforce the warnings about trusting first impressions, already given in chapter 5: considering that what we hear may well be influenced by the beat we choose to follow, by the way we move with the music, and by the ways we see the performer moving, it is important to listen with a variety of main beat levels and to check what we hear when we are watching the performer against what we hear when we close our eyes. In many cases, we may conclude that the sound is too ambiguous to allow us to judge focal impulse placement or type with any confidence. Bu in other cases, we may indeed conclude that there is a best fit. Although we can never be entirely certain about such judgments, it would be a mistake to retreat from reliance on our own hearing, instead trusting only things like algorithmic analysis of audio signals or visual inspection of wave forms. This is because listeners routinely make reliable auditory judgments—from the source of a sound to the emotional content of a vocalization—that make use of aspects of the sound signal that scientists have only begun the process of identifying. To take just a few examples, listeners have a decent ability to distinguish between men's and women's gait patterns by ear, with only some cases accounted for by the type of shoes being worn (Li, Logan, and Pastore 1991), and astronomers seeking to detect unexpected patterns in data regularly make use of sonification to "exploit the superior ability of the human auditory system to recognize temporal changes and patterns" (Walker and Nees 2011, 11). This is not proof for the reality of either focal impulses or their sonic traces, but it encourages us to temper our skepticism when thinking about just how much information we may be accurately perceiving.[10]

Furthermore, there is some good news about how our use of attention and of our bodies may assist in perception. Repp (2010) looked at the possibility that metrical accents could be illusory phenomenal accents—that notes heard as strong beats could be heard falsely as louder than they really are—and concluded that the results indicated instead heightened sensitivity on strong beats.[11] And Manning and Schutz (2013, 2015) demonstrated that the accuracy of temporal judgments improves when we move with the beat.[12] Taking these results together with dynamic attending theory, there is every reason to believe that moving with a beat allows us to hear some features with increased sensitivity—and makes us less aware of others. If we make a point of listening and moving with each of the plausible main beat levels, and having done so, if we feel that there are clear indications of the use of focal impulses, then there is no reason to think that we are merely hearing the echoes of our own preconceived notions.

13.4. Three Approaches to Motor Control and Three Experiments

In this section, we will examine relevant work in human movement science, also known as motor control, and review three sets of experiments that bear strongly on focal impulse theory: Bernstein and Popowa's examination of the relationship between rate and organization of motion in piano playing, Shaffer's work on hierarchical control of timing in music performance, and Sternad's experiments on discrete versus rhythmic organization of motion. In addition, because the dominant lines of thought in human movement science are not well known to musicians or scholars of music, I briefly introduce the three approaches on which the experiments are based: Bernstein's theory of motor control, the motor-programming approach, and the dynamic systems approach.

N. A. Bernstein's Approach to Motor Control

We begin with the pioneering Russian neurophysiologist Nikolai Aleksandrovitsch Bernstein (1896–1966). Although Bernstein's final works are already more than fifty years old, his thinking has experienced a renaissance in the past thirty years, with a number of his works being published for the first time or republished in translation; commentaries discussing the relevance of his work to contemporary motor control science have often described his ideas as being twenty to fifty years ahead of their time. [13]

At the most basic level, there are two lessons to learn from Bernstein. The first is that motor control is complex. In sketching the complexity, Bernstein focused on things such as the number of joints in the body, the number of muscles spanning each joint, and the fact that the force that a muscle exerts depends not only on the strength of the neural signal it receives but also on details about the state of the muscle. Today, this problem of complexity is often called the *Bernstein problem*. As one index of complexity, it has been twenty years since a computer defeated the reigning world chess champion, but robots have only recently gained the ability to walk with human-like gait patterns. The second lesson from Bernstein is that motor control is improvisatory. Bernstein's insistence on the improvisatory nature of motor control came in response to the more static views of his predecessor Ivan Petrovich Pavlov (1849–1936); Pavlov's theories may seem familiar to musicians, despite their age. Pavlov's basic idea was that each action corresponds to some set of neural pathways from the motor areas of the brain to the relevant body parts; if you want an action to become stable and habitual, you must practice the action in exact form to strengthen the neural connections. Bernstein had two problems with this static picture. The first problem was that even if we perform a familiar action, differences in contextual details will often require differences in motion. In many everyday tasks, although the specifics may be new, we succeed on the first try. For example, I like to run on irregular, bumpy trails used mainly by mountain bikers, and when I was recently joined by a friend from out of town, no one observing us could have known which of us was experienced with that particular terrain. Of course, none of this applies to the highly scripted movements of musicians; the violinist always puts her fingers down in exactly the same places—until the strings go out of tune. Bernstein's second problem was that real motor learning rarely looks like a process of static repetition. When children learn to ride bicycles, they spend a good amount of time swaying wildly back and forth and falling frequently until, at some point, there is a rapid transition to skilled riding. Somehow all of the unskilled attempts contribute to the sudden appearance of an ability to do something they had not done before. For Bernstein ([1991] 1996, 228), motor ability was the ability to come up with something new, and the pinnacle was dexterity, which he understood to be the ability to improvise rapid, graceful actions that effectively respond to unexpected challenges.

It should be clear that Bernstein's fundamentally improvisatory view of motor skill has implications for musicians. Bernstein saw motor improvisation as crucially guided by sensory information, and this on the basis of goals. It follows that the specifics of our goals will affect the outcomes. If we focus on consistent movement as a proxy for consistent sound, we will encounter difficulties when the usual movements are either impossible or useless (e.g., shaking hands, out-of-tune strings). But if we focus on sound, our bodies will be able to come up with novel solutions to novel challenges. The article from which this discussion is adapted (Ito 2013b) suggests ways to practice motor improvisation, making the desired sounds in new contexts of motion. For present purposes, however, we are ready to move on to Bernstein's experiment.

Many musicians, motivated by implicitly Pavlovian views of motor learning, go to great lengths to avoid ever looking like children learning to ride bicycles. If they cannot perform the motion correctly at tempo, they slow it down until they can. This may often be an effective practice technique, but it is not because they are performing exactly the same task at a slower rate. This was demonstrated by Bernstein and Popowa (1929). Using an early method of recording movement, they collected data from famous pianists performing two basic tasks, each of which involved playing repeated octaves in notes of equal notated duration and unchanging pitch. In the first task, the pianists were asked to play an accelerando followed by a ritardando, starting adagio, going to prestissimo, and returning. In the second task, they played at a constant, moderate tempo and played a crescendo followed by a diminuendo, starting *pianissimo*, going to *fortissimo*, and returning.

Bernstein and Popowa found that in the crescendo test, pianists showed only quantitative changes over the course of the task, changing amplitudes of motion but not the basic biodynamic construction of the movement. In the accelerando test, however, they found three distinct types of movement composition, corresponding to slow, medium, and fast tempi. When playing the octaves slowly, the pianists employed isolated impulses with pauses in between. At a medium tempo, these impulses united to form continuous chains, with active impulses coming from both the wrist and the elbow and with hand-arm coordination suggesting the dynamics of coupled pendula. At fast tempi, the wrist muscles abandoned the active impulses and simply produced static isotonic contractions, so that the hand underwent harmonic motion driven by the lower arm. Bernstein and Popowa thus disproved the theory that slow practice was advantageous on the grounds that it allowed careful self-observation by the pianist. Because the dynamic construction of the movement is radically altered by the change in tempo, a pianist playing slowly can observe himself carefully, but he is not performing the same movements.[14] The result that different speeds of motion require different kinds of organization will be important when we take up a larger-scale empirical evaluation of focal impulse theory in the final section of this chapter.

Motor Programming and Henry Shaffer

Turning to more contemporary approaches to human movement, we find that researchers have not agreed on a single overarching framework. This is not surprising, given the complexity of the topic. The field of motor control is currently in the aftermath of a major methodological conflict that occurred in the late 1970s through the early 1990s between the older motor-programming approach and the newer dynamic systems approach (Meijer and Roth 1988; Abernethy and Sparrow 1992). It is generally agreed that both approaches have important strengths and that any future consensus paradigm will need to incorporate aspects of both, but no consensus has yet emerged. Consequently, many current researchers focus mainly on specific cases, aware of larger questions but spending less effort theorizing at a high level of generality.[15]

The older approach is known variously as the motor-programming approach, motor-system theory, and the information-processing approach to motor control. Its development reached maturity in Schmidt (1975), with significant milestones in papers by Keele (1968), Adams (1971), and Pew (1974). According to Keele, "the concept of a motor program may be viewed as a set of muscle commands that are structured before a movement sequence begins" (387). Under Schmidt's theory (1975), a person preparing to move would activate a relevant schema—that is, a rule-based procedure for generating a motor program for any one of a general class of related actions (e.g., a forehand swing in tennis). The schema's input would include the initial conditions of the body and of the environment and also the precise details of the desired action. The schema would then generate two things: a motor program intended to produce the desired motion, and expectations about the sensory consequences of action. Given sufficient time, sensory information about the unfolding motion could be compared with predictions and used for real-time corrections.[16] This work had a strongly cognitive orientation, concerned mainly with high-level processes. A black box enclosed lower-level questions such as just how higher-level brain areas figured out what to tell the relevant body parts to do, a black box that was prominent in critiques of the approach.

The most relevant work within the motor-programming approach is by Henry Shaffer (1980, 1981, 1982, 1984; Shaffer, Clarke, and Todd 1985) on the hierarchical control of timing in music performance. (Though couched strongly in the paradigms of the motor-programming approach, the results also fit well within the dynamic systems approach.) Building on work by Lashley (1951), Shaffer (1980, 443) summarized his approach to motor programming as follows: "The basic idea of motor programming is that a sequence of movements can be coordinated in advance of their execution to form a single complex action. An extension of this idea is that a large-scale performance may be organized as a sequence of superordinate actions; another extension is that the principle of coordination may apply recursively, so that a motor program constructs an intended performance as a hierarchy of units." Shaffer believed that the construction of the higher-level action units was at least a two-stage process, with a first stage generating a relatively abstract structural description of the output, and a second generating the actual movements needed to bring about the desired output (Shaffer 1978).

Working within this framework, Shaffer, Clarke, and Todd (1985) proposed that time keeping in piano playing occurs on two levels. At the higher level, a timekeeper generates a clock-like sequence of temporal markers that is aligned with some level of the meter. These markers are not isochronous but rather expressively timed. At the lower level, timing is not controlled directly but is the result of motor procedures that are primarily concerned with generating patterns of movement (Shaffer 1982, 1984; Clarke 1985).[17] This theory has been supported with timing data from performances of Bach (Shaffer 1981), Beethoven and Chopin (Shaffer 1984), and Satie (Shaffer, Clarke, and Todd 1985).

The basic idea behind the data analysis is that if timing is indeed controlled at some level of beat, then variations in the timings of the next smaller metrical spans should be negatively correlated. That is, if timing is controlled at the level of the quarter note, then if the first eighth note within a quarter-note beat is performed slightly longer as a result of random fluctuation, the second eighth note should compensate by being slightly shorter, in order to preserve the duration of the quarter-note beat.[18] This basic idea of demonstrating hierarchical control of timing by comparing the variability of different temporal intervals was also pursued by Vorberg and Hambuch (1984), who showed that when tapping repeated nonisochronous rhythms, the measure-long spans from downbeat to downbeat (as opposed, e.g., to from beat 2 to beat 2) show the least variability.

In general, the theory of Shaffer, Clarke, and Todd (1985) seems friendly to focal impulse theory. Under their theory, timing control "lives" at one level of the metrical structure, just as I claim that focal impulses do, and in most cases the metrical levels identified by their timing analyses are musically sensible levels for the focal impulses to occupy. It is possible that timing control (at the level of beats) and motor control (at the level of the consequent spans) are two aspects of the same process, with focal impulses occupying the beats whose timing is controlled.

Enthusiasm for such a correspondence is tempered by tensions between Shaffer's results and focal impulse theory, however. In examining sight-read performances of a Bach fugue, the level identified as the level of timing control was not the same as the level at which the timing profile displayed typical indications of focal impulse placement (Shaffer 1981). And analysis of a performance of a Bartók dance with an asymmetrical meter in the same article did not find timing control at the mixed level, as would be predicted based on the discussion in chapter 8. I hope to run similar experiments at some point, looking at the relationship between hierarchical timing control and instructed main beat level. It would be particularly interesting to look at cases of triple meter in which two focal impulses are used in each measure, as this case of asymmetrical beat spans would be very different from the Bartók studied by Shaffer. Bengtsson and Gabrielsson (1980) speculated that, from a psychological point of view, a long-short pattern in triple meter might be understood in some cases as an unequal duple pattern, but to my knowledge this suggestion has not been pursued further.[19]

Dynamic Systems and Dagmar Sternad

The motor-programming approach was challenged starting in the late 1970s by what would become known as the dynamic systems approach. Two main streams came together to form the dynamic systems approach, one conceptual and philosophical and the other rooted in experimentation and mathematical modeling. The conceptual stream combined Bernstein's (1967, [1991] 1996) perspective on motion, discussed earlier, with Gibson's (1966, 1979) mature ecological psychology.[20] Bernsteinian and Gibsonian approaches were first combined by Turvey (1977), who proposed a model in which information about the environment is not processed by the central executive areas of the brain (as in Schmidt's schema theory) but rather fed directly to the relevant lower-level system, which both processes environmental information and generates movement commands. This new approach was called the *action-system* approach, in contrast to the earlier *motor-system* approach, because of its integrated view of perception, intention, and action. Action-system theorists distributed intelligence rather than centralizing it, and they took a more holistic view of action and perception, rejecting accounts in which "the motor system is the chattel of the sensory system" (Turvey 1977, 211–12).

The intellectual force of the action-system approach was greatly expanded with the publication of two key papers in 1980 (Kelso et al. 1980; Kugler, Kelso, and Turvey 1980). These papers marked the birth of the dynamic systems approach, which uses the dynamics of nonlinear systems to model voluntary motion. The basic idea is that when certain kinds of mathematics are used to model the dynamics of physical motion, certain typical patterns of coordinated motion emerge as stable regions within the systems of nonlinear differential equations. This approach can account, for example, for discrete phase relationships observed in quadruped locomotion, the motions of fish swimming, and human bimanual rhythmic activities (Turvey and Carello 1996). The demands on the intelligence of the central executive are greatly reduced in this approach, because typical patterns of movement coordination are revealed as emergent properties of dynamic systems. There is no need in such cases for control of the details of these patterns, only for selection from a finite set of possibilities.

One of the most prominent early papers in the dynamic systems approach is by Haken, Kelso, and Bunz (1985), who modeled the effects reported by Kelso (1984). The earlier paper provides a window into the dynamic systems approach because readers can replicate the experiment themselves. Hold up both hands with palms facing each other, extend the index fingers, and move them from back and forth, flexing and extending the base knuckle joint as if tapping. Begin at a comfortable tempo and move the fingers so that, with respect to the field of vision, both move right or left at the same time, like windshield wipers. Although the fingers move in the same direction at the same time from the perspective of the viewer, they are moving in opposite directions relative to the hands, as when the left index finger is moving toward the right hand, the right index finger is moving away from the left hand. Because of this, the windshield-wiper pattern is called *antiphase*, and the opposite, in which the fingers move symmetrically with respect to the hands, is called *in phase*. Kelso asked participants to start at a comfortable tempo and then gradually accelerate; at some point, the task would become difficult, and as the motion got faster and faster, the fingers would switch to an in-phase alignment, sometimes with a period of unstable patterning in between. In-phase motion is possible from very slow to very fast rates, but antiphase motion is possible only at slow to moderate rates.

The dynamic systems approach originated as an approach to movement, but it is now employed broadly in psychology (Thelen and Smith 1994; Port and van Gelder 1995). In music, its most prominent application is in modeling the attentional oscillators of dynamic attending theory.[21] Principal sources are Large and Jones (1999), Large (2000), and Large and Palmer (2002). Discussions of the mathematical aspects of the work intended for the nonspecialist are included in Large (2008) and Large (2010), the latter giving more detail.

Within human movement science, the dynamic systems work that is most relevant to focal impulse theory—and that provides a model for some experiments currently being conducted to test the theory—is a series of experiments by Dagmar Sternad and various collaborators (Sternad, Dean, and Schaal 2000; Sternad et al. 2002; de Rugy and Sternad 2003; Sternad and Dean 2003; Wei, Wertman, and Sternad 2003; Schaal et al. 2004). Together with several related papers (Adamovich, Levin, and Feldman 1994; Michaels and Bongers 1994; Latash 2000; Staude, Dengler, and Wolf 2002), this work examines the relationship between discrete and rhythmic motions. In the common terminology of movement science, a rhythmic motion is not rhythmic in the musical sense but rather a sequence of motion that involves periodic repetition; a discrete motion is a motion that is not repeated, sometimes but not necessarily performed in isolation from other movements. This research has probed the dynamic organization of repetitive, cyclical motions by means of discrete motions that are initiated while the rhythmic motions are in progress. Participants in Sternad's experiments made oscillatory motions of the forearm between two targets on a flat surface, paced at first by a metronomic signal. At random points within the cycle of motion, they heard an interrupting signal that cued them to respond with a discrete motion, in most conditions as quickly as possible.

In general, the results of Sternad's experiments showed an influence on the discrete motion from the previous periodic motion. Participants were not completely locked into the periodic motion, as there were no points within the phase of the ongoing motion at which no discrete responses occurred; however, the responses were also not evenly distributed with respect to the periodic motion, as they would have been if the periodic motion had had no influence on the discrete motion. Instead they found modal distributions, with responses tending to cluster in about a quarter of the phase space.[22]

At a simple level, these results show that an ongoing periodic motion has a pervasive influence on other motion, indicating its importance for motor organization. More fundamentally, in combination with results related to brain activation (Schaal et al. 2004), the results of Sternad's experiments demonstrated that repetitive motion involves a true hierarchy. A back-and-forth motion is not simply a series of discrete motions—forth + back + forth + back, etc.—but rather is organized in relation to complete periods of motion—(forth + back) + (forth + back), etc. This result invites exploration of deeper levels of motor hierarchy. If musicians were instructed to feel a main beat that had a period of four motions, would their motion be organized as (forth + back + forth + back) + (forth + back + forth + back)? I am currently investigating this question in one of the original experiments being carried out to test focal impulse theory.

A more recent result relating to Sternad's work with discrete and rhythmic motions looks at rate limits on rhythmic motions. In research that resonates strongly with Bernstein and Popowa's (1929) study of pianists, Park and his collaborators (2017) asked participants to synchronize a cyclical forearm motion with a metronome that varied in period between 1 and 6 seconds. They found evidence of a distinction between faster motions organized as continuous, periodic motions and slower motions organized by stringing together individual discrete motions, with a transition around 3 seconds. This result will be important when we consider how literally to take focal impulse theory in section 13.6.

13.5. Hierarchical Motor Organization in Speech

This section takes up the possibility that the motor organization of speech may offer support for the theory of focal impulses. Just as the theory of focal impulses holds that the motion of music performance is organized around focal impulses, these theories explore the possibility that speech may be organized around stressed syllables, proceeding at a physical level from stressed syllable to stressed syllable in a way that parallels a performer proceeding from focal impulse to focal impulse. We will look at the distinction between stress-timed and syllable-timed languages and at some studies of language from a dynamic systems perspective; I draw on the dynamic systems approaches to language in one of the original experiments currently under way.

When thinking about the rhythmic organization of speech, linguists often make use of a proposed distinction between stress-timed languages, such as English, and syllable-timed languages, such as French. It has been suggested that in stress-timed languages, the timing of speech is organized in terms of the stressed syllables, with the stressed syllables falling approximately evenly in time; in syllable-timed languages, the timing is proposed to be simpler, with each individual syllable approximately equally spaced and no special rhythmic role for the stressed syllables. This claim was introduced in linguistics by Kenneth L. Pike (1945), who drew on some significantly older precedents. Aniruddh Patel (2008, 118–54) gives a thorough and readable history of the distinction between stress-timed and syllable-timed languages in his book *Music, Language, and the Brain*, and one of the central points is that neither of Pike's claims about isochrony have turned out to be empirically accurate (Roach 1982; Bertinetto 1989). Although stress-timed languages are not currently understood to use equal temporal intervals between stresses, researchers continue to pursue the idea that the languages grouped together by Pike and subsequent investigators do share some basic rhythmic commonalities, with fruitful measures including the percentage of the speech signal occupied by vowels, the variability of stretches of sequential consonants, and the degree of contrast between successive vowel durations (Patel 2008, 126–35). Some of the best evidence for these language groupings comes from studies of perception in which the effects of contrasting phonemic vocabularies are eliminated or masked; neither adults (Ramus and Mehler 1999) nor infants (Nazzi, Bertoncini, and Mehler 1998) can distinguish between languages belonging to the same category (stress-timed or syllable-timed, and others in some cases), but they can distinguish between languages that belong to different categories.

From the standpoint of focal impulse theory, it is immaterial whether or not the stressed syllables in stress-timed languages are equally spaced in time; it is the idea of motor organization from stressed syllable to stressed syllable that makes the parallel striking. And although it has yet to be demonstrated that these languages are actually organized in this way, additional commonalities between stressed syllables and focal impulses motivate further pursuit of a possible link. For example, when English speakers omit a syllable, it is often an unstressed syllable that is dropped, and when a stressed syllable is omitted, the stress shifts to an adjacent syllable (Cutler 1980). It seems that it is easy to skip over an unstressed syllable in a run of them, but when a stressed syllable is omitted, the stress cannot simply disappear. Making a clear analogy with focal impulses on strong-beat rests, a stress around that location is still needed for organizational purposes, and so the stress shifts to a nearby syllable. In another parallel, here with the development from the note-to-note performance of beginners to the integrated sequences of advanced musicians, the speech of English-speaking toddlers has less syllable-to-syllable variation in timing than that of their mothers; French speaking children and adults show no such contrast (Grabe, Post, and Watson 1999). This result seems to point to the use of hierarchical motor organization as a developmental achievement in both music and language. But it also sounds a cautionary note: adult speakers of French should not be placed in a category with early childhood English speakers, both having a syllable-by-syllable organization of speech. Adult French speakers surely organize their speech into larger chunks, but however they do this, it does not seem to have a privileged place for stressed syllables. Similarly, as indicated in chapter 1, there may well exist ways of organizing motion in music performance that do not make use of focal impulses.

The second topic related to hierarchical motor organization in speech is the use of dynamic systems approaches to rhythm in language, particularly in work by Fred Cummins and Robert Port (1998) and Heather Rusiewicz (2011).

Although rhythm in language is not usually governed by a regular beat, Cummins and Port (1998) found that when English speakers were asked to repeat short phrases over and over, they naturally fell into patterns in which the stressed syllables aligned not only with a regular beat but also with larger metrical patterns—for example, falling on beats 1 and 3 in a triple meter. They further probed this phenomenon in an experiment in which participants were given short phrases such as "big for a duck" and asked to synchronize the stressed syllables with two auditory cues. The first cue was aligned with the first stressed syllable, and it defined a constant period with which the phrase was repeated. The second cue was specified as the location of the second syllable; with the full period represented by the interval from 0 to 1, the second cue ranged in phase position from 0.3 to 0.7. If participants had been able to match the verbal phrase to the auditory cues precisely, the distribution of their second stressed syllables would have been uniform across the segment explored. Instead, Cummins and Port found results similar to those of Sternad and her collaborators, discussed in the previous section. Figure 13.2, from Port (2003), presents data from the experiment of Cummins and Port (1998). This figure is a phase histogram. The *x*-axis displays the phase, scaled from 0 to 1, showing the full segment explored in the experiment. The *y*-axis displays the number of responses at each phase position. Although no portion of the phase segment shown entirely lacked responses, the response distribution was systematically skewed in favor of responses that made the simplest integer divisions of the phase space, equivalent to the beats of duple and triple measures. The work of Cummins and Port points strongly toward the centrality of stressed syllables for motor organization, as it is the stressed syllables that fall into regular metrical patterns when a phrase is repeated. The repetition creates the regular pattern, and as the model of Large and Jones (1999) would predict, the pattern is strongly influenced by nested beats with periods in small-integer ratios. Put another way, a duple or triple meter is found not as a result of notation or of musical training but rather as an emergent pattern created by the repetition. The parts of the speech signal that are most significant to motor organization (the stressed syllables) then entrain to this regular metrical pattern, showing that the beats in the meter serve as phase attractors.

A similar dynamic systems entrainment hypothesis, but without the regular context created by the repetition, has been put forward by Heather Rusiewicz (2011) in her theory of entrained manual and speech systems (TEMSS).

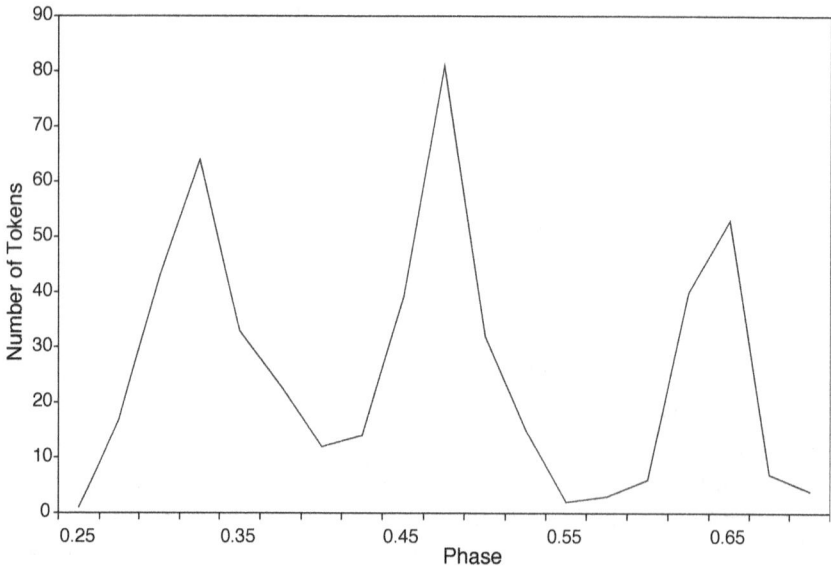

Fig. 13.2. Results from the experiment of Cummins and Port (1998), showing onset distribution of second stressed syllables in terms of phase. Figure 1 from Port (2003, 601). Reprinted from *Journal of Phonetics*, v. 31, Robert F. Port, "Meter and Speech," 599–611, © 2003, with permission from Elsevier.

Among other claims, TEMSS proposes that the most prominent syllable in a given unit of speech entrains the most salient portion of the accompanying gesture, resulting in the perceived temporal synchronization of speech and gesture. Claims and informal observations about alignment between speech and gesture have been made for some time (Dittmann and Llewellyn 1969; Kendon 1980; Bull and Connelly 1985), and they are supported by a significant body of empirical evidence (McClave 1994, 1998; Nobe 1996; de Ruiter 1998; Loehr 2004; Krahmer and Swerts 2007; Rochet-Capellan et al. 2008; Leonard and Cummins 2011; Rusiewicz et al. 2013, 2014; Esteve-Gibert et al. 2014). Evidence for the alignment of vocalization and manual movements also exists for infants (Iverson and Fagan 2004; Esteve-Gibert and Prieto 2014). Informed by the work of Cummins and Port (1998) and of Rusiewicz (2011), one of my original experiments currently under way to test focal impulse theory looks at metrical and motoric accents as competing phase attractors for strong syllables in a task that combines speech with music performance.

13.6. Focal Impulse Theory: Literal or Metaphorical?

As presented so far in this chapter, the relationship of the empirical litera-ture to focal impulse theory is one of qualified support: although scientific studies of music psychology, human movement science, and speech science raise some challenging questions, the picture presented is generally harmo-nious with the broader strokes of the theory. Nonetheless, this body of work leads me to conclude that while the theory's empirical hypotheses may be approximately accurate under some conditions, there are also conditions in which the theory likely functions as an extended metaphor, providing a help-ful guide to practice and interpretation that does not reflect the organization and control of motion at a root level. The reasons for this have to do with the wide range of temporal spacings between focal impulses, and especially with the slower end of focal impulse rates.

There are two potential challenges for widely spaced focal impulses; while the first does not seem severe, the second leads to my conclusion about the partially metaphorical status of the theory.

The first challenge to slow rates of focal impulses comes from the litera-ture on musical timescales, and especially from experiments involving tap-ping (either to music or to a metronome).[23] In looking at durational limits on pulses, the music psychological literature has tended to settle on 1.8 seconds, or 1,800 milliseconds (ms), as the slowest pulse that can be perceived as a main beat. Accordingly, London (2012, 30) places the limits of metrical hearing at around 4–6 seconds, based on grouping a 2-second pulse into units of two or three. For the majority of cases, this limit presents no obstacles to focal im-pulse theory, as it would be unusual for focal impulses to be placed more than 2 seconds apart. But there are cases in which this limit creates difficulties.

One example is the opening of the slow movement of Schubert's Arpeg-gione Sonata, shown in example 13.1. I have no great trouble singing this at a rate of 56 quarter-note beats per minute, or 1,070 ms. I feel it in one, conduct-ing in one with a large elliptical motion in my arm. Feeling it in one is crucial to making this tempo work—if I feel it in three, the quarter notes seem to plod along painfully slowly (probably because of the simplicity of the melody and the slow harmonic rhythm). Feeling the music in one, I believe that I am having an experience of pulse that lasts about 3,200 ms, which is more than 50 percent longer than the generally accepted limit on a main pulse. Given that quarter-note and eighth-note levels are present, accurate timekeeping is not the question. Rather, the issue is whether it is possible to direct primary

Example 13.1. Schubert, Arpeggione Sonata, D. 821, ii, mm. 1–11.

attention to the dotted-half level or whether the dotted-half level can exist only as a concatenation of quarters. (For London, 3,200 ms is within the range of metrical hearing but outside the bounds for a main pulse.)

Despite the general acceptance of the usual limit, the empirical literature strongly supports some gentle pushback against the notion of 1,800 ms as a firm outer bound on the length of pulses. While there is a marked drop off in pulse salience around 2 seconds, the real limit is probably between 3,600 and 4,800 ms. Strong evidence supports some kind of perceptual transition around 1,800 ms (Repp 2006b; Parncutt 1994; London 2012); for example, Repp (2006b) cites studies going back to the late nineteenth century indicating a limit on beat tracking around this threshold. And much of the evidence against 1,800 ms as an absolute limit strongly reinforces it as an effective limit, as most of the studies that acknowledge slower tapping rates have found them in a tiny minority of cases at most (van Noorden and Moelants 1999; McKinney and Moelants 2006; Martens 2011).

If the firmness of the 1800 ms limit is sometimes overstated, this is likely an instance of the common phenomenon in the psychological literature of nuanced findings becoming more black and white when they are cited.[24] Only

Drake, Penel, and Bigand (2000) report a larger number of slower tapping rates, with more than 10 percent of successful synchronizations by musicians at 2,500 ms or slower. The reason for this result is probably that they repeatedly asked participants to find both faster and slower beats to tap to in listening to music—by implication, until they could no longer do so. In contrast, most other studies looked at spontaneous tapping rates. Only a few more recent studies have been focused specifically on longer durations (Mates et al. 1994; Miyake, Onishi, and Pöppel 2004; Repp and Doggett 2007), and they support a much later cutoff. The data of Miyake, Onishi, and Pöppel (2004) indicate that the limit falls somewhere between their 3,600 and 4,800 ms conditions. Repp and Doggett's (2007) finer-grained examination of the region from 1,000 to 3,500 ms found no evidence of a firm cutoff on the ability to synchronize tapping.[25] Consequently, it seems likely that while pulse salience diminishes greatly beyond 1,800 ms or so, any true limit falls somewhere between 3,600 and 4,800 ms. This is at least provisional good news for my performance of the Schubert sonata, as a main pulse of 3200 ms seems clearly to fall inside any absolute cutoff on pulse duration. But pulse durations are not the only challenges for slow rates of focal impulses.

The second, more serious challenge for slow rates of focal impulses—the one that pushes me away from a purely empirical interpretation of focal impulse theory and toward an understanding of the theory as partially metaphorical—comes from the motor control literature. In general terms, the issue is that we have seen enough dichotomies in the organization of motion to conclude that any single, overarching theory of motion must be couched in general terms; focal impulse theory simply offers too many specifics to be empirically accurate with broad generality. One of the most important dichotomies is between short and long timescales: as demonstrated by Bernstein and Popowa (1929) and reinforced more recently by Park and his collaborators (2017), the same task performed at slow and fast rates will not have the same form or organization of motion. (Bernstein and Popowa found that medium rates are also different, so varying the rate can lead to more than two options for the organization of motion.) Likely related to this is the distinction between "ballistic" motions (in which the motion is prepared in advance and then proceeds with a minimum of sensory correction) and motions under continuous control; the type of control is probably related to the timescale because ballistic motions will often be faster than continuously controlled motions.[26] There is also the distinction between rhythmic (cyclical) and discrete motions, which again relates to timescales in that, as indicated by Bernstein and Popowa (1929) and Park and his collaborators (2017), there is almost certainly a lower limit on the rate at which a true cyclical motion can be performed. Focal impulse theory seems most likely to be accurate for music performance in which the motion is rapid, ballistic, and cyclical. For performance involving motion that is slow, continuously controlled, and discrete, I would expect the theory to be more metaphorical.

Why is the theory unlikely to be literally accurate for slower rates of motion? The most fundamental reason is that the heuristic physical models that we have been using do not support a connection between music performance and longer timescales. Returning to the half-pipe analogy, plenty of motions made in playing music could have some basic similarity to tossing some part of the body up into the air with each focal impulse. At many common rates of motion, such a model is intuitively reasonable, but it also makes sense in terms of basic physics. London (2012) cites 600 ms as the center of an average band of most preferred tempos. If you toss an object up into the air and want to catch it again after 600 ms, you will have to toss it a little less than eighteen inches into the air. This motion is bigger than most involved in playing music at a tempo of 100 beats per minute (the equivalent of 600 ms), but at least it seems to map to reality. For a flight time of 3,200 ms, the height reached would be over 40 feet; at the time of this writing, that is more than 25 percent higher than the current world-record height for a half-pipe jump and clearly on a scale that has nothing to do with music performance. More relevant periods could perhaps be obtained by modeling the body as a mass-spring system. Working this out in a realistic way would be complicated, but it is clear that no spontaneous spring- or pendulum-like bodily motions have periods of 3 seconds. To give some sense of a quantitative range, I made informal measurements of the rates of some of my own periodic movements. If I hold my forearm horizontally and make a spring-like back-and-forth motion in my wrist, the period is around 570 ms. If I pull my arm up and to the back so that it is approximately horizontal and allow it to act like a pendulum, using active motions only at the end of each cycle to bring it back to the starting position, the period is around 1,500 ms. If I do the same with my leg but with a range of motion closer to 90° than to 180°, the period is around 1,400 ms. If I hang from a bar and use my whole body as a pendulum, the period is around 2,250 ms. At least at this very basic level, I am unable to construct naturally periodic bodily motions whose timescales approach the longer intervals between focal impulses.

Hints to a metaphoric status can also be found in the theory of focal impulses itself. Recall how some discussions of motion from chapters 3 and 10 involved imagining being submersed in a viscous medium. Given that music is not usually performed in a vat of molasses, this scenario is not a literal description of motion but a metaphor intended to guide action. The theory provides musicians with a lens through which to view their own performance and with an image to guide their performance. Musicians need this kind of guidance. The so-called Bernstein problem discussed at the beginning of the chapter is a problem of degrees of freedom—there are many (too many) functionally equivalent ways of performing the same task. What Bernstein and many of those who followed him have agreed on is that there is a need for simplification, for a schema or organizing framework that drastically reduces the number of choices that need to be made (Bernstein 1967; Feldman 1986; Latash 2008).

A physical metaphor—such as making a ballistic, cyclical movement through a viscous medium with a long period—is one way to pare down the possible paths and to provide positive (albeit imagistic) guidance about how the motion is to be performed.[27] The kind of metaphor that focal impulse theory can provide is not an empty abstraction, an idea in the performer's head that makes no difference to how the music is actually performed. It is rather an image of physical motion that can be embodied, providing critically valuable guidance to unfolding motion at a detailed level. As a parallel case, consider a person attempting to imitate a slow-motion film of someone running; a mental picture of what it feels like and looks like to engage in the rapid, cyclical, ballistic activity of running would surely help in this task, even though it is slow, discrete, and under continuous control.

I am, furthermore, convinced that I am not introducing a new metaphor so much as making explicit a metaphor that is in wide, albeit often tacit, use. Musicians often talk about making unifying connections over multisecond time spans, using terms such as *line, shape,* or *gesture*.[28] If musicians attempt to make a smooth arc from one stronger beat until the next, they are already coming close to the kind of metaphor that focal impulse theory advances for slower rates of motion. We can compare this kind of embodied metaphor with the images a ballet dancer might use of almost weightless objects wafting through the air, images that exist apart from verbalization. Some analytically minded dancers might find it helpful to learn about how motions of the limbs can create an illusion of floating even while the center of mass is undergoing a ballistic trajectory (Laws 2002, 47–50); however, the physics lesson by itself will not lead to the graceful fluidity of motion that produces the illusion for an audience member.

An insightful metaphor offers a more direct road to a complex action than a detailed, literal description ever could. Surely this is why pianists use the image of playing with the weight of the arms alone, even though this is not possible outside of a limited range of rates and intensities. Similarly, when swimmers are told to "swim downhill," they are being asked to do something that will never be possible in a swimming pool—and yet it can help them with subtle aspects of the ways they feel and interact with the flow of the water, allowing them to improve body position, fluidity, efficiency, and speed. To say that the theory should not be taken literally for slower rates of motion is therefore not to diminish its value, but rather to see it more truly, and thereby to better appreciate the nature of its contribution.

Notes

1. This can even by detected with brain imaging (Iversen, Repp, and Patel 2009).
2. Unless noted here, these studies used piano and reported both loudness and durational patterns. Edlund (1985) examined many notational variants of "Twinkle Twinkle Little Star," and found the patterns often. Talley (1989) and Palmer, Jungers, and Jusczyk (2001) found the loudness patterns but not the durational patterns. Drake and Palmer (1993) found dynamic stresses on strong beats in $\frac{4}{4}$ and $\frac{6}{8}$ in the first of their experiments but not the second, and they found the timing patterns in the second experiment but not the first, and then not in all of the variants they used. Gabrielsson (1974), looking only at loudness, found louder strong beats in performances of piano, side drum, and bongo drum.
3. All studies used piano except Palmer and Kelley (1992), who used voice. Both loudness and duration patterns were reported only by Windsor and Clarke (1997), and because meter was not their main focus, they did not present statistical measures. In comparing real and algorithmic performances, however, they repeatedly stressed that effects of meter on loudness and timing were aspects of human performance that a more complete algorithm would need to produce. Henderson (1936) found the timing patterns but not the loudness patterns, and Drake and Palmer (1993) found the opposite. Of studies looking only at timing, three found the patterns (Shaffer 1984; Penel and Drake 1998; Windsor et al. 2006) and one found them in some passages but not in others (Shaffer 1981). Shaffer (1981) found the correlations with meter in a Bach fugue but not in a Chopin etude, but he later found hierarchical timing control at the level of the half note in that performance (Shaffer 1984), as we will see in sec. 13.4. Palmer and Kelly (1992), looking at vocal performance, found the timing patterns in two songs and the loudness patterns in one song but not in the other.
4. Although Repp (1998, 1091) attributed the results to grouping rather than to meter, one of his statistically extracted patterns (PC-IV) conforms exactly to the prediction that durations either beginning or ending with downbeats would be lengthened.
5. The fact that relatively high metrical levels were marked so consistently in so many studies (as opposed to, e.g., the quarter note in $\frac{3}{4}$ or common time) could be related to the use of predominately moderate to quick tempi, especially in the artificial musical sequences. Although not involving the primary sonic correlates of focal impulses, performers have been found to mark strong beats in performance in other ways. Both Sloboda (1983, 1985) and

Jungers (2007) found that notes on strong beats were performed more legato, and Palmer (1989, 1996) found greater melody lead in piano performance on strong beats. This last result connects somewhat more directly with the predictions about focal impulses, given that Goebl (2001) found that melody lead is correlated with hammer velocity, which directly affects loudness.

6. An interesting connection between sound and motion was noted by Eric Clarke (1993) in an experiment in which pianists imitated computer-generated performances. The computer performances were based on a human performance, but with transformed durations. When pianists attempted to imitate patterns that Clarke described as particularly perverse, he noticed that some moved in striking and idiosyncratic ways, leading him to propose some kind of bodily encoding of the timing patterns.

7. Although his original papers included little to characterize the temporal patterns, Repp (2006a, 65) states in a later essay that they were mainly related to the meter.

8. Infants indicated recognition by turning their heads for longer periods of time toward the familiar pattern than toward the unfamiliar pattern.

9. In a follow-up experiment that looked at passive motion, Phillips-Silver and Trainor (2008) found that both full-body and head motion produced this effect but leg motion alone did not, suggesting a role for the vestibular system. This result could suggest that conducting without moving the head might not influence hearing, but I would be surprised if that were shown to be the case, especially in light of some studies discussed below (Repp and Knoblich 2009; Manning and Schutz 2016; Manning, Harris, and Schutz 2017).

10. Gibson's (1966, 1979) ecological psychology is grounded in a similar confidence in the richness of available sensory information, having its origin in studies of how a pilot gauges the distance to the ground while landing an airplane (Gibson 1950, 6; Reed 1988).

11. This result will not surprise those familiar with London's (1993; 2012, 107–8) work on loud rests.

12. Interestingly, this result is stronger for musicians than for nonmusicians (Manning and Schutz 2016) and stronger for percussionists when they use a drumstick than when they tap their fingers (Manning, Harris, and Schutz 2017).

13. This discussion is based on an article (Ito 2013b) that has also appeared in revised and condensed form (Ito 2015). My account of Bernstein's work draws primarily on three sources: the 1996 English translation of Bernstein's book *On Dexterity and Its Development*, first published in Russian in 1991 (the original publication having been halted for political reasons in 1950); the abridged, edited, and translated version of Bernstein's 1935 paper, "The Problem of Interrelations between Coordination and Localization" ([1935] 2001), included in the collection *Classics of Movement Science*; and the commentaries on the relationships between *On Dexterity and Its Development* and contemporary human movement science that are published together with that book in a volume edited by Latash and Turvey (1996). Portions of text from Ito (2015) adapted by permission from Springer Nature Customer Service Centre GmbH: Springer, "Repetition without Repetition: How Bernstein Illumines Motor Skill in Music Performance," in *Anticipation: Learning from the Past; The Russian/Soviet Contributions to the Science of Anticipation*, ed. Mihai Nadin, 257–68, © Springer International Publishing Switzerland 2015.

14. As mentioned in chap. 1, Bernstein and Popowa (1929) also disproved a second theory: that of playing with the weight of the arms alone (i.e., with no active downward muscular forces applied). They demonstrated that gravity did not provide sufficient acceleration for playing at medium and fast tempi, and they observed that at slow tempi playing with weight alone occurred significantly less frequently than some pianists claimed.

15. A focus on specifics characterizes many studies of motor control in music performance, such as Askenfelt (1986), Winold, Thelen, and Ulrich (1994), and the chapters from pts. 3 and 4 of Altenmüller, Wiesendanger, and Kesselring (2006).

16. A more detailed discussion of Schmidt's work is offered by Abernethy and Sparrow (1992).

17. There is a strong connection here with the results of Repp (1999c), in which pianists played Chopin preludes both with a metronome and without, but intending to keep exactly in time; in both conditions, there was quite significant variation in the internal durations within the main beat, so attempts to be precisely regular in timing the main beat did not filter down to smaller metrical levels. This also connects with the performance results of using fewer focal impulses discussed in chap. 5, and especially with the discussion of historical performance styles that concludes that chapter. Note, however, that precise and consistent control of subtactus durations has been reported (e.g., in Malian Jembe music by Polak [2010]).

18. Because the timing of the beats is not isochronous, it is important to compare different performances of the same metrical span within the same measure across different performances by the same pianist. As many researchers have noted, timing profiles of the same piece by the same performer are extremely stable; this makes it feasible to perform the correlation analysis on multiple performances by the same pianist.

19. Other researchers have found different kinds of evidence for the importance of meter for motor planning (Palmer and Drake 1997; Drake and Palmer 2000; Palmer and Pfordresher 2003). But a number of other studies show that motor planning in music performance is not as simple as cuing up one consequent span at a time (Palmer and van de Sande 1995; Palmer and Drake 1997; Drake and Palmer 2000; Meyer and Palmer 2003). Recent research (Palmer and Pfordresher 2003; Palmer 2005) has given support to the older idea (Shaffer 1976) that different stages of motor planning may unfold at different rates at the same time.

20. An excellent source for Gibson is Reed (1988).

21. The use of the word *dynamic* in both the dynamic systems approach and dynamic attending theory appears to be coincidental. In the first dynamic attending paper to include the word in its title, Jones (1987, 621) stated that the term was used "to emphasize the integration of temporal relationships with other aspects of musical pattern structure."

22. In a modal distribution, data are unevenly clustered (see fig. 13.2); depending on how strongly modal the distribution is, the modes can look like waves or like spikes. Some readers may wish to return to the brief discussion of phase at the start of sect. 2.3.

23. Some of the best guides to the tapping literature are the surveys by Repp (2005b, 2006a, 2006b; Repp and Su 2013). He has also conducted many important experiments in this area.

24. In this case, overly stark statements of the limit often quote Richard Parncutt's (1994, 437) remark that beyond 1,800 ms, pulse sensations "cease to exist." Although standing firmly by the finding that pulse salience drops off markedly around 2 seconds, Parncutt (pers. comm. 2004) has acknowledged to me that he understands that phrase as having a degree of hyperbole.

25. Those wanting to pursue these results in more detail should give attention especially to Miyake, Onishi, and Pöppel's (2004) fig. 2 and its discussion, reading it in particular in light of Repp and Doggett's (2007) finding that the beginning of a transition to clustered responses can be accounted for in terms of a normal distribution of intended responses, but with a rapid reaction when the next metronome beat comes before the intended response. Based on this analysis, a true reactive strategy appears only in the 4,800 and 6,000 ms conditions, in which the formerly spread out response distribution is consolidated as a cluster of responses around usual reaction times after the beat (this is also seen at 3,600 ms in the most challenging of the memory conditions).

26. The distinction between ballistic and controlled motions is related to the long-known issue of the lag between electromyographic (EMG) signals and actual motions, with EMG leading motion for faster motions but being mostly synchronized for slower motions (Sternad 2001).

27. It seems possible that the brain could be well equipped to make use of this sort of imagistic guidance. Arnie Cox (2016) discusses the importance of mirror neurons for responses to music that involve imitation of the motions of producing the music and of motions implied by the music. And significant overlaps have been found in the brain areas recruited by playing music and by imagining playing (Meister et al. 2004). It would be interesting to know what brain areas are activated when a person imagines an action that is not physically possible.

28. For a fascinating account of some ways in which these arcs have been spatialized, see the discussion of Becking (1928), Truslit (1938), and some of their more recent successors in Shove and Repp (1995).

14

CONNECTIONS WITH OTHER MUSIC SCHOLARSHIP

THIS CHAPTER EXPLORES CONNECTIONS BETWEEN FOCAL IMPULSE THE-
ORY and other areas of music scholarship: approaches to embodiment
and gesture in music, Christopher Hasty's theory of metrical projection, and
studies of historical performance. These connections exist at a global level
and attach to focal impulse theory as a whole.

14.1. Embodiment and Gesture

The late nineteenth and early twentieth centuries saw significant interest in
the physical side of performance as integral to the nature and experience of
music; this interest declined markedly around the middle of the twentieth
century, as structural features of scores rose to almost unrivaled prominence.
Recent decades have seen a growing renewal of interest in this topic, and it has
become an active area of research. Some newer work has picked up strands
from the older tradition, and some has opened new paths (Godøy and Leman
2010; Cox 2016; Kim and Gilman, forthcoming). The following survey will
look first at the older line of work, including its more modern successors, and
then examine some relevant newer approaches.

There is a long tradition of combining attention to performance, embodiment, and gesture with a focus on practical application; this tradition includes Lussy (1874, [1885?]; Doğantan 2002), Riemann (1884; 1903; Hunnicutt
2000), Jaques-Dalcroze (1920; [1930] 1985; Moore 1992), Whiteside ([1955] 1997,
1969/1997), Zuckerkandl (1956), and Pierce (2007). Mathis Lussy belongs at
the head of this list both chronologically and because of his influence on
Riemann and on Jaques-Dalcroze (Doğantan 2002, 139–40, 144–45; Moore
1992, 31–37). Lussy sought a physiological basis for musical pulse and identified respiration as the source; his goal was to tie together musical structure,

performance variation, and affective expression. Despite the similarity of goals, Lussy's work is only indirectly comparable to focal impulse theory, for Lussy is concerned with larger structural units and with units of grouping, not meter. Of Hugo Riemann's works on meter, the most directly relevant is his *Musikalische Dynamik und Agogik* (1884). In this work Riemann is concerned with expressive performance variations that are organized in terms of the meter, and the measure is the main unit that attracts his attention. The downbeat is the locus of weight and always receives special treatment (except under certain carefully delimited circumstances). In *System der musikalischen Rhythmik und Metrik* (1903), Riemann pursues a physiological grounding of musical phenomena, seeing cardiovascular pulse as a source for musical pulse. Beyond these commonalities of general perspective, focal impulse theory largely diverges from Riemann, but a distinct sense of kinship remains, more directly than with Lussy.[1]

Lussy was both a teacher of and a major influence on Emile Jaques-Dalcroze, who is a central point of connection between the theoretical works of Lussy and Riemann and more pedagogical approaches that include, in addition to his own, those of Whiteside and Pierce. Jaques-Dalcroze's thinking is difficult to summarize. Chief among the difficulties is the fact that he saw in-person instruction as the only way in which his ideas could be conveyed; Jaques-Dalcroze (1916, 5) begins one of his books by stating that it exists as a supplement to experiential learning and that no one who has read the book apart from the guidance of an authorized instructor should presume to teach its contents.[2] Beyond this, his thinking evolved throughout his lifetime, his writings are largely unsystematic, and his approach has continued to evolve and diversify in the work of other Dalcroze practitioners (many of whom share his views on in-person transmission). It is clear, however, that Jaques-Dalcroze saw the organization of bodily motion as central to musical expressivity, and this is a central point of contact with focal impulse theory. A number of his exercises involve walking to music or synchronizing other motions of large body segments with music (Choksy et al. 1986, 30–41), and this approach seems like an excellent way to develop sensitivity to the musical features that guide focal impulse placement, even if the motions made by listeners in response to music will not necessarily correspond to the placement of focal impulses when performing. There are also more direct connections. Jaques-Dalcroze believed that motion always precedes sound, so that phrases that start on the downbeat are understood to have silent anacruses (Moore 1992, 54; cf. chap. 4). He also understood progressions of upbeat-downbeat-afterbeat (anacrusis-crusis-metacrusis, in his terminology) to have an essential continuity of bodily motion (Moore 1992, 85; cf. chap. 3, especially the analogy with half-pipe sports). A point of contrast is his lack of consistency regarding the relative importance of the notated meter and the various mixed meters that could be inferred from accentual patterns (Moore 1992, 127–34). Overall, however, Dalcroze practice is quite harmonious with the perspective advanced here.

Like Jacques-Dalcroze, Alexandra Pierce (2007) emphasizes attention to physical movement as a key to expressive shaping of music, in her case focusing especially on phrasing. Referring to earlier works, Moore (1992, 240) states that Pierce's and Jaques-Dalcroze's "ideas are so similar that one could mistake her writing for his own." The following quotation gives a sense of the scope of her concerns, which include those of focal impulse theory but go beyond them: "When the musical quality of the beat became vivid as movement and reverberated through a responsive body rather than, say, just an arm, a corresponding shift in musical expression could be expected. But the movement that replicated the beat was different from the movement that could bring out the life of melody. And expressing the kinetic quality of phrase called for yet another movement altogether" (Pierce 2007, 2). Many of her discussions of meter translate easily into the terms of focal impulse theory: focal impulses create what she calls "ping"; during their consequent spans, focal impulses guide what she calls "lilt"; and her exercise of balloon tapping removes the demands involved in playing notes, allowing musicians to focus on the expressive temporal trajectories that their focal impulses create (Pierce 2007, chap. 4). Pierce's (2007, chaps. 7–8) concepts of reverberation and juncture apply across too deep a hierarchy—from single notes to whole pieces—to allow any simple correlation with focal impulses, but there are interesting points of contact. Reverberation includes "the intention that precedes an action, commitment during the action . . . and fulfilment of the action" (121). It reflects the "paradox of resting while acting—the physical counterpart of dividing up the sound into notes, phrases, and measures while maintaining its continuity" (120). Juncture is "the moment of articulation, the time between parts" (120). Pierce applies these concepts to the spaces between notes; she observes how different those spaces can be depending on the hierarchical depth of the grouping boundary separating the notes, and she also observes the ways in which attention to those spaces can give shape not only to the spaces themselves but also to the units they articulate. Thinking about reverberation and juncture in relation to focal impulses and their consequent spans, we could turn our attention to the often full space that lies between focal impulses instead of considering the relatively empty spaces between notes. Giving attention to reverberation and juncture would then be a way of focusing on the unfolding quality of the consequent span, similar in many ways to the balloon-tapping exercise but emphasizing awareness rather than action. But we could also apply these concepts in the way Pierce uses them, focusing on the space between a new focal impulse and the final note of the preceding focal impulse's consequent span. Doing so would bring attention to an aspect of the succession of focal impulses that has not been emphasized so far, namely the degree to which one focal impulse prepares for the next. Perhaps one consequent span ends with significant reserves of energy, so that the note coinciding with the new focal impulse could have been performed as part of the preceding consequent span. When this happens, there is often a flowing sense of motion, with an awareness of the previous motion's momentum carrying the body into the new motion. Or the consequent span may end with the energy largely spent, so that the new focal impulse impels the body back into motion from a state approaching rest. Attention to reverberation and juncture leads us into awareness of the range of shapes that this space can have.[3]

The approach of Abby Whiteside ([1955] 1997, 1969/1997; Stevens, forthcoming) is also similar to Dalcroze's, and the way in which her exercises tie together meter and physical motion in performance comes quite close to focal impulse theory. Whiteside describes a process of playing only "the most important notes," which she calls variously "pulsing" or "outlining," as a key to gesture and musical fluidity; while she never specifies criteria for "important notes," it is clear that she is thinking metrically. In all examples shown, the notes chosen are on stronger beats than the notes removed, and she gradually fills in more notes by filling in the metrical hierarchy. It seems likely that what she called "outlining" was playing only the notes produced directly by focal impulses and that her examples therefore parallel example 1.2, which showed those notes in the opening of the "Ghost" Trio. Beyond this, she also emphasizes slow, whole-body motions as essential to giving the many smaller motions of the fingers, hands, and arms a convincing musical shape.

As a late echo of Lussy and Riemann, Victor Zuckerkandl rounds out this list of scholars exploring the gestural side of meter. In his *Sound and Symbol* (1956), Zuckerkandl suggested that we understand beats in relation to cyclical patterns of recurrence, depicted as waves. Here the waves are not beats but rather the time spans that connect the beats. Zuckerkandl wrote expressively of how the intervals between beats were always dynamically in motion: no dead intervals of time, they come out of one beat and then drive forward into the next. Although these descriptions harmonize well with the way in which one focal impulse leads to another, Zuckerkandl argued explicitly and at length against understanding these waves as reflecting bodily motion. Under his theory, all metrical levels that can be heard are all simultaneously sites of these dynamic processes; because the listener's physical investment in a metrical level is not made in all metrical levels at once, the phenomena he described could not be essentially physical. Although Zuckerkandl acknowledged the salience and importance of bodily responses to music, for him the waves represented the expression of the force of time itself.

Among more recent writings on embodiment and gesture, the earliest considered here is a paper by David Lidov (1987). Working within a semiotic framework, Lidov insisted that listening to and making music are bodily acts, so much so that interaction between music and the body may be taken as a primary point of departure for understanding reference in music. In one of the more direct parallels with focal impulse theory, and in accord with recent neuropsychological work on meter surveyed in chapter 13, Lidov (2005) has also suggested that hearing meter is first and foremost about physical motion in synchrony with salient beat levels; these motions may be so small as to be largely subliminal, but they may also be motions of performance. (The performer is included because the performer is also a listener.) This line of thinking has been developed further by Arnie Cox (2006, 2011, 2016). According to his mimetic hypothesis, a central part of the experience of listening to music is imagining or performing physical motions that could produce sounds similar to those being heard; moving with the beat is just one of the possibilities. The mimetic hypothesis fits well with focal impulse theory, which suggests that the various (often subtle) motions of engaged listeners will also often be organized around focal impulses. (The more difficult question of the extent to which performers' and listeners' focal impulse placements are likely to correspond is addressed in chap. 5.) Within *Music and Embodied Cognition* (2016), Cox's most extensive work on the mimetic hypothesis, the focus is primarily on aspects unrelated to focal impulse theory. He looks, for example, at the roles of embodied listener responses in metaphors of musical motion and in the achievement of musical goals. But he also discusses the many forms that a listener's mimetic responses might take, including imagining the motions of performance in great detail if the listener plays the same instrument—and misimagining them if the listener does not. Most interestingly for focal impulse theory, he suggests that the listener's mimesis may sometimes respond not to specific motions of performance but to a more generalized sense of effort, and that the motions involved in these more general mimetic responses may occur especially in the core muscles of the abdomen and back. If attention to the time-varying intensity profile of the music is focused especially on the characters of the main beats, this conception of mimetic response could be connected with the inflected focal impulses discussed in chapters 10 and 11.

The newer body of work on embodiment and gesture also includes work that is less closely related to focal impulse theory, for example, books by Naomi Cumming (2000) and Elisabeth Le Guin (2006). Both take relatively straightforward observations about performance as points of departure (e.g., the shape of the cellist's hand in thumb position) and build interpretations that function at a high conceptual level, pursuing such topics as cultural history and the construction of subjectivity. Focal impulse theory contrasts on both points. First, its claims about the mechanics of performance cannot be easily verified through simple observations. And second, although the theory builds bridges from expressive shaping to interpretation, the interpretive claims remain on a much more modest epistemological level. Focal impulse theory is more closely related to Robert Hatten's *Interpreting Musical Gestures, Topics, and Tropes* (2004) and Jonathan De Souza's *Mind and Hand: Instruments, Bodies, and Cognition* (2017). The foundational assumptions and perspectives of both works include psychology and the science of interactions among brain, body, and environment, as in this study. They also stay longer at lower levels than Cumming and Le Guin in analyzing scores and exploring topics including expressivity and meaning in music (Hatten 2004) and the ways in which the nature of specific instruments influences composition, improvisation, and listening (De Souza 2017). They still have higher epistemological centers of mass than this book, however, and neither work has empirical implications. In general, Hatten's and De Souza's books occupy something of a middle ground between focal impulse theory and the works of Cumming and Le Guin.[4]

In many ways, the spirit of focal impulse theory is closest to that of Lussy and Riemann in offering a general perspective on the interrelations among meter, performance, and musical expression, a perspective that has many practical implications for performing musicians. In some of its specifics, it comes quite close to Jaques-Dalcroze and Whiteside. It also has a degree of resemblance to the works of Cox and Hatten, both in content and in drawing connections with research in psychology; it takes a step further by attempting to contribute to an empirical understanding of music performance. Focal impulse theory is not, however, primarily a theory of music psychology. Its most basic impulse is not empirical but (in a general sense) phenomenological, as it tries to further understanding based mainly on careful examination of and reflection on the way things seem to be. Like most of the works surveyed here, at the end of the day it is to be judged primarily for its ability to offer insight in service of reflection and action.

14.2. Hasty's Theory of Metrical Projection

Another significant touchstone for the theory of focal impulses is Christopher Hasty's book *Meter as Rhythm* (1997). In that work Hasty argues against understandings of meter and rhythm that would place them in opposition to one another, with meter an almost contentless, abstract backdrop against which the drama of rhythm plays out. Instead, he wants to show that meter can be expressive, contingent, and highly varied. His central concept is projection, in which careful attention to unfolding processes of becoming in time leads to fine-grained sensitivity to a web of implications that situates the durations that are in process of becoming with respect to other durations, both past and potential.[5]

Many of Hasty's (1997) critiques of theories that separate meter from rhythm also apply to focal impulse theory; Hasty's theory and mine do nonetheless have several shared concerns and motivations, and even a few specific points of similarity. Focal impulse theory agrees that meter has an active component and is not just a passive default. Beyond this, focal impulse theory agrees in wanting to bring out lively and expressive qualities of meter, seeing meter as more than a dry abstraction. Notable points of convergence also exist in the ways in which the two theories deal with triple meter, with both departing significantly from standard metrical theory. For Hasty, the third beat in triple meter defers the completion of a metrical projection. It extends the realization of the implication that the duration of the first beat could reproduce itself in a second duration that brings a sense of completion (as in a $\frac{2}{4}$ measure turning out to contain a third beat), and it extends the completion of a longer duration that will itself carry the potential to reproduce itself in a second duration (as we wait for one measure to end so that we can expect how long the next measure will be). In focal impulse theory, while each of the three beats may be marked with focal impulses, so that the organization of motion simply follows a beat level within the metrical grid, it is also possible to feel two unequal beats, either the first and the second or the first and the third. The expressive contrast between the two possibilities for uneven placement will be enhanced if binary impulse cycles are used, and there are similarities between these two expressive characters and the differences of character that Hasty describes between rhythmic patterns in triple meter that mark either beats one and two or beats one and three (135–37). There are also clear corre-spondences between Hasty's arguments against what he calls "nonmediated unequal measures" (140–47), in which measures containing more than three beats are heard without internal groupings by twos or threes, and my account in chapter 8 of the reasons why focal impulses placed at the substrate level in asymmetrical meters will make the metrical organization of the measure unclear.

The similarities and differences between the two theories are crystalized in Hasty's central term, "projection." When first defining projection, Hasty emphasizes the meaning of the Latin root as a "throwing forth" (84), which provides an image strikingly similar to the throwing of the body into mo-tion accomplished by the focal impulse, and especially to half-pipe sports as a model. More fundamentally, both theories place great emphasis on begin-ning: for Hasty, beginning initiates duration and creates the possibility for various processes of projection; and in focal impulse theory, the focal impulse provides the motional context needed for all that will follow until the next focal impulse. But the natures of these beginnings are fundamentally dif-ferent. Projection is a process of expectation and interpretation of durations past, present, and potential, and it is radically open and vulnerable to the contingencies of an unknown future—or, if the future course of events may be said to be known with some degree of confidence, projection has a radical insistence on being present in the moment, with interpretations and expecta-tions rooted in the past and the present.[6] Furthermore, projection is first and foremost a mental process; although occasional references are made to move-ment (e.g., 94–95, 110–11, 141) and to kinetic energy (e.g., 111, 113–15), it is rare that Hasty's listeners need more than ears and a brain. This seems remarkable given how closely associated meter and rhythm are with physical motions both of production and of response. (To be fair, the same could be said of most music-theoretical treatments of meter.) In contrast, the focal impulse is produced by the performer's body. (And even if it should prove to be entirely metaphorical, and thus residing in the mind of the person perceiving it, it will be a metaphor about bodies and the ways in which they move.) Furthermore, the role of the focal impulse is not to open a wide field of temporal possibili-ties but to determine what will happen, or at least what can happen, within its consequent span. My main understanding of the relationship between the two theories is therefore not that they are in conflict but rather that they are orthogonal to one another—they are simply talking about different things.[7]

To return to the question of rhythm versus meter, I have not chosen to frame focal impulse theory, as Hasty does his theory of projection, around an attempt to move beyond an opposition between static meter and dynamic rhythm. While I see flexibility in the behaviors that occur around meter, I also affirm a sense of meter giving strong—and much less variably patterned—support to the rhythms that exist around and in relation to it. Focal impulse theory is intended to show how leaning on and pushing off from things that are stable and predictable makes possible the freedom, variety, and shape of rhythmic performance; without a skeleton to pull against, muscles can be nothing but twitching blobs. Hasty laments a history of seeing the opposition between meter and rhythm in terms of law and freedom (4). Rather than entirely countering that history, I would want to place those same oppositions in a tradition that sees law and freedom as mutually constituting one another (Ito 2011).

14.3. Focal Impulses and Historical Performance

Recorded performances of music offer abundant examples of patterns of accentuation that could well be sonic traces of focal impulses. As discussed in chapter 5, the clearest patterns involve notes on strong beats being louder or more pointedly articulated and lengthening durations that begin or end with strong beats. These same sonic patterns are also described in treatises on performance from before the age of recorded sound. To be clear, these reports cannot serve as direct evidence for organization in terms of focal impulses in past centuries. Primarily, as discussed in chapter 5, sonic evidence for focal impulse placement will always be uncertain and inferential, and it follows that this evidence cannot count strongly toward the existence of the focal impulse. Beyond this, there are a number of small conflicts with focal impulse theory; examples include the metrical levels highlighted and the nature of the processes that result in the sonic patterns. Although these historical accounts cannot serve as strong positive evidence, it would surely count as evidence against the theory if traces of focal impulses had not been observed regularly throughout the common-practice era. In fact, the opposite is the case.

In looking at the seventeenth and eighteenth centuries, George Houle (1987) is a particularly helpful guide. As explained by Houle, theorists of the seventeenth and early eighteenth centuries described metrically strong notes as differing in their inner duration or intrinsic sense of weight from metrically weaker notes. While greater intrinsic weight did not require expressive performance variations such as lengthening a note or giving it dynamic stress, authors of the time described the perceptions of listeners in those terms and said that such variations, though not strictly necessary, commonly occurred.

Many treatises describe one or both of those sonic patterns, and Houle suggests that a change occurred in the middle of the eighteenth century, with audible marking of meter shifting from temporal inflection in the first half of the century to dynamic stress in the second half (124).

One of the most famous descriptions of lengthening stronger beats is found in Johann Joachim Quantz's (1752, 105–6; [1752] 1966], 123–24) treatise on playing the flute. Quantz links these lengthenings explicitly to the meter. But while some metrical levels marked in this way would often carry focal impulses (e.g., quarter-note beats in $\frac{3}{4}$), others would not, with the marked beat levels seeming too fast (e.g., the eighth note in common time at a moderate tempo). There is good agreement among scholars that Baroque performers commonly marked the stronger beats of the meter with temporal inflections, but it is also clear that the exact nature of this practice was subject to considerable variation. This variation included which beats would be marked under which circumstances and the extent of the lengthening, which could range from mild emphasis to sharp overdotting, sometimes even reversing to include short-long patterns. In testimony to this somewhat chaotic picture, Robert Donington (1973, 255–9) offers a veritable barrage of often contradictory quotations from the period regarding inequality of duration. There is less agreement concerning the relationship between a widespread practice of emphasizing strong beats through duration and the French practice of *notes inégales*, which involved (under specific circumstances) the alternate lengthening and shortening of paired notes of short and equal notated duration (Donington 1973; Hefling 1993; Neumann 1993; Fuller 2001). The main issues concern the proper use of the term *notes inégales* and the extent to which conspicuous durational inequality was in widespread use; no one disputes the fact that inconspicuous lengthening of durations beginning or ending with strong beats was prevalent. Because of this, *notes inégales* may safely be set to the side for the purposes of evaluating possible historical evidence for the use of focal impulses.

Quantz, who stressed the lengthening of durations, also mentioned loudness accents in passing, speaking of the use of a "stronger tone" (1752 [1966], 123; see Quantz 1752, 106, "stärker im Tone"). In line with Houle's (1987) claim that the articulation of the meter shifts around the midcentury from time to loudness, this emphasis on loudness accents is significantly amplified in the discussions by Leopold Mozart (1756, 257–58; [1756] 1985, 219–20) and Daniel Gottlob Türk (1789, 335–36; [1789] 1982, 325), both of whom use examples in which dynamics change from one note to the next within a measure to indicate these contrasts. Mozart's chapter on bowing is heavily focused on maintaining the alignment between the down-bows and the notes on stronger beats, showing the continuing relevance of the "rule of the downbow" reported in 1698 by Georg Muffat (2001, 33–34). Houle discusses a number of other correspondences between meter and the performance techniques of specific instruments, focusing on string bowing, keyboard fingering, and woodwind tonguing; in each case, the manner of performance of notes is strongly influenced by metrical placement (91–109).

Moving into the nineteenth century, Clive Brown (1999) reports that musicians continued to assume that strong beats would be marked by dynamic stresses. He cites a passage by A. B. Marx from 1854 in which dynamic variation reflects a deeply nested metrical hierarchy, with accents on each eighth beat and nested diminuendos across each quarter-note beat, across each half-note beat, and across the entire measure (11). While such a pattern is not at all inconsistent with focal impulse theory, the present theory would single out only one (any one) of the three higher marked beat levels as carrying the sonic traces of focal impulses. As examples of performance treatises that report dynamic emphasis on strong beats, both Louis Spohr ([1832?], 41; [1843?], 28) and Carl Czerny ([1839?b], 1:89, 3:5–6; [1839?a], 1:119–20, 3:7) indicate that notes on strong beats will be somewhat louder in performance. Interestingly, Czerny attributes this to two separate causes. He states that there will often be a subtle, involuntary marking of the strong beat, which happens even when musicians count verbally "*one,* two, *three,* four" ([1839?b], 1:89; [1839?a], 1:119–20); in stating that this is automatic and involuntary, he comes close to the implications of focal impulse theory. But in a later passage, he states that it is one of the primary duties of the performer to make the metrical organization of the music clear to the listener, and that gentle accents should be added to this end, especially where the music may be unclear metrically ([1839?a], 3:5–6; [1839?b], 3:7). It is possible that the usual sonic traces of focal impulses could be emphasized voluntarily for purposes of communication, but Czerny's discussion does nothing to suggest that these loudness accents arise as organically as the sonic traces of focal impulses.

Given the general nature of the topic, many connections with other areas of scholarship in music are possible, and a number of other connections have been and will be noted briefly throughout the book as they arise. The topics addressed in this chapter have deeper significance for the theory. Among the meaningful connections with the literature on gesture and embodiment, Cox's (2016) mimetic hypothesis stands out because it lends weight to the possibility that listeners might use their own focal impulses to organize movement made in response to music. Christopher Hasty's (1997) important theory of metrical projection offers a fascinating counterpoint of similarities and contrasts with focal impulse theory. And the literature on performance practice of the eighteenth and nineteenth centuries allows us to examine the possibility that some authors may have been describing sonic traces of focal impulses. Taken together, I hope that these discussions offer not only a clearer picture of how focal impulse theory relates to its context, but also a richer sense of what it is.

Notes

1. Another cousin of focal impulse theory is found in the work of Riemann's student Gustav Becking (1928). Becking was interested in details of the shaping of downbeats and upbeats, and there is resonance between his work and the account of inflected focal impulses found in chaps. 10 and 11. The theories diverge at that point, however, because Becking, like Clynes (1995), was interested in composer-specific ways in which those beats would be characteristically shaped. He claimed, for example, that there exist different, most appropriate ways of shaping pulses in the music of Mozart and Beethoven. Becking's work is described in more detail by Shove and Repp (1995), who also discuss the work of Alexander Truslit (1938). Truslit was interested in connections between musical gesture and bodily motion, but he focused on melody at the phrase level, with meter playing no significant role in his theory.

2. I am grateful to Deanna Clement for bringing this passage to my attention.

3. I am indebted to David Lidov for suggesting this connection.

4. A few additional connections with more recent parts of the literature on music and embodiment are mentioned in the concluding chapter.

5. For those looking for a concise summary of Hasty's rather dense book, the most helpful source is probably Horlacher (1997).

6. In this respect, a clear kinship exists between Hasty's approach and the phenomenological work of David Lewin (1986). Their approach to perception sometimes reminds me of the "bullet time" effects associated with the 1999 film *The Matrix*.

7. This is not to say that the two cannot be put into relationship; the kind of analysis that Hasty models could be of great service to a performer wanting to make sensitive and informed choices about focal impulse placement. To cite only the most obvious of many examples, looking at two courantes from Bach's cello suites, Hasty (1997, chap. 10) examines the relationships among various temporal spans and their relative prominence in a way that could directly inform the choice of beats to receive focal impulses.

PART 5
APPLYING FOCAL IMPULSE THEORY

15

METRICAL DISSONANCE IN BRAHMS

Part 5 concludes the book by presenting further applications of focal impulse theory. Chapter 15 looks at several issues in the performance of metrical dissonance in Brahms. And Chapter 16 presents two complete movements from Brahms's clarinet sonatas, looking at interactions between focal impulse choices and other issues of analysis and performance.

At a fundamental level, part 5 deals with choices, and it is important to be clear that the discussion is unavoidably personal. These choices are not the logical consequences of focal impulse theory but rather examples of how someone might go about deciding among some of the multiple paths that focal impulse theory opens up. While I stand by the value and interest of the interpretations offered here, at the most fundamental level, they are presented not as products but as demonstrations of processes—as models of how close examination of the score, assessments of expressive character under various performance options, and personal taste can be combined in making considered decisions about focal impulse placement.

15.1. Interpretive Perspective

This chapter presents selected examples from a much longer study looking at metrical dissonance in all of Brahms's published works with opus numbers (Ito, in preparation c). A central question for this topic is the role of the notated meter; some scholars offer metrical frameworks that differ from the notated meter and provide renotated examples (Frisch 1990, Smith 2001), while others assert that the notated meter always retains primary importance (Cai 1986). John Rink (1995a) has attempted to split the difference, discussing how a performer's attention can move fluidly among contrasting metrical interpretations if each has been practiced on its own. In line with the more general discussion of metrical dissonance in chapter 12, the approach taken here also attempts to strike a balance between notated and alternative heard meters, but it does so rather differently, preferring decisive choices among competing options. The notated meter will be given the status of a strong default option, and significant efforts will be expended in finding ways to make it viable when challenged. Indeed, only one of the passages discussed here will depart from the notated meter for an alternative heard meter. The priority given to the notated meter results from having encountered many passages in which hearing and performing in the notated meter, although not on first encounter the most promising option, turns out to give the music a richly expressive quality. But there are also passages in which an alternative heard meter seems to be truly the better option, and in such cases, I generally adopt the alternative meter as the governing framework; while the notated meter may sometimes inflect the quality of motion within the heard meter, it does not continue to compete for attention in the way Rink advocates. The full study will include discussions of many passages in which an alternative heard meter is understood to prevail.

This approach rests to a large extent on personal aesthetic preference; however, there is also strong philological support for the legitimacy of alternative heard meters. An idiosyncratic feature of Brahms's metrical practice is his use of measures that are one-and-a-half times the length of the prevailing notated measures; these measures appear most frequently either singly or in pairs, and they may be either notated or unnotated. In reference to a term used in discussing hemiola in Handel (Wintersgill 1936; Willner 1991), I call them *1.5-length bars* (1.5LBs).

Two features of Brahms's use of 1.5LBs suggest that heard meter could validly depart from notated meter for Brahms. First, for the listener, a tenacious insistence on the notated meter will usually go hand-in-hand with adherence both to the first stable meter that is heard and to the placement of the bar lines in that first stable meter (allowances being made for ambiguity or metrical play in the initial measures). A listener without access to a score who wants to stay with the notated meter will need to assume that, like the great majority of common-practice works, the music heard has a single notated meter that continues without adjustment over the course of the movement. But if Brahms inserts a single, notated 1.5LB, the listener adopting the strategy of staying with the first stable meter will have no way of knowing this; the notated meter will sound like an instance of metrical dissonance. In some cases, this conflict between an originally heard metrical framework and the actual notation of the music is heightened, depending on the total number of 1.5LBs used across the course the movement. If the total number of notated 1.5LBs is even, any shifts will cancel each other out, leaving the bar line with no net change; but if the total number of 1.5LBs is odd, the bar line will change location from the beginning of the movement to the end. A little more than half of the time that Brahms uses odd-length stretches of notated 1.5LBs, the total number of 1.5LBs over the course of the movement is odd; for the listener who insists on the first stable position of heard bar lines, this results in the movement ending in a state of unresolved metrical dissonance. There are very few cases in which Brahms ends a movement with unresolved metrical dissonance with respect to the notated meter, all from the late works. This suggests that any supposed unresolved metrical dissonances resulting from odd numbers of 1.5LBs were not intended by Brahms, and that the listener should feel free to follow the clear auditory cues indicating a change in heard meter—for in these cases, such a mental adjustment is necessary to continue to hear in the notated meter. Paradoxically, this emphasis on the notated meter in these cases opens the door to alternative heard meters in other cases because the aural cues are indistinguishable. If the real metrical ground under our feet can shift—if there is not necessarily any one unchanging metrical framework that encompasses an entire movement—then the various possible departures from a metrical home base have the potential to receive a significantly enhanced status.[1]

The second reason that Brahms's use of 1.5LBs points to the legitimacy of alternative heard meters is that Brahms used notated and unnotated 1.5LBs with similar frequency and in similar ways. For example, 1.5LBs are often used shortly before cadences to create a broadening of pace, similar to that resulting from the hemiola. The populations of notated and unnotated 1.5LBs are statistically indistinguishable in the prevalence with which this use occurs. If a single notated 1.5LB is used, the bar lines will have shifted relative to their earlier positions, but the most obvious heard meter will correspond to the notated meter. And if a single unnotated 1.5LB is used, the bar lines will remain unchanged, but the most obvious heard meter will be out of phase with the notated meter. (In almost all cases, this shift will be resolved at some point later in the piece.) If a listener without a score is unable to distinguish between these cases, this suggests that the listener should be free to follow the often-fluctuating course of the heard meter, whether or not this corresponds to the actual notation. Cai (1986, 371) argued that for Brahms the notated meter should always be taken as perceptual bedrock, and that a performance that ceases to be grounded in the notated meter will always be impoverished. Based on my examination of his use of 1.5LBs, I am not convinced that that is always the case.[2]

Despite this robust defense of alternative heard meters, I will mainly play the role of champion of the notated meter in what follows, looking at cases in which a compelling approach to the notated meter can be found despite the strong indications of alternative meters. Because the great majority of performers sound like they are adopting alternative heard meters, original recordings have been made of most passages to demonstrate the mode of performance advocated here. The passages fall into three categories: shifted meter, hemiola, and shifted hemiola.

15.2. Shifted Meter

When Brahms writes music that strongly suggests metrical displacement, there is often no single point at which the bar lines clearly shift. In such cases, the weight of cues to shifted meter gradually accumulates until only listeners who make significant conscious efforts could retain the notated meter. The opening measures of Brahms's Capriccio op. 116, no. 1 (ex. 15.1), present the opposite scenario: a sudden, jarring, and seemingly unavoidable shift in meter. Frank Samarotto (2012) offers a detailed account of how a long history of compositional practice and discourse surrounding the capriccio genre could make this disorienting juxtaposition of meters (indicated below the staff in the example and often heard in performances) plausible as compositional intent.

For me, however, this approach sounds a bit too much like Stravinsky. If we insist on a well-formed, end-state metrical hearing of the passage, the early downbeat in measure 4 will imply the $\frac{2}{8}$ measure indicated below the staff in the example, which is extremely strange in context. A better solution—truer to the listener's experience and making better connections with other examples of Brahms's metrical practice—would be to say that the notated $\frac{3}{8}$ measure has simply been left incomplete, interrupted by the early assertion of the downbeat. This grants to beats in the heard meter some of the flexibility accorded to hyperbeats within hypermeasures in my schema-based approach to hypermeter, and several other passages by Brahms encourage this kind of midmeasure metrical reorientation (Ito, in preparation c). The return to the notated bar lines is somewhat more problematic. Samarotto's solution is to have an expanded eighth measure of the phrase, starting on the third eighth of the seventh measure (one measure later than shown below the staff); his justification is the similarity between the initial rolled chord and the triplet arpeggio in the left hand. But in practice, the great majority of pianists return to notated meter with the downbeat of measure 7, so that the hairpin swell and the arpeggiated chord both land in a clear heard downbeat at the start of measure 8, making the seventh heard measure of the phrase the expanded measure. This metrical interpretation is reflected in the meter signatures

Example 15.1. Brahms, Capriccio op. 116/1, mm. 1–9.

below the staff. If I hear a shift at all, this is where I hear the shift back; I have a hard time hearing it as Samarotto indicates.[3] But Samarotto's analysis has a consistency that the usual interpretation lacks; the third eighth beats are salient from the beginning because of the slurs that start on them, and once they begin to be heard as downbeats, they remain heard downbeats until the change of texture at the end of the phrase. There is no clear reason why the third beat of measure 7 (which, under the more usual hearing, is an extra up-beat preparing for the return to synchrony of heard and notated meters on the downbeat of measure 8) should not receive the same metrical interpretation as the third beats of the preceding measures. As a result, the usual shift back to notated meter feels just as capricious as the shift in—which is perfectly con-sistent with Samarotto's genre-centered reading of the piece. Although pas-sages exist in which Brahms's metrical practice resembles Stravinsky's, and even in which it resembles Messiaen's, in this passage it seems at least worth looking for other possibilities.[4]

As indicated above the staff in the example, my solution is to perform many of the beat 3 attack points as anticipations, sustaining the focal impuls-es into the notated downbeats that follow. Pianist David Keep can be heard in sound example 15.1 performing the passage in this way. A key to helping the listener hear the downbeat as notated in these measures is to allow the snap that comes from the release of the focal impulse to attach to the melodic attack point on the downbeat, producing a secondary stress. The sustaining of the focal impulses is also conveyed by agogic accents, as the third eighth beats within the measures that usually shift are consistently the longest beats within the measures.

The second example of a possible metrical shift is more complicated, both in terms of what happens in the score and in the manner of performance

Example 15.2. Brahms, Variations and Fugue on a Theme by Handel, op. 24, mm. 24–33.

required to project the notated meter. Example 15.2 shows the third of the Handel Variations, together with the music that immediately precedes and follows it. This example is extreme because the downbeat shifts to the second eighth-note beat in the common-time measure—an unusually weak beat for a heard downbeat. Recall the general discussion of metrical dissonance in chapter 12: the shift of the heard downbeat to the middle of the measure in duple meters is the most common case of shifted meter, with shifts to weaker metrical positions less frequently encountered. In Brahms's music, the frequency of various metrical shifts tracks with the strength of beat shifted to, so that a shift by an odd number of eighths of a measure in simple duple and quadruple meters occurs relatively infrequently—in a total of 17 passages, compared with around 120 shifts to the middle of the bar (Ito, in preparation c). The tendency to shift the bar lines is also unusually strong; in the great majority of recordings, it is extremely difficult if not impossible to hear in the notated meter. So why fight the current? There are three reasons. The first is simply that in looking at the page, it seems as if it should be perfectly straightforward to hear the music in the notated meter; the aural conflict is not visually apparent. The second reason has to do with the seams with the adjacent variations. The transition into the following variation does not present a problem; most pianists slow down the end of the third variation and insert a short fermata on the following rest, effectively reinserting the "missing" eighth-note beat that results from the return to notated meter at the start of the fourth variation. And even when time is kept more scrupulously, the sudden intrusion of the new variation can seem appropriately impetuous, a metrical discontinuity that works. The path into the shifted meter from the preceding variation is where the difficulties lie. The first downbeat of the third variation is clearly marked as a downbeat based on how it is approached from the end of the second, but then the heard downbeat simply moves over within a consistent pattern of motive and motion. The shift is neither disguised nor motivated, and especially in a context with such regular phrase rhythm, it seems rather inelegant. The third reason, in some ways the most persuasive for me, is the dolce indication. In shifted meter, the passage tends to prance with a mannered daintiness; in contrast, the dolce that Brahms asks for seems like it should be achievable if the notated meter is allowed to turn the slurs (syncopations in the shifted meter) into sighing figures—or at least it seems that way from singing the main line from one of the hands alone.

As it turns out, it is the relationship between the hands that makes it so extremely challenging to convey the notated meter in performance. No special focal impulse placement is needed to project the notated meter, but a straightforward performance in which the pianist hears and tries to bring out the notated meter is likely to end up simply reinforcing the shifted meter. The reason for this is that strong accents on the notated quarter-note beats serve only to create a more marked syncopation within the shifted meter. The key to conveying the notated meter turns out to be clearly feeling the focal impulses on the eighth rests. When this happens, the staccato eighths are not heard as on-beat accents; rather, they spring out of the silent focal impulses and lead into the slurs. It is this preparation that allows the start of the slur to be heard as a weighted strong beat and not as an accented syncopation. It is not extraordinarily difficult to achieve this result in each hand separately, but doing it in both hands at once is a different matter. In the process of rehearsing the passage with David Keep, the image that seemed particularly helpful was of two-handed juggling, with one hand catching a ball (playing the sighing figures) while the other threw a ball into the air (played the silent focal impulses). This is similar to imagining performing two different binary impulse cycles at once, with cycles aligned with the meter in the usual way in the right hand and with upward-oriented binary cycles in the left. Two different recordings of the passage as performed by Keep are provided as sound examples 15.2 and 15.3. Sound example 15.2 is more overt, the tempo is allowed more expressive freedom, and the sighing figures are often lingered over. This performance seems exaggerated in some ways, but given how difficult it can be to hear the notated meter and how unfamiliar an experience this may be for listeners well acquainted with the passage, it seemed a helpful aid—and even in this performance, there are moments when it becomes difficult to hang onto the notated meter. The performance in sound example 15.3 is more subtle, and it seems in many ways preferable, at least once listeners have become able (probably with the help of sound ex. 15.2) to hear the notated meter at all. Although still dolce, it is more circumspect in its treatment of the sighing figures, and the tempo is both more consistent and more typical than the slow tempo used in sound example 15.2.

15.3. Hemiola

A number of examples of hemiola were discussed in chapter 8, where we saw that most hemiolas offer two main options for placing focal impulses: in accord with the notated meter or on the three main beats of the hemiola. Although focal impulses aligned with the hemiola are often the most obvious option, retaining the notated meter can create more fluidity and forward motion. The notated meter can be a good default option unless some feature such as a syncopation within the hemiola (as in some examples from chaps. 7 and 12) gives the hemiola placement a strong advantage.

As noted, hemiolas are often used before cadences to create a broadening of pace; with cadences that want to be approached with significant momentum, the hemiola creates the danger of a loss of forward motion, especially if focal impulses follow the hemiola meter. The passage with the trombones near the end of the final movement of Brahms's Symphony No. 4 (mm. 273–80) is a case in point. Another hemiola passage that can dissipate momentum near the end is found in the final Capriccio from Brahms's op. 116 (ex. 15.3). Many pianists seem to place focal impulses with the hemiola in measures 82–89; this easily creates an effect of zooming out, broadening the pace and slackening the drive toward the cadence, and the effect is particularly pronounced when the tempo also slows down over these measures. For me, this sends a gestural message that we have already arrived, even as we are still waiting for the final tonic resolution, and it saps some of the force of the arrival. Granted, this may be what Brahms had in mind, as there *is* a real sense of

Example 15.3. Brahms, Capriccio op. 116/7, mm. 74–92, Allegro agitato.

already having arrived during those measures: the postcadential extension unfolds over a tonic pedal, and the repeated doubling of duration of the initially driving bass notes represents an undeniable slowing down. Nonetheless, focal impulses that stay with the notated meter can at least help maintain forward motion into the resolution.

This passage is further complicated in that the meter changes in measure 90 at the moment of the final tonic arrival, going to $\frac{2}{4}$ from $\frac{3}{8}$. This change strongly implies that the quarter-note beat of the hemiola meter has turned

Example 15.4. Robert Schumann, Piano Concerto op. 54, iii, mm. 80–88, Allegro vivace, reduced score.

into the main beat by the time the passage is over. Although this could serve as evidence that performers should feel the hemiola meter throughout, I prefer to maintain the notated meter until the final two hemiola measures 88–89, switching only at that point to the hemiola meter. Pianist David Keep performs the passage this way in sound example 15.4. As is often the case with potential heard meters, the alternative meter remains hearable in any performance; the difference between a performance that reflects the alternative meter and one that reflects the heard meter is not that the alternative meter is excluded if the heard meter is performed, but rather that hearing the notated meter becomes possible if it is also performed. It follows that the performance offered here will not exclude hearing the hemiola meter throughout the hemiola passage, but it may both help a listener inclined to maintain the notated meter and also help maintain the pace as the cadence is approached, even if a degree of broadening is inescapably written into the score.

Our final example of unshifted hemiola is an extended one, and it comes not from Brahms but from Robert Schumann; it is the second half of the exposition from the finale of the Piano Concerto op. 54. Referring to the beginning of the passage, Krebs (1999, 47) describes it as Schumann's "most celebrated example of subliminal dissonance" (his term for an alternative heard meter). Rarely performed in the notated meter, its various textures invite more than one kind of treatment of hemiola passages, and as the music proceeds, its hemiolas begin to alternate with passages that strongly suggest shifted meter.[5] A supplemental annotated score of the entire passage is available online.[6] In sound example 15.5, David Keep performs the solo part and William Davidson performs the orchestral reduction.

The second theme is shown in example 15.4. Focal impulses are usually placed following the hemiola meter, as demonstrated in video example 8.1, so that it sounds like a march in triple meter. But it is also possible to retain the

Example 15.5. Robert Schumann, Piano Concerto op. 54, iii, mm. 105–9, Allegro vivace, reduced score.

notated meter, a choice that seems supported by the slurring over the staccato dots. If the focal impulses fall on the downbeats, the hemiola will sound like a cross-rhythm (sound ex. 15.5, start). After appearances in the orchestra and in the solo piano (in the local dominant), the second theme returns to the orchestra with the solo piano playing a filigree (ex. 15.5). The orchestra will presumably continue as before, but now we discover that focal impulses on the downbeats worked in part because there were no attack points on the even downbeats of the phrase; here, because the piano has continuous eighth notes, focal impulses on all downbeats would tend to flatten out the hemiola, with the cross-rhythm too far in the background relative to the accents created by the focal impulses. To bring out the hemiola while remaining rooted in the notated meter, the solo pianist can articulate the second beat of the hemiola with focal impulses that are shifted in the manner of anticipations and sustained until the next strong beat (ex. 15.5; sound ex. 15.5, 0:22).

The remainder of the exposition has the character of an extended episode leading to the cadence in measure 251, which ends the exposition and introduces a brief fragment of the first theme. The first more metrically complex material encountered in this episode also has a hemiola rhythm (m. 144) and features the same rhythmic issues as the filigree at the end of the second theme; focal impulses are therefore placed in the same way (see the supplemental annotated score; sound example 15.5, 0:56).

In the episode's next material, the piano strongly suggests a shift of heard downbeat to the second quarter beat (ex. 15.6). Although the second

Example 15.6. Robert Schumann, Piano Concerto op. 54, iii, mm. 177–82, Allegro vivace, reduced score.

beat and the downbeat are both marked by contour accents, the accent on the second beat is stronger because of the extreme registral contrast; the motive also segments at that point, creating another kind of accent on the second beat. Despite these strong indications of a potential shift of meter, there are good reasons to retain the notated meter, the most obvious being that the orchestra is clearly in the notated meter with material based on the first theme.[7] The notated downbeats also have accents indicated in the piano part. Having the pianist stay in notated meter makes sense given the nature of the join between the previous hemiola and the potentially shifted material: if the shift is heard, an early downbeat will intrude awkwardly on the hemiola in progress, and the shift back will be equally abrupt. A pianist who remains in the notated meter will still want to vividly accentuate the dynamically plunging contour of the solo line, however. As with the previous two passages, shifting focal impulses to follow anticipations in an extended sense (supported here by harmonic rhythm) can help a performer give weight to a surface rhythmic event that is heard within the notated meter (ex. 15.6; sound ex. 15.5, 1:24, 1:40).[8]

These brief excerpts from the (much larger) second half of the exposition show that in a notoriously complex passage, performers can highlight the features that strain against the notated meter without ever departing from it in either hearing or physical motion (for the full passage, consult the supplemental annotated score and sound ex. 15.5).

15.4. Shifted Hemiola

Ryan McClelland (2018) has recently made the insightful observation that while hemiola is itself a form of metrical dissonance, it often functions in Brahms's music to clarify the notated meter after a period of instability or to return to notated meter from some alternative heard meter. This would imply that hemiola rarely occurs within shifted meters, an implication that is confirmed by my own survey of more complex hemiolas in Brahms (Ito, in preparation c; one example is mm. 57–58 of the first movement of the Symphony No. 3, op. 90, discussed briefly in sect. 12.2). Not uncommon, however, are hemiolas that feature conflicts with the notated meter. All hemiolas conflict with notated meter at a basic level, but they are most commonly in phase with the notated meter, with the strongest heard beat in the hemiola aligning with a strong beat in the notated meter (usually the downbeat). The issue here concerns hemiolas that are out of phase with the notated meter, in which the most strongly emphasized note within the hemiola falls on a weaker beat within the notated meter. How may these hemiolas be understood, apart from the few clear cases of shifted meter and the many clear cases of simple syncopation? Here we examine several out-of-phase hemiolas; ultimately, each will be reconciled with the notated meter, although the manner in which this occurs will vary.[9]

The middle section of the final Capriccio from op. 116, shown in example 15.7, features a hemiola melody that is displaced with respect to the bar lines. For Samarotto (2012), the heard meter follows the hemiola. The passage is frequently heard and performed in this way, and I used to hear it that way myself (although hearing the downbeat on the final eighth of the measure and not on the second, as Samarotto does). But two features of the music made me dissatisfied with this hearing. First, the movement begins and ends in $\frac{2}{4}$, and $\frac{6}{8}$ is used only for this middle section; if Brahms is willing to change meter signatures, why not find a way out of the shift and align hearing with notation in $\frac{3}{4}$? Second, the section ends clearly in the notated, unshifted $\frac{6}{8}$, especially in the first ending, but without any clear kind of metrical transition—rather, the notated meter emerges as if out of fog. Could this be a sign that notated meter is viable throughout? For me, the smoking gun was the observation of a few midbar chord changes (e.g., in mm. 26 and 28). As long as the harmonic rhythm corresponded to the measure, I could sweep the displacement of melody and accompaniment under the carpet as a composed-out example of nineteenth-century asynchrony between the hands. But the harmony's reinforcement of the second dotted-quarter beat

Example 15.7. Brahms, Capriccio op. 116/7, mm. 21–46, Allegro agitato.

in $\frac{6}{8}$ suggested that the notated meter might actually serve as an organizing framework for this music.

There followed a process of trying to find a way to convincingly hear the melody in relation to the notated $\frac{6}{8}$ meter. I started by conducting the meter and singing the melody as an unshifted hemiola, so starting with the C on the second of the hemiola's quarter-note beats in measure 21; I conducted dotted-quarter beats to reinforce the notated meter, but I felt the music in one. I then moved the melody one eighth earlier, to its actual notated position, and tried to sing and hear it as a version of the previous melody with anticipations added. With the hand that was not conducting, I performed the final eighth of the measure as an anticipation that was sustained into the downbeat, to connect with the release of weight that occurred on the downbeats in my previous, unshifted version of the melody. I again felt the melody in one, and I connected it with the unshifted version by placing no particular emphasis on any of the quarter notes except those felt as anticipations of the downbeats. I wanted to avoid emphasis in the middle of the measure created by what I saw as an essentially coinciden-tal alignment between the anticipation of the third hemiola beat in the melody and the second dotted-quarter beat of the notated meter—an emphasis that took effort to avoid, especially because I was conducting those dotted-quarter beats. But as with trying not to imagine a pink elephant, negatives are difficult; I found that the best way to avoid the midbar emphasis was by feeling more weight in the anticipation and letting the release of that weight energize the rest of the measure. This strategy placed the focus on the larger unit, rendering a new influx of energy in the middle of the bar superfluous.

Moving to the piano to explore the full texture, I found that an orchestral conception of the music was helpful. This conception allowed melody and accompaniment to be guided by the dynamic shapes of their own lines, and it also helped me to maintain a strong sense of the notated $\frac{6}{8}$, felt in one. The accompaniment parts were imagined as a dialogue between flutes and cellos, with expressive leaning on the downbeats lengthening the first notes of their entrances. The melody was heard as a midrange woodwind instrument such as an English horn, fitting the somewhat veiled quality of the melodic line. Hearing orchestrally was especially helpful in maintaining the character of each of the parts as they switched between the hands. In the rehearsal process with David Keep, we found that it was also helpful to allow the melody line to have fairly free rubato, especially around the climax in measure 35, so that the hands would often be somewhat asynchronous in the middle of the bar. Asynchronies on the second eighth were also common, in that case resulting from the shaping of the accompaniment.

The recording that resulted from this process is presented as sound example 15.6. Although some commercial recordings resemble this performance, it seems more common for pianists to be clear in projecting a shifted meter, cued especially by a loudness accent on the second of the eighths in the accompaniment.[10] There are many moving performances that project the shifted hemiola meter, but it does tend to ease the metrical conflict that Brahms has written into the passage. As we have seen, when a performer invests strongly in an alternative heard meter, it is often difficult for a listener to maintain the notated meter. And so the performer whose own metrical hearing follows the shifted hemiola in a straightforward way will tend to bring listeners along. This renders the shifted hemiola inaudible *as* a shifted hemiola; it becomes one of Krebs's (1999) subliminal dissonances. In overcoming the notated meter, the shifted hemiola loses its identity, becoming a simple metrical consonance in the heard $\frac{3}{4}$, with only the return of notated meter at the ends of the sections giving any hint of the metrical conflict. But if the passage is performed and heard in the notated meter, the quality of the shifted hemiola becomes very much a part of the character of the melody. I find this quality, floating and yet filled with a deeply troubled tension, to be compelling. As in many other instances, here metrical dissonance is best honored by resisting its most obvious implications.

The next passage is similar in many respects to the middle section of op. 116, no. 7; it is the return of the opening theme from the Capriccio op. 76, no. 5. This return must be understood in relation to the initial appearance of the theme (ex. 15.8). Like the previous example, it is an agitated hemiola melody, but in this case, the most likely hearing is in the notated meter of $\frac{6}{8}$; against the articulation of the dotted-quarter beats in the left hand, the unshifted hemiola will probably be heard as a cross-rhythm, and those emphatic dotted quarters also make it likely that the performer will feel the music in two.

When the theme returns in measure 87 (ex. 15.9), the melody is displaced; given the change of meter to $\frac{2}{4}$, the rhythm is as close to a shifted hemiola as Brahms could come without writing triplets. But a straightforward performance in the notated meter will sound very different from the shifted hemiola melody of op. 116, no. 7; with both main beats still strongly marked in the bass, the midbar emphasis, in several cases strongly reinforced by the contour of the melody, will tend to replace sinuous fluidity with a sharply etched rhythmic profile. Midbar emphasis is also reinforced by the obvious option of using focal impulses on the quarter-note beats; this is shown in example 15.9 and demonstrated by David Keep in sound example 15.7. This passage is strongly linked to the displaced hemiola, both in its durational patterning

Example 15.8. Brahms, Capriccio op. 76/5, mm. 1–4.

Example 15.9. Brahms, Capriccio op. 76/5, mm. 86–90, Agitato, ma non troppo presto, focal impulses following meter.

and because of its original meter and rhythm, and yet in terms of expressive character, it is worlds away. This incongruity motivated a search for a new interpretive lens.

The key that led into a new perspective turned out to be the observation of a further parallel between the rhythm in the thematic return and the shifted hemiola. The shifted hemiola in ⅜ can be viewed as two half-measure cells; if the order of the cells is reversed, the result is the simple hemiola. This is illustrated in example 15.10a.[11] Similarly, as illustrated in example 15.10b, the rhythm of measures 86–94 can be understood as consisting of two half-measure cells that, when permuted, result in a rhythm similar to the hemiola. The syncopation created by a juxtaposition of the two orderings is illustrated in example 15.10c. The unsyncopated version of this rhythm should look familiar; it is half of the clave pattern, the part called the *tresillo*. And when the tresillo is combined with steady quarter notes in ²⁄₄, quarter notes of the sort supplied by the bass in the passage at hand, the composite rhythm that results is the habanera rhythm shown in example 15.10d. Given the popularity of the habanera among (especially French) European composers of the

Example 15.10. Related rhythmic patterns: (a) hemiola, with half-bar modules than can be reversed to form syncopation within the hemiola; (b) *tresillo*, again with reversible half-bar modules; (c) *tresillo* in lower voice, syncopation in *tresillo* in upper voice; and (d) habanera rhythm.

late nineteenth and early twentieth centuries, it is quite likely that Brahms would have encountered it at some point.[12]

These observations led to an attempt to read the left hand in terms of the habanera, and especially the tresillo, with this providing a ground for the figure of the melody in the right hand. When hemiolas feature simple syncopations, I usually prefer to place focal impulses with the hemiola; in parallel to this, a performance was first envisioned in which focal impulses followed the tresillo; this placement is given above the staff as option *a* in example 15.11. This way of performing the passage was not entirely successful. No longer aligned with focal impulses, the right hand's rhythm was free to float gracefully over the surface, but because the patterning of the left hand's sixteenth notes gives only occasional support to this focal impulse placement, the accentuation often felt arbitrary.

The first attempt brought the habanera rhythm to the fore; a more convincing performance was crafted by allowing it to recede while still exerting influence. This was done by putting the focal impulses back in alignment with the notated meter, but with adjustments that reflect the tresillo. As shown as option *b* in example 15.11, the second focal impulse still falls on the fourth sixteenth, but now it is performed as an anticipation, sustained into the second beat and then released. And in place of a full focal impulse on the third sixteenth of the second beat, a secondary focal impulse is used to gently inflect the flow and to bind together the final two sixteenths. As in the straightforward performance in the notated meter, the melodic note in the middle of the bar coincides with a focal impulse, but now it coincides only with the release of a sustained focal impulse, not also with the attack. Especially in the context of the tresillo, the motional quality of the shifted, sustained focal impulse

Example 15.11. Brahms, Capriccio op. 76/5, mm. 86–94, Agitato, ma non troppo presto; in (a) focal impulses follow the habanera rhythm, and in (b) they respond both to the habanera and to the notated meter.

resonated with my (non-expert) experiences observing and participating in Latin dance, and so this became a source of inspiration for the specific character of motion I imagined, having to do primarily with a combination of fluidity with a strong rhythmic sense.[13]

The resulting performance is heard in sound example 15.8. The midbar melody notes do receive some accentuation—quite appropriately, given the swells and contour accents—but unlike the performance in the notated meter without adjustments, this accentuation does not dispel the floating sense that helps connect it with the syncopated hemiola. As part of the expressive emphasis on these notes, there was often asynchrony with the left hand; this seemed generally appropriate, and it also made the notes less rhythmically pointed. This way of performing the passage responds to the more purposefully striding bass line while still connecting with the expressive world of the shifted hemiola as it appeared in op. 116, no. 7. Although the emotional spaces

Example 15.12. Brahms, Clarinet Quintet op. 115, i, mm. 25–41, Allegro. (*Cont.*)

of the two passages are not the same, both are able to use metrical dissonance to convey a heartbreaking inner conflict.

Our final passage, the transition and the start of the second theme from the first movement of the Clarinet Quintet (ex. 15.12), includes several kinds of metrical dissonance. As indicated in the example, most of the transition, specifically measures 25–33, can be heard in 1.5LBs. Although this hearing may

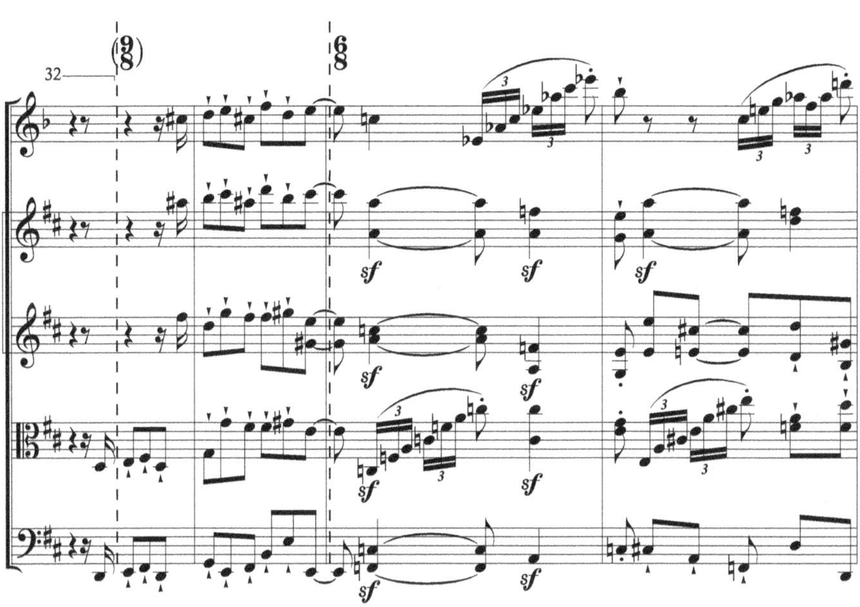
32
(9/8)
6/8
sf
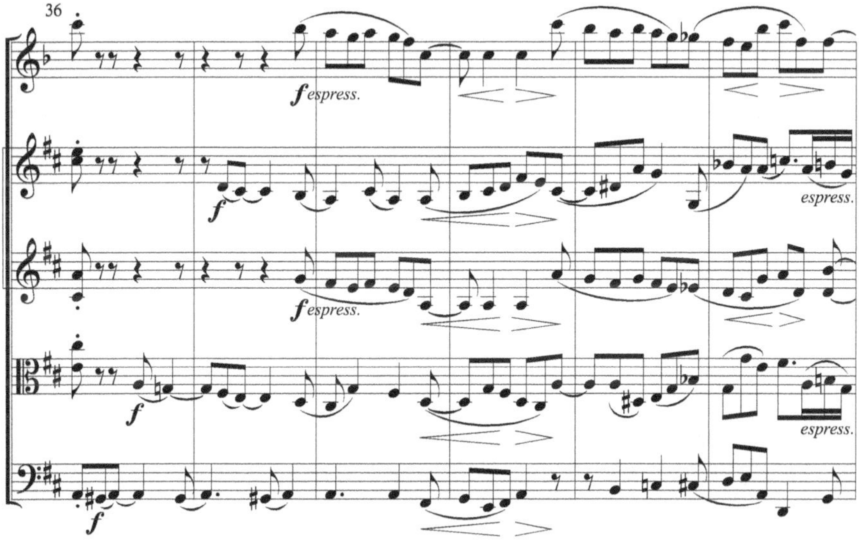
36
f espress.
f
espress.

seem somewhat tenuous, it is strongly confirmed by the parallel passage in the recapitulation (mm. 149–54), in which the 1.5LBs are obvious. John Rink (1995a) observed with respect to op. 116 that Brahms often allows metrical implications to emerge gradually, so that initially latent possibilities become manifest later. This is indeed something seen frequently in Brahms's output (Ito, in preparation c); it is one facet of his much-discussed love of ambiguity (Epstein 1979; Dunsby 1981; Smith 2006). In this passage, performing in terms of a mental rebarring seems wholly appropriate. One positive outcome is that it becomes easier to perceive a hemiola that is at least suggested in the fourth and fifth heard measures of the passage, indicated above the staff in the example. This hemiola is not as simple as a return to the notated $\frac{6}{8}$ because the hemiola is shifted with respect to the bar lines. One might ask why the passage should be heard in terms of the rebarring if the possibility of $\frac{9}{4}$ is only latent or emergent in this passage, waiting to become manifest later. The reason has to do with the balance of power between the two hearings. As we have seen, alternative metrical hearings are often quite robust, hearable no matter how a passage is performed, with the notated meter more likely to need help from the performers. This case is different; because the features pointing toward the alternative meter are subtle, there is no danger of the performers giving away Brahms's game too early. If the performers simply hear in the alternative meter themselves, most listeners will either continue in the notated meter or else be somewhat underoriented—or even disoriented—metrically. At most, the performers will be giving slightly stronger hints of things to come, and perhaps allowing listeners who know what will follow in the recapitulation to recognize that it is possible here as well.

The two measures that immediately follow the 1.5LBs, measures 34 and 35, are metrically confusing on a number of grounds. The crucial features of these measures are the ties across the bar line into measure 34 and then the sforzandi that fall on the second eighths of the next three dotted-quarter beats; these features create the strong possibility of hearing a meter that is shifted by one eighth note, so that the downbeat is heard on the second eighth-beat of each measure. Passages that are disorienting metrically are not uncommon in Brahms, but these measures stand out because their alternative implications can reach across the formal boundary that follows and into the new theme; it is much more common for alternative meters to resolve to the notated meter before the ends of their formal sections.[14] Because of the salience of the cello's G♯ on the second eighth of measure 36, it is possible that the shifted meter could be heard as continuing into the second theme area; given the quarter-note periodicities, a shifted meter would probably be organized in

Example 15.13. Brahms, Clarinet Quintet op. 115, i, mm. 32–41, Allegro, alternative metrical notation.

terms of a $\frac{3}{4}$ hemiola (ex. 15.13). Within this heard meter of the shifted hemiola, a further hemiola is created by the half-note periodicity defined by the cello's G♯s and the answers in the upper strings a quarter-beat later. Although it would have been possible to notate these measures in $\frac{3}{2}$ in the example, the hemiola is such a standard feature of Brahms's music that it seemed unnecessary to further rebar the music; instead, the hemiola is indicated above the staff, with the expectation that performers would be in the hemiola meter for those measures, which is to say in a shifted double hemiola with respect to the notated $\frac{6}{8}$.[15] When the second theme proper enters in m. 38, it is malleable enough metrically that it too can be heard in the $\frac{3}{4}$ shifted hemiola meter, as indicated in the example. In sound example 15.9, the passage is performed as in Example 15.13 (and using parts rebarred in that way) by clarinetist Bixby Kennedy and the Verona Quartet, violinists Jonathan Ong and Dorothy Ro, violist Abigail Rojansky, and cellist Warren Hagerty. As indicated by the dashed bar lines, the $\frac{10}{8}$ measure was felt in four, 3 + 3 + 2 + 2.

It will probably come as no surprise that I do not find this way of performing the passage entirely satisfactory. The $\frac{10}{8}$ measure is one reason, as it does seem too Stravinskian for Brahms, but a reason less reliant on taste is that the downbeat of measure 36 is a very significant cadence; it is the half cadence that prepares for the second theme group, a medial caesura in the influential terms of Hepokoski and Darcy (2006). For this cadence to fall on a final weak eighth beat in $\frac{6}{8}$ seems bizarre, for the good reason that in music of the eighteenth and nineteenth centuries, cadences fall on strong beats in the overwhelming majority of cases. Most performers seem to hear this as well. I know of no commercial recordings in which the passage is performed as in example 15.13 and sound example 15.9. The most common way of understanding the passage, at least judging from the sound of the performances, is to hear the metrical shift in measures 34 and 35 but then to shift back, so that the cadence in measure 36 is heard as falling on the downbeat.

But this approach also has problems. Granted, the $\frac{10}{8}$ measure can be improved by hearing it as $\frac{9}{8}$ with an extra eighth, either with a bit of a hesitation or as 3 + 3 + 4 eighths. What is harder to work around is the lack of parallelism in the metrical interpretations of the downbeats of measures 35 and 36. A high degree of similarity exists between measures 34 and 35, especially in the first violin part. It would seem that the notes that directly follow these measures, the downbeats of 35 and 36, should also be similar in metrical interpretation and degree of accentual weight; but the most common way of performing the passage makes the first a weak-beat eighth and the second a downbeat. Returning to that first violin part, the melodic approach to the two downbeats is identical, and there is also a shared harmonic meaning, both chords being local dominants: measure 36 is a half cadence in D major, and in measure 35, the C chord is V in relation to the F-major chord that just deceptively resolved V/V to ♮VI/V. We could even imagine this V chord taking part in a half cadence, a possibility that is realized in example 15.14, with the chord on the downbeat of measure 35 receiving the continuation that follows the downbeat of measure 36. Given how strange a tritone key relationship would

Example 15.14. Brahms, Clarinet Quintet op. 115, i, mm. 32–38, Allegro, first alternative version, omitting m. 35 and modulating to F major.

be between first and second themes, example 15.14 does not show a viable alternative course for the piece but rather underscores the role of the downbeat of measure 35 as a feint, embedded in the rhetoric of a failed attempt.

If the downbeat of measure 35 is understood as gesturing toward the medial caesura that will arrive on the following downbeat, this strongly suggests that both measures 34 and 35 can be performed in the notated meter; the ties

Example 15.15. Brahms, Clarinet Quintet op. 115, i, mm. 32–38, Allegro, second alternative version, omitting mm. 34–35.

across the bar line into measure 34 and the strong dynamic, articulatory, and durational accents on the second and fifth eighth beats of measures 34 and 35 would then all be understood as contributing to strong metrical dissonance in those measures, not as indications of a different heard meter. No matter what the performers do, many listeners will probably hear a shift in those measures, but how can the performers help themselves to hear and project the notated meter? Playing through a few more alternative versions of the passage can help in clarifying the meanings that the ties and sforzandi have in the interpretation put forward here. In example 15.15, measures 34 and 35 have been removed altogether, showing that the half cadence could perfectly well have arrived two measures earlier; this is heard in sound example 15.10. In example 15.16, heard in sound example 15.11, measures 34 and 35 have been restored, but the deceptive resolution of the secondary chord arrives squarely on the downbeat of measure 34, eliminating the tie over the bar line. This significantly clarifies the sforzandi as syncopations. Finally, having absorbed the implications of the alternative versions, in sound example 15.12 Bixby Kennedy and the members of the Verona Quartet perform the original passage as it appears in op. 115; their performance reflects the change of notation for the 1.5LBs in the transition, but otherwise their intention was to project the notated meter.

This way of performing the passage is rare. A handful of commercial recordings make the downbeat of measure 35 sound like a downbeat, and a very few make the second eighth beat of measure 34 sound like a syncopation.

Example 15.16. Brahms, Clarinet Quintet op. 115, i, mm. 32–38, Allegro, third alternative version, clarifying notated meter.

Among them, I would single out the recording by Anthony McGill and the Pacifica Quartet (2013, 1:06). In addition to the moments just mentioned, the transition's 1.5LBs and the hemiola within them both emerge with particular clarity, and these features fit into an extremely moving overall conception.

Attentive listeners to sound example 15.12 may notice in the performance of the start of the second theme that not every trace of the possibility of a shifted hemiola rhythm has vanished. But rather than being the real heard and performed meter, as in sound example 15.9, it is now a subtle cross-rhythm. The fluid shape of the shifted hemiola rhythm, as heard above, especially in the central section of op. 116, no. 7, comes through in the gentle emphases given to the beats that define it (the strong beats in ex. 15.13). It has become a shadow meter, to use Samarotto's (1999) evocative term in Rothstein's sense (1995).[16] Performances of the start of the second theme balance the notated meter with the shifted hemiola in various ways, and many are quite compelling. What makes sound example 15.12 unique among the performances I have heard, and what makes me particularly grateful to Kennedy and the members of the Verona Quartet for their beautiful rendition, is the combination of two things: the clear projection of my interpretation of meter in the transition, and in the second theme a particular way of balancing the notated meter as the primary frame of reference with the shifted hemiola as a cross-rhythm. Alternative heard meters can certainly be fully valid, and sometimes they are clearly preferable. But this passage has shown once more that even when an alternative heard meter may seem inevitable, hearing and performing in the notated meter can turn out to be deeply rewarding.

Notes

1. When a movement does not end in the key in which it began, the status of subsidiary keys is enhanced in a similar way. The implications of this observation for the metaphor of metrical dissonance are discussed in the full study (Ito, in preparation c).

2. In my future work on Brahms (Ito, in preparation c), I will discuss a few ways in which performers who switch to an alternative heard meter can allow the notated meter to affect their performance and their hearing (see chap. 8, n. 14).

3. The most disorienting features of Samarotto's interpretation are the lack of an attack point in the middle of the implied $\frac{2}{4}$ measure and the fact that this measure directly precedes the plagal cadence, significantly destabilizing it. These are not necessarily problems from the standpoint of Samarotto's interpretation.

4. For the passage resembling Messiaen, see chap. 8, n. 5.

5. It seems that the notated meter is rarely taken seriously as a live option. Frisch (1984, 92) says of this passage, "for about forty measures the theme floats blithely in $\frac{3}{2}$, disregarding the written $\frac{3}{4}$ meter." And Joel Sheveloff (2000, 154), describing the difficulties of returning to the notated meter after the hemiola sections, recounts that he has "witnessed great artists in states of deep distress here." When he advocates having the conductor remain in the notated meter, "though no sound matche[s] his perverse-seeming beat" (154), it is clear that he is describing a hypothetical situation. He suggests that a visual cue to an aurally irrelevant meter could help in returning to that meter when it regains relevance; the reading of the passage offered here goes substantially further in reducing the difficulties.

6. The supplemental annotated score is available on KiltHub, Carnegie Mellon University's online data repository. An internet search for *KiltHub, Ito, focal impulse theory,* and *Schumann concerto* should bring it up.

7. One of the best pieces of evidence that many musicians hear a metrical shift in this material can be heard in a number of recordings by leading orchestras; as this passage continues, the synchronization between piano and orchestra often becomes increasingly imprecise, suggesting that the potential for confusion inherent in alternating between hemiola meter and shifted meter is taking its toll.

8. Note that although the technique is the same, placing the sustained, shifted focal impulse on beat 2 rather than on beat 3 creates a more dramatic effect, as the anticipation must begin so hard on the heels of the downbeat's release.

9. Other examples of shifted hemiolas reconciled with the notated meter have already been seen, from Beethoven's Symphony No. 3 (chap. 7) and from "Grillen" from Schumann's *Phantasiestücke* (chap. 12).

10. Wilhelm Kempff's (1963) recording is particularly overt because his arpeggios have loudness accents on each of the quarter beats of the shifted $\frac{3}{4}$ meter.

11. The versions of these patterns in which the eighth rest is replaced with an eighth note are used frequently in Brahms's music. Because these patterns can fit within the notated meter, they can be used to open a door to hemiola or to shifted hemiola without stating those rhythms unambiguously. This property is often exploited by Brahms when transitioning into or out of hemiola (Ito, in preparation c).

12. He certainly encountered it in Bizet's *Carmen*, but although it seems likely he knew it before the 1878 composition of op. 76, no. 5 (Clive 2006, 47-48), the most direct evidence for this is anecdotal (de Ternant 1924).

13. Neither option *a* nor option *b* represented an attempt to imitate actual performance practices of clave-based musics, which seem to be quite different; see the concluding chapter, n. 5.

14. I am indebted to Le Lu for the observation that the shifted meter could be heard to continue into the second theme. A similar analysis of possible alternative heard meters is offered by Ellenwood (1996, 51–61), who also gives rebarrings similar to ex. 15.13.

15. Nested hemiolas, even rather deeply nested hemiolas, appear a number of times in Brahms's music (Ito, in preparation c); they have also been discussed by Cohn (2001) and Murphy (2007).

16. See chap. 12, n. 16.

16

THE FIRST MOVEMENTS OF THE BRAHMS
SONATAS OP. 120

THIS CHAPTER PUTS THE APPLICATION OF FOCAL IMPULSE theory in a larger context, showing how focal impulse choices interact with other factors in performances of two entire movements, the first movements of Brahms's two clarinet sonatas, op. 120. Although these movements contrast in many ways, the analyses presented here reveal that the movements feature remarkably similar progressions of temporal intensity, including in both cases codas that must reconcile otherwise unresolved temporal conflicts and contrasts. Because rhythm and meter are central to the narrative arcs of these movements, focal impulse choices can amplify their dramatic trajectories, thereby highlighting the contributions of rhythm and meter to form (Krebs 1999; Temperley 2003; McClelland 2010; Ng 2012; Klorman 2016). In the sound examples, I play the viola and David Keep plays the piano, performing Brahms's own versions for viola and piano. Although my own performance abilities do not rank with those of the musicians who have been kind enough to record the other examples for this book, an important advantage is that I can discuss the performance process from a first-person perspective.[1]

Complete supplemental annotated scores of both movements are available online. They show the choices for focal impulse placement and hypermeter that were used in the recordings, and they also show major formal segments.[2] It will be helpful to have these at hand while reading the chapter. Printed examples are provided for a few key passages.

16.1. Sonata in F Minor, op. 120, no. 1, Allegro appassionato

Exposition

The exposition of the first movement of op. 120, no. 1, unfolds as a long, gradual crescendo of metrical dissonance. To heighten the contrast with the strong metrical conflicts at the end of the third (C minor) theme area, the calmness of the opening was accentuated by using cyclical focal impulses placed one per measure, a choice that would have been likely in any case, given the prevalent harmonic rhythm of one chord per measure and the similarly slow rate of melodic motion.[3] The first theme area was also calibrated in relation to the return of the piano's introductory statement near the end of the coda (mm. 227–30). Because it follows the final cadence in measure 227, this passage was interpreted as the movement's final state; with its bare fifths and octaves, it defines a cold, dark place of death, defeat, and despair. The six warmer bars that follow seem more like a wistful reflection on what might have been than like meaningful comfort or redemption. In relation to the end of the movement, then, the expressive character often heard when the opening theme is played on the clarinet seemed more appropriate than the sound used in many viola performances, which, to my ears, can take too much pleasure in the richness of the lower register. We therefore strove for a more reserved and austere sound in the beginning, wanting to project something along the lines of a protagonist entering a situation that can be expected to end badly. As can be seen in the supplemental annotated score, the first theme area was treated straightforwardly in terms of focal impulse placement and hypermeter. The hypermeter proceeded in regular four-bar units, and only two passages raised the possibility of adjusting focal impulses. They were adjusted in the piano in measures 12–17, responding to the ties with shifted, sustained focal impulses. They were not adjusted for the hemiola of measures 21 and 22; this choice made the notes tied across the bar line into syncopations, and it also fostered forward motion in those measures.

While the transition and the second theme begin to move away from the stability of the first theme area, they only mildly anticipate the conflict that will follow in the third theme area. Tables 16.1 and 16.2 chart the body of the movement, with exposition and recapitulation in table 16.1 and development in table 16.2. For each formal/thematic area, they show metrical dissonance, hypermeter, and the main proposed focal impulse use. It may be helpful to refer to these tables periodically in the course of this discussion.

The transition begins in measure 33 with first theme material, now appearing as a five-bar unit that presents the movement's first disruption of regular four-bar hypermeter. As illustrated in the supplemental annotated score, it is straightforward using the schema approach (chap. 2; Ito 2013a) to understand an extra hyperbeat 2/4 leading into the clear hyperbeats 3/4 and 4/4 that end the unit. In measure 38, the second theme arrives in D-flat major (ex. 16.1). Metrically, the theme's main interest comes from the canonic

Table 16.1. Form, metrical dissonance, hypermeter, and focal impulse use in the exposition and recapitulation of Brahms's Clarinet Sonata no. 1, op. 120/1, i.

Theme	Measures: Key	Metrical Dissonance	Hypermeter	Focal Impulse Use
1	1–32: f / 138–45: f	Minimal	Mostly stable	*(musical notation)*
Trans. (from 1)	33–37: f →D♭ / 146–52: f	Minimal	Mostly stable	*(musical notation)*
2	38–52: D♭ / 153–67: F	Syncopation in hemiola	Frequent adjustments	*(musical notation)*
3a	53–60: c / 168–75: f	Minimal	Stable	*(musical notation)*
3b	61–68: c / 176–83: f	Notated meter in clarinet vs. shifted hemiola in piano	Stable, but not aligned with hemiola	*(musical notation)*
3c	68–76: c / 183–91: f	Heard meter 4/4, heard and notated hypermeters align at endings; 3x16th pattern in recap	Four-bar units in notated meter, triple hypermeter in heard meter	c! *(musical notation)*
Closing	77–89: c / 192–205: f	Mostly consonant except for weak hemiola	Some adjustments	*(musical notation)*

imitation within the hemiola of its first two bars, measures 38–39 and 46–47; this is a pattern that Brahms used extensively (Ito, in preparation c). As discussed in chapter 15, feeling a syncopated hemiola within the notated meter can be somewhat complicated; because nothing in these measures makes it important to bring out the notated meter, focal impulses were placed on the main beats of the hemiola, and this choice made it straightforward to perform

Table 16.2. Form, metrical dissonance, hypermeter, and focal impulse use in the development of Brahms's Clarinet Sonata no. 1, op. 120/1, i.

Theme	Measures: Key	Metrical Dissonance	Hypermeter	Focal Impulse Use
2	90–115: A♭→F♭ →d♭	Syncopation in hemiola	Frequent adjustments	*[musical notation]*
3a (first derived from)	116–22: d♭	Syncopation	Stable	*[musical notation]*
3b	123–29: d♭→g♭	Hemiola with very abrupt phase resetting; also some syncopation	Mostly stable, though alignment with hemiola changes	*[musical notation]*
1	131–37: g♭→f	Mostly consonant	Stable	*[musical notation]*

the notes of the melodic line as syncopations. The beginning of the second theme is heard at 1:10 in sound example 16.1. Although the theme begins with an eight-bar unit, regular hypermeter is disrupted by the modified repetition of the material from the third and fourth bars in the fifth and sixth bars. Consequently, those measures were heard as "extra" hyperbeats 3/4 and 4/4, followed by another pair of those same hyperbeats motivated by the concluding function of measures 44–45, which lead into the second statement of the theme via the evaded cadence in measure 46. That second statement was understood in similar terms hypermetrically, with the augmentation of measure 49 in measures 51–52 providing clear motivation for an extra hyperbeat 4/4 at the very end of the theme. That hemiola is a clear example of the kind of augmentation hemiola discussed by Mirka (2009, 159–64); there are many other examples in Brahms (Ito, in preparation c). I often prefer to keep focal impulses aligned with the notated meter for hemiolas that do not contain syncopation, but in this case, the sense of forward motion fostered by that placement did not seem helpful; the eerie stillness and suspense of those measures seemed better served by focal impulses aligned with the hemiola. This choice

Example 16.1. Brahms, Clarinet Sonata No. 1, op. 120/1, i, mm. 38–41, Allegro appassionato.

Example 16.2. Brahms, Clarinet Sonata No. 1, op. 120/1, i, mm. 53–56, Allegro appassionato.

also allowed the third theme's pointed focal impulses on each quarter-note beat to emerge as a doubling of the previous rate.

The beginning of the third theme, which starts in measure 53, emphasizes a quarter-note pulse in a way that no previous material has (ex. 16.2). The downbeat is marked by contour accents in the piano's left hand and by the start of the slur. The second beat is marked by the note with which the slur ends; more importantly, the sixteenth rest and sixteenth note that follow need a source of energy on the second beat to give them a rhythmic snap into the third beat. Finally, the third beat is marked with the long duration on which the snapped rhythm lands. Taken together with the emphatic indication of "ma ben marcato," this invites focal impulses on the quarter-note beats. The third theme draws us forward; it is more about moving toward something to follow than about presenting itself as a primary locus of attention. This is heard most straightforwardly in its dominant-chord beginning and tendency to avoid the tonic. The theme's dynamism makes binary impulse cycles a clear choice, but given three focal impulses per measure, mixed impulse cycles are required. This raises a further question: Should the second or the third beat receive the contrast created by the transition from downward-oriented to upward-oriented focal impulses? A number of factors point to the more usual emphasis on beat 3: it has the longest melody notes, it is marked by harmonic change more consistently than beat 2, and it would help prepare the hemiola that begins in measure 60. Despite this, I chose to place the move to upward orientation on beat 2; as shown in example 16.2, this required the use of the focal impulse succession ↓∩↑, inserting the upward cyclical focal impulse in the middle of the binary impulse cycle, as discussed in chapter 11. This choice was based on the perception of beat 2 as the rhythmic focal point of the theme. Beyond the rhythmic snap, the contour of the motive rises to a high point on beat 2 and then subsides; beat 2 is further emphasized in the second statement of the theme by the entry of the piano's sixteenth-note arpeggios following silent or tied-over downbeats. The expressive character of a rhythmic focal point that is not well marked harmonically also seemed to fit the ominous character of this theme, with the tension that is about to erupt still simmering beneath the surface. The start of the third theme is heard at 1:41 in sound example 16.1.

In the next stages of the third theme group, the suppressed tension boils over in strong metrical dissonance. This is announced by the very unexpected entrance of the clarinet (viola) in an imitation of the end of the theme; this entrance initiates a series of hemiolas that is both metrically and hypermetrically dissonant (ex. 16.3). Hypermetrically, a single hemiola fits most prototypically in the second and third bars of a four-bar unit, as in the example from *Eine kleine Nachtmusik* discussed in chapter 8.[4] Longer strings of hemiolas, however, are more usually aligned with the grouping units (occupying the first and second or the third and fourth bars). This series of hemiolas is aligned in the opposite way, coming into phase with the notated meter on the second and fourth notated downbeats, not on the first and third. As a result, the hyperdownbeat is marked very weakly, not coinciding with a focal impulse. At the metrical level, beyond the hemiolas themselves, two other features contribute to metrical dissonance. First, the clarinet abandons the hemiola after announcing it, so that the straight notated meter of the clarinet conflicts with the hemiolas of the piano. Second, the piano's hemiolas present the initial material of the second theme group in augmentation, but

Example 16.3. Brahms, Clarinet Sonata No. 1, op. 120/1, i, mm. 60–63, Allegro appassionato.

with material previously on the crucial second beat now falling on the notated downbeat, which is also the downbeat in the large triple meter implied by the hemiolas. This divergence of parts seemed sufficient grounds to allow each to go its own way. The clarinet creates impulse polyphony when it returns to the notated meter in measure 62, with the piano continuing to place focal impulses to follow the hemiolas (ex. 16.3). This second stage of the third theme group begins at 1:57 in sound example 16.1.

The final stage of the third theme group presents the climax of the traumatic conflict; although framed by clear cadences, it intensifies the metrical and hypermetrical dissonances already present. As shown in example 16.4, the third section is prepared by a stabilization within the second. The motive of descent from A-flat to D, which had appeared previously in the fourth bars of hypermeasures in measures 56 and 60, is moved to the third bar and ushers in a strong half cadence in the following measure. At this point, the heard meter departs from the notated meter, changing the size of the heard measure—but in a way that maintains a frame of four notated bars, as occurs in a number of other passages in Brahms (Ito, in preparation c). One feature marks this passage as more unusual, however: heard and notated meters come into alignment not at the beginnings of four-bar units but at their ends, continuing the pattern of conflicting meters aligning on weak hyperbeats. Example 16.4 shows hypermeter in both notated and heard meters, with the hypermeter of the notated measures in square brackets above the hypermeter of the heard meter. The heard meter is understood as common time, starting in measure 68 and returning to the notated meter in measure 76. As can be seen in the example, the heard meter has a triple hypermetrical organization that amounts to a double hemiola ($\frac{3}{1}$) with respect to the notated meter, with the points of alignment between the two occurring in measures 68, 72, and 76, always on final hyperbeats. Metrical dissonance is further intensified by the canon between the clarinet and the right hand of the piano, both based initially on the same descent from A-flat to D.

This passage is heard starting at 2:12 in sound example 16.1. Focal impulses have been placed to follow the heard meter, with two cyclical focal impulses per heard measure. This choice was made because one would have been too few for music of such intensity, while four would have sounded beaty, also obscuring the larger shape of the canon at the half note. In performing this passage, I wanted to give primary attention to the heard meter but also to have some consciousness of the notated four-bar frame. To that end, I practiced singing the passage while conducting the two hypermeters with one in each arm, triple hypermeter for the common-time heard measures and quadruple hypermeter for the $\frac{3}{4}$ notated measures, with the two coming into alignment on the final beats of each hypermeasure.

The closing theme, which starts in measure 77, represents a refocusing after the preceding outburst; meter is stabilized, metrical dissonance mostly goes away, and hypermeter is mostly regular. Although the harmonic rhythm is relatively quick, the quarter-note beats do not seem weighted in the way they had been in the start of the third theme, and so focal impulses once per measure seemed a good choice to reflect this ratcheting down of tension. The closing theme begins at 2:30 in sound example 16.1.

To summarize: as interpreted here (table 16.1), the movement opens in a place of relative stability and placidity, metrically and hypermetrically consonant and with focal impulses only once per measure. The second (transitional) theme (in D♭ major) expresses a yearning for a positive outcome that will not be possible in this movement; it also increases tension temporally, with some metrical dissonance reflected in focal impulse placement and some hypermetrical irregularity. With the arrival of the third theme in the structurally oppositional key of the minor dominant (C minor), the pace and intensity pick up noticeably, with focal impulses every quarter note and the use of a complex form of mixed impulse cycle. As the third theme group continues, its tensions turn into open conflict, with striking forms of metrical and hypermetrical dissonance; the metrical dissonance is emphasized here by means of focal impulse placements. The closing theme is a place of regrouping and of regained stability, mostly consonant metrically and hypermetrically, with a return to focal impulses placed only on downbeats. This is the context for the start of the development section.

Example 16.4. Brahms, Clarinet Sonata No. 1, op. 120/1, i, mm. 65–78, Allegro appassionato. (*Cont.*)

Development and Recapitulation

The development section begins on a hopeful note, with the second theme material. Because the final cadence of the exposition in measure 88 seems so clearly a hyperdownbeat, I have labeled the start of the second theme in the development with hyperbeats 3/4 and 4/4, and then resumed the hypermetrical interpretation used previously. This raises an interesting question: Should the second theme in the exposition have begun with a hyperbeat 3/4? In the original context, beginning with a hyperbeat 3/4 would not have been an obvious choice; however, doing so could eliminate almost all of the hyper-metrical adjustments until the arrival of the third theme, leaving only the extra hyperbeat 4/4 brought about by the augmentation at the end. Measures 40–43, for example, clearly do not want a hyperdownbeat in measure 42, but they make perfect sense as a single hypermeasure. The reason this more straightforward reading was not used in the original passage, or even allowed to continue past the first two measures in the development, is that the repetition of hyperbeats 3/4 and 4/4 contributes to a sense of continual forward motion, of yearning for a positive outcome that seems impossible in this context.

In its grounded stability, the simpler reading seems to realize the unrealizable in ways that do not fit the larger narrative of the movement.

One moment in the performance that involves time but neither focal impulse placement nor hypermeter is the downbeat of measure 100. Many performances convey this downbeat mainly as the start of a new presentation of the second theme, down a major third from the one just heard. What such performances obscure is the fact that for one quarter note, it is possible to hear that moment as a surprising and deflating cadential arrival on the tonic minor, like a reverse Picardy third. There is something like a denial of reality in the way in which this minor arrival, which we did not foresee but perhaps should have, is quickly covered over by the reinterpretation in terms of a new major key. To give ourselves and the listener time to absorb that which will soon be denied, we lingered on that chord for a moment longer than would have been called for if it had functioned only to start the theme.

As in the exposition, the more hopeful state of the second (transitional) theme proves short lived. A contraction in measure 110 in a canon at the measure between the clarinet and the left hand of the piano introduces a hemiola, reinforced here by focal impulses, that leads to a return of third theme material in measure 116. Not yet an overt return of themes from the third theme group, this material recalls the third theme by its linear descent through a third and its return to the minor mode (a more direct reference lurks in the piano part). Significantly, given its expressive contradiction of the second theme, its key is the parallel minor of the key in which the second theme was heard in the exposition. With the return to marcato articulation and heavily marked quarter-note beats, three focal impulses per measure were an appropriate choice, using cyclical focal impulses except in measures 117 and 119, where the strong contour and rhythmic accents on beat 2 suggested the same mixed impulse cycles that were used for the start of the third theme in the exposition.

With the literal return of third theme material in measure 120, the development begins to mirror the exposition more closely than is common in a development (tables 16.1 and 16.2). The clarinet even begins the transition into the final stage of the third theme with the interrupting statement of the fifth descent—as before, forming a hemiola—with measures 123 and 124 closely paralleling measures 60 and 61. In measure 125, however, the piano takes control and averts a repetition of the climactic conclusion of the third theme. In an even more jarring intrusion by the same material, the motive enters on the second beat, resetting the phase of the hemiola. Because the hemiola had previously been out of phase with the hypermeter, this seizing of control puts the strong beats of the hemiola into alignment with the hypermetrically strong downbeats; it will lead before long into the recapitulation. It is like a violent effort of will that prevents the music from replaying the catastrophe of the exposition.

In a normal sonata form, the success of any such efforts will be short lived, especially if the catastrophe is more metrical than tonal. And here, as with many of Brahms's sonata forms, the recapitulation follows the exposition quite closely, with larger alterations confined to the first theme area (the alteration relevant here is the use of double-length heard measures in measures 147–52, suggested by the harmonic stasis of those bars). The trauma of the third theme area in the exposition is, if anything, even worse in the recapitulation, with a cross-rhythm created by groupings of three sixteenths added to the piano part in measures 184–86, an addition that complicates the music without (for me) altering its metrical interpretation. Although the normal tonal/harmonic tasks of the recapitulation have all been accomplished, there is little sense of resolution at an emotional level as the closing area draws to a close. It is left to the coda to provide whatever resolution may be possible.

Coda

The sostenuto ed espressivo section forms the larger portion of the coda, and its role may be compared with therapeutic transference: it transposes a traumatic event to a less charged context in which it can begin to be processed. This section is shown in example 16.5, and it begins at 7:15 in sound example 16.1.

There are some pitch relationships between the third theme and the final sostenuto section; for example, the motive of a linear third with which it begins recalls the slurred notes at the beginning of the third group, and the long dominant harmony of the first four measures could recall the key area of its appearance in the exposition. The primary resemblances, however, have to do with rhythm and meter. From the outset, the arpeggiated chords suggest the quarter-note pulse that has been associated exclusively with the initial theme of the third group. As shown in example 16.5, I chose to mark the weak beats of the measure not with focal impulses but with secondary focal impulses. These were used both because the marking of the beats seems only moderate, with the harmony basically static, and because the expressive quality of the opening of the section seems somewhat distant, not yet fully in touch with the place it is about to explore.

The intensification begins already in the third measure, as the registral expansion of the motive is joined by a hemiola and a hypermetrical expansion of

Example 16.5. Brahms, Clarinet Sonata No. 1, op. 120/1, i, mm. 214–36, Allegro appassionato. (*Cont.*)

the phrase, tracing a path similar to the one followed in the exposition. With the second statement of this material, starting in measure 219, the intensification picks up steam. Based on both melodic and harmonic considerations, I hear a meter of common time starting in that measure and continuing until a return to notated meter coinciding with hyperbeat 4/4 in measure 223; this is, of course, quite similar to the climactic section of the third theme group. As shown in example 16.5, focal impulses followed the heard meter at this point, using the same frequency and type as at the climax of the third theme group but with secondary focal impulses used on the weak beats in the piano part. The music builds in dynamic, registral, and emotional intensity until the apex in measure 224, a hyperdownbeat. In the one salient contrast with the trajectory of the third theme, metrically conflicted music has now been able to build to a climatic, hypermetrically weighted tonic arrival (though not to a perfect authentic cadence); in the exposition, tonic arrived with the start of the closing group, with the third theme already spent by its end. After this, the music seems to need to catch its breath, and I hear the hypermeter accelerating, following the small $\frac{2}{4}$ meter of the hemiola in measures 225 and 226. And this brings us to the desolate measures that were in mind as a destination from the outset.

Words like *acceptance* and *resignation* seem too strong to describe the hint of something resembling peace that hangs over these measures; it would be closer to say that the biting edge of desperation has been taken away. What today might be achieved through medication seems to have been won through the indirect reliving of the trauma in the previous part of the sostenuto ed espressivo, and perhaps by a hint that conflicted music has achieved something beyond its own exhaustion. Appropriate to their position following the final cadence, measures 227–30 seem like the true inner destination of the movement; the stereotyped tag that follows, though using the melodic material of the introductory measures, belongs with its greater warmth and final major sonority to the expressive world of the second theme. Does it relieve the pain to contemplate, for a final time, the illusory hope that could never be realized, or is the pain merely intensified? This is not an uncommon question for a piece by Brahms to raise, and as usual, he gives us no clear answer.

16.2. Sonata in E-flat Major, op. 120, no. 2, Allegro amabile

Expressively, the first movement of the Sonata in E-flat Major, op. 120, no. 2, belongs to a different universe from that of the Sonata in F Minor; in terms of rhythmic and metrical profile, however, there are clear similarities. These can be seen by comparing tables 16.1 and 16.3, both charting the expositions and recapitulations of their respective movements.

Exposition

Like op. 120, no. 1, the E-flat-major sonata begins with slow harmonic rhythm corresponding to the measure. Although the middle of the measure becomes somewhat more marked starting with measures 3 and 4, these contour accents seem best understood as graceful afterbeats, receding from the primary

Table 16.3. Form, metrical dissonance, hypermeter, and focal impulse use in the exposition and recapitulation of Brahms's Clarinet Sonata no. 2, op. 120/2, i.

Theme	Measures: Key	Metrical Dissonance	Hypermeter	Focal Impulse Use
1, trans.	1–21: Eb→Bb 103–19: Eb→Bb	Minimal	Some extra 3/4 4/4 bar pairs	*(musical notation)*
2a	22–27: Bb 120–25: Cb→Eb	Canon at the quarter note between clarinet and piano left hand	All hypermeasures have extra 3/4 4/4 bar pairs	*(musical notation)*
2b	28–39: Bb 126–37: Eb	Persistent syncopation in piano	More extra 3/4 4/4 bar pairs	*(musical notation)*
Closing	40–51: Bb 138–49: Eb	Minimal	Stable, no extra bars	*(musical notation)*
Codetta	52–55: Bb 150–53: Eb	Mostly consonant except for piano left hand, delay of midbar attack	Stable, no extra bars	*(musical notation)*

weight on the downbeats. In accord with this understanding, cyclical focal impulses on the downbeats were chosen for the opening theme. As shown in the supplemental annotated score, the only adjustment to the hypermeter in the first theme area is found in the measures of extension that lead from the half cadence in measure 8 into the second statement of the theme at the start of the transition. Within the first theme area, measure 10 invites comment not on musical grounds but because of the challenges it presents in performance.

Example 16.6. Brahms, Clarinet Sonata No. 2, op. 120/2, i, mm. 22–25, Allegro amabile.

Arpeggios that span multiple registers seem to be straightforward on the clarinet, but on the viola, they are quite challenging. In student performances, it
is common to hear clear signs of a focal impulse in the middle of the measure,
put there for the simple reason that it both breaks up the passage into two
smaller chunks and injects new energy in the middle of the measure. Because
this solution was not deemed acceptable on musical grounds—the measure
clearly consists of one seamless gesture—this measure required more extensive practice. Returning to examination of the score, metrical dissonance
first appears in measures 15–17, as those three notated measures are occupied
by two unnotated 1.5LBs. Responding to the more emphatic quality of these
measures, they were performed using binary impulse cycles, with the upward
focal impulses on the third beats of the 1.5LBs.

There is both a quickening of pace and an increase in metrical dissonance
with the arrival of the second theme in measure 22 (ex. 16.6).[5] This moment is
already surprising because the preceding German augmented-sixth chord has
received a common-tone resolution, skipping the expected dominant. It can
also be surprising if the canon between the clarinet and the left hand of the
piano is allowed to create questions about the true location of the downbeat, as
Edward Klorman (2016) has advocated. There is certainly much to enjoy and
admire in the performance in which Klorman illustrates this possibility; however, in the end, the complexity and strength of metrical dissonance in the passage does not rise to the level that, for me, would justify such widely divergent
metrical hearings between two performers. I hope to give a more grounded
aesthetic defense of this position in the future (Ito, in preparation c). For now,
let it suffice to say that I chose to explore different possibilities for the passage.

Example 16.7. Brahms, Clarinet Sonata No. 2, op. 120/2, i, mm. 27–31, Allegro amabile.

The clarinet part was performed using two cyclical focal impulses per measure (ex. 16.6; upward-oriented cyclical focal impulses could also work nicely here). The rate of focal impulses was determined mainly by the degree of presence that was desired in the eighths in the second half of the measure. Without a focal impulse on the third beat, those notes would still be drawing down the energy injected by the focal impulse on the downbeat, and they would have a rather inconspicuous profile. Cyclical focal impulses were chosen because of the gentle quality heard in the passage; binary impulse cycles would give the passage an intensity and forward direction that seemed out of place. The task with the piano part was to find a focal impulse placement that both brought out the canon with the clarinet and kept the piano grounded in the notated meter. The solution was to use focal impulses that are shifted, as though following anticipations, and then sustained into the beat on which they would otherwise have occurred (ex. 16.6; sound ex. 16.2, 0:58). This appeal to the anticipation in an extended sense was often supported by the pitch content.

The texture changes significantly for the second statement of the second theme, and focal impulse placements were adjusted accordingly (ex. 16.7). In the clarinet part, the more legato line with more regular rhythm suggests a more intense and continuously sung-though quality that is served well by binary impulse cycles. In the piano, the end of the canon removes the motivation for the shifted focal impulses, but the rather neutral quality of the accompaniment at this point suggests that it might continue to go its own way, using unitary impulse cycles rather than binary. From here, the music begins a long and gradual intensification toward the closing theme. At some point, it

Example 16.8. Brahms, Clarinet Sonata No. 2, op. 120/2, i, mm. 40–43, Allegro amabile.

will be appropriate for the piano to join the clarinet in using binary impulse cycles; the moment chosen for this performance was measure 34. The right hand of the piano briefly takes the melody line at that point, and the rhythm of the left hand changes, putting consistent attack points on the strong beats for the first time within the second theme area.

The cadence in measure 40 is the most heavily emphasized cadence of the exposition, and it begins the closing theme, which has the most intense quality of motion of the sonata's themes; it is the climactic goal of the exposition (ex. 16.8; sound ex. 16.2, 1:50). Although in this performance binary impulse cycles have already been present in both instruments, it is here that the alternation of releasing and pulling characters becomes most emphatic. Especially in the opening measures of the theme, the half-note beats are extremely strongly marked in the score—by the registral and durational accents in the bass, by the harmonic rhythm, and by the linear descent in half notes through a tetrachord that undergirds the melody. The tonic pedal in the bass only increases the tension rather than dampening it, as it is clear that the forces driving toward cadence must soon overcome the recalcitrance of the pianist's left hand. Not all of Brahms's late music is autumnal; here, we find youthful vigor, verdant and vernal.

For all its initial vehemence, the intensity of the closing theme dissipates rapidly during the second statement, which takes an unexpected detour to the local major mediant for the cadence. Although the rising octaves that follow in the second halves of measures 48–50 are still served well by upward focal impulses, the upward quality now issues a playful invitation rather than preparing for a forceful release. Like many codettas, the one found here strongly recalls the opening theme, and in our performance, a return to cyclical focal impulses on downbeats, arriving in the measure before the codetta, helped cement the connection.[6] Although the harmonic rhythm marks the half note in a way that the opening did not, this greater emphasis on the half bar is somewhat submerged by the late arrival of left hand, following the eighth rests on the third beats.

Although there is certainly nothing traumatic or catastrophic about this exposition, it has nonetheless followed a similar arc to that of the F-minor sonata in its motional quality. Again, this can be seen by comparing tables 16.1 and 16.3. The movement began at a place of relative repose, with slow harmonic rhythm and, in this performance, one cyclical focal impulse per measure. From there, the movement gradually added a bit of metrical dissonance and hypermetrical irregularity, still within material from the first theme group. The second theme increased both the level of metrical dissonance and the degree of marking of the half-note beats, both features that were reflected here using focal impulse placements. Further intensification across the second theme led to the closing theme, which to some extent parallels the third theme in the first movement of op. 120, no. 1. Both are climactic; in the F-minor sonata, the climax is a catastrophe expressed not least through extreme metrical and hypermetrical dissonance, while here the climax sheds metrical dissonance and (in this performance) uses binary impulse cycles aligned with the measure to help convey uninhibited lyrical strength. The codetta, paralleling the closing theme of the F-minor sonata, then ratchets down the intensity, returning in this performance to the focal impulse placement of the opening of the movement.

Development and Recapitulation

Perhaps because the exposition had relatively little metrical dissonance, the development section of op. 120, no. 2, has more metrical play than that of the F-minor sonata. But because it does not participate in obvious ways in the movement's rhythmic and metrical narrative (unlike the development of op. 120, no. 1), it will pass largely without comment. Interesting features of the development and of our performance include the following: a passage in which the extensive use of shifted, sustained focal impulses continues out of a statement of the theme 2 material for which these impulses were originally used (mm. 73–86, 69–72); two unnotated 1.5LBs that result in a brief half-bar shift (81–84); and several passages in which an intense forward drive leads to a sudden and unexpected stasis.[7] The supplemental annotated score contains the full hypermetrical analysis and the focal impulse placements.

Example 16.9. Brahms, Clarinet Sonata No. 2, op. 120/2, i, mm. 152–66, Allegro amabile. (*Cont.*)

Like the recapitulation of the F-minor sonata, the one found here is fairly literal, and so the temporal drama of the exposition plays out again; in this movement, however, the basically sunny character leaves no unresolved crises. Nonetheless, there is a sense in which, at least with the performance choices made here, the expressive and motional characters of the first and closing themes represent opposite poles that are not adequately integrated into a whole. There is a clear, gradual progression from one to the other, but the relaxation back to the character of the first theme that comes in the codetta simply results in a more direct juxtaposition; it does not put them into closer relationship.[8]

Coda

As in the F-minor sonata, it will fall to the coda to reconcile the unresolved issues (ex. 16.9; sound example 16.2, 7:13). Interestingly, this coda also works its way to a climactic final section that has a slower tempo. The coda begins with a harmonic twist that created special performance issues. Paralleling the end of the exposition, the final cadence in the recapitulation adds a seventh to the tonic chord; in the exposition, this leads the music back to the tonic for the start of the development, imitating an exposition repeat, as Brahms was fond of doing. At the end of the recapitulation, the tonic as V_7/IV resolves deceptively to ♭VI/IV, resulting in a modulation to ♭II, or F-flat major. For the sake of readability, Brahms spells the music that follows in E major, but E major is a bright and warm key, far removed from the cool darkness of F-flat major. To help myself to hear this music in the key of the Neapolitan, I preceded work on this passage by playing F-flat major scales in first position. This led to disorienting fingerings on the A string: the fourth finger was used on the D string for A-flat, followed by the open string in place of the first finger for B-double-flat; the second finger was then used for C-flat, just where the first finger is often placed in first position. Although strange, I found this exercise helpful in hearing the passage as F-flat major and not E major, which in turn helped with the crucial arrival of the tranquillo.

The coda opens in measure 154 with a new incarnation of material from the first theme, in the form taken at the start of the transition. The extremely placid character of the initial measures led to the choice of cyclical focal impulses on the downbeats. The music then becomes more insistent, turning into a sequence and doubling the rate of motion of the underlying counterpoint; this was reflected in a doubling of the rate of focal impulses, although still using cyclical focal impulses for their more neutral quality. A crescendo supports the rise in register and in tension; so far, the coda's path is similar to the arc of motion found in the exposition and recapitulation.

This forward motion is unexpectedly arrested in measure 158, with a subito *piano* and the indication "molto dolce sempre." In a straightforward sense, the coda still follows the path of the exposition and recapitulation, as the initial first-theme material is followed in measure 158 by second-theme material: the melody's motive comes from the second statement of the second theme, and the rhythmic canon at the quarter note in the piano is drawn from the first statement. In our performance, a connection with the second theme area was also emphasized by using two cyclical focal impulses per measure. In another sense, however, we are moving in the opposite direction, for while the second theme continued to build tension and intensity, measure 158 clearly represents an expressive volte-face. Measure 158 could have been a climactic arrival; instead, the music abruptly ratchets down tension without a moment of powerful release, floating down through seventh chords in an adjusted circle-of-fifths sequence, two of them with the highly expressive major-major quality. Each strong beat in the clarinet part is marked by poignant appoggiaturas that invite lingering, even as these appoggiaturas help define lines that make stepwise tetrachordal descents, recalling the much more dynamic closing theme.[9] In measure 161 the piano stays on the dominant instead of following the sequence on to tonic; the clarinet has descended through more than an octave and then dropped out altogether. Near the nadir of a long diminuendo, it appears that the energy that had been built up is now fully spent. Despite the lingering question mark of the distant key, it is time to cadence and be finished.

What happens instead is the most magical moment in the piece. Recalling the arrival of the second theme in the exposition, the dominant seventh in the key of the Neapolitan is reinterpreted as a German augmented-sixth chord in E-flat major, but the dominant implications of the apparent cadential 6/4 that it ushers in seem to vanish like mist as the bass moves down to scale-degree 1, clearly grounding the chord as tonic harmony. In a gentle way, the music of the tranquillo seems to have been reenergized by the miraculous return to the tonic key, and so this circle of fifth sequence in seventh chords (again, with one adjustment) has a very different character from the one we have just heard. In the confident striding of the bass and the gently accented chord tones of the melody's strong beats, there is a sense of purpose and direction that was absent from the more passively floating music that preceded it.[10] In terms of melodic content, the sequence that begins the tranquillo is actually a transformation of the same material from the second theme group that was used for the previous sequence, differing in rhythm, metric position, and status of notes as chord versus nonchord tones. But in gestural character, it seems very much like a transfigured version of the closing theme; this was emphasized in our performance by using the same focal impulse choices, binary impulse cycles corresponding to the measures.

In relation to the exposition and recapitulation, the coda has taken a similar trajectory in terms of metrical dissonance and (in this performance) focal impulse deployments, but it has taken almost an opposite path in terms of energy and dynamism. As a result, the tranquillo can be simultaneously an apotheosis and a reconciliation of the two main motional characters of the body of the movement. The first theme was peaceful but mildly passive; it seemed to yawn and stretch as if it had just woken up. And the closing theme, while vigorous and energetic, had perhaps a touch of youthful naiveté; certainly it didn't seem to know what to do with its energy, as it ebbed gently away without reaching the kind of climactic arrival that we might have expected.

The theme of the tranquillo is peaceful and content but also purposeful, and it leads to one of the most magnificent cadences in all of Brahms's music, as the clarinet—an expressive backdrop for most of the phrase—suddenly rides a soaring scale-degree 6 into a melodic arabesque with an exquisitely vocal quality.

With the movement's one nagging tension fully resolved and complete tonal and hypermetrical closure having been achieved, the music's last remaining energy can spin out into the night sky, still recalling the coordinated linear third motions into that last cadence. A return here to the cyclical focal impulses on downbeats of the opening music can be at once a satisfied homecoming and the final step in the journey of relating the characters of the first and closing themes.

The analyses and performances presented in this chapter have shown how, on the scale of entire movements, focal impulse choices can contribute to the strategic design of performances, by making vivid the rhythmic, metric, and gestural shapes found within the score. By breathing the life of motion into these shapes, focal impulses can help them to realize their potential to be full partners with formal, harmonic, and thematic processes in shaping musical narratives.

Notes

1. News of my teacher George Neikrug's death on the second day of his second century reached me as I was putting the final touches on this book. That the passage I am most pleased with from these recordings (the approach to the cadence in m. 166 in the second sonata) is also the passage that shows Mr. Neikrug's influence most clearly is no coincidence.

2. These supplemental annotated scores are available on KiltHub, Carnegie Mellon University's online data repository. An internet search for *KiltHub, Ito, focal impulse theory*, and *Brahms sonata* should bring them up.

3. Because the exposition has three key areas, it is analyzed in terms of three-theme sonata form, with the third key being the primary contrasting key. Peter H. Smith (1998) discusses good reasons for understanding only two main keys, with the D-flat major material (here the second theme) part of the linear and harmonic path to the dominant.

4. The hypermetrical dissonance this creates is discussed by Channan Willner (2013).

5. Alternative understandings of some formal boundaries in this movement are discussed by Sprick (2013).

6. This movement takes an unusual path to the recollection of the opening theme, as it makes telescoped references to the second theme along the way (mm. 48–51, rising octaves in canon between clarinet and piano left hand, rhythm of right-hand accompaniment), as if moving backward through time.

7. My observation of this pattern is likely due to conversations with and unpublished work by David Keep on temporal stasis and lyric time in Brahms.

8. As in the F-minor sonata, the disparity may be more acute in the recapitulation, here because of a tonal detour for the first half of the second theme. The distant key used for this music mitigates the effects of its role in mediating between the placidity of the first theme and the vigor of the closing theme. Because the return to tonic for the second half coincides with the introduction of the binary impulse cycles that will characterize the closing theme, the spare cyclical focal impulses of the first theme are juxtaposed more directly with the faster binary impulse cycles of the second half of the second theme and of the closing theme.

9. This sequence is examined in detail by McClelland (2012), who shows that the appoggiaturas represent suspensions in the underlying voice leading.

10. McClelland (2012) understands the relationship between the two sequences differently, hearing the first as transcendent and the second as more pedestrian. He also discusses in more depth the relationship between the two salient augmented-sixth resolutions, as does Sprick (2013).

CONCLUSIONS

Placing Focal Impulse Theory in Larger Contexts

THIS BRIEF CONCLUDING CHAPTER REVISITS THE CENTRAL CLAIMS and perspectives of focal impulse theory and considers the theory's potential contributions to studies of human movement, speech, embodiment, dance, non-Western musics, and popular musics. At the end, it returns to general questions about meter.

Focal impulse theory is, first and foremost, a theory about the body. It claims that complex sequences of physical motion are organized around certain key moments in time—the moments at which focal impulses occur. Focal impulses are muscular contractions with noticeable onsets that help to organize motion until the next focal impulse. While a focal impulse will often directly produce some desired result (e.g., a sonic attack point in music), its larger role is to set the body in motion in ways that will be conducive to producing the other desired motions that fall between it and the next focal impulse. Focal impulses inject energy into the physical system of the body, and because the body is not perfectly elastic, this energy will dissipate over time. When a more energetic sequence of motion is desired, focal impulses will need to occur more frequently. When a more placid effect is the goal, focal impulses are likely to be spaced more widely in time, subject to some limit on the maximum spacing. A basic analogy for focal impulses was provided in chapter 3, which discussed half-pipe snowboarding. Without minimizing the importance of motions initiated during the aerial phase of motion, the fact that the body is a projectile means that for any given flight, some tricks will be possible and others impossible, depending on the momentum and angular momentum of the various parts of the body at the moment the athlete pushes off from the ground.

Focal impulse theory claims that bodily motion is organized hierarchically, with some of the individual motions produced directly by focal impulses and others not. The theory does not make rigid claims about the frequency of focal impulses (e.g., one focal impulse for every three individual motions). To the contrary, a central tenet of the theory is that within a sequence of motion that may seem "the same" at the most obvious level of observation, there will always be multiple options for where focal impulses are placed. A simple, though by no means complete, analogy is the activity of pushing a child in a swing on a playground. The most common option is pushing each time the child reaches the apex of motion nearest to us, but we could also push every second apex, or every third. These options for pushing create a set of discrete possibilities for the motion of the swing, assuming the child's own active motions are the same in each case. These possibilities may appear quite similar at a broad level of observation, but the details of motion will be different.

These different details of motion lead to the second main topic addressed by the theory, which is musical expression. As John Baily (1985, 242) has pointed out, musical instruments are transducers, converting patterns of energy in the physical motion of the body into patterns of energy in the vibrations that give rise to sound. Subtle, detailed changes in the motion of the body lead to subtle changes in the sound produced—though as we have seen, the sonic effects of focal impulses are not always subtle. It is not only in music that different focal impulse placements can lead to different expressive qualities. In dance, one can readily imagine the same sequence of motion being performed in a vigorous, energetic way, with more focal impulses, or in a gentle and fluid way, with fewer. To make this contrast more concrete, we can consider some particularly simple forms of dance. The YMCA and the Macarena both involve quick transitions between discrete postures. These dances often give the impression that each move to a new posture is performed using its own focal impulse; however, they could also be performed with focal impulses occurring every other posture or even every fourth. Speech, at least in English, also seems to proceed from stressed syllable to stressed syllable, and changes of expression result from using more or fewer stressed syllables (e.g., "BRUSH YOUR TEETH!"). And even with a mundane activity like hammering a nail, in which we do not usually pay attention to potentially expressive aspects of the motion, differences in frequency of focal impulses will lead to observable differences in the details of the motion.

In generalizing focal impulse theory beyond music, meter recedes in prominence. Regular periodicity is central to the use of focal impulses in the repertoire discussed in this book, but it is not central to what a focal impulse is. Even with respect to Western classical music, we have seen that focal impulses need not simply duplicate the regularity of a beat. The simplest example was seen in the case of triple meter, which is often felt in an uneven duple meter, with the second focal impulse on either beat 2 or beat 3. More complex examples include asymmetrical meters and cases in which focal impulses are shifted forward to align with anticipations. I have argued that when the music has a regular pulse, focal impulses will very often align with some level of pulse. But there is nothing in the central claim—that some motions play a special role in organizing other motions—that presupposes temporal regularity in the superordinate motions. Many examples of simple physical systems used to illustrate the theory (e.g., the child on the swing) involve periodic motion; therefore, an example from the eurhythmics pedagogy of my colleague Stephen Neely may help bridge the gap between periodic and temporally irregular motions. Dalcroze Eurhythmics aligns closely with focal impulse theory in emphasizing smooth physical motion that proceeds in a clear and purposeful way from one motion to another. To help students move fluidly at slow tempos, Neely uses the image of a pendulum. The period of a pendulum depends on its length, so if we want a slower rate, we have to have a longer pendulum. Neely has students imagine that they are swinging a heavy weight on the end of a rope; if they want to get slower, they need to let out more rope. This exercise can be helpful for achieving slow, continuous motions, as opposed to movements that arrive at the target early and then wait, and it is particularly valuable for shaping a ritard in a more natural way. Focal impulses may involve something fundamentally periodic, but if so, it must be possible to continually adjust the period. We might imagine a large, hollow metal ball swinging at the end of a long cable, with a spool and a motorized winch inside that make it possible to wind more of the cable into the ball or to let more out. If the winch were in continuous operation, winding in and letting out the cable, the period of the pendulum might be quite irregular, even though the governing dynamics were those of simple pendular motion.

For human movement scientists, the range of potential applications of the theory is wide, including the performing arts, sports, and many day-to-day activities. Viewed in the broadest terms, the theory could encourage research into higher-level hierarchical organization in movement. Dagmar Sternad and various collaborators (Sternad, Dean, and Schaal 2000; de Rugy and Sternad 2003; Schaal et al. 2004) have shown, for example, that periodic motions are not simply strings of discrete motions. Like the swing being pushed every other cycle, could some periodic motions be organized in terms of a longer period than one cycle of the basic motion? The central challenge for scientists would lie in determining more specifically what the theory's claims might mean. For despite the liberal use of terms from basic physics, the theory is explored primarily on the basis of experience, using and framing observations about our own actions and those of others. These observations may be careful, detailed, and even penetrating, but they lack the objective controls and quantitative measures of scientific experimentation. And as discussed at the end of chapter 13, which situates the theory in relation to the empirical literature, there are good reasons to think the theory may be metaphorical at slower rates of motion—though not introducing a new metaphor so much as making explicit a metaphor that seems to be in wide, if often tacit, use among musicians. Some initial experiments testing the theory are in progress, but this represents only a modest beginning.

As discussed in chapter 13, focal impulse theory could potentially be used in speech science to inform the vexed question of stress-timed languages. It is clear that stressed syllables are not equally spaced in time, as originally claimed, but substantial evidence suggests some meaningful temporal distinction between so-called stress-timed and syllable-timed languages. With its claims of organization in terms of key moments and focal movements that are not necessarily isochronous, focal impulse theory could point to a helpful way of looking at that distinction.[1]

Moving from the sciences to the humanities, studies of embodiment are one area in which the central ideas behind focal impulse theory might be put to use—again, for their focus on hierarchy in the organization of motion in time—but in quite different ways. (A more detailed discussion of the literature on music and embodiment is offered in chap. 14.) Until recently, studies of embodiment in music focused more on space than on time, examining questions such as the physical layout of instruments (Baily 1985) or the postures involved in playing certain passages (Le Guin 2006). And outside of music, space is the central concern of Lakoff and Johnson's (1980) landmark study. Focal impulse theory provides a way to make time more central in examinations of embodiment because it provides a way of conceptualizing the experience of moving in time, focusing on directed sequences of motion whose goals include both the end states (readiness to perform the next focal impulse) and the motional paths traversed along the way. Focal impulse theory may thus join a diverse chorus of voices drawing attention to temporal aspects of embodiment in music (De Souza 2017; Zbikowski 2018; Montague, forthcoming; Stevens, forthcoming).[2]

Two of this book's central concerns, bodily motion and rhythm, are also central to dance and to the relationship between music and dance (Jordan 2011, 52; Zbikowski 2018). Like the motions made by musicians, the motions made by dancers could potentially be understood in terms of sequences of motion that include more than one individual unit of motion, sequences that are set in motion by strong initiating impulses. Like a musical score (or even more like a tablature), systems of dance notation such as Labanotation (Bartenieff and Lewis 1980; Guest 2005) and Benesh movement notation (Benesh and Benesh 1977) tend to describe individual motions and postures, leaving any larger units of organization unspecified.[3] Just as there are multiple options for focal impulse placement when performing music, two dancers performing the same choreography could well use focal impulses differently, with expressive details varying accordingly. A hint in this direction is offered by the dance critic Edwin Denby, who observes that changing the beat on which a specific ballet step is used can change the impression that step gives, in exact parallel with the argument pursued here regarding contrasting metrical interpretations (Jordan 2000, 84).

Looking at the literature on dance-music relationships from the perspective of focal impulse theory raises many new questions. Is (was) the minuet felt in three by its dancers, and the Viennese waltz in one (McKee 2012, esp. 159)? Is the effect of passages in which dancers' motions are out of alignment with the music's meter modulated when dancers change their focal impulse placements, aligning either with the meter or with their salient motions (Zbikowski 2018)? Does the salsa break step feel different depending on whether it is placed on beat 1 or beat 2, and if it is placed on beat 2, does the body feel something significant on the downbeat (Simpson-Likte and Stover 2019)? In light of the many accounts of the importance of the bass-register beat in dancing to electronic dance music (Butler 2006, 92; Van Dyck et al. 2013; Solberg and Jensenius 2016), can Zeiner-Henriksen's (2010) reports about synchronization between dancers' whole-body motions and the beat be correlated with the use of focal impulses?

The possibilities are intriguing, but there are also good reasons to be cautious about the extent to which focal impulse theory might apply to dance. When dancers and musicians try to talk about meter, they often seem to be at cross-purposes (Benford 2000; Still 2015). And while dance involving quick, energetic motions can seem compatible with focal impulse theory, in other cases smooth motions unfold over such long timescales that even a metaphorical appeal to focal impulses would seem unlikely, the governing metaphors probably taking other forms. A potential objection is also raised by the fact that choreographers since the middle of the twentieth century have often avoided aligning the gestures of dance too closely with the gestures of music, a practice referred to derisively as "Mickey Mousing" (Damsholt 2006; White 2006). By itself, this does not create significant difficulties, however, as it could simply point to a polyphonic use of focal impulses by musicians and dancers. And viewing a contrapuntal relationship between music and dance through the lens of focal impulse theory could be interesting for choreomusical analysis (Hodgins 1991; Jordan 2010).

The literature on non-Western musics is another area of scholarship containing threads that also run through focal impulse theory. One of these is formed by silent beats and salient syncopations, which are encountered particularly frequently in accounts of West African drumming. In coming to grips with a highly complex musical surface, many earlier (Western) ethnomusicologists employed frequent metrical shifts and multiple simultaneous meters in trying to align salient attack points with strong beats (Agawu 1995, 187–95). In the past forty years or so, however, a clear consensus has developed holding that all of these complex patterns exist in relation to simple, unchanging meters (Locke 1982; Agawu 1995, 2006). Locke's statement is representative: "no matter how prominently a countermeter is mentally or acoustically accented . . . the primary duple/quadruple stream of beats is never negated or replaced. On the contrary, the cross-rhythmic stream of beats derives its powerful effect from its interaction with the inexorable flow of dotted-quarter-note beats" (224). Examples of strong syncopation from other cultures include the rapid and highly syncopated *sangsih* part in Balinese gamelan music, which is felt in relation to the basic timekeeping beat of the *kajar* (Vitale 1990; Tenzer 2000, 212–31), and a syncopated melody from Iranian classical music discussed by Azadehfar (2006, 34–36).[4]

Another shared thread is physical motion that occurs on a silent strong beat—or, more accurately, on a strong beat that carries a rest or a tie. There are many cases in the literature on non-Western musics in which such physical motion—whether of dancers or of musicians—is considered a much surer guide to emic metrical understanding than the often complex and ambiguous musical surface. In West African music, this motion can include claps, shakes of a rattle, and swinging a child (Agawu 1995, 67–73, 80–83, 188–91), and if the music includes dancing, the dancers' feet are the best guide to the governing meter (Agawu 2006, 18–19, 23; Kubik 1985, 35, 38). In Iranian music, in addition to silent strong-beat motion in the example cited above, a particularly interesting case is the *ṣawt khatm*, in which the defining (silent) strong beat in a highly syncopated drum and clapping pattern is marked by bodily shaking, with children explicitly instructed in this practice (Azadehfar 2006, 31–33). A physical aspect is also often imputed to feeling a silent beat, even when no overt motion is described (Locke 1982, 220; Agawu 1995, 192).

I would hope that scholars of non-Western musics might find the focal impulse concept helpful in investigating these and other phenomena, and I would be curious about the degree of confirmation the theory might find, whether experiential or experimental. So far I have emphasized mainly findings that are consonant with the theory, but plenty of cases raise challenging questions. For example, in video 1 from Rainer Polak's (2010) first study of microtiming in Malian jembe music, the first *dunun* player (leftmost in the video) performs a highly syncopated pattern, and I see no visual evidence that the one stroke occurring on a strong beat is any different from a motor perspective than any of the other strokes, all of which occur on weak subdivisions of the beat. It would be tempting to claim that, as an expert, this musician may be able to minimize any motions not relating directly to sound production, just as some Western classical (especially orchestral) musicians sometimes do; however, I find that when I approximate the same pattern, I do not feel the need for strong-beat focal impulses, even while clearly feeling the meter. It is a helpful reminder that given the enormous variety and complexity of metrical performance across the world, it is no surprise if some patterns of motion are organized in rather different terms.[5]

Studies of popular musics (usually of the industrialized West, although often having roots elsewhere) also offer points of contact with focal impulse theory. One area of research on popular music comes close in spirit to focal impulse theory by looking at the intersection of physical motion and the expressive shaping of sound—indeed, this book's use of the phrase "sonic traces" is drawn from this literature (Iyer 2002). Focusing on what are sometimes called "participatory discrepancies" (Keil and Feld 1994), this research looks especially at the synchronization between musicians and its effect on groove. Popular music has also been examined for the details of event timing within a single part (Butterfield 2006; Chor 2010). As we have seen, such details cannot determine a listener's metrical hearing, but a strong connection between meter and details of timing is reinforced by the fact that electronic dance music—the kind of popular music that features shifts of metrical perception most frequently—often involves exact metronomic regularity (Butler 2006; Danielsen 2010). Another parallel has to do with anticipations representing a main event arriving early, not merely foreshadowing that main event. As David Temperley (1999; 2001, 243–53) has shown, this understanding of the anticipation is reflected in rock music, with accented syllables often placed on anticipations; in focal impulse theory it is found in the practice of emphasizing an anticipation by shifting a focal impulse to coincide with it. The rock anticipations bring together meter and salient physical motion, and they connect accented events in music and speech in ways that fit well with the perspectives developed in chapter 13, given that stressed syllables are not drawn by just any syncopations but specifically by displacements of strong beats.

Especially in light of the close connections and overlaps between the cultures of classical and popular musics in the contemporary West, focal impulse theory has the potential to shed light on the interrelations of meter, rhythmic feel, and expressive profile in popular music, just as it does for classical music. A nice illustration of this potential is presented by three versions of "Stop in the Name of Love": the original by the Supremes (1965) and the covers by Jonell Mosser (1998) and by the Sons of Serendip (2017). Close attention to expressive shaping indicates that each lead singer adopts a stable level for focal impulses in the song, with Diana Ross and Jonell Mosser feeling it in four and Micah Christian, the lead singer of the Sons of Serendip, feeling it in two.[6] Against the backdrop of this consistency of focal impulse placement in the lead vocals, each version creates interesting interplays of metrical levels. Over the heavy and even accentuation of quarter-note beats in the instrumental parts in the recording by the Supremes, feeling the vocal part in four could have made the song sound choppy; instead, Diana Ross creates a longer, more legato line that projects a smooth motion from half-note beat to half-note beat.[7] Jonell Mosser also consistently marks the half measure as an organizing periodicity for the voice; among other things, she avoids attack points on beats 2 or 4, often with anticipation or hemiola, and she uses gentle articulations in those passages, suggesting floating syncopations.[8] Beyond this, the instrumental parts in her recording use rhythmic feel to project an arc of intensity, opening with a single acoustic guitar, adding bass guitar on downbeats only, and gradually building emphasis on beats 2 and 4. The Sons of Serendip create a different interplay of levels, centered on the early dramatic contrast between cellist Kendall Ramseur's declamatory introduction, with focal impulses on quarter-note beats, and the instrumental marking of only downbeats as the vocals enter.

These three recordings—each so different, and each so effective in its own way—have provided a final example, in a new repertoire, of this book's central concern. Different ways of organizing the movements involved in performance—here, again, involving feeling the music in four versus in two—leave traces in the sound, affecting the expressive character of the music. Not simply a matter of minute details, decisions about focal impulses can help drive significant, holistic emotional contrasts. These contrasts have been particularly salient in cases involving metrical dissonance and in cases in which multiple metrical interpretations are possible. Although I have certainly argued for ways of performing that I find particularly compelling, especially when those ways of performing have not been in common use, the basic purpose of the theory throughout has been to bring to light multiple interpretive possibilities. The theory is not meant to turn the analyzing theorist into a kingmaker or an umpire, but rather to enhance the personal agency of anyone who performs music or who thinks about how it might be performed.

Because of the close relationship between focal impulses and meter—at least for the music that this book has primarily addressed—the theory can also speak to the question of what meter is. As discussed in chapter 6, I do not believe that meter is just one thing, but rather a network of interrelated behaviors. The central node is Lerdahl and Jackendoff's (1983) metrical grid, understood in terms of psychological processes of entrainment (Large and Jones 1999). Justin London (2012) has charted some of the behaviors that build out from this core by pointing to the importance of specific durational thresholds, by arguing that specific rhythmic grooves involving systematic deviations from isochrony should count as different meters (the Viennese waltz being a classic example), and by allowing for and theorizing meters with no nominally isochronous smallest beat unit (with credit for the final point shared with a number of scholars of meter in non-Western musics). A purely grid-based conception of meter has also been expanded through my concepts of metrical and hypermetrical orientation, which explain how a listener without a score could bind tactus beats into measures and measures into hypermeasures (Ito 2013a).[9]

The use of focal impulses is then one more behavior that helps constitute meter for those who engage in it. While using focal impulses could be seen as a physical process that occurs in relation to the purely psychological processes of meter, such an approach would be needlessly—and anachronistically—mentalistic. Several psychological theories of the origins and nature of entrainment hold that it is an outgrowth of motor behaviors such as locomotion (Patel and Iversen 2014; Large, Herrera and Velasco 2015; Todd and Lee 2015). And if a musician has an awareness that the motions of performance are flowing from half-note beat to half-note beat, how could this experience not be part of the experience of meter? Focal impulses could also have an important role in organizing the experience of the listener. I often find myself making slow-period muscular contractions that are synchronized with some layer of the metrical hierarchy; depending on the context, and on whether I am being observed, these motions may be more or less overt, but I generally feel that they are shaped in ways that respond to flows of energy within the music (Cox 2016). This might seem simply a reinforcement of the tactus, but the beats I feel are often slow for a tactus (and in some cases, I track a faster, more tactus-like beat in other ways, e.g., by contracting muscles in my toes). There are many good reasons to think that these motions are shaping and helping to constitute my experience as a listener in significant ways, including but not limited to the ones discussed in chapters 5 and 13. Focal impulses contribute to meter on many levels, then: as part of the experience of the performer, as an influence on the expressive shaping of the sound produced, through the ways that sonic shaping influences (but does not determine) the experience of the listener, and as part of the experience of the listener in responding actively to the music.

In these pages I have tried to explain and illustrate the focal impulse concept and to show something of its utility for experiencing music and for thinking about it, for performing music, and for its academic study. My intention has been to offer a new conceptual framework for an old, familiar experience, in hopes that as we give focused attention to a trusty companion who has often gone unnoticed, familiar experiences may be made new.

Notes

1. Given the prevalence of coarticulation, it is clear that this discretized mode of motor organization could not be the only one.

2. Stern (2010) focuses on dynamic temporal processes more generally (not specifically applied to music). Kubik's (1979, 228–29) discussion of embodiment in music is one of the few I have encountered that engages with focal impulse theory's attention to expressive performance.

3. Labanotation includes a concept of impulse that has some similarities to the concept as used here (as a larger category including both focal and subsidiary impulses). In Laban's use, the term *impulse* seems to have a more restricted meaning, but some have extended it in ways that bring it closer to focal impulse theory (Jordan 2000, 78–84; Guest 2005, 108–109, 415, 426). Both systems include qualitative designations for expressive quality, but these are analogous to similar terms used in scores; even if occasional comments could hint at the use of focal impulses (Bartenieff and Lewis 1980, 80–82), these indications do not offer any direct clues to their placement.

4. An interesting case is found in some performances of the slow opening of the initial *ālāp* section in North Indian *dhrupad*, often described as without either pulse or meter. Richard Widdess (1994, 1995; see also Clayton 2000, 97–98) offers accounts of musicians who do feel pulse and meter in this music, with the existence of the pulse concealed by a slow and somewhat flexible rate and by frequent nonalignment between salient events and beats (Widdess 1994, 65–68). It would be interesting to know the extent to which focal impulse theory might resonate with musicians who describe performing both silent beats and salient syncopations. In this connection, it is worth noting again that focal impulse theory does not speak only to situations in which a governing beat exists. In arguing that notes that do or do not coincide with focal impulses will be different both from the experiential perspective of the performer and in the expressive qualities of the sound, focal impulse theory could offer an organizing framework for understanding temporal organization apart from a regular pulse (Clayton 1996).

5. Along these lines, I would be interested in exploring the potential connections between focal impulse theory and Simpson-Litke and Stover's (2019, 78) conception of clave as a timeline rhythm that is not quite either rhythm or meter: "clave simultaneously requires a metric frame and partially determines the rhythmic behaviors that occupy this frame." This concept is developed further by Chris Stover (in preparation).

6. Key factors include the quality of the syncopation on "Stop" (grounded vs. vigorous), the weight of attack given to notes on beats 2 and 4 (e.g., "before you"), and the weight given to the eighth notes in dotted rhythms (cf., discussion of dotted rhythms in the Overture to Don Giovanni in chap. 7, n. 5). Mosser's website (http://www.jonellmosser.com/about.html, accessed February 1, 2019) describes the song as in $\frac{6}{8}$, but to facilitate the comparison, I shall discuss it as if it were in $\frac{12}{8}$.

7. This is done by means including dynamic emphases, rhythmic trajectories, and vocal ornaments. In light of this projection of the half measure, is it not surprising to see the Supremes using a legato body sway synchronized with the half notes (although with evidence of a felt quarter-note pulse as well) in a performance of this song on a 1965 British television broadcast, easily available on the internet.

8. While some occasional notes on beat 2 or 4 show signs of the focal impulses placed there ("Stop!" "Baby baby," 0:04; "run to her," 0:34; "secluded nights," 1:44), others receive little or no accentuation ("my heart," 1:08).

9. While the theory of metrical orientation is directed in the first instance toward Western music of the past several centuries, in general terms, it could be useful in accounting for non-Western musics (e.g., of Northern India or Indonesia) that are organized in terms of periodicities far longer than can be accounted for in terms of entrainment (Clayton 2000; Tenzer 2000, 254–61).

GLOSSARY

Focal Impulse Symbols and Their Definitions

Figure G.1 displays the graphic symbols used in focal impulse theory:

(a) Focal impulse.

(b) Vertical dashed lines are a visual guide, indicating alignment between focal impulses and lower staves.

(c) Dots above staves represent beats at some metrical level; they are used to show the placement of focal impulses when the beats on which they are placed are not marked visually, falling in the middle of some longer note or rest.

(d) The dashed-line version of the focal impulse symbol indicates that a focal impulse that (for consistency) would normally have occurred has instead been omitted. This happens when the focal impulse would have no new motion to organize, motion resuming after some subsequent focal impulse.

(e) Secondary focal impulse. The slur is extended to cover the secondary consequent span.

(f) Arrow proceeds from a focal impulse that has been shifted to coincide with an anticipation and points to the beat on which the focal impulse would normally have occurred.

(g) Downward focal impulse.

(h) Upward focal impulse.

(i) (Downward) cyclical focal impulse.

(j) Upward cyclical focal impulse.

(k) Large-font dot used below a midbar focal impulse to indicate a heard downbeat in cases in which the heard and notated meters conflict. It is also used below focal impulses on notated downbeats to indicate alignment of heard and notated downbeats just before and just after metrical shifts. (This clarifies whether the measure that accomplishes the shift is shorter or longer than the prevailing measures.)

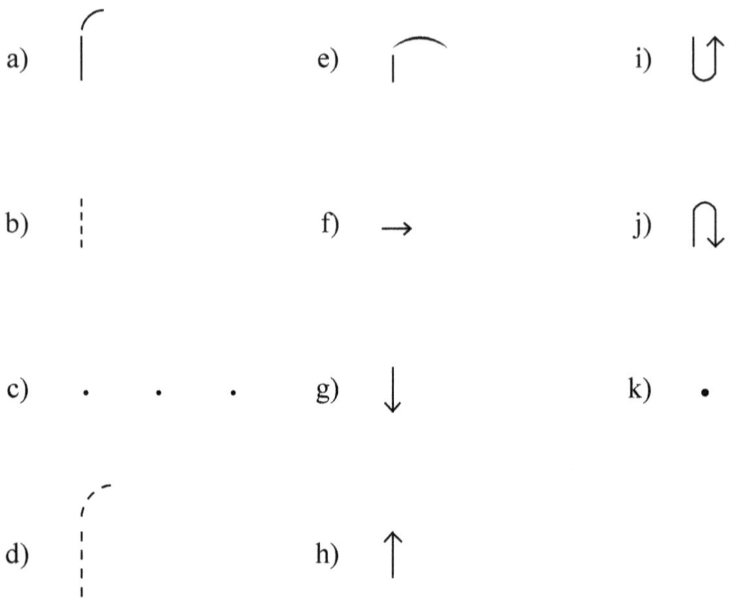

a)

b)

c) .   .   .

d)

e)

f) →

g) ↓

h) ↑

i)

j)

k) •

Fig. G.1. Focal impulse symbols.

REFERENCES

Abernethy, Bruce, and W. A. Sparrow. 1992. "The Rise and Fall of Dominant Paradigms in Motor Behaviour Research." In *Approaches to the Study of Motor Control and Learning*, edited by Jeffery J. Summers, 3–45. Amsterdam: North-Holland.

Adamovich, Sergei V., Mindy F. Levin, and Anatol G. Feldman. 1994. "Merging Different Motor Patterns: Coordination between Rhythmical and Discrete Single-Joint Movements." *Experimental Brain Research* 99 (2): 325–37.

Adams, Jack A. 1971. "A Closed-Loop Theory of Motor Learning." *Journal of Motor Behavior* 3 (2): 111–49.

Agawu, Kofi. 1995. *African Rhythm: A Northern Ewe Perspective*. Cambridge: Cambridge University Press.

———. 2006. "Structural Analysis or Cultural Analysis? Competing Perspectives on the 'Standard Pattern' of West African Rhythm." *Journal of the American Musicological Society* 59 (1): 1–46.

Altenmüller, Eckart, Mario Wiesendanger, and Jürg Kesselring, eds. 2006. *Music, Motor Control, and the Brain*. Oxford, Oxford University Press.

Askenfelt, Anders. 1986. "Measurement of Bow Motion and Bow Force in Violin Playing." *Journal of the Acoustical Society of America* 80 (4): 1007–15.

Azadehfar, Mohammad Reza. 2006. *Rhythmic Structure in Iranian Music*. Tehran: University of Art Press.

Baily, John. 1985. "Music Structure and Human Movement." In *Musical Structure and Cognition*, edited by Peter Howell, Ian Cross, and Robert West, 237–58. London: Academic.

Barolsky, Daniel G. 2007. "The Performer as Analyst." *Music Theory Online* 13 (1). http://www.mtosmt.org/issues/mto.07.13.1/mto.07.13.1.barolsky.html.

Barolsky, Daniel G., and Edward Klorman. 2016 "Performance and Analysis Today: New Horizons." *Music Theory Online* 22 (2). http://mtosmt.org/issues/mto.16.22.2/mto.16.22.2.barolsky_klorman.html.

Bartenieff, Irmgard, and Dori Lewis. 1980. *Body Movement: Coping with the Environment*. New York: Gordon & Breach.

Becking, Gustav. 1928. *Der musikalische Rhythmus als Erkenntnisquelle*. Augsburg: Benno Filser.

Benesh, Rudolf, and Joan Benesh. 1977. *Reading Dance: The Birth of Choreology*. London: Souvenir.

Benford, Robert. 2000. "16 Ways to Explore Meter and Rhythm in Sound and Movement." *International Guild of Musicians in Dance Journal* 6:16–19.

Bengtsson, Ingmar, and Alf Gabrielsson. 1980. "Methods for Analyzing Performance of Musical Rhythm." *Scandinavian Journal of Psychology* 21 (1): 257–68.

Benson, Bruce Ellis. 2003 *The Improvisation of Musical Dialogue: A Phenomenology of Music*. Cambridge: Cambridge University Press.

Bent, Ian. 1987. *Analysis*. New York: Norton.

Bernstein, Nikolai Aleksandrovitsch. 1967. *The Co-ordination and Regulation of Movements.* Oxford: Pergamon.

———. (1991) 1996. "On Dexterity and Its Development." In *Dexterity and Its Development,* edited by Mark L. Latash and Michael T. Turvey, 1–244. Mahwah, NJ: Erlbaum.

———. (1935) 2001. "The Problem of Interrelations between Coordination and Localization." In *Classics in Movement Science,* edited by Mark L. Latash and Vladimir M. Zatsiorsky, 64–84. Champaign, IL: Human Kinetics.

Bernstein, Nikolai Aleksandrovitsch, and Tatiana Popowa. 1929. "Untersuchung über die Biodynamik des Klavieranschlags." *Arbeitsphysiologie* 1 (5): 396–432.

Berry, Wallace. 1976. *Structural Functions in Music.* Englewood Cliffs, NJ: Prentice-Hall.

———. 1989. *Musical Structure and Performance.* New Haven, CT: Yale University Press.

Bertinetto, Pier Marco. 1989. "Reflections on the Dichotomy 'Stress' vs. 'Syllable-Timing.'" *Revue de phonétique appliquée* 91–93:99–130.

Bijeljac-Babic, Ranka, Josiane Bertoncini, and Jacques Mehler. 1993. "How Do 4-Day-Old Infants Categorize Multisyllabic Utterances?" *Developmental Psychology* 29 (4): 711–21.

Brown, Clive. 1999. *Classical and Romantic Performing Practice 1750–1900.* Oxford: Oxford University Press.

Bull, Peter, and Gerry Connelly. 1985. "Body Movement and Emphasis in Speech." *Journal of Nonverbal Behavior* 9 (3): 169–87.

Burger, Birgitta, Marc R. Thompson, Geoff Luck, Suvi H. Saarikallio, and Petri Toiviainen. 2014. "Hunting for the Beat in the Body: On Period and Phase Locking in Music-Induced Movement." *Frontiers in Human Neuroscience* 8: article 903. http://journal.frontiersin.org /article/10.3389/fnhum.2014.00903/full.

Butler, Mark J. 2006 *Unlocking the Groove: Rhythm, Meter, and Musical Design in Electronic Dance Music.* Bloomington: Indiana University Press.

Butterfield, Matthew W. 2006. "The Power of Anacrusis: Engendered Feeling in Groove-Based Musics." *Music Theory Online* 12 (4). http://www.mtosmt.org/issues/mto.06.12.4/mto.06 .12.4.butterfield.html.

Cai, Camilla. 1986. "Brahms' Short Late Piano Pieces—Opus Numbers 116–118: A Source Study, an Analysis and Performance Practice." PhD diss., Boston University.

Cannam, Chris, Christian Landone, and Mark Sandler. 2010. "Sonic Visualiser: An Open Source Application for Viewing, Analysing, and Annotating Music Audio Files." In *Proceedings of the 18th ACM International Conference on Multimedia,* edited by Alberto del Bimbo and Shih-Fu Chang, 1467–68. New York: ACM. http://dl.acm.org/citation.cfm ?id=1873951.1874248.

Choksy, Lois, Robert M. Abramson, Avon E. Gillespie, and David Woods. 1986. *Teaching Music in the Twentieth Century.* Englewood Cliffs, NJ: Prentice-Hall.

Chor, Ives. 2010. "Microtiming and Rhythmic Structure in Clave-Based Music: A Quantitative Study." In *Musical Rhythm in the Age of Digital Reproduction,* edited by Anne Danielsen, 37–50. Farnham, UK: Ashgate.

Clarke, Eric F. 1985. "Structure and Expression in Rhythmic Performance." In *Musical Structure and Cognition,* edited by Peter Howell, Ian Cross, and Robert West, 209–36. London: Academic.

———. 1988. "Generative Principles in Music Performance." In *Generative Processes in Music,* edited by John A. Sloboda, 1–26. Oxford: Clarendon.

———. 1993. "Imitating and Evaluating Real and Transformed Musical Performances." *Music Perception* 10 (3): 317–41.

Clarke, Eric F., Nicholas Cook, Bryn Harrison, and Philip Thomas. 2005. "Interpretation and Performance in Bryn Harrison's *être temps.*" *Musicae Scientiae* 19 (1): 31–74.

Clarke, Eric F., and Jane W. Davidson. 1998. "The Body in Performance." In *Composition, Performance, Reception: Studies in the Creative Process in Music*, edited by Wyndham Thomas, 74–92. Aldershot, UK: Ashgate.

Clayton, Martin. 1996. "Free Rhythm: Ethnomusicology and the Study of Music without Metre." *Bulletin of the School of Oriental and African Studies, University of London* 59 (2): 323–32.

———. 2000. *Time in Indian Music: Rhythm, Metre, and Form in North Indian Rāg Performance*. Oxford: Oxford University Press.

Clifton, Thomas. 1983. *Music as Heard: A Study in Applied Phenomenology*. New Haven, CT: Yale University Press.

Clive, Peter. 2006. *Brahms and His World: A Biographical Dictionary*. Lanham, MD: Scarecrow.

Clynes, Manfred. 1977. *Sentics: The Touch of the Emotions*. Garden City, NY: Anchor.

———. 1995. "Microstructural Musical Linguistics: Composers' Pulses Are Liked Most by the Best Musicians." *Cognition* 55 (3): 269–310.

Cohn, Richard. 2001. "Complex Hemiolas, Ski-Hill Graphs and Metric Spaces." *Music Analysis* 20 (3): 295–326.

———. 2018. "Brahms at Twenty: Hemiolic Varietals and Metric Malleability in an Early Sonata." In *Brahms and the Shaping of Time*, edited by Scott Murphy, 178–204. Rochester, NY: University of Rochester Press.

Cone, Edward T. 1968. *Musical Form and Musical Performance*. New York: Norton.

———. 1974. *The Composer's Voice*. Berkeley: University of California Press.

———. 1985. "*Musical Form and Musical Performance* Reconsidered." *Music Theory Spectrum* 7:149–58.

Cook, Nicholas. 1999. "Analysing Performance and Performing Analysis." In *Rethinking Music*, edited by Nicholas Cook and Mark Everist, 239–61. Oxford: Oxford University Press.

———. 2013. *Beyond the Score: Music as Performance*. New York: Oxford University Press.

Cooper, Grosvenor, and Leonard B. Meyer. 1960. *The Rhythmic Structure of Music*. Chicago: University of Chicago Press.

Copland, Aaron. 1943–44. "On the Notation of Rhythm." *Modern Music* 21:217–20.

Cox, Arnie. 2006. "Hearing, Feeling, Grasping Gestures." In *Music and Gesture*, edited by Anthony Gritten and Elaine King, 45–60. Aldershot, UK: Ashgate.

———. 2011. "Embodying Music: Principles of the Mimetic Hypothesis." *Music Theory Online* 17 (2). http://www.mtosmt.org/issues/mto.11.17.2/mto.11.17.2.cox.html.

———. 2016. *Music and Embodied Cognition: Listening, Moving, Feeling, and Thinking*. Bloomington: Indiana University Press.

Cumming, Naomi. 2000. *The Sonic Self: Musical Subjectivity and Signification*. Bloomington: Indiana University Press.

Cummins, Fred, and Robert F. Port. 1998. "Rhythmic Constraints on Stress Timing in English." *Journal of Phonetics* 26 (2): 145–71.

Cutler, Anne. 1980. "Syllable Omission Errors and Isochrony." In *Temporal Variables in Speech: Studies in Honour of Frieda Goldman-Eisler*, edited by Hans W. Dechert and Manfred Raupach, 183–190. The Hague: Mouton.

Czerny, Carl. [1839?a]. *Complete Theoretical and Practical Piano Forte School, from the First Rudiments of Playing to the Highest and Most Refined State of Cultivation, with the Requisite Numerous Examples, Newly and Expressly Composed for the Occasion*. 3 vols. London: R. Cocks.

———. [1839?b]. *Vollständige theoretisch-practische Pianoforte-Schule von dem ersten Anfange bis zur höchsten Ausbildung fortschreitend, und mit allen nöthigen, zu diesem Zwecke eigends componirten zahlreichen Beispielen*. 4 vols. Vienna: A. Diabelli.

Damsholt, Inger. 2006. "Mark Morris, Mickey Mouse, and Choreomusical Polemic." *Opera Quarterly* 22 (1): 4–21.

Danielsen, Anne. 2010. "Introduction: Rhythm in the Age of Digital Reproduction." In *Musical Rhythm in the Age of Digital Reproduction*, edited by Anne Danielsen, 1–16. Farnham, UK: Ashgate.

Day, Timothy. 2000. *A Century of Recorded Music: Listening to Musical History*. New Haven, CT: Yale University Press.

DeBellis, Mark. 1999. "The Paradox of Musical Analysis." *Journal of Music Theory* 43 (1): 83–99.

Dehaene, Stanislas. 2011. *The Number Sense: How the Mind Creates Mathematics*. Rev. ed. New York: Oxford University Press.

de Rugy, Aymar, and Dagmar Sternad. 2003. "Interaction between Discrete and Rhythmic Movements: Reaction Time and Phase of Discrete Movement Initiation during Oscillatory Movements." *Brain Research* 994 (2): 160–74.

de Ruiter, Jan Peter. 1998. "Gesture and Speech Production." PhD diss., Katholieke Universiteit, Nijmegen, the Netherlands.

De Souza, Jonathan. 2017. *Music at Hand: Instruments, Bodies, and Cognition*. New York: Oxford University Press.

de Ternant, Andrew. 1924. "Debussy and Brahms." *Musical Times* 65 (July): 608–9.

Deutsch, Diana. 1986. "A Musical Paradox." *Music Perception* 3 (3): 275–80.

Dittmann, Allen T., and Lynn G. Llewellyn. 1969. "Body Movement and Speech Rhythm in Social Conversation." *Journal of Personality and Social Psychology* 11 (2): 98–106.

Doğantan, Mine. 2002. *Mathis Lussy: A Pioneer in Studies of Expressive Performance*. Bern: Lang.

Donington, Robert. 1973. *A Performer's Guide to Baroque Music*. London: Faber & Faber.

Downs, Philip G. 1970. "Beethoven's 'New Way' and the 'Eroica.'" *Musical Quarterly* 56 (4): 585–604.

Drake, Carolyn, and Caroline Palmer. 1993. "Accent Structures in Music Performance." *Music Perception* 10 (3): 343–78.

———. 2000. "Skill Acquisition in Music Performance: Relations between Planning and Temporal Control." *Cognition* 74 (1): 1–32.

Drake, Carolyn, Amandine Penel, and Emmanuel Bigand. 2000. "Tapping in Time with Mechanically and Expressively Performed Music." *Music Perception* 18 (1): 1–23.

Dunsby, Jonathan. 1981. *Structural Ambiguity in Brahms: Analytical Approaches to Four Works*. Ann Arbor, MI: UMI Research Press.

———. 1995. *Performing Music: Shared Concerns*. Oxford: Clarendon.

Edlund, Bengt. 1985. *Performance and Perception of Notational Variants: A Study of Rhythmic Patterning in Music*. Uppsala: Almqvist & Wiksell.

Ellenwood, Christian Kent. 1996. "Metric Displacement in the First Movement of Brahms's Clarinet Quintet, op. 115: An Analysis for Performance." DMA diss., University of North Carolina at Greensboro.

Epstein, David. 1979. *Beyond Orpheus: Studies in Musical Structure*. Cambridge, MA: MIT Press.

———. 1990. "Brahms and the Mechanisms of Motion: The Composition of Performance." In *Brahms Studies: Analytical and Historical Perspectives*, edited by George S. Bozarth, 191–226. Oxford: Clarendon.

———. 1995. *Shaping Time: Music, the Brain, and Performance*. New York: Schirmer.

Esteve-Gibert, Núria, Joan Borràs-Comes, Marc Swerts, and Pilar Prieto. 2014. "Head Gesture Timing Is Constrained by Prosodic Structure." In *Social and Linguistic Speech Prosody:*

Proceedings of the 7th International Conference on Speech Prosody, edited by Nick Campbell, Dafydd Gibbon, and Daniel Hirst, 356–60. Urbana, IL: Speech Prosody Special Interest Group. http://fastnet.netsoc.ie/sp7/sp7book.pdf.

Esteve-Gibert, Núria, and Pilar Prieto. 2014. "Infants Temporally Coordinate Gesture-Speech Combinations before They Produce Their First Words." *Speech Communication* 57:301–16.

Feldman, Anatol G. 1986. "Once More on the Equilibrium-Point Hypothesis (λ-Model) for Motor Control." *Journal of Motor Behavior* 18 (1): 17–54.

Fisher, George, and Judy Lockhead. 2002. "Analyzing from the Body." *Theory and Practice* 27:37–67.

Friedman, William J. 1990. *About Time: Inventing the Fourth Dimension.* Cambridge, MA: MIT Press.

Frisch, Walter. 1984. *Brahms and the Principle of Developing Variation.* Berkeley: University of California Press.

———. 1990. "The Shifting Barline: Metrical Displacement in Brahms." In *Brahms Studies: Analytical and Historical Perspectives*, edited by George S. Bozarth, 139–63. Oxford: Clarendon.

Fuller, David. 2001. "Notes inégales." In vol. 18 of *The New Grove Dictionary of Music and Musicians*, 2nd ed., edited by Stanley Sadie, 190–200. London: Macmillan.

Gabrielsson, Alf. 1974. "Performance of Rhythm Patterns." *Scandinavian Journal of Psychology* 15 (1): 63–72.

———. 1987. "Once Again: The Theme from Mozart's Piano Sonata in A Major (K. 331): A Comparison of Five Performances." In *Action and Perception in Rhythm and Music*, edited by Alf Gabrielsson, 81–103. Stockholm: Royal Swedish Academy of Music.

———. 1999. "The Performance of Music." In *The Psychology of Music*, edited by Diana Deutsch, 501–602. 2nd ed. San Diego, CA: Academic.

Geeraerts, Dirk. 1989. "Prospects and Problems of Prototype Theory." *Linguistics* 27 (4): 587–612.

———. 1997. *Diachronic Prototype Semantics: A Contribution to Historical Lexicology.* Oxford: Oxford University Press.

Gibson, James J. 1950. *The Perception of the Visual World.* Boston: Houghton Mifflin.

———. 1966. *The Senses Considered as Perceptual Systems.* Boston: Houghton Mifflin.

———. 1979. *The Ecological Approach to Visual Perception.* Boston: Houghton Mifflin.

Godøy, Rolf Inge. 2017a. "Key-Postures, Trajectories and Sonic Shapes." In *Music and Shape*, edited by Daniel Leech-Wilkinson and Helen M. Prior, 4–29. New York: Oxford University Press.

———. 2017b. "Postures and Motion Shaping Musical Experience." In *The Routledge Companion to Embodied Music Interaction*, edited by Micheline Lesaffre, Pieter-Jan Maes, and Marc Leman, 113–21. New York: Routledge.

———. 2018. "Sonic Object Cognition." In *The Springer Handbook of Systematic Musicology*, edited by Rolf Bader, 761–77. Cham, Switzerland: Springer.

Godøy, Rolf Inge, and Marc Leman, eds. 2010. *Musical Gestures: Sound, Movement, and Meaning.* New York: Routledge.

Goebl, Werner. 2001. "Melody Lead in Piano Performance: Expressive Device or Artifact?" *Journal of the Acoustical Society of America* 110 (1): 563–72.

Gotham, Mark. 2015. "Meter Metrics: Characterizing Relationships among (Mixed) Metrical Structures." *Music Theory Online* 21 (2). http://www.mtosmt.org/issues/mto.15.21.2/mto.15.21.2.gotham.html.

———. Forthcoming. "Towards a Cognitively-Based Quantification of Metrical Dissonance." In *The Oxford Handbook of Time in Music*, edited by Mark Doffman, Emily Payne, and Toby Young. Oxford: Oxford University Press.

Grabe, Esther, Brechtje Post, and Ian Watson. 1999. "The Acquisition of Rhythmic Patterns in English and French." In *Proceedings of the 14th International Congress of Phonetic Sciences*, edited by John Ohala, 1201–1204. Berkeley: Linguistics Department, University of California, Berkeley.

Grave, Floyd K. 1984. "Common-Time Displacement in Mozart." *Journal of Musicology* 3 (4): 423–42.

———. 1985. "Metrical Displacement and the Compound Measure in Eighteenth-Century Theory and Practice." *Theoria* 1:25–60.

Guest, Ann Hutchinson. 2005. *Labanotation: The System of Analyzing and Recording Movement*, 4th ed. New York: Routledge.

Haken, Hermann, J. A. Scott Kelso, and Helmut Bunz. 1985. "A Theoretical Model of Phase Transitions in Human Hand Movements." *Biological Cybernetics* 51 (5): 347–56.

Handel, Stephen. 1989. *Listening: An Introduction to the Perception of Auditory Events*. Cambridge, MA: MIT Press.

Hasty, Christopher F. 1997. *Meter as Rhythm*. New York: Oxford University Press.

Hatten, Robert S. 2002. Review of *Fantasy Pieces: Metrical Dissonance in the Music of Robert Schumann*, by Harald Krebs. *Music Theory Spectrum* 24 (2): 273–82.

———. 2004. *Interpreting Musical Gestures, Topics, and Tropes: Mozart, Beethoven, Schubert*. Bloomington: Indiana University Press.

———. 2012. "Musical Forces and Agential Energies: An Expansion of Steve Larson's Model." *Music Theory Online* 18 (3). http://mtosmt.org/issues/mto.12.18.3/mto.12.18.3.hatten .php.

———. 2015. "Commentary: 'Up' within 'Down.'" *Empirical Musicology Review* 10 (1–2): 138–39. http://emusicology.org/article/view/4578.

———. 2018. *A Theory of Virtual Agency for Western Art Music*. Bloomington: Indiana University Press.

Hefling, Stephen E. 1993. *Rhythmic Alteration in Seventeenth- and Eighteenth-Century Music: Notes inégales and Overdotting*. New York: Schirmer.

Henderson, M. T. 1936. "Rhythmic Organization in Artistic Piano Performance." In *Objective Analysis of Musical Performance*, edited by Carl E. Seashore, 281–305. Iowa City, IA: University Press.

Hepokoski, James, and Warren Darcy. 2006. *Elements of Sonata Theory: Norms, Types, and Deformations in the Late-Eighteenth-Century Sonata*. Oxford: Oxford University Press.

Hodgins, Paul. 1991. "Making Sense of the Dance-Music Partnership: A Paradigm for Choreomusical Analysis." *International Guild of Musicians in Dance Journal* 1:38–41.

Horlacher, Gretchen. 1997. Review of *Meter as Rhythm*, by Christopher F. Hasty. *Intégral* 11:181–90.

Houle, George. 1987. *Meter in Music, 1600–1800: Performance, Perception, and Notation*. Bloomington: Indiana University Press.

Hudson, Richard. 1994. *Stolen Time: The History of Tempo Rubato*. Oxford: Clarendon.

Hunnicutt, Bradley Clark. 2000. "Hugo Riemann's *System der musikalischen Rhythmik und Metrik*, Part Two: A Translation Preceded by Commentary." PhD diss., University of Wisconsin–Madison.

Ito, John Paul. 2011. "On Music, Mathematics, and Theology: Pythagoras, the Mind, and Human Agency." In *Resonant Witness: Conversations between Music and Theology*, edited by Jeremy Begbie and Steven Guthrie, 109–34. Grand Rapids, MI: Eerdmans.

———. 2013a. "Hypermetrical Schemas, Metrical Orientation, and Cognitive-Linguistic Paradigms." *Journal of Music Theory* 57 (1): 47–85.

———. 2013b. "Repetition without Repetition: Bernsteinian Perspectives on Motor Learning for Musicians." *College Music Symposium* 51. https://symposium.music.org/index.php/51/item/11-repetition-without-repetition-bernsteinian-perspectives-on-motor-learning-for-musicians.

———. 2013c. "Focal Impulses and Expressive Performance." In *From Sounds to Music and Emotions: 9th International Symposium, CMMR 2012, London, UK, June 2012; Revised Selected Papers*, edited by Mitsuko Aramaki, Mathieu Barthet, Richard Kronland-Martinet, and Sølvi Ystad, 480–89. Berlin: Springer.

———. 2014. "Koch's Metrical Theory and Mozart's Music: A Corpus Study." *Music Perception* 31 (3): 205–22.

———. 2015. "Repetition without Repetition: How Bernstein Illumines Motor Skill in Music Performance." In *Anticipation: Learning from the Past; The Russian/Soviet Contributions to the Science of Anticipation*, edited by Mihai Nadin, 257–68. Cham, Switzerland: Springer.

———. In preparation a. "Bach and the Rationalization of Musical Time." Unpublished manuscript.

———. In preparation b. "*Kennenschaft*: Imagination, Empiricism, and a Greater Whole." Unpublished manuscript.

———. In preparation c. "Metrical Dissonance in Brahms." Unpublished manuscript.

Iversen, John R., Bruno H. Repp, and Aniruddh D. Patel. 2009. "Top-Down Control of Rhythm Perception Modulates Early Auditory Responses." *Annals of the New York Academy of Sciences* 1169 (1): 58–73.

Iverson, Jana M., and Mary K. Fagan. 2004. "Infant Vocal-Motor Coordination: Precursor to the Gesture-Speech System?" *Child Development* 75 (4): 1053–66.

Iyer, Vijay. 2002. "Embodied Mind, Situated Cognition, and Expressive Timing in African-American Music." *Music Perception* 19 (3): 387–414.

Jaques-Dalcroze, Emile. 1916. *La Rythmique: Enseignement pour le Développement de l'Instinct rythmique et métrique, du sens de l'Harmonie plastique et de l'Equilibre des mouvements, et pour la Régularisation des Habitudes motrices*, vol. 1. Lausanne: Jobin.

———. 1920. *Le rythme, la musique et l'éducation*. Paris: Fischbacher.

———. (1930) 1985. *Eurythmics, Art and Education*. Translated by Frederick Rothwell, edited by Cynthia Cox. London: Chatto & Windus. Reprint, Salem, NH: Ayer. Citations refer to the Ayer edition.

Jones, Mari Riess. 1976. "Time, Our Lost Dimension." *Psychological Review* 83 (5): 323–55.

———. 1984. "The Patterning of Time and Its Effects on Perceiving." *Annals of the New York Academy of Sciences* 423 (1): 158–67.

———. 1987. "Dynamic Pattern Structure in Music: Recent Theory and Research." *Perception and Psychophysics* 41 (6): 621–34.

———. 1992. "Attending to Musical Events." In *Cognitive Bases of Musical Communication*, edited by Mari Riess Jones and Susan Holleran, 91–110. Washington, DC: American Psychological Association.

———. 2016. "Musical Time." In *The Oxford Handbook of Music Psychology*, 2nd ed., edited by Susan Hallam, Ian Cross, and Michael Thaut, 125–41. Oxford: Oxford University Press.

Jones, Mari Riess, and Marilyn Boltz. 1989. "Dynamic Attending and Responses to Time." *Psychological Review* 96 (3): 459–91.

Jones, Mari Riess, Marilyn Boltz, and Gary Kidd. 1982. "Controlled Attending as a Function of Melodic and Temporal Context." *Perception and Psychophysics* 32 (3): 211–18.

Jones, Mari Riess, and William Yee. 1997. "Sensitivity to Time Change: The Role of Context and Skill." *Journal of Experimental Psychology: Human Perception and Performance* 23 (3): 693–709.

Jordan, Stephanie. 2000. *Moving Music: Dialogues with Music in Twentieth-Century Ballet*. London: Dance Books.

———. 2011. "Choreomusical Conversations: Facing a Double Challenge." *Dance Research Journal* 43 (1): 43–64.

Jungers, Melissa Kay. 2007. "Performance Priming in Music." *Music Perception* 24 (4): 395–99.

Kallio, Tapio. 2001. "Meter in the Opening of the Second Symphony." In *Sibelius Studies*, edited by Timothy L. Jackson and Veijo Murtomäki, 275–95. Cambridge: Cambridge University Press.

Kaminsky, Peter M. 1989. "Aspects of Harmony, Rhythm, and Form in Schumann's *Papillons, Carnaval*, and *Davidsbündlertänze*." PhD diss., University of Rochester.

Keele, S. W. 1968. "Movement Control in Skilled Motor Performance." *Psychological Bulletin* 70 (6, Pt. 1): 387–403.

Keil, Charles, and Steven Feld. 1994. *Music Grooves: Essays and Dialogues*. Chicago: University of Chicago Press.

Kelso, J. A. Scott. 1984. "Phase Transitions and Critical Behavior in Human Bimanual Coordination." *American Journal of Physiology: Regulatory, Integrative and Comparative Physiology* 246 (6): R1000–R1004.

Kelso, J. A. Scott, K. G. Holt, Peter N. Kugler, and Michael T. Turvey. 1980. "On the Concept of Coordinative Structures as Dissipative Structures: II. Empirical Lines of Convergence." In *Tutorials in Motor Behavior*, edited by George E. Stelmach and Jean Requin, 49–70. Amsterdam: North Holland.

Kendon, Adam. 1980. "Gesticulation and Speech: Two Aspects of the Process of Utterance." In *The Relationship of Verbal and Nonverbal Communication*, edited by Mary R. Key, 207–27. The Hague: Mouton.

Kilpeläinen, Kari. 2000a. "Critical Commentary." In *Jean Sibelius: Symphony No. 2 in D Major*, edited by Kari Kilpeläinen, 215–39. Wiesbaden: Breitkopf und Härtel.

———, ed. 2000b. "Facsimiles." In *Jean Sibelius: Symphony No. 2 in D Major*, edited by Kari Kilpeläinen, 207–13. Wiesbaden: Breitkopf und Härtel.

Kim, Youn, and Sander L. Gilman, eds. Forthcoming. *The Oxford Handbook of Music and the Body*. New York: Oxford University Press.

Klorman, Edward. 2016. *Mozart's Music of Friends: Social Interplay in the Chamber Works*. Cambridge: Cambridge University Press.

Kozak, Mariusz. 2015. "Listeners' Bodies in Music Analysis: Gestures, Motor Intentionality, and Models." *Music Theory Online* 21 (3). http://www.mtosmt.org/issues/mto.15.21.3/mto.15.21.3.kozak.html.

Krahmer, Emiel, and Marc Swerts. 2007. "The Effects of Visual Beats on Prosodic Prominence: Acoustic Analyses, Auditory Perception and Visual Perception." *Journal of Memory and Language* 57 (3): 396–414.

Krebs, Harald. 1987. "Some Extensions of the Concepts of Metrical Consonance and Dissonance." *Journal of Music Theory* 31 (1): 99–120.

———. 1999. *Fantasy Pieces: Metrical Dissonance in the Music of Robert Schumann*. New York: Oxford University Press.

Kubik, Gerhard. 1979. "Pattern Perception and Recognition in African Music." In *The Performing Arts: Music and Dance*, edited by John Blacking and Joann W. Kealiinohomoku, 221–49. The Hague: Mouton.

———. 1985. "The Emics of African Musical Rhythm." In *Cross Rhythms 2*, edited by Daniel Avorgbedor and Kwesi Yankah, 26–66. Bloomington, IN: Trickster.

Kugler, Peter N., J. A. Scott Kelso, and Michael T. Turvey. 1980. "On the Concept of Coordinative Structures as Dissipative Structures: I. Theoretical Lines of Convergence." In *Tutorials in Motor Behavior*, edited by George E. Stelmach and Jean Requin, 3–47. Amsterdam: North Holland.

Lakoff, George. 1987. *Women, Fire, and Dangerous Things: What Categories Reveal about the Mind*. Chicago: University of Chicago Press.

Lakoff, George, and Mark Johnson. 1980. *Metaphors We Live By*. Chicago: University of Chicago Press.

Large, Edward W. 2000. "On Synchronizing Movements to Music." *Human Movement Science* 19 (4): 527–66.

———. 2008. "Resonating to Musical Rhythm: Theory and Experiment." In *Psychology of Time*, edited by Simon Grondin, 189–231. Bingley, UK: Emerald.

———. 2010. "Neurodynamics of Music." In *Music Perception*, edited by Mari Riess Jones, Richard R. Fay, and Arthur N. Popper, 201–31. New York: Springer.

Large, Edward W., Jorge A. Herrera, and Marc J. Velasco. 2015. "Neural Networks for Beat Perception in Musical Rhythm." *Frontiers in Systems Neuroscience* 9: article 159. http://journal.frontiersin.org/article/10.3389/fnsys.2015.00159/full.

Large, Edward W., and Mari Riess Jones. 1999. "The Dynamics of Attending: How People Track Time-Varying Events." *Psychological Review* 106 (1): 119–59.

Large, Edward W., and Carolyn Palmer. 2002. "Perceiving Temporal Regularity in Music." *Cognitive Science* 26 (1): 1–37.

Larson, Steve. 2012. *Musical Forces: Motion, Metaphor, and Meaning in Music*. Bloomington: Indiana University Press.

Lashley, K. S. 1951. "The Problem of Serial Order in Behavior." In *Cerebral Mechanisms in Behavior: The Hixon Symposium*, edited by Lloyd A. Jeffress, 112–36. New York: Wiley.

Laskowski, Larry. 1990. "Voice Leading and Meter: An Unusual Mozart Autograph." In *Trends in Schenkerian Research*, edited by Allen Cadwallader, 41–49. New York: Schirmer.

Latash, Mark L. 2000. "Modulation of Simple Reaction Time on the Background of an Oscillatory Action: Implications for Synergy Organization." *Experimental Brain Research* 131 (1): 85–100.

———. 2008. *Synergy*. Oxford: Oxford University Press.

Latash, Mark L., and Michael T. Turvey, eds. 1996. *Dexterity and Its Development*. Mahwah, NJ: Erlbaum.

Laws, Kenneth. 2002. *Physics and the Art of Dance: Understanding Movement*. Oxford: Oxford University Press.

Le Guin, Elisabeth. 2006. *Boccherini's Body: An Essay in Carnal Musicology*. Berkeley: University of California Press.

Leonard, Thomas, and Fred Cummins. 2011. "The Temporal Relation between Beat Gestures and Speech." *Language and Cognitive Processes* 26 (10): 1457–71.

Lerdahl, Fred, and Ray Jackendoff. 1983. *A Generative Theory of Tonal Music*. Cambridge, MA: MIT Press.

Lester, Joel. 1986. *The Rhythms of Tonal Music*. Carbondale: Southern Illinois University Press.

———. 1992. Review of *Musical Structure and Performance*, by Wallace Berry. *Music Theory Spectrum* 14 (1): 75–81.

———. 1995. "Performance and Analysis: Interaction and Interpretation." In *The Practice of Performance: Studies in Musical Interpretation*, edited by John Rink, 197–216. Cambridge: Cambridge University Press.

Lewin, David.1986. "Music Theory, Phenomenology, and Modes of Perception." *Music Perception* 3 (4): 327–92.

Li, Xiaofeng, Robert J. Logan, and Richard E. Pastore. 1991. "Perception of Acoustic Source Characteristics: Walking Sounds." *Journal of the Acoustical Society of America* 90 (6): 3036–49.

Lidov, David. 1987. "Mind and Body in Music." *Semiotica* 66 (1): 69–97.

———. 2005. "Repairing Errors in the Musical Theory of Meter." In *Aus dem Takt: Rhythmus in Kunst, Kultur und Natur,* edited by Christa Brüstle, Nadia Ghattas, Clemens Risi, and Sabine Schouten, 161–173. Bielefeld: Transcript.

Little, Meredith, and Natalie Jenne. 2001. *Dance and the Music of J. S. Bach,* 2nd ed. Bloomington: Indiana University Press.

Livingstone, Steven R., Ralf Muhlberger, Andrew R. Brown, and William F. Thompson. 2010. "Changing Musical Emotion: A Computational Rule System for Modifying Score and Performance." *Computer Music Journal* 34 (1): 41–64.

Locke, David. 1982. "Principles of Offbeat Timing and Cross-Rhythm in Southern Eʋe Dance Drumming." *Ethnomusicology* 26 (2): 217–46.

Loehr, Daniel P. 2004. "Gesture and Intonation." PhD diss., Georgetown University, Washington, DC.

London, Justin. 1993. "Loud Rests and Other Strange Metric Phenomena (or, Meter as Heard)." *Music Theory Online* 0 (2). http://www.mtosmt.org/issues/mto.93.0.2/mto.93.0.2.london .art.

———. 2012. *Hearing in Time: Psychological Aspects of Musical Meter.* 2nd ed. Oxford: Oxford University Press.

Lussy, Mathis. 1874. *Traité de l'expression musicale: accents, nuances et mouvements dans la musique vocale et instrumentale.* 2nd ed. Paris: Heugel.

———. [1885?]. *Musical Expression, Accents, Nuances, and Tempo, in Vocal and Instrumental Music.* Translated by M. E. von Glehn. London: Novello.

Ma, Yo-Yo. 2015. "Cellist Yo-Yo Ma Gives Prokofiev Masterclass." *The Strad,* October 6. https:// www.thestrad.com/cellist-yo-yo-ma-gives-prokofiev-masterclass/1467.article.

Maes, Pieter-Jan, Marc Leman, Caroline Palmer, and Marcelo M. Wanderley. 2014. "Action-Based Effects on Music Perception." *Frontiers in Psychology* 4: article 1008. http://journal .frontiersin.org/article/10.3389/fpsyg.2013.01008/full.

Malin, Yonatan. 2005. "Multilayered Metric Dissonances: Applications and Extensions for the Theories of Krebs and Cohn." Presented at the annual meeting of the Society for Music Theory, Cambridge, MA.

Manning, Fiona C., Jennifer Harris, and Michael Schutz. 2017. "Temporal Prediction Abilities Are Mediated by Motor Effector and Rhythmic Expertise." *Experimental Brain Research* 235 (3): 861–71.

Manning, Fiona C., and Michael Schutz. 2013. "'Moving to the Beat' Improves Timing Perception." *Psychonomic Bulletin and Review* 20 (6): 1133–39.

———. 2015. "Movement Enhances Perceived Timing in the Absence of Auditory Feedback." *Timing and Time Perception* 3 (1–2): 1–10.

———. 2016. "Trained to Keep a Beat: Movement-Related Enhancements to Timing Perception in Percussionists and Non-percussionists." *Psychological Research* 80 (4): 532–42.

Martens, Peter. 2011. "The Ambiguous Tactus: Tempo, Subdivision Benefit, and Three Listener Strategies." *Music Perception* 28 (5): 433–48.

———. 2012. "*Tactus* in Performance: Constraints and Possibilities." *Music Theory Online* 18 (1). http://mtosmt.org/issues/mto.12.18.1/mto.12.18.1.martens.php.

Mates, Jiří, Ulrike Müller, Tomáš Radil, and Ernst Pöppel. 1994. "Temporal Integration in Sensorimotor Synchronization." *Journal of Cognitive Neuroscience* 6 (4): 332–40.

Maurer Zenck, Claudia. 2001. *Vom Takt: Untersuchungen zur Theorie und kompositorischen Praxis im ausgehenden 18. und beginnenden 19. Jahrhundert.* Vienna: Böhlau.

McClave, Evelyn. 1994. "Gestural Beats: The Rhythm Hypothesis." *Journal of Psycholinguistic Research* 23 (1): 45–66.

———. 1998. "Pitch and Manual Gestures." *Journal of Psycholinguistic Research* 27 (1): 69–89.

McClelland, Ryan. 2003. "Performance and Analysis Studies: An Overview and Bibliography." *Indiana Theory Review* 24:95–106.

———. 2006. "Extended Upbeats in the Classical Minuet: Interactions with Hypermeter and Phrase Structure." *Music Theory Spectrum* 28 (1): 23–56.

———. 2010. *Brahms and the Scherzo: Studies in Musical Narrative.* Farnham, UK: Ashgate.

———. 2012. "Sequence as Expressive Culmination in the Chamber Music of Brahms." In *Expressive Intersections in Brahms: Essays in Analysis and Meaning*, edited by Heather Platt and Peter H. Smith, 147–85. Bloomington: Indiana University Press.

———. 2018. "Hemiola as Agent of Metric Resolution in the Music of Brahms." In *Brahms and the Shaping of Time*, edited by Scott Murphy, 143–77. Rochester, NY: University of Rochester Press.

McKee, Eric. 2004. "Extended Anacruses in Mozart's Instrumental Music." *Theory and Practice* 29:1–37.

———. 2012. *Decorum of the Minuet, Delirium of the Waltz: A Study of Dance-Music Relations in ¾ Time.* Bloomington: Indiana University Press.

McKinney, Martin F., and Dirk Moelants. 2006. "Ambiguity in Tempo Perception: What Draws Listeners to Different Metrical Levels?" *Music Perception* 24 (2): 155–66.

Meijer, Onno G., and Klaus Roth. 1988. *Complex Movement Behaviour: "The" Motor-Action Controversy.* Amsterdam: North-Holland.

Meister, I. G., T. Krings, H. Foltys, B. Boroojerdi, M. Müller, R. Töpper, and A. Thron. 2004. "Playing Piano in the Mind: An fMRI Study on Music Imagery and Performance in Pianists. *Cognitive Brain Research* 19 (3): 219–28.

Mervis, Carolyn B., and Eleanor Rosch. 1981. "Categorization of Natural Objects." *Annual Review of Psychology* 32:89–115.

Meyer, Rosalee K., and Caroline Palmer. 2003. "Temporal and Motor Transfer in Music Performance." *Music Perception* 21 (1): 81–104.

Michaels, Claire F., and Raoul M. Bongers. 1994. "The Dependence of Discrete Movements on Rhythmic Movements: Simple RT during Oscillatory Tracking." *Human Movement Science* 13 (3–4): 473–93.

Mirka, Danuta. 2009. *Metric Manipulations in Haydn and Mozart: Chamber Music for Strings, 1787–1791.* New York: Oxford University Press.

Miyake, Yoshihiro, Yohei Onishi, and Ernst Pöppel. 2004. "Two Types of Anticipation in Synchronization Tapping." *Acta Neurobiologiae Experimentalis* 64 (3): 415–26.

Monahan, Seth. 2013. "Action and Agency Revisited." *Journal of Music Theory* 57 (2): 321–71.

Montague, Eugene. 2011. "Phenomenology and the 'Hard Problem' of Consciousness and Music." In *Music and Consciousness: Philosophical, Psychological, and Cultural Perspectives*, edited by David Clarke and Eric Clarke, 29–46. Oxford: Oxford University Press.

———. Forthcoming. "Entrainment and Embodiment in Musical Performance." In *The Oxford Handbook of Music and the Body*, edited by Youn Kim and Sander L. Gilman. New York: Oxford University Press.

Moore, Stephen Fred. 1992. "The Writings of Emile Jaques-Dalcroze: Toward a Theory for the Performance of Musical Rhythm." PhD diss., Indiana University, Bloomington.

Mozart, Leopold. 1756. *Versuch einer gründlichen Violinschule.* Augsburg: Johann Jacob Lotter.

———. (1756) 1985. *A Treatise on the Fundamental Principles of Violin Playing,* 2nd ed. Translated by Editha Knocker. Oxford: Oxford University Press.

Muffat, Georg. 2001. "Texts from *Florilegium Secundum,* 1698." In *Georg Muffat on Performance Practice: The Texts from* Florilegium Primum, Florilegium Secundum, *and* Auserlesene Instrumentalmusik, edited and translated by David K. Wilson, 23–65. Bloomington: Indiana University Press.

Murphy, Scott. 2007. "On Metre in the Rondo of Brahms's Op. 25." *Music Analysis* 26 (3): 323–53.

——— 2009. "Metric Cubes in Some Music of Brahms." *Journal of Music Theory* 53 (1): 1–56.

Nazzi, Thierry, Josiane Bertoncini, and Jacques Mehler. 1998. "Language Discrimination by Newborns: Toward an Understanding of the Role of Rhythm." *Journal of Experimental Psychology: Human Perception and Performance* 24 (3): 756–66.

Neumann, Frederick. 1993. *Performance Practices of the Seventeenth and Eighteenth Centuries.* New York: Schirmer.

Nobe, Shuichi. 1996. "Representational Gestures, Cognitive Rhythms, and Acoustic Aspects of Speech: A Network/Threshold Model of Gesture Production." PhD diss., University of Chicago.

Nowotny, Rudolf. 1996. "Das Duett Nr. 7 aus der Zauberflöte: Periode und Takt." In *Mozart-Jahrbuch,* 85–126.

Ng, Samuel. 2006. "The Hemiolic Cycle and Metric Dissonance in the First Movement of Brahms's Cello Sonata in F Major, op. 99." *Theory and Practice* 31:65–95.

———. 2009. "Reinterpreting Metrical Reinterpretation." *Intégral* 23:121–61.

———. 2012. "Phrase Rhythm as Form in Classical Instrumental Music." *Music Theory Spectrum* 34 (1): 51–77.

Palmer, Caroline. 1989. "Mapping Musical Thought to Musical Performance." *Journal of Experimental Psychology: Human Perception and Performance* 15 (2): 331–46.

———. 1996. "On the Assignment of Structure in Music Performance." *Music Perception* 14 (1): 23–56.

———. 1997. "Music Performance." *Annual Review of Psychology* 48:115–38.

———. 2005. "Time Course of Retrieval and Movement Preparation in Music Performance." *Annals of the New York Academy of Sciences* 1060 (1): 360–67.

Palmer, Caroline, and Carolyn Drake. 1997. "Monitoring and Planning Capacities in the Acquisition of Music Performance Skills." *Canadian Journal of Experimental Psychology* 51 (4): 369–84.

Palmer, Caroline, Melissa K. Jungers, and Peter W. Jusczyk. 2001. "Episodic Memory for Musical Prosody." *Journal of Memory and Language* 45 (4): 526–45.

Palmer, Caroline, and Michael H. Kelly. 1992. "Linguistic Prosody and Musical Meter in Song." *Journal of Memory and Language* 31 (4): 525–42.

Palmer, Caroline, and Carol L. Krumhansl. 1990. "Mental Representations for Musical Meter." *Journal of Experimental Psychology: Human Perception and Performance* 16 (4): 728–41.

Palmer, Caroline, and Peter Q. Pfordresher. 2003. "Incremental Planning in Sequence Production." *Psychological Review* 110 (4): 683–712.

Palmer, Caroline, and Carla van de Sande. 1995. "Range of Planning in Music Performance." *Journal of Experimental Psychology: Human Perception and Performance* 21 (5): 947–62.

Park, Se-Woong, Hamal Marino, Steven K. Charles, Dagmar Sternad, and Neville Hogan. 2017. "Moving Slowly Is Hard for Humans: Limitations of Dynamic Primitives." *Journal of Neurophysiology* 118 (1): 69–83.

Parncutt, Richard. 1989. *Harmony: A Psychoacoustical Approach*. Berlin: Springer.

———. 1994. "A Perceptual Model of Pulse Salience and Metrical Accent in Musical Rhythms." *Music Perception* 11 (4): 409–64.

Patel, Aniruddh D. 2008. *Music, Language, and the Brain*. Oxford: Oxford University Press.

Patel, Aniruddh D., and John R. Iversen. 2014. "The Evolutionary Neuroscience of Musical Beat Perception: The Action Simulation for Auditory Prediction (ASAP) Hypothesis." *Frontiers in Systems Neuroscience* 8: article 57. http://journal.frontiersin.org/article/10.3389/fnsys.2014.00057/full.

Patel, Aniruddh D., John R. Iversen, Yanqing Chen, and Bruno H. Repp. 2005. "The Influence of Metricality and Modality on Synchronization with a Beat." *Experimental Brain Research* 163 (2): 226–38.

Penel, Amandine, and Carolyn Drake. 1998. "Sources of Timing Variation in Music Performance: A Psychological Segmentation Model." *Psychological Research* 61 (1): 12–32.

Perl, Benjamin. 1998. "Wo soll man bei 6/8 die Taktstriche ziehen? Weitere Gedanken zum Duett as der 'Zauberflöte.'" *Mozart-Jahrbuch*, 85–101.

Pew, Richard W. 1974. "Human Perceptual-Motor Performance." In *Human Information Processing: Tutorials in Performance and Cognition*, edited by Barry H. Kantowitz, 1–39. Hillsdale, NJ: Erlbaum.

Philip, Robert. 1992. *Early Recordings and Musical Style: Changing Tastes in Instrumental Performance, 1900–1950*. Cambridge: Cambridge University Press.

———. 2004. *Performing Music in the Age of Recording*. New Haven, CT: Yale University Press.

Phillips-Silver, Jessica, and Laurel J. Trainor. 2005. "Feeling the Beat: Movement Influences Infant Rhythm Perception." *Science* 308 (5727): 1430.

———. 2007. "Hearing What the Body Feels: Auditory Encoding of Rhythmic Movement." *Cognition* 105 (3): 533–46.

———. 2008. "Vestibular Influence on Auditory Metrical Interpretation." *Brain and Cognition* 67 (1): 94–102.

Pierce, Alexandra. 2007. *Deepening Musical Performance through Movement: The Theory and Practice of Embodied Interpretation*. Bloomington: Indiana University Press.

Pike, Kenneth. 1945. *The Intonation of American English*. Ann Arbor: University of Michigan Press.

Polak, Rainer. 2010. "Rhythmic Feel as Meter: Non-isochronous Beat Subdivision in Jembe Music from Mali." *Music Theory Online* 10 (4). http://www.mtosmt.org/issues/mto.10.16.4/mto.10.16.4.polak.html.

Polanyi, Michael. 1962. *Personal Knowledge: Towards a Post-critical Philosophy*. Corr. ed. Chicago: University of Chicago Press.

Port, Robert F. 2003. "Meter and Speech." *Journal of Phonetics* 31 (3–4): 599–611.

Port, Robert F., and Timothy van Gelder, eds. 1995. *Mind as Motion: Explorations in the Dynamics of Cognition*. Cambridge, MA: MIT Press.

Potter, Tully. 2010. *Adolf Busch: The Life on an Honest Musician*. 2 vols. London: Toccata.

Poudrier, Ève, and Bruno H. Repp. 2013. "Can Musicians Track Two Different Beats Simultaneously?" *Music Perception* 30 (4): 369–90.

Povel, Dirk-Jan. 1977. "Temporal Structure of Performed Music: Some Preliminary Observations." *Acta Psychologica* 41 (4): 309–20.

Quantz, Johann Joachim. 1752. *Versuch einer Anweisung die Flöte traversiere zu spielen: Mit verschiedenen, zur Beförderung des guten Geschmackes in der praktischen Musik dienlichen Anmerkungen begleitet, und mit Exempeln erläutert*. Berlin: Johann Friedrich Voss.

———. (1752) 1966. *On Playing the Flute*. Translated by Edward R. Reilly. New York: Schirmer.

Ramus, Franck, and Jacques Mehler. 1999. "Language Identification with Suprasegmental Cues: A Study Based on Speech Resynthesis." *Journal of the Acoustical Society of America* 105 (1): 512–21.

Reed, Edward S. 1988. *James J. Gibson and the Psychology of Perception*. New Haven, CT: Yale University Press.

Repp, Bruno H. 1990. "Patterns of Expressive Timing in Performances of a Beethoven Minuet by Nineteen Famous Pianists." *Journal of the Acoustical Society of America* 88 (2): 622–41.

———. 1997 "The Aesthetic Quality of a Quantitatively Average Music Performance: Two Preliminary Experiments." *Music Perception* 14 (4): 419–44.

———. 1998. "A Microcosm of Musical Expression: I. Quantitative Analysis of Pianists' Timing in the Initial Measures of Chopin's Etude in E Major." *Journal of the Acoustical Society of America* 104 (2): 1085–1100.

———. 1999a. "Control of Expressive and Metronomic Timing in Pianists." *Journal of Motor Behavior* 31 (2): 145–64.

———. 1999b. "Detecting Deviations from Metronomic Timing in Music: Effects of Perceptual Structure on the Mental Timekeeper." *Perception and Psychophysics* 61 (3): 529–48.

———. 1999c. "Relationships between Performance Timing, Perception of Timing Perturbations, and Perceptual-Motor Synchronization in Two Chopin Preludes." *Australian Journal of Psychology* 51 (3): 188–203.

———. 2002. "The Embodiment of Musical Structure: Effects of Musical Context on Sensorimotor Synchronization with Complex Timing Patterns." In *Common Mechanisms in Perception and Action*, edited by Wolfgang Prinz and Bernhard Hommel, 245–65. Oxford: Oxford University Press.

———. 2005a. "Rate Limits of On-beat and Off-beat Tapping with Simple Auditory Rhythms: 2. The Roles of Different Kinds of Accent." *Music Perception* 23 (2): 165–87.

———. 2005b. "Sensorimotor Synchronization: A Review of the Tapping Literature." *Psychonomic Bulletin and Review* 12 (6): 969–92.

———. 2006a. "Musical Synchronization." In *Music, Motor Control, and the Brain*, edited by Eckart Altenmüller, Mario Wiesendanger, and Jürg Kesselring, 55–76. Oxford: Oxford University Press.

———. 2006b. "Rate Limits of Sensorimotor Synchronization." *Advances in Cognitive Psychology* 2 (2): 163–81.

———. 2010. "Do Metrical Accents Create Illusory Phenomenal Accents?" *Attention, Perception, and Psychophysics* 72 (5): 1390–403.

Repp, Bruno H., and Rebecca Doggett. 2007. "Tapping to a Very Slow Beat: A Comparison of Musicians and Nonmusicians." *Music Perception* 24 (4): 367–76.

Repp, Bruno H., and Günther Knoblich. 2009. "Performed or Observed Keyboard Actions Affect Pianists' Judgments of Relative Pitch." *Quarterly Journal of Experimental Psychology* 62 (11): 2156–70.

Repp, Bruno H., and Yi-Huang Su. 2013. "Sensorimotor Synchronization: A Review of Recent Research (2006–2012)." *Psychonomic Bulletin and Review* 20 (3): 403–52.

Riemann, Hugo. 1884. *Musikalische Dynamik und Agogik: Lehrbuch der musikalischen Phrasierung auf Grund einer Revision der Lehre von der Musikalischen Metrik und Rhythmik*. Hamburg: D. Rahter.

———. 1903. *System der musikalischen Rhythmik und Metrik*. Leipzig: Breitkopf & Härtel.

Rink, John. 1990. Review of *Musical Structure and Performance*, by Wallace Berry. *Music Analysis* 9 (3): 319–39.

———. 1995a. "Playing in Time: Rhythm, Metre and Tempo in Brahms's Fantasien op. 116." In *The Practice of Performance: Studies in Musical Interpretation*, edited by John Rink, 254–82. Cambridge: Cambridge University Press.

———, ed. 1995b. *The Practice of Performance: Studies in Musical Interpretation*. Cambridge: Cambridge University Press.

———. 2002. "Analysis and (or?) Performance." In *Musical Performance: A Guide to Understanding*, edited by John Rink, 35–58. Cambridge: Cambridge University Press.

———. 2015. "Chopin's Study in Syncopation." In *Bach to Brahms: Essays on Musical Design and Structure*, edited by David Beach and Yosef Goldenberg, 132–42. Rochester, NY: University of Rochester Press.

Roach, Peter. 1982. "On the Distinction between 'Stress-Timed' and 'Syllable-Timed' Languages." In *Linguistic Controversies: Essays in Linguistic Theory and Practice in Honour of F. R. Palmer*, edited by David Crystal, 73–79. London: Edward Arnold.

Rochet-Capellan, Amélie, Rafael Laboissièrre, Arturo Galván, and Lean-Luc Schwartz. 2008. "The Speech Focus Position Effect on Jaw-Finger Coordination in a Pointing Task." *Journal of Speech, Language, and Hearing Research* 51 (6): 1507–21.

Rosch, Eleanor. 1978. "Principles of Categorization." In *Cognition and Categorization*, edited by Eleanor Rosch and Barbara B. Lloyd, 27–48. Hillsdale, NJ: Erlbaum.

Rosenblum, Sandra P. 1992. "The Uses of Rubato in Music, Eighteenth to Twentieth Centuries." *Performance Practice Review* 7 (1): 33–53.

Rothstein, William. 1989. *Phrase Rhythm in Tonal Music*. New York: Schirmer.

———. 1995. "Beethoven with and without *Kunstgepräng'*: Metrical Ambiguity Reconsidered." In *Beethoven Forum 4*, edited by Christopher Reynolds, Lewis Lockwood and James Webster, 165–93. Lincoln: University of Nebraska Press.

———. 2008. "National Metrical Types in Music of the Eighteenth and Early Nineteenth Centuries." In *Communication in Eighteenth-Century Music*, edited by Danuta Mirka and Kofi Agawu, 112–59. New York: Cambridge University Press.

Rusiewicz, Heather L. 2011. "Synchronization of Speech and Gesture: A Dynamic Systems Perspective." In *Proceedings from the 2nd Gesture and Speech in Interaction (GESPIN) Conference, Bielefeld, Germany*. http://gespin.amu.edu.pl/?page_id=46.

Rusiewicz, Heather L., Susan Shaiman, Jana M. Iverson, and Neil Szuminsky. 2013. "Effects of Prosody and Position on the Timing of Deictic Gestures." *Journal of Speech, Language, and Hearing Research* 56 (2): 458–70.

———. 2014. "Effects of Perturbation and Prosody on the Coordination of Speech and Gesture." *Speech Communication* 57:283–300.

Saldaña, Helena M., and Lawrence D. Rosenblum. 1993. "Visual Influences on Auditory Pluck and Bow Judgments." *Perception and Psychophysics* 54 (3): 406–16.

Samarotto, Frank. 1999. "Strange Dimensions: Regularity and Irregularity in Deep Levels of Rhythmic Reduction." In *Schenker Studies 2*, edited by Carl Schachter and Hedi Siegel, 222–38. Cambridge: Cambridge University Press.

———. 2012. "'Fantasia subitanea': Temporal Caprice in Brahms's Op. 116, Nos. 1 and 7." In *Expressive Intersections in Brahms: Essays in Analysis and Meaning*, edited by Heather Platt and Peter H. Smith, 186–216. Bloomington: Indiana University.

Schaal, Stefan, Dagmar Sternad, Reiko Osu, and Mitsuo Kawato. 2004. "Rhythmic Arm Movement Is Not Discrete." *Nature Neuroscience* 7 (10): 1136–43.

Schmalfeldt, Janet. 1992. "Cadential Processes: The Evaded Cadence and the 'One More Time' Technique." *Journal of Musicological Research* 12 (1–2): 1–52.

———. 2016. "Response." *Music Theory Online* 22 (2). http://mtosmt.org/issues/mto.16.22.2/mto .16.22.2.schmalfeldt.html.

Schmidt, Richard A. 1975. "A Schema Theory of Discrete Motor Skill Learning." *Psychological Review* 82 (4): 225–60.

Schutz, Michael, and Scott Lipscomb. 2007. "Hearing Gestures, Seeing Music: Vision Influences Perceived Tone Duration." *Perception* 36 (6): 888–97.

Shaffer, L. H. 1976. "Intention and Performance." *Psychological Review* 83 (5): 375–93.

———. 1978. "Timing in the Motor Programming of Typing." *Quarterly Journal of Experimental Psychology* 30 (2): 333–45.

———. 1980. "Analysing Piano Performance: A Study of Concert Pianists." In *Tutorials in Motor Behavior*, edited by George E. Stelmach and Jean Requin, 443–55. Amsterdam: North-Holland.

———. 1981. "Performances of Chopin, Bach, and Bartók: Studies in Motor Programming." *Cognitive Psychology* 13 (3): 326–76.

———. 1982. "Rhythm and Timing in Skill." *Psychological Review* 89 (2): 109–23.

———. 1984. "Timing in Solo and Duet Piano Performances." *Quarterly Journal of Experimental Psychology* 36A (4): 577–95.

Shaffer, L. H., Eric F. Clarke, and Neil P. McAngus Todd. 1985. "Metre and Rhythm in Piano Playing." *Cognition* 20 (1): 61–77.

Sheveloff, Joel. 2000. "Dance, Gypsy, Dance!" in *The Varieties of Musicology: Essays in Honor of Murray Lefkowitz*, edited by John Daverio and John Ogasapian, 151–65. Warren, MI: Harmonie Park Press.

Shove, Patrick, and Bruno H. Repp. 1995. "Musical Motion and Performance: Theoretical and Empirical Perspectives." In *The Practice of Performance: Studies in Musical Interpretation*, edited by John Rink, 55–83. Cambridge: Cambridge University Press.

Simpson-Litke, Rebecca, and Chris Stover. 2019. "Theorizing Fundamental Music/Dance Interactions in Salsa." *Music Theory Spectrum* 41 (1): 74–103.

Sloboda, John A. 1983. "The Communication of Musical Metre in Piano Performance." *Quarterly Journal of Experimental Psychology* 35A (2): 377–96.

———. 1985. "Expressive Skill in Two Pianists: Metrical Communication in Real and Simulated Performances." *Canadian Journal of Psychology* 39 (2): 273–93.

Smith, Linda B. 2005. "Emerging Ideas about Categories." In *Building Object Categories in Developmental Time*, edited by Lisa Gershkoff-Stowe and David H. Rakison, 159–173. Mahwah, NJ: Erlbaum.

Smith, Peter H. 1997. "Brahms and Motivic 6/3 Chords." *Music Analysis* 16 (2): 175–217.

———. 1998. "Brahms and the Neapolitan Complex: ♭II, ♭VI, and Their Multiple Functions in the First Movement of the F-Minor Clarinet Sonata." In *Brahms Studies*, vol. 2, edited by David Brodbeck, 169–208. Lincoln: University of Nebraska Press.

———. 2001. "Brahms and the Shifting Barline: Metric Displacement and Formal Process in the Trios with Wind Instruments." In *Brahms Studies*, vol. 3, edited by David Brodbeck, 191–229. Lincoln: University of Nebraska Press.

———. 2006. "You Reap What You Sow: Some Instances of Rhythmic and Harmonic Ambiguity in Brahms." *Music Theory Spectrum* 28 (1): 57–97.

Solberg, Ragnhild Torvanger, and Alexander Refsum Jensenius. 2016. "Pleasurable and Intersubjectively Embodied Experiences of Electronic Dance Music." *Empirical Musicology Review* 11 (3–4): 301–18. http://emusicology.org/article/view/5023/4601.

Spencer, Herbert. 1857. "The Origin and Function of Music." *Fraser's Magazine* 56 (October): 396–408.

Spohr, Louis. [1832?]. *Violinschule*. Vienna: Haslinger.

———. [1843?]. *Violin School*. Translated by John Bishop. London: R. Cocks.

Sprick, Jan Philipp. 2013. "Wiederholung und Symmetrie im Kopfsatz von Johannes Brahms' Sonate Es-Dur op. 120/2." *Zeitschrift der Gesellschaft für Musiktheorie* 10 (1): 147–58.

Staude, Gerhard, Reinhard Dengler, and Werner Wolf. 2002. "The Discontinuous Nature of Motor Execution II. Merging Discrete and Rhythmic Movements in a Single-Joint System—The Phase Entrainment Effect." *Biological Cybernetics* 86 (6): 427–43.

Stein, Erwin. 1962. *Form and Performance*. London: Faber & Faber.

Stern, Daniel N. 2010. *Forms of Vitality: Exploring Dynamic Experience in Psychology, the Arts, Psychotherapy, and Development*. Oxford: Oxford University Press.

Sternad, Dagmar. 2001. "Kurt Wachholder: Pioneering Electrophysiological Studies of Voluntary Movements." In *Classics in Movement Science*, edited by Mark L. Latash and Vladimir M. Zatsiorsky, 375–407. Champaign, IL: Human Kinetics.

Sternad, Dagmar, and William J. Dean. 2003. "Rhythmic and Discrete Elements in Multi-Joint Coordination." *Brain Research* 989 (2): 152–71.

Sternad, Dagmar, William J. Dean, and Stefan Schaal. 2000. "Interaction of Rhythmic and Discrete Pattern Generators in Single-Joint Movements." *Human Movement Science* 19 (4): 627–64.

Sternad, Dagmar, Aymar de Rugy, Todd Pataky, and William J. Dean. 2002. "Interaction of Discrete and Rhythmic Movements over a Wide Range of Periods." *Experimental Brain Research* 147 (2): 162–74.

Stevens, Daniel B. Forthcoming. "Rhythm and the Performer's Body." In *The Oxford Handbook of Music and the Body*, edited by Youn Kim and Sander L. Gilman. New York: Oxford University Press.

Still, Jonathan. 2015. "How Down is a Downbeat? Feeling Meter and Gravity in Music and Dance." *Empirical Musicology Review* 10 (1–2):121–34. http://emusicology.org/article/view /4577.

Stover, Chris. In preparation. "Timeline Spaces: A Theory of Temporal Processes in Afro-Diasporic Music." Unpublished manuscript.

Talley, James Tazewell. 1989. "Minor Variations in Performance as Indicators of Musical Meter." PhD diss., The Ohio State University, Columbus.

Taylor, Charles. 2004. *Modern Social Imaginaries*. Durham, NC: Duke University Press.

Taylor, John R. 2004. "The Ecology of Constructions." In *Studies in Linguistic Motivation*, edited by Günther Radden and Klaus-Uwe Panther, 49–73. Berlin: Mouton de Gruyter.

———. 2006. "Polysemy and the Lexicon." In *Cognitive Linguistics: Current Applications and Future Perspectives*, edited by Gitte Kristiansen, Michel Achard, René Dirven, and Francisco J. Ruiz de Mendoza Ibáñez, 51–80. Berlin: Mouton de Gruyter.

Temperley, David. 1996. "Hypermetrical Ambiguity and Sonata Form Closing Groups." Paper presented at the annual meeting of the Society for Music Theory, Baton Rouge, LA. http:// www.theory.esm.rochester.edu/temperley/hyp-amb-clo.pdf.

———. 1999. "Syncopation in Rock: A Perceptual Perspective." *Popular Music* 18:19–40.

———. 2001. *The Cognition of Basic Musical Structures*. Cambridge, MA: MIT Press.

———. 2003. "End-Accented Phrases: An Analytical Exploration." *Journal of Music Theory* 47 (1): 125–54.

———. 2008. "Hypermetrical Transitions." *Music Theory Spectrum* 30 (2): 305–25.

Tenzer, Michael. 2000. *Gamelan Gong Kebyar: The Art of Twentieth-Century Balinese Music*. Chicago: University of Chicago Press.

Thelen, Esther, and Linda B. Smith. 1994. *A Dynamic Systems Approach to the Development of Cognition and Action*. Cambridge, MA: MIT Press.

Todd, Neil P. McAngus. 1992. "The Dynamics of Dynamics: A Model of Musical Expression." *Journal of the Acoustical Society of America* 91 (6): 3540–50.

Todd, Neil P. McAngus, and Christopher S. Lee. 2015. "The Sensory-Motor Theory of Rhythm and Beat Induction 20 Years On: A New Synthesis and Future Perspectives." *Frontiers in Human Neuroscience* 9: article 444. https://www.frontiersin.org/articles/10.3389/fnhum.2015.00444/full.

Toiviainen, Petri, Geoff Luck, and Marc R. Thompson. 2010. "Embodied Meter: Hierarchical Eigenmodes in Music-Induced Movement." *Music Perception* 28 (1): 59–70.

Truslit, Alexander. 1938. *Gestaltung und Bewegung in der Musik: Ein tönendes Buch vom musikalischen Vortrag und seinem bewegungserlebten Gestalten und Hören*. Berlin: Christian Friedrich Veiweg.

Türk, Daniel Gottlob. 1789. *Klavierschule, oder Anweisung zum Klavierspielen für Lehrer und Lernende, mit kritischen Anmerkungen*. Leipzig: Schwickert.

———. (1789) 1982. *School of Clavier Playing, or Instructions in Playing the Clavier for Teachers and Students*. Translated by Raymond H. Haggh. Lincoln: University of Nebraska Press.

Turvey, Michael T. 1977. "Preliminaries to a Theory of Action with Reference to Vision." In *Perceiving, Acting, and Knowing: Toward an Ecological Psychology*, edited by Robert Shaw and John Bransford, 211–65. Hillsdale, NJ: Erlbaum.

Turvey, Michael T., and Claudia Carello. 1996. "Dynamics of Bernstein's Level of Synergies." In *Dexterity and Its Development*, edited by Mark L. Latash and Michael T. Turvey, 339–76. Mahwah, NJ: Erlbaum.

Van Dyck, Edith, Dirk Moelants, Michiel Demey, Alexander Deweppe, Pieter Coussement, and Marc Leman. 2013. "The Impact of the Bass Drum on Human Dance Movement." *Music Perception* 30 (4): 349–59.

van Noorden, Leon, and Dirk Moelants. 1999. "Resonance in the Perception of Musical Pulse." *Journal of New Music Research* 28 (1): 43–66.

Vitale, Wayne. 1990. "Kotekan: The Technique of Interlocking Parts in Balinese Music." *Balungan* 4 (2): 2–15.

Vorberg, Dirk, and Rolf Hambuch. 1984. "Timing of Two-Handed Rhythmic Performance." *Annals of the New York Academy of Sciences* 423 (1): 390–406.

Walker, Bruce N., and Michael A. Nees. 2011. "Theory of Sonification." In *The Sonification Handbook*, edited by Thomas Hermann, Andy Hunt, and John G. Neuhoff, 9–39. Berlin: Logos.

Wanderley, Marcelo M. 2002. "Quantitative Analysis of Non-obvious Performer Gestures." In *Gesture and Sign Language in Human-Computer Interaction: International Gesture Workshop, GW 2001, London, UK, April 18–20, 2001; Revised Papers*, edited by Ipke Wachsmuth and Timo Sowa, 241–53. Berlin: Springer.

Wanderley, Marcelo M., Bradley W. Vines, Neil Middleton, Cory McKay, and Wesley Hatch. 2005. "The Musical Significance of Clarinetists' Ancillary Gestures: An Exploration of the Field." *Journal of New Music Research* 34 (1): 97–113.

Wei, Kunlin, Gary Wertman, and Dagmar Sternad. 2003. "Interactions between Rhythmic and Discrete Components in a Bimanual Task." *Motor Control* 7 (2): 134–54.

White, Barbara. 2006. "'As If They Didn't Hear the Music,' Or: How I Learned to Stop Worrying and Love Mickey Mouse." *Opera Quarterly* 22 (1): 65–89.

Whiteside, Abby. (1955) 1997. *Indispensibles of Piano Playing*. In *Abby Whiteside on Piano Playing: Indispensables of Piano Playing & Mastering the Chopin Etudes and Other Essays*, edited by Joseph Prostakoff and Sophia Rosoff. Portland, OR: Amadeus.

———. (1969) 1997. *Mastering the Chopin Etudes and Other Essays*. In *Abby Whiteside on Piano Playing: Indispensables of Piano Playing & Mastering the Chopin Etudes and Other Essays*, edited by Joseph Prostakoff and Sophia Rosoff. Portland, OR: Amadeus.

Wick, Norman L. 1994. "Shifted Downbeats in Classic and Romantic Music." *Indiana Theory Review* 15 (2): 73–87.

Widdess, Richard. 1994. "Involving the Performers in Transcription and Analysis: A Collaborative Approach to Dhrupad." *Ethnomusicology* 38 (1): 59–79.

———. 1995. "'Free Rhythm' in Indian Music." *EM: Annuario degli Archivi di Etnomusicologia dell'Accademia Nazionale di Santa Cecilia* 3:77–95.

Willner, Channan. 1991. "The Two-Length Bar Revisited: Handel and the Hemiola." *Göttinger Händel-Beiträge* 4:208–31.

———. 2013. "Metrical Displacement and Metrically Dissonant Hemiolas." *Journal of Music Theory* 57 (1): 87–118.

Windsor, W. Luke. 2011. "Gestures in Music-Making: Action, Information and Perception." In *New Perspectives on Music and Gesture*, edited by Anthony Gritten and Elaine King, 45–66. Farnham, UK: Ashgate.

Windsor, W. Luke, and Eric F. Clarke. 1997. "Expressive Timing and Dynamics in Real and Artificial Musical Performances: Using an Algorithm as an Analytical Tool." *Music Perception* 15 (2): 127–52.

Windsor, W. Luke, Peter Desain, Amandine Penel, and Michiel Borkent. 2006. "A Structurally Guided Method for the Decomposition of Expression in Music Performance." *Journal of the Acoustical Society of America* 119 (2): 1182–93.

Windsor, W. Luke, Kia Ng, Jane W. Davidson, and A. Utley. 2003. "Investigating Musicians' Natural Upper Body Movements." Paper presented at the First International Conference on Music and Gesture, Norwich, UK.

Winold, Helga, Esther Thelen, and Beverly D. Ulrich. 1994. "Coordination and Control in the Bow Arm Movements of Highly Skilled Cellists." *Ecological Psychology* 6 (1): 1–31.

Wintersgill, H. H. 1936. "Handel's Two-Length Bar." *Music and Letters* 17 (1): 1–12.

Zander, Benjamin. 2008. "The Transformative Power of Classical Music." *TED: Ideas Worth Spreading*. https://www.ted.com/talks/benjamin_zander_on_music_and_passion.

Zbikowski, Lawrence M. 2018. "Ways of Knowing: Social Dance, Music, and Grounded Cognition." In *Music-Dance: Sound and Motion in Contemporary Discourse*, edited by Patrizia Veroli and Gianfranco Vinay, 57–75. Abingdon, UK: Routledge.

Zeiner-Henriksen, Hans T. 2010. "Moved by the Groove: Bass Drum Sounds and Body Movements in Electronic Dance Music." In *Musical Rhythm in the Age of Digital Reproduction*, edited by Anne Danielsen, 121–39. Farnham, UK: Ashgate.

Zuckerkandl, Victor. 1956. *Sound and Symbol: Music and the External World*. Translated by Willard R. Trask. Princeton, NJ: Princeton University Press.

DISCOGRAPHY

Items in the discography are listed by performers' last names, using the common orderings from recordings (e.g., soloist first, then conductor, then orchestra). In some cases, the discussion in the text focuses on one performer in particular; in such cases, that performer will come first in the listing. The primary date listed is the earliest available, with recording date used where possible. Phonogram copyright and regular copyright dates (℗ and ©) are given at the end of the reference where available.

Abbado, Claudio, and the Chamber Orchestra of Europe. Rec. 1997. Mozart, Overture, from *Don Giovanni*. Deutsche Grammophon 457 601-2. ℗ and ©1998.

Alban Berg Quartet. ℗ 1983. String Quartet in B-flat Major, op. 130, Adagio ma non troppo – Allegro, from *Beethoven: The Late String Quartets*. EMI 7 47135 8.

Amadeus Quartet. Rec. 1959. String Quartet in A Minor, op. 51, no. 2, Finale, Allegro non assai, from *Johannes Brahms: String Quartets, Quintets, Sextets, Clarinet Trio*. Deutsche Grammophon 474 358-2. ℗ 1960.

Argerich, Martha. Rec. 1979. Schumann, *Fantasiestücke*, op. 12, "Grillen," from *Martha Argerich: 5 Classic Albums*. Warner 50999 9 84441 2 0. ℗ 2000, 2013, © 2013.

Bernstein, Leonard, and the New York Philharmonic. Rec. 1966. Symphony No. 2 in D Major, op. 43, iv, from *Sibelius: Symphonies Nos. 1, 2, and 3, Luonnotar, Pohjola's Daughter*. Sony SM2K 47619. ℗ 1965/68/70, © 1993.

Böhm, Henryk, Uwe Theimer, and the Mörbisch Festival Orchestra. Rec. 2013. "Und da soll man noch galant sein," from *Der Bettelstudent von Carl Millöcker*. Oehms 432. ℗ and ©2013.

Brendel, Alfred. Rec. 1971. Piano Sonata in B-flat Major, D. 960, Andante Sostenuto, from *Schubert: Piano Sonata in B-flat, D. 960, "Wanderer" Fantasy*. Philips 420 644-2. ℗ 1972.

Busch Quartet. Rec. 1938. String Quartet in G Major, D. 887, Allegro assai, from *Schubert: String Quartets Nos. 14 'Death and the Maiden' and 15*. EMI 0946 3 61589 2 1. ℗ 1940, 2006, © 2006.

Busch Quartet. Rec. 1941. String Quartet in B-flat Major, op. 130, Adagio ma non troppo, from *Beethoven: Quartets op. 59, no. 1, and op. 130*. Sony Classical MPK 47687. ℗ 1941, © 1991.

Bylsma, Anner. 1979. Suite No. 5 in C Minor for Violoncello Solo, BWV 1011, Sarabande, from *Johann Sebastian Bach: Unaccompanied Suites for Cello*. Pro Arte CDG 3227. ℗ 1979, © 1985.

Cahn-Lipman, Kivie. ℗ and ©2014. Suite No. 4 in E-flat Major for Violoncello Solo, BWV 1010, Prelude, from *Johann Sebastian Bach: Six Suites for Solo Violoncello without Bass*. New Focus FCR142.

Central Band of the RAF and Keith Brion. Rec. 2012. "President Garfield's Inaugural March," from *John Philip Sousa: Music for Wind Band*, vol. 13. Naxos 8.559729. ℗ and ©2014.

Concerto Köln and Anton Steck. Rec. 2005. Serenade in G Major, K. 525, "Eine kleine Nachtmusik," Menuetto, from *Mozart*. Archiv 00289 477 5800. ℗ and ©2006.

Davis, Miles, and the Miles Davis Nonet. Rec. 1949. *The Birth of the Cool*. Capitol 7243 5 30117 2 7. ℗ 1957, © 2001.

Dreyfus, Laurence, and Ketil Haugsand. Rec. 1985. Sonata in G major, BWV 1027, Adagio, from *Johann Sebastian Bach: Sonatas for Viola da gamba and Harpsichord, BWV 1027-1029*. Simax PSC 1024. ℗ and ©1986.

Eklund, Niklas, Roy Goodman, and the Swedish Chamber Orchestra. Rec. 1999. Neruda, Trumpet Concerto in E-flat Major, Vivace, from *Trumpet Concertos: Haydn, Hummel, Neruda.* Naxos 8.554806. ℗ 2002, © 2003.

Eschenbach, Christoph. Rec. 1968. Sonata for Piano No. 9 in D Major, K. 311 (284c), Allegro con spirito, from *Mozart: The Piano Sonatas.* Deutsche Grammophon 463 139-2. © 1999.

Fournier, Pierre. Rec. 1960. Suite No. 5 in C Minor for Violoncello Solo, Courante, from *Johann Sebastian Bach: Suites for Solo Cello.* Archiv 449 711-2. ℗ 1961, © 1996.

Fournier, Pierre, and Friedrich Gulda. Rec. 1959. Sonata No. 3 in A Major for Cello and Piano, Scherzo: Allegro molto, from *Beethoven: Complete Works for Cello and Piano.* Deutsche Grammophon 00289 477 6266. ℗ 1960, © 2006.

Freiburger Barockorchester. Rec. 2000. *Johann Sebastian Bach: Brandenburg Concertos.* EuroArts 2050316. © 2000.

Gerhardt, Alban, and Markus Groh. Rec. 1997. Sonata No. 2 for Cello and Piano in F Major, op. 99, Allegro passionato, from *Brahms: Sonates Violoncelle-Piano.* Harmonia Mundi HMN 911641. ℗ 1998.

Gibbons, John, Frans Brüggen, and the Orchestra of the Eighteenth Century. Rec. 1986. Piano Concerto No. 20 in D Minor, K. 466, Allegro, from *Mozart Piano Concertos KV 466 and 491.* Philips 420 823-2. ℗ 1987.

Hagen Quartet. Rec. 1994. Serenade in G Major, K. 525, "Eine kleine Nachtmusik," Menuetto, from *Mozart: The String Quartets.* Deutsche Grammophon 00289 477 6253 GB7. ℗ 1994, 2006.

Heifetz, Jascha. Rec. 1952. Partita No. 3 in E Major, BWV 1006, Loure, from *J. S. Bach: Sonatas and Partitas for Unaccompanied Violin.* RCA Victor 7708-2-RG. ℗ 1988.

Hellmich, Wolfgang, Günther Herbig ,and the Leipzig Radio Symphony Orchestra. ℗ 1968. "Und da soll man noch galant sein," from *Carl Millöcker: Der Bettelstudent.* Philips 422 143-2.

Helseth, Tine Thing, and the Norwegian Chamber Orchestra. Rec. 2007. Neruda, Trumpet Concerto in E-flat Major, Vivace, from *Trumpet Concertos: Haydn, Albinoni, Neruda, Hummel.* Simax PSC 1292. ℗ 2007, © 2007.

Kempff, Wilhelm. Rec. 1963. Capriccio in D Minor, op. 116, no. 7, from *Johannes Brahms: Fantasien op. 116; Intermezzi op. 117; Klavierstücke op. 118 und 119.* Deutsche Grammophon 437 249-2. ℗ 964.

Kremer, Gidon, and the Kremerata Baltica. Rec. 1999. Serenade in G Major, K. 525, "Eine kleine Nachtmusik," Menuetto, from *After Mozart.* Nonesuch 79633-2. ℗ and ©2001.

Kuijken, Sigiswald, and La petite Bande. ℗ 1982. Orchestral Suite No. 3 in D Major, BWV 1068, Gigue, from *J. S. Bach: Suites (Overtures) BWV 1066-1069.* Deutsche Harmonia Mundi 77008-2-RG. © 1990.

Leonhardt, Gustav. Rec. 1975. *J. S. Bach: Französische Suiten.* Sony SBK 60717. ℗ 1975, © 1998.

Lilye, Peter, and the Moscow RTV Symphony Orchestra. © 2015. Symphony No. 3 in E-flat Major, op. 97, "Rhenish," i, Lebhaft, from *Schumann Symphony No. 3.* Denon.

Luca, Sergiu. ℗ 1977. Partita No. 3 in E, BWV 1006, Loure, from *Johann Sebastian Bach: The Sonatas and Partitas for Unaccompanied Violin.* Elektra Nonesuch 9 73030-2.

Ma, Yo-Yo. ℗ and ©1983. *J. S. Bach: The Six Unaccompanied Cello Suites.* CBS M2K 37867.

Ma, Yo-Yo, and Emmanuel Ax. Rec. 1983. Sonata No. 3 in A Major for Cello and Piano, Scherzo: Allegro molto, from *Beethoven Sonatas Volume 2: No. 3, op. 69, and No. 5, op. 102, no. 2.* Sony Classical 88697 54730 2. ℗ 1984, © 2013.

Maisky, Mischa. Rec. 1999. *Johann Sebastian Bach: 6 Cello-Suiten.* Deutsche Grammophon 463 314-2. ℗ and ©1999.

Marriner, Neville, and the Academy of St. Martin in the Fields. Rec. 1998. Symphony No. 3 in E-flat Major, op. 97, "Rhenish," i, Lebhaft, from *Schumann Symphonies Nos. 1 and 3.* Hänssler 98.191. ℗ and ©1999.

McGill, Anthony, and the Pacifica Quartet. Rec. 2013. Brahms, Quintet in B minor for Clarinet and Strings, op. 115, Allegro, from *Mozart and Brahms Clarinet Quintets.* Cedille CDR 90000 147. ℗ and ©2014.

Mørk, Truls, and Juhani Lagerspetz. Rec. 1988. Sonata No. 2 for Cello and Piano in F Major, op. 99, Allegro passionato, from *Brahms Sonatas for Cello and Piano.* Simax PSC 1029. ℗ and ©1988.

Mosser, Jonell. ℗ 1998 "Stop in the Name of Love," from *Music from the Motion Picture "Hope Floats."* Capitol CDP 7243 4 93402 2 0. ℗ and ©1998.

Nézet-Séguin, Yannick, and the Mahler Chamber Orchestra. Rec. 2011. Mozart, Overture, from *Don Giovanni.* Deutsche Grammophon 477 9878. ℗ and ©2012.

Norman, Jessye, and Daniel Barenboim. Rec. 1981/1982. "Geistliches Wiegenlied," op. 91, no. 2, from *Brahms Lieder.* Deutsche Grammophon 459 469. ℗ 1983, © 2001.

Norman, Jessye, and Geoffrey Parsons. Rec. 1985. "Wie sollten wir geheim sie halten," op. 19, no. 4, from *Richard Strauss: Lieder.* Philips 416 298-2.

Norman, Jessye, Ulrich von Wrochem, and Geoffrey Parsons. Rec. 1980. "Geistliches Wiegenlied," op. 91, no. 2, from *Brahms Lieder.* Philips 416 439-2.

Ollendorff, Fritz, Robert Stolz , Chor der Deutschen Oper Berlin, and the Berliner Symphoniker. [Rec. 1966?] *Der Bettelstudent,* "Und da soll man noch galant sein," from *Carl Millöcker:* Der Bettelstudent *(Gesamtaufnahme),* Die Dubarry *(Querschnitt).* Eurodisc 610330-232.

Pahud, Emmanuel, and Eric Le Sage. Rec. 1997. Dutilleux, Sonatine for Flute and Piano, i, from *Paris.* EMI 7243 5 56488 2 2. ℗ and ©1997.

Pienaar, Daniel-Ben. Rec. 2009. Piano Sonata No. 8 in D Major, K. 311, Allegro con spirito, from *Mozart: Piano Sonatas.* Avie AV2209. ℗ and ©2010.

Pinnock, Trevor, and the English Concert. Rec. 1978. Orchestral Suite No. 3 in D Major, BWV 1068, Gigue, from *Bach: Overtures.* Deutsche Grammophon 477 6348. ℗ 1979/80.

Pratsch-Kaufmann, Kurt, Robert Stolz, Chor der Deutschen Oper Berlin, and the Berliner Symphoniker. [Rec. 1966?] *Der Bettelstudent,* "Ach guter Meister Enterich," from *Carl Millöcker:* Der Bettelstudent *(Gesamtaufnahme),* Die Dubarry *(Querschnitt).* Eurodisc 610330-232.

"The President's Own" United States Marine Band. ℗ and ©2014. "President Garfield's Inaugural March (John Philip Sousa)," from *100 Famous Marches: United States Military Bands.* Altissimo ALT01072.

Prey, Hermann, Kiri Te Kanawa, Paul Crook, Zubin Mehta, and the Orchestra of the Royal Opera House Covent Garden. Rec. 1977. The television broadcast is documented at http://www.rohcollections.org.uk/performance.aspx?performance=12023&row=8&searchtype=performance&page=1&person=Robert%20Tear

Rachmaninoff, Sergei. Rec. 1930. Piano Sonata No. 2 in B-flat Minor, op. 35, Presto, from *Rachmaninoff Plays Chopin.* BMG 09026-62533-2. ℗ and ©1994.

Schiff, Heinrich. Rec. 1984. Suite No. 4 for Solo Violoncello, BWV 1010, Prelude, from *Bach Cello Suites Nos. 1-6.* EMI CDS 7 47471 8. ℗ 1985.

Schnabel, Artur. Rec. 1939. Piano Sonata in B-flat Major, D. 960, Andante Sostenuto, from *Schubert: Sonaten D. 850, D. 959, D. 960, Moments musicaux D. 780, Marsch D. 606.* EMI ZDHB 7 64259 2. ℗ 1992.

Schuricht, Carl, and the Stuttgart Radio Symphony Orchestra. Rec. 1960. Symphony No. 3 in E-flat Major, op. 97, "Rhenish," i, Lebhaft, from *Schumann Symphonie No. 3, "Rhénane."* Adès 13.276-2. ℗ 1960 - 1988.

Skrowaczewski, Stanislaw, and the Deutsche Radio Philharmonie. Rec. 2007. Symphony No. 3 in E-flat Major, op. 97, "Rhenish," i, Lebhaft, from *Schumann Symphonies 2 and 3*. Oehms OC 708. ℗ 2007, © 2008.

Solti, Georg, and the London Philharmonic Orchestra. Rec. 1996. Mozart, Overture, from *Don Giovanni*. London 455 500-2. ℗ and ©1997.

Sons of Serendip. ℗ and ©2017. "Stop in the Name of Love," from *Life + Love*. Independently produced.

Supremes. Rec. 1965. "Stop in the Name of Love," from *Motown 1960s*, vol. 2. Motown 440 016 160-2. ℗ and © 2001.

Thedéen, Torleif, and Roland Pöntinen. Rec. 2006. Sonata No. 2 for Cello and Piano in F Major, op. 99, Allegro passionato, from *Brahms: Cello Sonatas*. BIS BIS-SACD-1606. ℗ and ©2010.

Thompson, Marcus, Mihae Lee, Arturo Delmoni, and Ronald Thomas. Rec. 1990. Quartet in C minor for Piano and Strings, opus 60, Allegro non troppo, from *Johannes Brahms: Piano Trio in B major, opus 8, and Piano Quartet in C minor, opus 60*. Northeastern NR 244-CD. ℗ and © 1990.

Vienna Philharmonic Orchestra and Leonard Bernstein. Rec. 1981. Symphony No. 3 in F Major, op. 90, i, from *Brahms: The Symphonies*. Deutsche Grammophon 0440 073 4331. ℗ 2007.

Walter, Bruno, and the Columbia Symphony Orchestra. Rec. 1954. Symphony No. 25 in G Minor, K. 183, Allegro con brio, from *Bruno Walter Conducts Mozart*. Sony Classical 8 86979 06832 2. ℗ and ©2011.

INDEX

JOHN PAUL ITO is Associate Professor of Music Theory in the School of Music at Carnegie Mellon University.

www.ingramcontent.com/pod-product-compliance
Lightning Source LLC
Chambersburg PA
CBHW020601270326
41927CB00005B/129